משנה

ArtScroll Mishnah Series®

A rabbinic commentary to the Six Orders of the Mishnah

Rabbis Nosson Scherman / Meir Zlotowitz

General Editors

the mishnah

ARTSCROLL MISHNAH SERIES / A NEW TRANSLATION WITH A COMMENTARY **YAD AVRAHAM** ANTHOLOGIZED FROM TALMUDIC SOURCES AND CLASSIC COMMENTATORS.

Published by

Mesorah Publications, ltd

THE COMMENTARY HAS BEEN NAMED **YAD AVRAHAM**
AS AN EVERLASTING MEMORIAL AND SOURCE OF MERIT
FOR THE *NESHAMAH* OF
אברהם יוסף ע"ה בן הר"ר אליעזר הכהן גליק נ"י
AVRAHAM YOSEF GLICK ע"ה
WHOSE LIFE WAS CUT SHORT ON 3 TEVES, 5735

FIRST EDITION
First Impression . . . December, 1990

Published and Distributed by
MESORAH PUBLICATIONS, Ltd.
Brooklyn, New York 11232

Distributed in Israel by
MESORAH MAFITZIM / J. GROSSMAN
Rechov Harav Uziel 117
Jerusalem, Israel

Distributed in Europe by
J. LEHMANN HEBREW BOOKSELLERS
20 Cambridge Terrace
Gateshead, Tyne and Wear
England NE8 1RP

Distributed in Australia & New Zealand by
GOLD'S BOOK & GIFT CO.
36 William Street
Balaclava 3183, Vic., Australia

Distributed in South Africa by
KOLLEL BOOKSHOP
22 Muller Street
Yeoville 2198
Johannesburg, South Africa

THE ARTSCROLL MISHNAH SERIES®
SEDER KODASHIM Vol. III(c); *KEREISOS*

ISBN
0-89906-309-8 (hard cover)
0-89906-310-1 (paperback)

Typography by Compuscribe at ArtScroll Studios, Ltd.
4401 Second Avenue / Brooklyn, NY 11232 / (718) 921-9000

Printed in the United States of America by Moriah Offset
Bound by Sefercraft Inc., Quality Bookbinders, Brooklyn, N.Y.

◆ מסכת כריתות

◆ Tractate Kereisos

Translation and anthologized commentary by

Rabbi Avrohom Yoseif Rosenberg

Edited by

Rabbi Naftoli Kempler

דּוֹדִי יָרַד לְגַנּוֹ . . . וְלִלְקֹט שׁוֹשַׁנִּים

My Beloved has gone down to His garden . . . to pick roses (Shir Hashirim 6:2)

Like a gardener who knows when to pluck his fruit, the Almighty knows when to remove the righteous from this world *(Midrash)*.

This volume is dedicated to the memory of a dear friend

ר׳ דוד ע״ה בן ר׳ שמעון נ״י

David Litman ע״ה

June 17, 1955 — August 17, 1990

נפטר כ״ו מנחם אב תש״ן

He lived a life of hard work — loving work — for his family and his people.

Much of his love was for learning, an exuberant love for the words of the Torah and the satisfaction of victory whenever he achieved a new milestone in his learning.

He believed that no Jewish child should be without a Jewish education, and he worked tirelessly to guarantee them that birthright.

The Gardener plucked him before we were ready to spare him, but we are left with a radiant legacy of striving and accomplishment.

תנצב״ה

הסכמה

RABBI MOSES FEINSTEIN
455 F. D. R. DRIVE
NEW YORK, N. Y. 10002

OREGON 7-1222

משה פיינשטיין
ר״מ תפארת ירושלים
בנוא יארק

בע״ה

הנה ידידי הרב הגאון ר׳ אברהם יוסף ראזענבערג שליט״א אשר היה מתלמידי החשובים ביותר וגם הרביץ תורה בכמה ישיבות ואצלינו בישיבתנו בסטעטן איילאנד, ובזמן האחרון הוא מתעסק בתרגום ספרי קודש ללשון אנגלית המדוברת ומובנת לבני מדינה זו, וכבר איתמחי גברא בענין תרגום לאנגלית וכעת תרגם משניות לשפת אנגלית וגם לקוטים מדברי רבותינו מפרשי משניות על כל משנה ומשנה בערך, והוא לתועלת גדול להרבה אינשי ממדינה זו שלא התרגלו מילדותם ללמוד המשנה וגם יש הרבה שבעזר השי״ת התקרבו לתורה ויראת שמים כשכבר נתגדלו ורוצים ללמוד שיוכלו ללמוד משניות בנקל בשפה המורגלת להם, שהוא ממזכי הרבים בלמוד משניות וזכותו גדול. ואני מברכו שיצליחהו השי״ת בחבורו זה. וגם אני מברך את חברת ארטסקרול אשר תחת הנהלת הרב הנכבד ידידי מוהר״ר מאיר יעקב בן ידידי הגאון ר׳ אהרן שליט״א זלאטאוויץ אשר הוציאו כבר הרבה חבורים חשובים לזכות את הרבים וכעת הם מוציאים לאור את המשניות הנ״ל.

ועל זה באתי על החתום בז׳ אדר תשל״ט בנוא יארק.

נאום משה פיינשטיין

מכתב ברכה

יעקב קמנצקי

RABBI J. KAMENECKI

38 SADDLE RIVER ROAD

MONSEY, NEW YORK 10952

בע"ה

יום ה' ערב חג השבועות תשל"ס, פה מאנסי.

כבוד הרבני איש החסד שוע ונדיב מוקיר רבנן מר אלעזר נ"י גליק
שלו' וברכת כל טוב.

מה מאד שמחתי בהודעי כי כבודו רכש לעצמו הזכות שייקרא ע"ש בנו המנוח הפירוש מבואר על כל ששת סדרי משנה ע"י "ארטסקראל" והנה חברה זו יצאה לה מוניטין בפירושה על תנ"ך, והנה בקוה שכשם שהצליחה בתורה שבכתב כן תצליח בתורה שבע"פ. ובהיות שאותיות "משנה" הן כאותיות "נשמה" לפיכך טוב עשה בכוונתו לעשות זאת לעילוי נשמת בנו המנוח אברהם יוסף ע"ה, ומאד מתאים השם "יד אברהם" לזה הפירוש, כדמצינו במקרא (ש"ב י"ח) כי אמר אין לי בן בעבור הזכיר שמי וגו'. ואין לך דבר גדול מזה להפיץ ידיעת תורה שבע"פ בקרב אחינו שאינם רגילים בלשון הקדש. וד' הטוב יהי' בעזרו ויוכל לברך על המוגמר. ויראה רוב נחת מכל אשר אתו כנפש מברכו.

יעקב קמנצקי

מכתב ברכה

ישיבת טלז
קרית טלז-סטון
ירושלים

YESHIVAT TELSHE
Kiryat Telshe Stone
Jerusalem, Israel

בע״ה — ד׳ בהעלותך — לבני א״י, תשל״ט — פה קרית טלז, באה״ק

מע״כ ידידי האהובים הרב ר׳ מאיר והרב ר׳ נתן, נר״ו, שלום וברכה נצח!

אחדשה״ט באהבה ויקר,

לשמחה רבה היא לי להודע שהרחבתם גדול עבודתכם בקודש לתורה שבע״פ, בהוצאת המשנה בתרגום וביאור באנגלית, וראשית עבודתכם במס׳ מגילה.

אני תקוה שתשימו לב שיצאו הדברים מתוקנים מנקודת ההלכה, וחזקה עליכם שתוציאו דבר נאה ומתוקן.

בפנותכם לתורה שבע״פ יפתח אופק חדש בתורת ה׳ לאלה שקשה עליהם ללמוד הדברים במקורם, ואלה שכבר נתעשרו מעבודתכם במגילת אסתר יכנסו עתה לטרקלין חדש וישמשו להם הדברים דחף ללימוד המשנה, וגדול יהי׳ שכרכם.

יהא ה׳ בעזרכם בהוספת טבעת חדשה באותה שלשלת זהב של הפצת תורת ה׳ להמוני עם לקרב לב ישראל לאבינו שבשמים בתורה ואמונה טהורה.

אוהבכם מלונ״ח,
מרדכי

מכתב ברכה

RABBI SHNEUR KOTLER
BETH MEDRASH GOVOHA
LAKEWOOD, N. J.

בע"ה

שניאור קוטלר
בית מדרש גבוה
לייקוואוד, נ. דז.

בשורת התרחבות עבודתם הגדולה של סגל חבורת ,,ארטסקרול״, המעתיקים ומפרשים, לתחומי התושבע״פ, לשים אלה המשפטים לפני הציבור כשלחן ערוך ומוכן לאכול לפני האדם [ל׳ רש״י], ולשימה בפיהם — לפתוח אוצרות בשנות בצורת ולהשמיעם בכל לשון שהם שומעים — מבשרת צבא רב לתורה ולימודה [ע׳ תהלים ס״ח י״ב בתרגום יונתן], והיא מאותות ההתעוררות ללימוד התורה, וזאת התעודה על התנוצצות קיום ההבטחה ,,כי לא תשכח מפי זרעו״. אשרי הזוכים להיות בין שלוחי ההשגחה לקיומה וביצועה.

יה״ר כי תצליח מלאכת שמים בידם, ויזכו ללמוד וללמד ולשמור מסורת הקבלה כי בהרקת המים החיים מכלי אל כלי תשתמר חיותם, יעמוד טעמם בם וריחם לא נמר. [וע׳ משאחז״ל בכ״מ ושמרתם זו משנה — וע׳ חי׳ מרן רי״ז הלוי עה״ת בפ׳ ואתחנן] ותהי׳ משנתם שלמה וברורה, ישמחו בעבודתם חברים ותלמידים, ,,ישוטטו רבים ותרבה הדעת״, עד יקויים ,,אז אהפוך אל העמים שפה ברורה וגו׳ ״ [צפני׳ ג׳ ט׳, עי׳ פי׳ אבן עזרא ומצודת דוד שם].

ונזכה כולנו לראות בהתכנסות הגליות בזכות המשניות כל׳ חז״ל עפ״י הכתוב ,,גם כי יתנו בגוים עתה אקבצם״, בגאולה השלמה בב״א.

הכו״ח לכבוד התורה, יום ו׳ עש״ק לס׳ ,,ויוצא פרח ויצץ ציץ ויגמול שקדים״, ד׳ תמוז התשל״ט

יוסף חיים שניאור קוטלר
בלאאמו״ר הגר״א זצוק״ל

מכתב ברכה

ב״ה

ישיבה דפילאדעלפיא

ב״ה

לכבוד ידידי וידיד ישיבתנו, מהראשונים לכל דבר שבקדושה
הרבני הנדיב המפורסם ר׳ אליעזר הכהן גליק נ״י
אחדש״ה באהבה,

בשורה טובה שמעתי שכב׳ מצא את המקום המתאים לעשות יד ושם להנציח זכרו של בנו אברהם יוסף ע״ה שנקטף בנעוריו. ,,ונתתי להם בביתי ובחומתי יד ושם״. אין לו להקב״ה אלא ד׳ אמות של הלכה בלבד. א״כ זהו בית ד׳ לימוד תורה שבע״פ וזהו המקום לעשות יד ושם לנשמת בנו ע״ה.

נר ד׳ נשמת אדם אמר הקב״ה נרי בידך ונרך בידי. נר מצוה ותורה אור, תורה זהו הנר של הקב״ה וכששומרים נר של הקב״ה שעל ידי הפירוש ,,**יד אברהם**״ בשפה הלעוזית יתרבה ויתפשט לימוד ושקיעת התורה בבתי ישראל. ד׳ ישמור נשמת אדם.

בנו אברהם יוסף ע״ה נתברך בהמדה שבו נכללות כל המדות, לב טוב והיה אהוב לחבריו. בלמדו בישיבתנו היה לו הרצון לעלות במעלות התורה וכשעלה לארצנו הקדושה היתה מבוקשו להמשיך בלמודיו. ביקוש זה ימצא מלואו על ידי הרבים המבקשים דרך ד׳, שהפירוש ,,**יד אברהם**״ יהא מפתח להם לים התלמוד.

התורה נקראת ,,אש דת״ ונמשלה לאש ויש לה הכח לפעפע ברזל לפצוץ כוחות האדם, הניצוץ שהאיר בך רבנו הרב שרגא פייוועל מנדלויץ זצ״ל שמרת עליו, ועשה חיל. עכשיו אתה מסייע להאיר נצוצות בנשמות בני ישראל שיעשה חיל ויהא לאור גדול.

תקותי עזה שכל התלמידי חכמים שנדבה רוחם להוציא לפועל מלאכה ענקית זו לפרש המשניות כולה, יצא עבודתם ברוח פאר והדר ויכוונו לאמיתה של תורה ויתקדש ויתרבה שם שמים על ידי מלאכה זו.

יתברך כב׳ וב״ב לראות ולרוות נחת רוח מצאצאיו.
הכו״ח לכבוד התורה ותומכיה עש״ק במדבר תשל״ט

אלי׳ שווי

מכתב ברכה

דוד קאהן

ביהמ״ד גבול יעבץ
ברוקלין, נוא יארק

בס״ד כ״ה למטמונים תשל״ט

כבוד רחימא דנפשאי, עושה ומעשה
ר׳ אלעזר הכהן גליק נטריה רחמנא ופרקיה

שמוע שמעתי שכבר תקעת כפיך לתמוך במפעל האדיר של חברת ארטסקרול — הידוע בכל קצווי תבל ע״י עבודתה הכבירה בהפצת תורה — לתרגם ולבאר ששה סדרי משנה באנגלית. כוונתך להנציח זכר בנך הנחמד אברהם יוסף ז״ל שנקטף באבו בזמן שעלה לארץ הקודש בתקופת התרוממות הנפש ושאיפה לקדושה, ולמטרה זו יכונה הפירוש בשם „**יד אברהם**״; וגם האיר ה׳ רוחך לגרום עילוי לנשמתו הטהורה שעי״ז יתרבה לימוד התורה שניתנה בשבעים לשון, על ידי כלי מפואר זה.

מכיוון שהנני מכיר היטיב שני הצדדים, אוכל לומר לדבק טוב, והנני תקוה שיצליח המפעל הלזה לתת יד ושם וזכות לנשמת אברהם יוסף ז״ל. חזקה על חברת ארטסקרול שתוציא דבר נאה מתוקן ומתקבל מתחת ידה להגדיל תורה ולהאדירה.

והנני מברך אותך שתמצא נוחם לנפשך, שהאבא זוכה לברא, ותשבע נחת — אתה עם רעיתך תחיה — מכל צאצאיכם היקרים אכי״ר

ידידך עז
דוד קאהן

Preface

אָמַר ר׳ יוֹחָנָן: לֹא כָּרַת הקב״ה בְּרִית עִם יִשְׂרָאֵל אֶלָּא עַל־תּוֹרָה שֶׁבְּעַל פֶּה שֶׁנֶּאֱמַר: ,,כִּי עַל־פִּי הַדְּבָרִים הָאֵלֶּה כָּרַתִּי אִתְּךָ בְּרִית . . .״

R' Yochanan said: The Holy One, Blessed is He, sealed a covenant with Israel only because of the Oral Torah, as it is said [Exodus 34:27]: For according to these words have I sealed a covenant with you . . . (Gittin 60b).

With gratitude to Hashem Yisborach *we present the Jewish public with* Kereisos, *the seventh tractate in* Seder Kodashim, *This* Seder *is now more than half done,* baruch Hashem, *and work is proceeding on the remainder, as well as on* Seder Zeraim *and* Toharos. *All of this is thanks to the vision and commitment of* MR. AND MRS. LOUIS GLICK. *In their quiet, self-effacing way, they have been a major force for the propagation of Torah knowledge and the enhancement of Jewish life for a generation. The commentary to the mishnayos bears the name* YAD AVRAHAM, *in memory of their son* AVRAHAM YOSEF GLICK ע״ה. *An appreciation of the* niftar *will appear in Tractate* Berachos. *May this dissemination of the Mishnah in his memory be a source of merit for his soul.* תנצב״ה.

By dedicating the ArtScroll Mishnah Series, the Glicks have added a new dimension to their tradition of service. The many Mishnah *study groups in synagogues, schools, and offices throughout the English-speaking world are the most eloquent testimony to the fact that thousands of people thirst for Torah learning, presented in a challenging, comprehensive, and comprehensible manner.*

We are proud and grateful that such venerable luminaries as MARAN HAGAON HARAV YAAKOV KAMENETZKI זצ״ל *and* להבל״ח MARAN HAGAON HARAV MORDECHAI GIFTER שליט״א *have declared that this series should be translated into Hebrew.* Baruch Hashem, *it has stimulated readers to echo the words of King David:* גַּל־עֵינַי וְאַבִּיטָה נִפְלָאוֹת מִתּוֹרָתֶךָ, *Uncover my eyes that I may see wonders of Your Torah (Psalms 119:18).*

May we inject two words of caution:

First, although the Mishnah, by definition, is a compendium of laws, the final halachah does not necessarily follow the Mishnah. The development of halachah proceeds through the Gemara, commentators, codifiers, responsa, and the acknowledged poskim. *Even when our commentary cites the* Shulchan Aruch, *the intention is to sharpen the reader's understanding of the Mishnah, but not to be a basis for actual practice. In short, this work is meant as a first step in the study of our recorded Oral Law — no more.*

Second, as we have stressed in our other books, the ArtScroll commentary is not meant as a substitute for the study of the sources. While this commentary, like others in the various series, will be immensely useful even to accomplished scholars and will often bring to light ideas and sources they may have overlooked, we strongly urge those who can, to study the classic sefarim *in the original. It has been said that every droplet of ink coming from* Rashi's *pen is worthy of seven days' contemplation. Despite the exceptional caliber of our authors, none of us pretends to replace the study of the greatest minds in Jewish history.*

This volume was written by RABBI AVROHOM YOSEIF ROSENBERG, *who has contributed many fine volumes to the ArtScroll Mishnah Series. His manuscript was edited by* RABBI NAFTOLI KEMPLER. *Also contributing to this volume were* RABBI YEHEZKEL DANZIGER, RABBI AVIE GOLD, *and* RABBI HERSH GOLDWURM. MRS. JUDI DICK *and* MRS. FAYGIE WEINBAUM *read the galleys meticulously and contributed mightily.*

We are also grateful to the staff of Mesorah Publications: REB SHEAH BRANDER, *who remains the leader in bringing beauty of presentation to Torah literature;* REB ELI KROEN *who is responsible for the layout;* RABBI YOSEF GESSER, RABBI SHIMON GOLDING, AVROHOM BIDERMAN, YOSEF TIMINSKY, MICHAEL ZIVITZ, SAID KOHANFOLAD, YITZCHOK SAFTLAS, YEHUDA GORDON, LEA FREIER, SHEILA TENNENBAUM, MRS. ESTHER FEIERSTEIN, MRS. ZISSI LANDAU, BASSIE GOLDSTEIN, ESTI KUSHNER, *and* RAIZY BRANDER. *May we mention, as well, our intense pride in the members of our staff, old and new, whose work on the ArtScroll Edition of Talmud Bavli has evoked so much praise from scholar and layman alike.*

Finally, our gratitude goes to RABBI DAVID FEINSTEIN שליט״א *and* RABBI DAVID COHEN שליט״א, *whose concern, interest, and guidance throughout the history of the ArtScroll Series have been essential to its success.*

Rabbi Nosson Scherman / Rabbi Meir Zlotowitz

ג׳ טבת תשנ״א */ December 20, 1991*
Brooklyn, New York

◈ Seder Kodashim Vol. III (c):

מסכת כריתות
Tractate Kereisos

The Publishers are grateful to

TORAH UMESORAH

and

YAD AVRAHAM INSTITUTE

for their efforts in the publication of the

ARTSCROLL MISHNAH SERIES

חַטָּאת קְבוּעָה

(ויקרא ד:כז-כט . . . לב)

כז וְאִם־נֶפֶשׁ אַחַת תֶּחֱטָא בִשְׁגָגָה מֵעַם הָאָרֶץ בַּעֲשֹׂתָהּ אַחַת
מִמִּצְוֺת ה׳ אֲשֶׁר לֹא־תֵעָשֶׂינָה וְאָשֵׁם: כח אוֹ הוֹדַע אֵלָיו חַטָּאתוֹ
אֲשֶׁר חָטָא וְהֵבִיא קָרְבָּנוֹ שְׂעִירַת עִזִּים תְּמִימָה נְקֵבָה עַל־
חַטָּאתוֹ אֲשֶׁר חָטָא: כט וְסָמַךְ . . . לב וְאִם־כֶּבֶשׂ יָבִיא קָרְבָּנוֹ
לְחַטָּאת נְקֵבָה תְמִימָה יְבִיאֶנָּה:

קָרְבָּן עוֹלֶה וְיוֹרֵד

(ויקרא ה:א-ח . . .)

א וְנֶפֶשׁ כִּי־תֶחֱטָא וְשָׁמְעָה קוֹל אָלָה וְהוּא עֵד אוֹ רָאָה אוֹ יָדָע
אִם־לוֹא יַגִּיד וְנָשָׂא עֲוֺנוֹ: ב אוֹ נֶפֶשׁ אֲשֶׁר תִּגַּע בְּכָל־דָּבָר טָמֵא
אוֹ בְנִבְלַת חַיָּה טְמֵאָה אוֹ בְּנִבְלַת בְּהֵמָה טְמֵאָה אוֹ בְּנִבְלַת שֶׁרֶץ
טָמֵא וְנֶעְלַם מִמֶּנּוּ וְהוּא טָמֵא וְאָשֵׁם: ג אוֹ כִי יִגַּע בְּטֻמְאַת אָדָם
לְכֹל טֻמְאָתוֹ אֲשֶׁר יִטְמָא בָּהּ וְנֶעְלַם מִמֶּנּוּ וְהוּא יָדַע וְאָשֵׁם: ד אוֹ
נֶפֶשׁ כִּי תִשָּׁבַע לְבַטֵּא בִשְׂפָתַיִם לְהָרַע ׀ אוֹ לְהֵיטִיב לְכֹל אֲשֶׁר
יְבַטֵּא הָאָדָם בִּשְׁבֻעָה וְנֶעְלַם מִמֶּנּוּ וְהוּא־יָדַע וְאָשֵׁם לְאַחַת
מֵאֵלֶּה: ה וְהָיָה כִי־יֶאְשַׁם לְאַחַת מֵאֵלֶּה וְהִתְוַדָּה אֲשֶׁר חָטָא
עָלֶיהָ: ו וְהֵבִיא אֶת־אֲשָׁמוֹ לַה׳ עַל חַטָּאתוֹ אֲשֶׁר חָטָא נְקֵבָה
מִן־הַצֹּאן כִּשְׂבָּה אוֹ־שְׂעִירַת עִזִּים לְחַטָּאת וְכִפֶּר עָלָיו הַכֹּהֵן
מֵחַטָּאתוֹ: ז וְאִם־לֹא תַגִּיעַ יָדוֹ דֵּי שֶׂה וְהֵבִיא אֶת־אֲשָׁמוֹ אֲשֶׁר
חָטָא שְׁתֵּי תֹרִים אוֹ־שְׁנֵי בְנֵי־יוֹנָה לַה׳ אֶחָד לְחַטָּאת וְאֶחָד
לְעֹלָה: ח וְהֵבִיא . . .

אָשָׁם תָּלוּי

(ויקרא ה:יז-יח)

יז וְאִם־נֶפֶשׁ כִּי תֶחֱטָא וְעָשְׂתָה אַחַת מִכָּל־מִצְוֺת ה׳ אֲשֶׁר לֹא
תֵעָשֶׂינָה וְלֹא־יָדַע וְאָשֵׁם וְנָשָׂא עֲוֺנוֹ: יח וְהֵבִיא אַיִל תָּמִים
מִן־הַצֹּאן בְּעֶרְכְּךָ לְאָשָׁם אֶל־הַכֹּהֵן וְכִפֶּר עָלָיו הַכֹּהֵן עַל שִׁגְגָתוֹ
אֲשֶׁר־שָׁגָג וְהוּא לֹא־יָדַע וְנִסְלַח לוֹ:

Fixed Chatas

(Leviticus 4:27-29 . . . 32)

27 If an individual person from among the people of the land shall sin unintentionally, by committing one of the commandments of HASHEM *that may not be done, and he becomes guilty; 28 if the sin that he committed becomes known to him, he shall bring as his offering an unblemished she-goat for the sin that he had committed. 29 He shall lean . . . 32 If he shall bring a sheep as his offering for a sin offering, he shall bring an unblemished female.*

Variable Chatas

(Leviticus 5:1-8 . . .)

1 If a person will sin: If he accepted a demand for an oath, and he is a witness — either he saw or he knew — if he does not testify he shall bear his sin. 2 Or if a person will have touched any contaminated object — whether the contaminating carcass of a beast, the contaminating carcass of an animal, or the contaminating carcass of a creeping animal — but it was concealed from him, and he is contaminated and had become guilty; 3 or if he will touch a human contamination in any manner of its contamination through which he can become contaminated, but this fact was concealed from him — and then he knew — and he had become guilty. 4 Or if a person will swear, expressing with his lips to do harm or to do good, anything that a person will express in an oath, but it was concealed from him, and then he knew — and he became guilty regarding one of these matters. 5 When one shall become guilty regarding one of these matters, he shall confess what he had sinned. 6 He who sinned shall bring as his guilt offering to HASHEM *for his sin: a female from the flock, a sheep or a goat, for a sin offering; and the Kohen shall provide him atonement for his sin. 7 But if his means are insufficient for a sheep or goat, then the one who sinned shall bring as his guilt offering: two turtledoves or two young pigeons to* HASHEM*, one for a sin offering and one for an elevation offering. 8 He shall bring . . .*

Suspensive Asham

(Leviticus 5:17-18)

17 If a person will sin and will commit one of all the commandments of HASHEM *that may not be done, but is unaware and became guilty, and bears his iniquity. 18 He shall bring an unblemished ram from the flock of the proper value for a guilt offering to the Kohen; and the Kohen shall provide him atonement for the inadvertence that he committed unwittingly, and it shall be forgiven him.*

אֲשַׁם מְעִילוֹת

(ויקרא ה:יד-טו)

יד וַיְדַבֵּר ה׳ אֶל־מֹשֶׁה לֵּאמֹר: טו נֶפֶשׁ כִּי־תִמְעֹל מַעַל וְחָטְאָה
בִּשְׁגָגָה מִקָּדְשֵׁי ה׳ וְהֵבִיא אֶת־אֲשָׁמוֹ לַה׳ אַיִל תָּמִים מִן־הַצֹּאן
בְּעֶרְכְּךָ כֶּסֶף־שְׁקָלִים בְּשֶׁקֶל־הַקֹּדֶשׁ לְאָשָׁם:

אֲשַׁם גְּזֵלוֹת

(ויקרא ה:כא-כו)

כא נֶפֶשׁ כִּי תֶחֱטָא וּמָעֲלָה מַעַל בַּה׳ וְכִחֵשׁ בַּעֲמִיתוֹ בְּפִקָּדוֹן
אוֹ־בִתְשׂוּמֶת יָד אוֹ בְגָזֵל אוֹ עָשַׁק אֶת־עֲמִיתוֹ: כב אוֹ־מָצָא אֲבֵדָה
וְכִחֶשׁ בָּהּ וְנִשְׁבַּע עַל־שָׁקֶר עַל־אַחַת מִכֹּל אֲשֶׁר־יַעֲשֶׂה הָאָדָם
לַחֲטֹא בָהֵנָּה: כג וְהָיָה כִּי־יֶחֱטָא וְאָשֵׁם וְהֵשִׁיב אֶת־הַגְּזֵלָה אֲשֶׁר
גָּזָל אוֹ אֶת־הָעֹשֶׁק אֲשֶׁר עָשָׁק אוֹ אֶת־הַפִּקָּדוֹן אֲשֶׁר הָפְקַד אִתּוֹ
אוֹ אֶת־הָאֲבֵדָה אֲשֶׁר מָצָא: כד אוֹ מִכֹּל אֲשֶׁר־יִשָּׁבַע עָלָיו לַשֶּׁקֶר
וְשִׁלַּם אֹתוֹ בְּרֹאשׁוֹ וַחֲמִשִׁתָיו יֹסֵף עָלָיו לַאֲשֶׁר הוּא לוֹ יִתְּנֶנּוּ בְּיוֹם
אַשְׁמָתוֹ: כה וְאֶת־אֲשָׁמוֹ יָבִיא לַה׳ אַיִל תָּמִים מִן־הַצֹּאן בְּעֶרְכְּךָ
לְאָשָׁם אֶל־הַכֹּהֵן: כו וְכִפֶּר עָלָיו הַכֹּהֵן לִפְנֵי ה׳ וְנִסְלַח לוֹ
עַל־אַחַת מִכֹּל אֲשֶׁר־יַעֲשֶׂה לְאַשְׁמָה בָהּ:

אֲשַׁם שִׁפְחָה חֲרוּפָה

(ויקרא יט:כ-כב)

כ וְאִישׁ כִּי־יִשְׁכַּב אֶת־אִשָּׁה שִׁכְבַת־זֶרַע וְהִוא שִׁפְחָה נֶחֱרֶפֶת
לְאִישׁ וְהָפְדֵּה לֹא נִפְדָּתָה אוֹ חֻפְשָׁה לֹא נִתַּן־לָהּ בִּקֹּרֶת תִּהְיֶה לֹא
יוּמְתוּ כִּי־לֹא חֻפָּשָׁה: כא וְהֵבִיא אֶת־אֲשָׁמוֹ לַה׳ אֶל־פֶּתַח אֹהֶל
מוֹעֵד אֵיל אָשָׁם: כב וְכִפֶּר עָלָיו הַכֹּהֵן בְּאֵיל הָאָשָׁם לִפְנֵי ה׳
עַל־חַטָּאתוֹ אֲשֶׁר חָטָא וְנִסְלַח לוֹ מֵחַטָּאתוֹ אֲשֶׁר חָטָא:

יוֹלֶדֶת

(ויקרא יב:א-ח)

א וַיְדַבֵּר ה׳ אֶל־מֹשֶׁה לֵּאמֹר: ב דַּבֵּר אֶל־בְּנֵי יִשְׂרָאֵל לֵאמֹר אִשָּׁה
כִּי תַזְרִיעַ וְיָלְדָה זָכָר וְטָמְאָה שִׁבְעַת יָמִים כִּימֵי נִדַּת דְּוֹתָהּ
תִּטְמָא: ג וּבַיּוֹם הַשְּׁמִינִי יִמּוֹל בְּשַׂר עָרְלָתוֹ: ד וּשְׁלֹשִׁים יוֹם
וּשְׁלֹשֶׁת יָמִים תֵּשֵׁב בִּדְמֵי טָהֳרָה בְּכָל־קֹדֶשׁ לֹא־תִגָּע וְאֶל־
הַמִּקְדָּשׁ לֹא תָבֹא עַד־מְלֹאת יְמֵי טָהֳרָהּ: ה וְאִם־נְקֵבָה תֵלֵד

Asham of Me'ilah

(Leviticus 5:14-15)

14 HASHEM spoke to Moses, saying: 15 If a person commits treachery against HASHEM's holies, sinning unintentionally; he shall bring as his guilt offering to HASHEM an unblemished ram from the flock, with a value of silver shekels, according to the shekel of the Sanctuary, for a guilt offering.

Asham of Theft

(Leviticus 5:21-26)

21 If a person will sin and commit a treachery against HASHEM by lying to his comrade regarding a pledge, a loan, a robbery, or by defrauding his comrade; 22 or he found a lost item and lied about it — and he swore falsely about any of all the things that a person can do and sin thereby. 23 So it shall be that when he will sin and become guilty, he shall return the robbed item that he robbed, or the proceeds of his fraud, or the pledge that was left with him, or the lost item that he found; 24 or anything about which he had sworn falsely — he shall repay its principal and add its fifth to it; he shall give it to its owner on the day he admits his guilt. 25 And he shall bring his guilt offering to HASHEM — an unblemished ram from the flock, of the proper value, as a guilt offering — to the Kohen. 26 The Kohen shall provide him atonement before HASHEM, and it shall be forgiven him; for any of all the things he might do to incur guilt.

Asham of the Betrothed Maidservant

(Leviticus 19:20-22)

20 If a man lies carnally with a woman, and she is a slavewoman who has been designated for another man, and who has not been redeemed, or whose freedom has not been granted her; there shall be an investigation — they shall not be put to death, for she has not been freed. 21 He shall bring his guilt offering to HASHEM, to the entrance of the Tent of the Meeting, a ram guilt offering. 22 The Kohen shall atone for him with the ram guilt offering before HASHEM for the sin that he had committed; and the sin that he had committed shall be forgiven him.

The Woman Who Has Given Birth

(Leviticus 12:1-8)

1 HASHEM spoke to Moses, saying: 2 Speak to the Children of Israel, saying: When a woman conceives and gives birth to a male, she shall be contaminated for a seven-day period, as during the days of her separation infirmity shall she be contaminated. 3 On the eighth day, the flesh of his foreskin shall be circumcised. 4 For thirty-three days she shall remain in blood of purity; she may not touch anything sacred and she may not enter the Sanctuary, until the completion of her days of purity. 5 If she gives birth to

וְטָמְאָה שְׁבֻעַיִם כְּנִדָּתָהּ וְשִׁשִּׁים יוֹם וְשֵׁשֶׁת יָמִים תֵּשֵׁב עַל־דְּמֵי
טָהֳרָה׃ ו וּבִמְלֹאת ׀ יְמֵי טָהֳרָהּ לְבֵן אוֹ לְבַת תָּבִיא כֶּבֶשׂ
בֶּן־שְׁנָתוֹ לְעֹלָה וּבֶן־יוֹנָה אוֹ־תֹר לְחַטָּאת אֶל־פֶּתַח אֹהֶל־מוֹעֵד
אֶל־הַכֹּהֵן׃ ז וְהִקְרִיבוֹ לִפְנֵי ה׳ וְכִפֶּר עָלֶיהָ וְטָהֲרָה מִמְּקֹר דָּמֶיהָ
זֹאת תּוֹרַת הַיֹּלֶדֶת לַזָּכָר אוֹ לַנְּקֵבָה׃ ח וְאִם־לֹא תִמְצָא יָדָהּ דֵּי
שֶׂה וְלָקְחָה שְׁתֵּי־תֹרִים אוֹ שְׁנֵי בְּנֵי יוֹנָה אֶחָד לְעֹלָה וְאֶחָד
לְחַטָּאת וְכִפֶּר עָלֶיהָ הַכֹּהֵן וְטָהֵרָה׃

מְצוֹרָע

(ויקרא יד:א־ב . . . י־לב)

א וַיְדַבֵּר ה׳ אֶל־מֹשֶׁה לֵּאמֹר׃ ב זֹאת תִּהְיֶה תּוֹרַת הַמְּצֹרָע בְּיוֹם
טָהֳרָתוֹ וְהוּבָא אֶל־הַכֹּהֵן . . . י וּבַיּוֹם הַשְּׁמִינִי יִקַּח שְׁנֵי־כְבָשִׂים
תְּמִימִם וְכַבְשָׂה אַחַת בַּת־שְׁנָתָהּ תְּמִימָה וּשְׁלֹשָׁה עֶשְׂרֹנִים
סֹלֶת מִנְחָה בְּלוּלָה בַשֶּׁמֶן וְלֹג אֶחָד שָׁמֶן׃ יא וְהֶעֱמִיד הַכֹּהֵן
הַמְטַהֵר אֵת הָאִישׁ הַמִּטַּהֵר וְאֹתָם לִפְנֵי ה׳ פֶּתַח אֹהֶל מוֹעֵד׃
יב וְלָקַח הַכֹּהֵן אֶת־הַכֶּבֶשׂ הָאֶחָד וְהִקְרִיב אֹתוֹ לְאָשָׁם וְאֶת־לֹג
הַשָּׁמֶן וְהֵנִיף אֹתָם תְּנוּפָה לִפְנֵי ה׳׃ יג וְשָׁחַט אֶת־הַכֶּבֶשׂ בִּמְקוֹם
אֲשֶׁר יִשְׁחַט אֶת־הַחַטָּאת וְאֶת־הָעֹלָה בִּמְקוֹם הַקֹּדֶשׁ כִּי
כַּחַטָּאת הָאָשָׁם הוּא לַכֹּהֵן קֹדֶשׁ קָדָשִׁים הוּא׃ יד וְלָקַח הַכֹּהֵן
מִדַּם הָאָשָׁם וְנָתַן הַכֹּהֵן עַל־תְּנוּךְ אֹזֶן הַמִּטַּהֵר הַיְמָנִית
וְעַל־בֹּהֶן יָדוֹ הַיְמָנִית וְעַל־בֹּהֶן רַגְלוֹ הַיְמָנִית׃ טו וְלָקַח הַכֹּהֵן
מִלֹּג הַשָּׁמֶן וְיָצַק עַל־כַּף הַכֹּהֵן הַשְּׂמָאלִית׃ טז וְטָבַל הַכֹּהֵן
אֶת־אֶצְבָּעוֹ הַיְמָנִית מִן־הַשֶּׁמֶן אֲשֶׁר עַל־כַּפּוֹ הַשְּׂמָאלִית וְהִזָּה
מִן־הַשֶּׁמֶן בְּאֶצְבָּעוֹ שֶׁבַע פְּעָמִים לִפְנֵי ה׳׃ יז וּמִיֶּתֶר הַשֶּׁמֶן אֲשֶׁר
עַל־כַּפּוֹ יִתֵּן הַכֹּהֵן עַל־תְּנוּךְ אֹזֶן הַמִּטַּהֵר הַיְמָנִית וְעַל־בֹּהֶן יָדוֹ
הַיְמָנִית וְעַל־בֹּהֶן רַגְלוֹ הַיְמָנִית עַל דַּם הָאָשָׁם׃ יח וְהַנּוֹתָר בַּשֶּׁמֶן
אֲשֶׁר עַל־כַּף הַכֹּהֵן יִתֵּן עַל־רֹאשׁ הַמִּטַּהֵר וְכִפֶּר עָלָיו הַכֹּהֵן
לִפְנֵי ה׳׃ יט וְעָשָׂה הַכֹּהֵן אֶת־הַחַטָּאת וְכִפֶּר עַל־הַמִּטַּהֵר
מִטֻּמְאָתוֹ וְאַחַר יִשְׁחַט אֶת־הָעֹלָה׃ כ וְהֶעֱלָה הַכֹּהֵן אֶת־הָעֹלָה
וְאֶת־הַמִּנְחָה הַמִּזְבֵּחָה וְכִפֶּר עָלָיו הַכֹּהֵן וְטָהֵר׃ כא וְאִם־דַּל הוּא
וְאֵין יָדוֹ מַשֶּׂגֶת וְלָקַח כֶּבֶשׂ אֶחָד אָשָׁם לִתְנוּפָה לְכַפֵּר עָלָיו
וְעִשָּׂרוֹן סֹלֶת אֶחָד בָּלוּל בַּשֶּׁמֶן לְמִנְחָה וְלֹג שָׁמֶן׃ כב וּשְׁתֵּי
תֹרִים אוֹ שְׁנֵי בְּנֵי יוֹנָה אֲשֶׁר תַּשִּׂיג יָדוֹ וְהָיָה אֶחָד חַטָּאת

a female, she shall be contaminated for two weeks, as during her separation; and for sixty-six days she shall remain in blood of purity. 6 Upon the completion of the days of her purity for a son or for a daughter, she shall bring a sheep within its first year for an elevation offering, and a young dove or a turtledove for a sin offering, to the entrance of the Tent of Meeting, to the Kohen. 7 He shall offer it before HASHEM and atone for her, and she becomes purified from the source of her blood; this is the law of one who gives birth to a male or to a female. 8 But if she cannot afford a sheep, then she shall take two turtledoves or two young doves, one for an elevation offering and one for a sin offering; and the Kohen shall atone for her and she shall become purified.

The Metzora

(Leviticus 14:1-2 . . . 10-32)

1 HASHEM spoke to Moses saying: 2 This shall be the law of the metzora on the day of his purification. He shall be brought to the Kohen . . . 10 On the eighth day, he shall take two unblemished sheep and one unblemished ewe in its first year, three tenth-ephas of fine flour mixed with oil, and one log of oil. 11 The Kohen who purifies shall place the person being purified along with them before HASHEM at the entrance of the Tent of Meeting. 12 The Kohen shall take the one sheep and bring it near for a guilt offering, with the log of oil; and he shall wave them as a wave offering before HASHEM. 13 He shall slaughter the sheep in the place where he will slaughter the sin offering and the elevation offering, in the holy place; for the guilt offering is like the sin offering, it is the Kohen's, it is most holy. 14 The Kohen shall take from the blood of the guilt offering, and the Kohen shall place it on the middle part of the right ear of the person being purified and on the thumb of his right hand and the big toe of his right foot. 15 The Kohen shall take from the log of oil and he shall pour it upon the Kohen's left palm. 16 The Kohen shall dip his right index finger into the oil that is in his left palm; and he shall sprinkle from the oil with his finger seven times before HASHEM. 17 Some of the oil remaining on his palm, the Kohen shall put on the middle part of the right ear of the man being purified, on his right thumb and on the big toe of his right foot; on the blood of the guilt offering. 18 And the rest of the oil that is on the Kohen's palm, he shall place upon the head of the person being purified; and the Kohen shall atone for him before HASHEM. 19 The Kohen shall perform the sin offering service and atone for the person being purified from his contamination; and then he shall slaughter the elevation offering. 20 The Kohen shall bring the elevation offering and the meal offering up to the Altar; and the Kohen shall atone for him, and he becomes pure. 21 If he is poor and his means are not sufficient, then he shall take one sheep as a guilt offering for a waving to atone for him; and one tenth-ephah of fine flour mixed with oil for a meal offering, and a log of oil. 22 And two turtledoves or two young pigeons — for whichever his means are sufficient — one shall be a sin offering and

וְהָאֶחָד עֹלָה: כג וְהֵבִיא אֹתָם בַּיּוֹם הַשְּׁמִינִי לְטָהֳרָתוֹ אֶל־הַכֹּהֵן
אֶל־פֶּתַח אֹהֶל־מוֹעֵד לִפְנֵי ה׳: כד וְלָקַח הַכֹּהֵן אֶת־כֶּבֶשׂ הָאָשָׁם
וְאֶת־לֹג הַשָּׁמֶן וְהֵנִיף אֹתָם הַכֹּהֵן תְּנוּפָה לִפְנֵי ה׳: כה וְשָׁחַט
אֶת־כֶּבֶשׂ הָאָשָׁם וְלָקַח הַכֹּהֵן מִדַּם הָאָשָׁם וְנָתַן עַל־תְּנוּךְ
אֹזֶן־הַמִּטַּהֵר הַיְמָנִית וְעַל־בֹּהֶן יָדוֹ הַיְמָנִית וְעַל־בֹּהֶן רַגְלוֹ
הַיְמָנִית: כו וּמִן־הַשֶּׁמֶן יִצֹק הַכֹּהֵן עַל־כַּף הַכֹּהֵן הַשְּׂמָאלִית:
כז וְהִזָּה הַכֹּהֵן בְּאֶצְבָּעוֹ הַיְמָנִית מִן־הַשֶּׁמֶן אֲשֶׁר עַל־כַּפּוֹ
הַשְּׂמָאלִית שֶׁבַע פְּעָמִים לִפְנֵי ה׳: כח וְנָתַן הַכֹּהֵן מִן־הַשֶּׁמֶן | אֲשֶׁר
עַל־כַּפּוֹ עַל־תְּנוּךְ אֹזֶן הַמִּטַּהֵר הַיְמָנִית וְעַל־בֹּהֶן יָדוֹ הַיְמָנִית
וְעַל־בֹּהֶן רַגְלוֹ הַיְמָנִית עַל־מְקוֹם דַּם הָאָשָׁם: כט וְהַנּוֹתָר
מִן־הַשֶּׁמֶן אֲשֶׁר עַל־כַּף הַכֹּהֵן יִתֵּן עַל־רֹאשׁ הַמִּטַּהֵר לְכַפֵּר עָלָיו
לִפְנֵי ה׳: ל וְעָשָׂה אֶת־הָאֶחָד מִן־הַתֹּרִים אוֹ מִן־בְּנֵי הַיּוֹנָה מֵאֲשֶׁר
תַּשִּׂיג יָדוֹ: לא אֵת אֲשֶׁר־תַּשִּׂיג יָדוֹ אֶת־הָאֶחָד חַטָּאת וְאֶת־
הָאֶחָד עֹלָה עַל־הַמִּנְחָה וְכִפֶּר הַכֹּהֵן עַל הַמִּטַּהֵר לִפְנֵי ה׳:
לב זֹאת תּוֹרַת אֲשֶׁר־בּוֹ נֶגַע צָרָעַת אֲשֶׁר לֹא־תַשִּׂיג יָדוֹ בְּטָהֳרָתוֹ:

זָב

(ויקרא יד:א־ב . . . יג־טו)

א וַיְדַבֵּר ה׳ אֶל־מֹשֶׁה לֵּאמֹר: ב זֹאת תִּהְיֶה תּוֹרַת הַמְּצֹרָע בְּיוֹם
טָהֳרָתוֹ וְהוּבָא אֶל־הַכֹּהֵן . . . יג וְשָׁחַט אֶת־הַכֶּבֶשׂ בִּמְקוֹם אֲשֶׁר
יִשְׁחַט אֶת־הַחַטָּאת וְאֶת־הָעֹלָה בִּמְקוֹם הַקֹּדֶשׁ כִּי כַּחַטָּאת
הָאָשָׁם הוּא לַכֹּהֵן קֹדֶשׁ קָדָשִׁים הוּא: יד וְלָקַח הַכֹּהֵן מִדַּם הָאָשָׁם
וְנָתַן הַכֹּהֵן עַל־תְּנוּךְ אֹזֶן הַמִּטַּהֵר הַיְמָנִית וְעַל־בֹּהֶן יָדוֹ הַיְמָנִית
וְעַל־בֹּהֶן רַגְלוֹ הַיְמָנִית: טו וְלָקַח הַכֹּהֵן מִלֹּג הַשָּׁמֶן וְיָצַק עַל־כַּף
הַכֹּהֵן הַשְּׂמָאלִית:

זָבָה

(ויקרא טו:כה . . . כט־ל)

כה וְאִשָּׁה כִּי־יָזוּב זוֹב דָּמָהּ יָמִים רַבִּים בְּלֹא עֶת־נִדָּתָהּ אוֹ
כִי־תָזוּב עַל־נִדָּתָהּ כָּל־יְמֵי זוֹב טֻמְאָתָהּ כִּימֵי נִדָּתָהּ תִּהְיֶה
טְמֵאָה הִוא . . . כט וּבַיּוֹם הַשְּׁמִינִי תִּקַּח־לָהּ שְׁתֵּי תֹרִים אוֹ שְׁנֵי
בְּנֵי יוֹנָה וְהֵבִיאָה אוֹתָם אֶל־הַכֹּהֵן אֶל־פֶּתַח אֹהֶל מוֹעֵד: ל וְעָשָׂה
הַכֹּהֵן אֶת־הָאֶחָד חַטָּאת וְאֶת־הָאֶחָד עֹלָה וְכִפֶּר עָלֶיהָ הַכֹּהֵן
לִפְנֵי ה׳ מִזּוֹב טֻמְאָתָהּ:

one an elevation offering. 23 *He shall bring them to the Kohen, on the eighth day of his purification, to the entrance of the Tent of Meeting, before* Hashem. 24 *The Kohen shall take the guilt offering sheep and the log of oil; and the Kohen shall wave them as a waving before* Hashem. 25 *He shall slaughter the guilt offering sheep and the Kohen shall take some of the guilt offering's blood and place it on the middle part of the right ear of the man being purified and on the thumb of his right hand and on the big toe of his right foot.* 26 *From the oil the Kohen shall pour upon the Kohen's left palm.* 27 *The Kohen shall sprinkle with his right index finger some of the oil that is in his left palm seven times before* Hashem. 28 *The Kohen shall place some of the oil that is on his palm upon the middle of the right ear of the person being purified, on the thumb of his right hand and on the big toe of his right foot — on the place of the guilt offering's blood.* 29 *And the rest of the oil that is on the Kohen's palm, he shall place upon the head of the person being purified; to atone for him before* Hashem. 30 *He shall then perform the service of one of the turtledoves or of the young pigeons, for whichever his means are sufficient.* 31 *Of whichever his means are sufficient — one is a sin offering and one is an elevation offering — along with the meal offering; and the Kohen shall atone for the one being purified, before* Hashem. 32 *This is the law of one in whom there is a tzaraas affliction — whose means are not sufficient — for his purification.*

The Zav

(Leviticus 14:1-2 . . . 13-15)

1 Hashem *spoke to Moses saying:* 2 *This shall be the law of the metzora on the day of his purification. He shall be brought to the Kohen . . .* 13 *He shall slaughter the sheep in the place where he will slaughter the sin offering and the elevation offering, in the holy place; for the guilt offering is like the sin offering, it is the Kohen's, it is most holy.* 14 *The Kohen shall take from the blood of the guilt offering, and the Kohen shall place it on the middle part of the right ear of the person being purified and on the thumb of his right hand and the big toe of his right foot.* 15 *The Kohen shall take from the log of oil and he shall pour it upon the Kohen's left palm.*

The Zavah

(Leviticus 15:25 . . . 29-30)

25 *If a woman's blood flows for many days outside of her period of separation, or if she has a flow after her separation, all the days of her contaminated flow shall be like the days of her separation; she is contaminated . . .* 29 *On the eighth day she shall take for herself two turtledoves or two young pigeons; she shall bring them to the Kohen, to the entrance of the Tent of Meeting.* 30 *The Kohen shall make one a sin offering and one an elevation offering; the Kohen shall atone for her before* Hashem *from her contaminating flow.*

General Introduction to Kereisos

I. The Kares Punishment[1]

Kares is a form of Heavenly retribution for the transgression of certain *mitzvos* enumerated in the first mishnah of this tractate. The title *Kereisos* [the plural of *kares*] notwithstanding, a clarification of exactly what *kares* is is not provided in this tractate, probably because the actual nature of the Heavenly punishment has no halachic ramifications. From its description in the Torah, *kares* is a spiritual punishment which affects the transgressor's soul. Often, the Torah uses a phrase such as וְנִכְרְתָה הַנֶּפֶשׁ, *the soul shall be cut off*, to describe this punishment, making it apparent that *kares* is primarily a spiritual phenomenon. At the same time, it is likewise apparent that this spiritual death has physical ramification, resulting in the premature death of the violator. This is indicated by the Torah's use of the term וְהַאֲבַדְתִּי, *and I will destroy* in conjunction with the term *kares* (*Toras Kohanim, Emor* 14:4)

Ramban (*commentary* to *Leviticus* 18:29) offers an exposition regarding the *kares* punishment:

> One who eats *cheilev* (forbidden fats) or blood, but is otherwise righteous, and committed the transgression only because he was momentarily overcome with lust, will have his life cut off and die before he is the age of sixty. He will, however, have a place in *Olam Haba* (the World to Come) in the ultimate Resurrection. Concerning this type of sin the Torah states, וְנִכְרַת הָאִישׁ הַהוּא, *that person will be cut off*. If, in addition to this serious transgression, the violator has a greater number of sins [than *mitzvos*], the punishment affects his soul after its departure from his body by being excised from Heavenly life. This is indicated by the phrase, וְהַאֲבַדְתִּי אֶת הַנֶּפֶשׁ הַהִיא, *I will destroy that soul*. Sinners of this category experience no physical *kares;* they often live to old age. There is a third category of *kares* concerning which the Torah uses the double phrase, הִכָּרֵת תִּכָּרֵת, *it will surely be cut off*, to indicate a double *kares:* early death

1. This introduction is limited to the punishment of *kares* meted out by the Heavenly court. To deserve this punishment one must intentionally violate the prohibition for which *kares* is prescribed. The discussion includes certain *korbanos* (Temple offerings) as they relate to *kares*-bearing sins and their atonement, but should not be taken as a complete exposition of *korbanos*.

and the loss of any share in *Olam Haba* (see also at length *Ramban's* treatise *Shaar HaGemul*). This punishment is reserved for the sins of idolatory and blasphemy.

There is also a punishment similar to *kares* known as מִיתָה בִּידֵי שָׁמַיִם, [*misah bidei shamayim*], *death at the hands of Heaven*. This, too, is a spiritual death of the soul but one for which the term כָּרֵת is not used by the Torah. Of the two punishments, *kares* is considered the more severe. It is apparent that the punishments of both *kares* and *misah bidei shamayim* are not limited to the spiritual sphere: they result in physical death. However, the difference between the two punishments is the subject of discussion in the Talmud and by the *Rishonim*.

According to *Yerushalmi* (*Bikkurim* 2:1), both *kares* and *misah bidei shamayim* are premature death. One who is liable to *kares* dies before the age of fifty; one liable to *misah bidei shamayim* dies before the age of sixty. The Talmud Bavli (*Moed Katan* 28a) apparently disagrees, stating that the punishment of *kares* brings about death between the age of fifty and sixty. After the age of sixty, *kares* takes the form of sudden death. *Misah bidei shamayim* simply means earlier death, without a fixed time (*Tos. Shabbos* 25a; *Yevamos* 2a s.v. אשת).

In some opinions, the differences between the categories of Heavenly punishment center on the persons involved: *Kares* affects not only the transgressor but his young children as well (*Rashi* 22a, s.v. כרת, *Shabbos* 25a; *Tos., Moed Katan* 28a; *Rabbeinu Yonah, Shaarei Teshuvah, sha'ar* 3:107). Others contend that this is true only for those transgressions for which the Torah uses the words עֲרִירִי, *childless*, indicating that the transgressor will lose his children during his lifetime. This punishment is reserved for incestuous relationships (see *Lev.* 20:21,22; *Yevamos* 55a). *Kares* for other transgressions, however, results in the premature death of the transgressor only (*Tos. Yevamos* 1a).[1]

Others distinguish between the *kares* and *misah bidei shamayim* punishments in terms of lingering effect: One who violated a *kares* offense may be subject to further punishment in *Olam Haba*, if he did not repent properly; but the punishment of *misah bidei shamayim* is completed with the transgressor's death (*Rav, Sanhedrin* 6:9). On the other hand, *misah bidei shamayim* may be preceded by the death of the violator's livestock or the loss of his possessions [to arouse him to repentance] prior to his own death (*Rabbeinu Yonah, Shaarei Teshuvah* loc. cit.).

---

1. *Aruch Laner* (*Yevamos* 2a) submits that even according to *Rashi*, there is a difference between the *kares* punishment and that for which the Torah mentions עֲרִירִי: The word עֲרִירִי indicates a punishment that involves the sinner's children, who will die during his lifetime. However, the term כָּרֵת means that his children may die prematurely, yet after him.

II. Atonement for Kereisos

The name *Kereisos* as an indicator of the subject matter of this tractate does not refer to the plural form of *kares*. Rather it alludes to the transgressions punishable by *kares* if they are committed deliberately. Moreover, the tractate discusses not the *kares* aspect of these transgressions, but the atonement offerings brought to atone for their inadvertent transgression. This atonement is the חַטָּאת [*chatas*], *sin offering*. The circumstances that occasion other offerings of atonement are also discussed, as will be elaborated upon below. Related to these sacrifices is a status known as מְחוּסַר כַּפָּרָה, *lacking atonement*, individuals who, for a variety of reasons, must bring offerings to enable them to partake of sacrificial food and enter the Temple grounds (see IV, below). Taken as a whole, these laws form a distinct category of sacrificial obligations — those of atonement for individuals, hence, the placing of this tractate in the order of *Kodashim* (*Rambam*, Introduction to *Commentary on the Mishnah*).

Since the most common atonement offering is the *chatas*, which is brought to atone for the inadvertent transgression of prohibitions punishable by *kares*, therefore the mishnah begins with a listing of those prohibitions, which gives the tractate its name — *Kereisos*.

III. Other Atonement Offerings

Aside from the *chatas*, another atonement offering directly related to prohibitions punishable by *kares* (and hence discussed extensively in this tractate) is the אָשָׁם תָּלוּי [*asham talui*], *the guilt offering of doubt*. This offering is brought by someone who is in doubt as to whether he inadvertently transgressed a *kares*-punishable prohibition. To forestall any Divine retribution until he determines whether he has sinned, he brings an *asham talui*. The differences between the *chatas* offering and the *asham talui* will be discussed below.

There are other transgressions mentioned in this tractate, which call for atonement offerings. Herewith is a brief listing and description of all atonement offerings and the circumstances that create the obligation to bring them.

☙ **Chatas** — The offering brought for the inadvertent transgression of any prohibition which is punishable by *kares* if violated deliberately. It consists of a ewe or she-goat in its first year. It is also known as a חַטָּאת קָבוּעַ, *a fixed chatas offering*, because the offering is the same regardless of the violator's financial status. It is thus distinguished from the *olah v'yored*, described below.

Olah v'yored — The variable sin offering which is a *chatas* that is adjusted in accord with the financial circumstances of the violator — for the rich it consists of a ewe or she-goat as in other *chatas* offerings. For the less prosperous it consists of a pair of birds — one for an *olah* and one for *chatas*. In cases of extreme poverty, a *minchah* (meal offering) is brought.

This offering is brought for only three sins: an unfulfilled or false oath; an oath taken to falsely deny knowledge of testimony on someone's behalf; and the transgression of entering the Temple grounds or eating *kodashim* (sacred food) while in a state of *tumah* (ritual impurity). Of these three transgressions, only the last is punishable by *kares*.

Asham talui — This offering is brought for cases of questionable *chatas* liability; i.e., one is not certain whether he inadvertently transgressed a *kares*-punishable transgression. Like any *asham*, it consists of a ram in its second year with a minimal value of two *selaim*, the mishnaic equivalent of the two silver *shekel* of the Torah's monetary system.

Asham — A personal atonement offering prescribed by the Torah for the violation of the following transgressions: *theft*, by falsely denying under oath the possession of money belonging to another; *me'ilah*, misappropriation of funds or property belonging to the Temple treasury; *shifchah charufah*, cohabitation with a non-Jewish female slave (שִׁפְחָה כְּנַעֲנִית) in a state of betrothal. (A more detailed description of this transgression is provided at the end of the first chapter in this tractate.) Unlike the *chatas*, the *asham* can be brought for a deliberate transgression.

IV. Mechusrei Kapparah — Those Who Lack Atonement

In addition to offerings brought to atone for transgressions, there is a category of offerings which serve the function of providing atonement as part of the purification process, to enable the owner of the offering to partake of *kodashim* (sacrificial foods) and enter the *Temple* grounds, after a period of *tumah*. The individual's in this category are:

Zav — a man experiencing a gonorrheal issue in a manner that causes *tumah*.

Zavah — a woman who enters a state of *tumah* as the result of an extra-menstrual issue of blood.

For both of these, the offering consists of a pair of birds. One for an *olah* and one for a *chatas*.

ও **Metzora** — one who contracted *tzaraas*, the symptom of which is a white-spotted skin disorder. Upon completing his *taharah* (purification process) the cured *metzora* brings a number of offerings which include an *asham*, a *minchah*, an *olah*, and a *chatas*. The latter two vary according to his financial circumstances.

The woman who has given birth — after childbirth a woman undergoes a period of *tumah* (forty days for a boy, eighty for a girl) during which she may not eat *kodashim*). At the end of this period, she brings offerings of a *chatas* and an *olah* which likewise vary according to financial circumstances.

V. Other Obligation Offerings

Beyond the four instances which comprise the category known as *mechusrei kapparah* there are two other occasions when offerings are brought as part of ritual obligations:

ও **Nazir** — The *nazir*, who became *tamei* by contact with a corpse during the period of his vow must bring a pair of birds — one for an *olah* and one for a *chatas*, in addition to an *asham*, before resuming his *nazir* vow. When a *nazir's* period of *nezeirus* (abstinence from wine, haircutting, and contact with the dead) comes to an end, he brings a group of offerings which include an *olah* lamb, a *chatas* ewe and a *shelamim* ram.

ও **Ger** — A proselyte must bring an offering in conjunction with his conversion.

These offerings are discussed briefly in the second chapter of this tractate.

כריתות א/א

[א] שְׁלֹשִׁים וְשֵׁשׁ כְּרֵיתוֹת בַּתּוֹרָה: הַבָּא עַל הָאֵם, וְעַל אֵשֶׁת הָאָב, וְעַל הַכַּלָּה; הַבָּא עַל הַזָּכוּר, וְעַל הַבְּהֵמָה, וְאִשָּׁה הַמְבִיאָה אֶת הַבְּהֵמָה עָלֶיהָ; הַבָּא עַל אִשָּׁה וּבִתָּהּ,

יד אברהם

Chapter 1

1.

שְׁלֹשִׁים וְשֵׁשׁ כְּרֵיתוֹת בַּתּוֹרָה: — *Thirty-six kereisos [are mentioned] in the Torah:*

The deliberate transgression of any of the thirty-six *mitzvos* listed in this mishnah incurs the punishment of *kares* (excision) [a form of Divine retribution described in the General Introduction] (*Rav; Tif. Yis.*).

However, in most cases the punishment is not limited to *kares*. If the violator was forewarned [and the act was witnessed by two valid witnesses] these transgressions are, in fact, punishable by *beis din* (Rabbinical court) — either capital punishment or *malkus*, [thirty-nine] lashes.[1] It is only in the absence of either a warning or witnesses, when the transgressor cannot be punished by the בֵּית דִּין שֶׁל מַטָּה, *earthly tribunal*, that the punishment of *kares* is meted out by the בֵּית דִּין שֶׁל מַעְלָה, *heavenly tribunal*.

Our mishnah, then, which groups all these transgressions together as punishable by *kares*, discusses only instances in which the transgression was deliberate, but was committed either without a warning or without the presence of witnesses (*Rashi; Rav; Tos. Yom Tov; Tif. Yis.*).

[If the transgression was committed inadvertently, the perpetrator is required to bring a *chatas* (sin) offering for all but the last two *mitzvos* on the list.]

The mention of the number of transgressions [thirty-six *kereisos*] seems superfluous; a simple tally of the enumerated prohibitions would be sufficient to know that. The number is stated to emphasize that one who in a single lapse of awareness commits all the sins mentioned in the mishnah must bring a separate *chatas* for each of them [except for the last two listed]. Each of the listed prohibitions, then, is a separate entity as far as the *chatas* obligation is concerned (*Gemara* 2b, cf. *Rabbeinu Gershom; Rambam, Shegagos* 4:1).

The phrase *in the Torah* indicates that the mishnah includes only the *kares*-transgressions mentioned in the Torah. However, there are *kares*-transgressions which are first mentioned in Prophets, such as intimacy with a non-Jewish woman [whose punishment is derived from *Malachi* 2:11-12]. These are not listed in the mishnah (see *Sanhedrin* 9:6).

הַבָּא עַל הָאֵם, — *[1] he who cohabits with his mother,*[2]

1. In the Torah's justice system, in order for a sin to be subject to court-imposed corporal punishment, the Torah must not only clearly establish the punishment for that activity, but it must also clearly state the prohibition of that activity. While such a prohibitive statement is not required for the *kares* punishment, it is the view of some commentators that a clearly stated prohibition is necessary for the obligation to bring a *chatas* to be in force (*Rashi* to *Eruvin* 96a, *Zevachim* 107a). In this view, each *kares*-transgression of the mishnah, which is mentioned in connection with the obligation to offer a *chatas*, must be associated with at least two Torah verses — one that states the אַזְהָרָה, *prohibition*, and one that states the עוֹנֶשׁ, *punishment*. The commentary will give the appropriate pair of verses in each case.

2. Although the mishnah mentions only that the male partner in illicit unions incurs punishment, the same punishment applies to the female partner (see below 2:4; *Bava Kamma* 32a).

1 **1.** Thirty-six *kereisos* [are mentioned] in the Torah: [1]
1 he who cohabits with his mother, [2] or with his
father's wife, [3] or with his daughter-in-law; [4] he who
cohabits with a male, [5] or with an animal, [6] or a
woman who allows herself to be mounted by an animal;

YAD AVRAHAM

This intimacy is prohibited by the Torah section dealing with the prohibition of incestuous relationships (*Lev.* 18:1ff). There, the Torah distinguishes between his mother (v. 7) and his father's wife (v. 8).

The *kares* punishment for this transgression is stated at the end of the aforementioned section, where the Torah makes a general statement (v. 29): כִּי כָל־אֲשֶׁר יַעֲשֶׂה מִכֹּל הַתּוֹעֵבֹת הָאֵלֶּה וְנִכְרְתוּ הַנְּפָשׁוֹת הָעֹשֹׂת מִקֶּרֶב עַמָּם, *For whoever shall commit any of these abominations, the persons who committed them shall be cut off from the midst of their people.* This generalization teaches that atransgression of any of the previously listed prohibitions is punishable by *kares*, even those not specified by the Torah in its section dealing with the punishments for these forbidden relations (see *Lev.* 20:1ff).

If committed in the presence of witnesses and with a warning, this transgression — as well as the next five — carries the punishment of סְקִילָה, *[death by] stoning.*[1] They are listed first because *stoning* is the most severe of the four capital punishments meted out by the *beis din*. See *Sanhedrin* 7:1 (*Rashi; Tos. Yom Tov*).

וְעַל אֵשֶׁת הָאָב, — *[2] or with his father's wife,*

This intimacy is prohibited by *Lev.* 18:8. This prohibition applies to any wife of his father, not only his mother. The prohibition remains in force even after the father's death, or after a divorce (*Sanhedrin* 54a).

As mentioned above, the penalty of *kares* is stated at the end of the passage prohibiting illicit relations.

With a warning and the presence of witnesses, this transgression is liable to *sekilah*, death by stoning (*Lev.* 20:11).

וְעַל הַכַּלָּה; — *[3] or with his daughter-in-law;*

This intimacy is prohibited by *Lev.* 18:15. She, too, is forbidden to him even if she is no longer married to his son (*Sanhedrin* 54a).

Here, too, the *kares* penalty is indicated in the aforementioned verse at the end of the chapter.

With warning and witnesses, the transgressors are liable to *sekilah* [death by stoning] (*Lev.* 20:12).

הַבָּא עַל הַזָּכוּר, — *[4] he who cohabits with a male,*

Homosexual relations are explicitly prohibited by *Lev.* 18:22. As is the case with the previous transgressions, the Torah proclaims the penalty of *kares* at the end of the chapter, including this in the phrase וְנִכְרְתוּ הַנְּפָשׁוֹת הָעֹשֹׂת, *the persons doing so shall be cut off.*

With warning and witnesses, this sin, too, is punishable by *sekilah* (*Lev.* 20:13).

וְעַל הַבְּהֵמָה, וְאִשָּׁה הַמְּבִיאָה אֶת הַבְּהֵמָה עָלֶיהָ; — *[5] or with an animal, [6] or a woman who allows herself to be mounted by an animal;*

Sexual intimacy with an animal is prohibited by *Lev.* 18:23. The *kares* penalty is derived from the same verse that refers to previous transgressions (ibid. v. 29).

This sin, too, may incur the death penalty of *sekilah* (ibid. 20:15).

1. The capital penalty for intimacy with one's mother is not written explicitly in the Torah. The Sages derive it exegetically from the punishment specified for his father's wife (*Lev.* 20:11; see *Sanhedrin* 53b).

כריתות וְעַל אֵשֶׁת אִישׁ; הַבָּא עַל־אֲחוֹתוֹ, וְעַל אֲחוֹת אָבִיו,
א/א וְעַל־אֲחוֹת אִמּוֹ, וְעַל־אֲחוֹת אִשְׁתּוֹ, וְעַל־אֵשֶׁת
אָחִיו, וְעַל־אֵשֶׁת אֲחִי אָבִיו, וְעַל־הַנִּדָּה; הַמְגַדֵּף,

יד אברהם

הַבָּא עַל אִשָּׁה וּבִתָּהּ, — *[7] he who cohabits with a woman and her daughter,*

The mother-and-daughter prohibition is stated in *Lev.* 18:17. The phrase *a woman and her daughter* includes: his wife's daughter from another man [i.e., his stepdaughter]; his wife's mother [i.e., his mother-in-law]; his wife's paternal or maternal grandmother; and his wife's granddaughter. His own daughter [even one born out of wedlock] and granddaughter are included as well (*Rav; Sanhedrin* 9:1).

Rather than state *'he who cohabits with his mother-in-law or with his wife's daughter'* as separate *chatas* categories, the mishnah used only the Torah's phrase one who cohabits *with a woman and her daughter* because it includes all these relationships (*Tif. Yis.*).[1]

The *kares* penalty for this prohibition is included in the same verse (ibid. 29) as are all the other sins of immorality. With warning and witnesses, this transgression is liable to שְׂרֵפָה, *death by burning* (*Lev.* 20:14). Since this is a less severe form of capital punishment than death by stoning, it is listed after the previous six, which are punishable by stoning.

The death penalty appears in *Lev.* 20:14 only with reference to a mother-in-law. However, it is extended exegetically to include the other variations of the mother-and-daughter prohibition mentioned above (*Sanhedrin* 9:1).

This prohibition includes his wife's daughter regardless of whether he or another man is the father. However, it does not include the daughter [by another man] of a woman with whom he had extra-marital relations.

וְעַל אֵשֶׁת אִישׁ; — *[8] or with a married woman;*

This is prohibited by the Torah (*Lev.* 18:20) and is included in the verse (ibid. v. 29) that prescribes *kares* for all the other illicit relations.

With warning and witnesses, this sin is punishable by חֶנֶק, *death by strangulation* (*Lev.* 20:10). Since this is the mildest of the four forms of capital punishment, it is listed as the last of the immoral acts punishable by death (*Tos. Yom Tov*).

[The mishnah now continues to complete the listing of the other incestuous relations that are subject to *kares*, but not to capital punishment (ibid.; see also *Makkos* 4:1).]

הַבָּא עַל־אֲחוֹתוֹ, וְעַל אֲחוֹת אָבִיו, וְעַל־אֲחוֹת אִמּוֹ, — *[9] he who cohabits with his sister, [10] or with his father's sister, [11] or with his mother's sister,*

[Relations with these women are subject to *kares*, as stated in *Leviticus* 20:17,19, regardless of whether they are full sisters or half sisters.]

וְעַל־אֲחוֹת אִשְׁתּוֹ, — *[12] or with his wife's sister,*

This prohibition, stated in *Leviticus* 18:18, is included in the general *kares* penalty stated for incestuous relationships (ibid. v. 29). [However, this prohibition is in force only during the wife's

1. *Rambam* (*Shegagos* 1:4), by contrast, does enumerate the prohibitions of the mishnah in terms of the nine individuals involved. Thus he lists separately a wife's mother, a wife's grandmother, a wife's daughter, etc., even though all these offenses are derived from the same phrase: עֶרְוַת אִשָּׁה וּבִתָּהּ לֹא תְגַלֵּה — *Do not expose the nakedness of a woman and her daughter* (*Lev.* 18:17). Thus the listing of *kereisos* as they appear in *Rambam's Mishneh Torah* includes more than the thirty-six prohibitions of *kares* mentioned by the mishnah.

1
1

[7] he who cohabits with a woman and her daughter, [8] or with a married woman; [9] one who cohabits with his sister, [10] or with his father's sister, [11] or with his mother's sister, [12] or with his wife's sister, [13] or with his brother's wife, [14] or with his father's brother's wife, [15] or with a menstruant; [16] the blasphemer,

YAD AVRAHAM

lifetime. After his wife's death, a man is permitted to marry her sister (*Yevamos* 4:13).]

In the Torah, the prohibition of intimacy with one's brother's wife precedes the prohibition of taking two sisters (*Lev.* 18:14,16). The *Tanna*, however, reversed the order to keep the prohibitions of sisters in one series and the prohibitions of wives in a separate series (*Lechem Shamayim* to *Makkos* 3:1).

וְעַל־אֵשֶׁת אָחִיו, — *[13] or with his brother's wife,*

Since a woman married to one's brother is included in the capital offense of אֵשֶׁת אִישׁ, *a married woman*, mentioned previously, the reference here obviously is to a woman who *was* married to a brother but is now divorced or widowed.

[The widow of a brother from one father, who died without any surviving children, is subject to the laws of *yibum* (levirate marriage) and is, of course, excluded from this prohibition.]

The prohibition for taking a brother's wife is stated in *Leviticus* 18:16; the penalty of *kares* in verse 29.

In the presence of witnesses and with a warning, the punishment for this offense is *malkus* (lashes).

וְעַל־אֵשֶׁת אֲחִי אָבִיו, — *[14] or with his father's brother's wife,*

[This, too, applies only to a divorcee or a widow.] The prohibition appears in *Leviticus* 18:14; the penalty of *kares* in verse 29.

This prohibition applies only to the wife of the father's paternal brother. The wife of the father's maternal half-brother and the wife of the mother's brother are included in the category of שְׁנִיּוֹת, *secondary arayos*, prohibited by Rabbinic decree (*Tif. Yis.* from *Rambam, Hil. Ishus* 1:6).

וְעַל־הַנִּדָּה; — *[15] or with a menstruant;*

[A *niddah* is a woman who has menstruated and has not purified herself by immersion in a *mikveh*. It is immaterial whether she is still menstruating at the time of the intimacy.]

The prohibition of intimacy with a *niddah* is stated in *Leviticus* 18:19; the *kares* penalty in 20:18.

As mentioned above, the last six relationships mentioned in this section are not subject to the death penalty. An intentional transgression bears the *kares* punishment. If the transgressor was forewarned and witnessed, he is punished by *malkus* (lashes), as explained in *Makkos* 3:1 (*Tos. Yom Tov*).

In the event that a person received the *malkus* punishment, he is exempted from the punishment of *kares*, as explained in *Makkos* 3:15.

Having completed the series of *kares* offenses included in the category of עֲרָיוֹת, *forbidden relations*, the *Tanna* now continues with the listing of other *kares* offenses, beginning with those subject to the penalty of death by stoning (*Tif. Yis.*).

הַמְגַדֵּף, — *[16] the blasphemer,*

One who blasphemes by uttering Hashem's[1] Name and cursing it (*Rav*).

1. Elsewhere (*Sanhedrin* 7:5) the mishnah stipulates: *The blasphemer is not liable unless he utters the Divine Name*, that is, the Name of God must be clearly enunciated in order for the blasphemer to be liable for the death penalty. According to one view, this refers to the Ineffable Name, known in Hebrew as the שֵׁם הַמְיוּחָד, the Tetragrammaton written in Hebrew as *yud*

יד אברהם

In an alternate explanation, this means an oral form of idolatry, i.e., he sings praises to a pagan deity (*Rashi* from *Gem.* 7b). Since this is the form of worship for this deity, he is liable to the death penalty and *kares*, despite the fact that it is merely an oral expression rather than a concrete action usually associated with the idolatry prohibition (*Tif. Yis.*).

According to the alternate explanation it is not clear, though, why the mishnah lists this as a distinct category of *kares*; it should be included in the prohibition of *one who worships idols* (*Rashash* 2a).

The prohibition against blaspheming is stated in *Exodus* 22:27: אֱלֹהִים לֹא תְקַלֵּל, *do not curse God.* The *kares* and death penalty are spelled out in *Leviticus* 24:15-16 (see *Sanhedrin* 56a).

וְהָעוֹבֵד עֲבוֹדָה זָרָה; — *[17] the idol worshiper;*

The Torah prohibits idolatry in *Exodus* 34:14: כִּי לֹא תִשְׁתַּחֲוֶה לְאֵל אַחֵר, *For you shall not prostrate yourself to another god* (*Rashi*). Others cite the verse in the Decalogue (*Ex.* 20:5): לֹא תִשְׁתַּחֲוֶה לָהֶם וְלֹא תָעָבְדֵם — *Do not prostrate yourself to them nor worship them* (*Rambam Sefer HaMitzvos*, Prohibition #5 and #6; *Mishnah Torah, Avodah Zarah* 3:3; see *Sanhedrin* 60b).

Kares for this sin is stated in *Numbers* 15:31: כִּי דְבַר־ה׳ בָּזָה וְאֶת־מִצְוָתוֹ הֵפַר הִכָּרֵת תִּכָּרֵת הַנֶּפֶשׁ הַהִוא עֲוֹנָה בָהּ, *For he has despised the word of HASHEM, and he has broken His commandment; that soul shall utterly be cut off, his iniquity upon him*. The phrase דְּבַר־ה׳, *the word of HASHEM*, alludes to the second commandment which prohibits idolatry[1] [*Sanhedrin* 99a] (*Rashi*).

With a warning and witnesses, the penalty for idolatry is stoning, as expressly stated in *Deut.* 17:5.

There are two forms to the transgression of idolatry:

(a) If one worships any deity other than *Hashem* in its customary manner — whatever that ritual happens to be. For example, even an act of desecration such as throwing stones at the deity is considered *avodah zarah* if that is the manner in which it is normally worshiped. This is the case if one throws stones at the pagan god *Markulis* (Mercurius). Worshiping any other deity in this manner, however, is not liable to this punishment, even if performed as an act of reverence.

(b) If one worships any deity with one of the standard methods of worship, i.e., one of four acts of worship practiced in the Temple in the service of God. These are: שְׁחִיטָה, *slaughtering* (a sacrifice); קִטּוּר, *burning* (an offering or incense); נִסּוּךְ, *pouring libations*, and הִשְׁתַּחֲוָאָה, *prostrating* oneself. The worship of any deity by performing one of these four acts of worship is liable to the penalty of stoning or *kares* even if this is not the manner in which this particular deity is customarily worshiped. Thus, for example, if one slaughtered an offering to

kei vav kei (*Meiri, Sanhedrin* loc. cit.; opinion cited by *Rambam*, *Hilchos Avodah Zarah* 7:2). According to others, the Name spelled *aleph dalet nun yud* [i.e., the way the Four-Letter Name is commonly pronounced] is in the same category [*Rambam*, ibid.]. As far as *kares* is concerned, though, all names of *Hashem*, even those classified as merely כִּנּוּיִם (e.g. אֵל or אֱלוֹהַּ), are included in the prohibition (*Tosafos Sanhedrin* 56a s.v. ועל) (see ArtScroll *Shevuos* 4:13, *Sanhedrin* 7:5 and footnote there).

1. Although all 613 *mitzvos* are actually *Hashem's* commands, the prohibition of idolatry is singled out by the phrase *the word of Hashem*. This is because all *mitzvos* were transmitted to us through Moses; the prohibition against idolatry contained in the first two of the Ten Commandments was heard by all of Israel directly from *Hashem* (*Gem.* ibid., cf. the emendations of the Vilna Gaon, ad loc.).

1 [17] the idol worshiper; [18] the one who gives of his
1 offspring to the *Molech*, [19] the practitioner of *ov;*

YAD AVRAHAM

Markulis, he would incur the death penalty of *kares*, even though the customary form of worship for this deity is stone throwing (*Rav* from *Sanhedrin* 6:9).

Actually, then, there is more than one act that incurs the *kares* penalty for idolatry. The *Tanna* could have stated: *One who slaughters to avodah zarah; one who burns an offering to avodah zarah*, etc., counting four forms of idolatry. However, the *Tanna* counts it as one for it is the *prohibition* that is being listed, not the action. For the same reason the sin of desecration of the Sabbath is counted as one although there are numerous actions that are included in the thirty-nine אֲבוֹת מְלָאכוֹת, *primary labor categories* (*Tos. Yom Tov* from *Gem.* 3a).

וְהַנּוֹתֵן מִזַּרְעוֹ לַמֹּלֶךְ, — *[18] the one who gives of his offspring to the Molech,*

The Torah states (*Lev.* 18:21): וּמִזַּרְעֲךָ לֹא־תִתֵּן לְהַעֲבִיר לַמֹּלֶךְ, *do not give any of your children to pass through for the Molech.* What is meant is a pagan rite in which a person passed one or more of his children through a flame in honor of an entity called *Molech.*

[There are a number of opinions among the commentators concerning the exact description of the *Molech* rite. See *Yad Avraham* commentary in ArtScroll *Sanhedrin* 7:7. According to all, it involved some form of passing a child through fire, although not necessarily burning him to death. The *Tanna* of this mishnah apparently follows the view that *Molech* was not deemed a deity and its service is thus not included in the previously listed category of idolatry (see *Sanhedrin* 64a).]

וּבַעַל אוֹב; — *[19] the practitioner of ov;*

The ancients were knowledgeable in certain acts of sorcery which enabled one to communicate with the dead.[1] One form of this art was known as אוֹב, *ov*, and its practitioner called a בַּעַל אוֹב, *baal ov.* It is a form of necromancy that involves the use of a human skull [*ov*, plural *ovos*] and incense to raise the spirit of the dead person being consulted. The voice of the spirit is heard from the armpit of the necromancer.[2]

The prohibition against the practice of this art is stated in *Lev.* 19:31: אַל־תִּפְנוּ אֶל־הָאֹבֹת, *Do not turn to the ovos*, and is liable to *kares* or the penalty of death by stoning, as stated in *Lev.* 20:6 and 27[3] (see *Tosafos, Sanhedrin* 65a, s.v. והנשאל).

There is another form of necromancy mentioned in the Torah (ibid.) performed by a practitioner called the יִדְּעוֹנִי, *yidoni.* As described by the mishnah in *Sanhedrin* 7:7, this was performed by using the bone of a certain animal [or bird] called *yedua*. The practitioner placed the bone in his mouth, from where the voice of the spirit emanated. This form of necromancy has the same status

1. According to most commentators, the ability of these practitioners to communicate with the dead was *real*, not simply an effect created by black magic; it was reality. This is evidenced by the narrative in *I Samuel* (28:7ff) describing King Saul's use of a practitioner of *ov* to communicate with the deceased prophet Samuel (*Beur HaGra Y.D.* 179:13).

There are, however, opinions among the early *Rishonim* that all the acts of sorcery described in the Torah are actually illusions (*Rambam, Avodah Zarah* 11:16; *Radak, I Samuel* 28:24; see footnote to ArtScroll *Sanhedrin* 7:11).

2. The description of the *ov* process is found in *Sanhedrin* 7:7. See ArtScroll *Sanhedrin* and *Yad Avraham* commentary there for a fuller discussion of the different views of the commentators concerning the details of this practice.

3. The penalty of stoning or *kares* is only for the practitioner of the *ov*; the individual who inquires of them violates a prohibition and the penalty of מַכַּת מַרְדּוּת, *rabbinically ordained lashes* (*Sanhedrin* 7:7; *Rambam, Avodah Zarah* 11:14).

אוֹב; הַמְחַלֵּל אֶת־הַשַּׁבָּת; וְטָמֵא שֶׁאָכַל אֶת־הַקֹּדֶשׁ, וְהַבָּא לַמִּקְדָּשׁ טָמֵא; הָאוֹכֵל חֵלֶב, וְדָם,

יד אברהם

as the *ovos*; it is prohibited by the verse (*Lev.* 19:31): אַל־תִּפְנוּ אֶל־הָאוֹבֹת וְאֶל־הַיִּדְּעֹנִים, *Do not turn to the ovos or to the yidonim*, and is liable to the penalty of death by stoning and *kares*, as stated in *Lev.* 20:6 and 7.

The mishnah in *Sanhedrin* (7:7) that mentions the categories of prohibitions punishable by death lists the *yidoni* as a separate category. Our mishnah, in dealing with *kares*, lists only the prohibition of the *ov*, although the *yidoni* is equally liable to *kares*. This is because the *yidoni* does not have a separately stated prohibition in the Torah; it is included in the prohibition for the *baal ov*. Therefore, as far as *kares* is concerned, both these forms of necromancy are really one category, i.e., if one performed both of them in one period of forgetfulness he is liable to only one *chatas*. The *Tanna* listed only the *baal ov* because it is mentioned first in the Torah's prohibition. What is really meant is that one is liable for *kares* [and, as a result, a *chatas*] for *either* the *ov* or the *yidoni* (*Rav*; *Tos. Yom Tov* citing the view of R' Yochanan in the *Gemara* 3b and *Sanhedrin* 61b cf. *Rashash;* see also commentary to mishnah 2, s.v. יָצָא מְגַדֵּף).

הַמְחַלֵּל אֶת־הַשַּׁבָּת; — *[20] one who desecrates the Sabbath;*

This refers to the performance of any of the thirty-nine *avos melachos* [main categories of labor] listed in *Shabbos* 7:2, or any of their *tolados* [secondary labors] (*Rav*).

These labors are forbidden to be performed on the Sabbath by the verse (*Ex.* 20:10): לֹא־תַעֲשֶׂה כָל־מְלָאכָה, *You may not do any work*. The penalty of *kares* as well as the death penalty are stated in *Ex.* 31:14 (*Rashi*).

This sin can be committed in numerous ways, viz., by performing any of various forms of labor that comprise the thirty-nine *avos* and their numerous subcategories, the *tolados*. The *Tanna*, however, lists it merely as one *kares* penalty since all of these diverse actions fall under the category of one prohibition: חִלּוּל שַׁבָּת, *desecration of the Sabbath*. As a result, if one performs all thirty-nine labors in one lapse of awareness, i.e., he forgets that it is the Sabbath, he is liable for only one *chatas*. [As already explained above (s.v. והעובד), the *Tanna* lists the various *prohibitions* that bring *kares*, not physical actions. The various *avos melachos* are alternate forms of the violation of the Torah's prohibition *You may not do any work* (*Tos. Yom Tov* from *Gem.* 3a).]

Actually, it *is* possible to bring many *chatas* offerings for performing a number of *melachos*. This is true when he was aware that it was the Sabbath but unaware that the *melachos* in question were forbidden. For example, if one wrote and cooked on the Sabbath, not being aware that either of these actions is forbidden, he will be obligated to bring two *chatas* offerings although in essence both these actions are a repetition of the same prohibition: לֹא־תַעֲשֶׂה כָל־מְלָאכָה, *You may not do any work*. The distinctive category of each *av melachah* causes us to regard each action as a separate prohibition (cf. 3:7 below; see also ArtScroll *Shabbos* 7:1; with *Yad Avraham* comm., the prefatory remarks there, and 12:6 for a fuller exposition of this concept). Thus, in the above situation it is possible to bring as many as thirty-nine *chatas* offerings for the sin of *chillul Shabbos* [desecration of the Sabbath].

Our mishnah, which lists the sin of *chillul Shabbos* as the cause of only one *chatas*, is referring to a case where a person performed a number of labors because he was unaware that it was the Sabbath. Since all of his transgressions are the result of only one error — the mistake in the day — he is liable for only one *chatas*.

Our mishnah chose this situation [rather than one when he erred concerning the permissibility of the labors themselves] to emphasize that under all circumstances one is obligated for at least one *chatas* for the desecration of the Sabbath (*Gem.* 3a).

1 [20] one who desecrates the Sabbath; [21] a *tamei*
1 [person] who eats consecrated foods, [22] or one who
enters the Temple grounds while *tamei;* [23] one who
eats *cheilev* fat, [24] or blood, [25] leftover [sacrificial

YAD AVRAHAM

The remaining transgressions listed by the mishnah are punishable by *kares* only, and are not liable to the death penalty. However, with a warning and witnesses the transgressor is liable to *malkus* (lashes). After receiving *malkus*, the violator is then exempted from *kares*, as explained in *Makkos* 3:15.

וְטָמֵא שֶׁאָכַל אֶת־הַקֹּדֶשׁ, — *[21] a tamei [person] who eats consecrated foods,*

[A *tamei* person is one who is in a legally defined state of impurity known as *tumah*. This can be caused by such physical phenomena as menstruation or the emission of semen, or it can be transmitted by physical contact with a *tamei* person or object, such as a human corpse, the carcass of an unslaughtered kosher animal, and certain rodents. The *tamei* is enjoined from eating sacrificial foods or entering the Temple grounds, as explained below.]

The prohibition against a *tamei* person partaking of sacrificial food, e.g., the meat of a *korban* or the remainder of a *minchah*, is punishable by *kares*, as stated explicitly in *Lev.* 7:20.

The admonition against a *tamei* eating consecrated food is not stated explicitly; it is derived exegetically by the Talmud (*Makkos* 14b) from the verse (*Lev.* 12:4): בְּכָל־קֹדֶשׁ לֹא־תִגָּע, *she* [i.e., a woman after childbirth, who is *tamei*] *shall touch no consecrated foods*. According to the *Gemara's* interpretation, this means that a *tamei* may not *eat* any consecrated foods; nowhere is it stated that one who is *tamei* is liable to *kares* for touching consecrated foods (*Tos. Yom Tov, Makkos* 3:2).

וְהַבָּא לַמִּקְדָּשׁ טָמֵא; — *[22] or one who enters the Temple grounds while tamei;*

As already stated above, a *tamei* may not enter the Temple precincts. This, too, is derived from the verse concerning a woman after childbirth (*Lev.* 12:4), which states וְאֶל־הַמִּקְדָּשׁ לֹא תָבֹא, *nor shall she enter the Sanctuary.* This is punishable by *kares* (*Num.* 19:13). The admonition is stated in *Num.* 5:3: וְלֹא יְטַמְּאוּ אֶת־מַחֲנֵיהֶם, *And they shall not contaminate their camps* (*Makkos* 14b).

The second word טָמֵא, *while tamei*, seems superfluous in this clause of the mishnah; it would have sufficed to say *a tamei that ate sacrificial foods or entered the Temple*. The point of this repetition, however, is to include in this prohibition an instance in which the person became *tamei* in the Temple grounds. If he then tarries in the Temple grounds it is considered as if he entered when he was *tamei* [see *Shevuos* 2:1] (*Tif. Yis.*).

הָאוֹכֵל חֵלֶב, וְדָם, — *[23] one who eats cheilev fat, [24] or blood,*

The Torah prohibits the eating of two parts of an animal's body, viz., חֵלֶב [*cheilev*], *fat,* and דָּם, *blood.* [The fats prohibited by the Torah are those fats that were placed on the Temple Altar in the case of sacrificial animals — see *Lev.* 3:3-4. Basically, these fats are the ones that drape over the meat and can be peeled away, rather than those that are marbled with the meat. These prohibited fats are delineated in *Yoreh Deah* 64. The animal's other fats, usually referred to as שׁוּמָן, *shuman,* are permitted.] Eating either the animal's *cheilev* or its blood is punishable with *kares* [excision]. [Only the 'lifeblood' carries the penalty of *kares;* the other bloods carry only the penalty of lashes — see 5:1 below with commentary; see also *Yad Avraham* commentary in ArtScroll *Chullin* 8:3 and 2:1.]

Both the penalties of *kares* and the admonition against eating *cheilev* and blood are stated in *Lev.* 7:22-27 (*Tos. Yom Tov*).

נוֹתָר, פִּגּוּל; הַשּׁוֹחֵט וְהַמַּעֲלֶה בַחוּץ; הָאוֹכֵל חָמֵץ בַּפֶּסַח; וְהָאוֹכֵל וְהָעוֹשֶׂה מְלָאכָה בְּיוֹם הַכִּפּוּרִים;

יד אברהם

נוֹתָר, — [25] *leftover [sacrificial meat],*

All sacrifices must be eaten within an allotted time frame. Some must be eaten by the end of the night following their slaughtering; others by the end of the next day, i.e., they may be eaten during the day of slaughter, the following day and the night between them (see *Zevachim* 5:3ff).

The meat of a *korban* that was left beyond its allotted time is called נוֹתָר, *leftover,* and becomes disqualified and forbidden to be eaten; it must be burned instead. This is stated in *Exodus* 29:34: וְשָׂרַפְתָּ אֶת־הַנּוֹתָר בָּאֵשׁ לֹא יֵאָכֵל כִּי־קֹדֶשׁ הוּא, *and you shall burn the leftover in a fire; it shall not be eaten for it is holy* (*Tos. Yom Tov; Rashi* ibid.).

The *kares* penalty for eating leftover is stated in *Lev.* 19:8. With a warning and witnesses this transgression is punishable by *malkus* (since the admonition is expressed with a negative expression, as above).

פִּגּוּל; — [26] *or piggul* [lit. *abomination*];

Piggul, which means abomination, is the Torah's term for a sacrifice disqualified during its service because of the intent on the part of the *Kohen* performing the service to eat the sacrifice (or burn it on the Altar) beyond its allotted time.[1] Once this intention is expressed, the sacrifice is invalid even if, in actuality, it was consumed within the proper time. Consumption of such an offering is forbidden under the penalty of *kares*.

Rav defines *piggul* as: *'sacrifices which he intended to eat beyond their allotted time or beyond their allotted place.'*

The fact that *Rav* included in his definition the invalidation of חוּץ לִמְקוֹמוֹ, *intention to eat beyond its allotted place,* is very difficult to understand. For while it is true that an offering brought with such an intention is invalid, it is clear from many mishnayos that the consumption of a sacrifice invalidated in this manner is exempt from *kares*. Thus, in the context of our mishnah, which discusses actions punishable by *kares*, eating *piggul* can refer only to the invalidation created by the intent of חוּץ לִזְמַנּוֹ, *beyond its allotted time* (*Tos. Yom Tov*).

The *kares* punishment for eating *piggul* is explicit in the Torah (*Lev.* 7:18).

The prohibition is derived from the generality used by the Torah regarding leftover sacrificial meat (*Ex.* 29:34): לֹא יֵאָכֵל כִּי־קֹדֶשׁ הוּא, *it shall not be eaten for it is holy*. The implication is that whatever is holy and becomes disqualified is included in this prohibition (*Tos. Yom Tov, Makkos* 3:2; *Rashi* ad loc.).

הַשּׁוֹחֵט וְהַמַּעֲלֶה בַחוּץ; — [27] *one who slaughters [a sacrificial animal], or [28] offers [it] up, outside [the Temple grounds];*

Bringing an offering outside the place designated for its service, i.e., the Temple courtyard, is a violation of Torah law for which the punishment is *kares*.

There are two separate and distinct prohibitions involved in this ban — one is *slaughtering* outside the Temple grounds an animal that has been designated as an offering, and the other is *offering*, i.e., burning the offering on an altar, outside the Temple (see *Zevachim* 13:1ff).

Slaughtering a sacrificial animal outside of the Temple is in itself liable to *kares* even if he never burnt the offering. This is stated in *Lev.* (17:3ff) where the Torah states: אִישׁ אִישׁ ... אֲשֶׁר יִשְׁחַט שׁוֹר אוֹ־כֶשֶׂב אוֹ־עֵז בַּמַּחֲנֶה אוֹ אֲשֶׁר יִשְׁחָט מִחוּץ לַמַּחֲנֶה, וְאֶל־פֶּתַח אֹהֶל מוֹעֵד לֹא הֱבִיאוֹ ... דָּם יֵחָשֵׁב לָאִישׁ הַהוּא, דָּם שָׁפָךְ וְנִכְרַת הָאִישׁ הַהוּא, *anyone ... who slaughters a bull or*

1. The laws of *piggul* are quite detailed and are the subject of extensive discussion in the tractates *Zevachim* (chapters 2-4) and *Menachos* (chapters 2-3). The interested reader is directed to the prefatory remarks in ArtScroll Mishnah *Zevachim* 2:3 for a brief compendium of these laws.

1
1 meat], [26] or *piggul;* [27] one who slaughters [a sacrificial animal], [28] or offers [it] up, outside [the Temple grounds]; [29] one who eats *chametz* on Pesach; [30] one who eats [31] or performs work on Yom Kippur;

YAD AVRAHAM

a sheep or a goat in the camp or who slaughters outside the camp and did not bring it to the Tabernacle . . . it shall be counted for that man as bloodshed; he has shed blood, and he shall be cut off.

Similarly, burning an offering on an altar outside of the Temple is punishable by *kares* [even if he did not slaughter it outside the Temple] as stated in the Torah (ibid. 8,9): ... אִישׁ אִישׁ מִבֵּית יִשְׂרָאֵל ... אֲשֶׁר־יַעֲלֶה עֹלָה אוֹ־זָבַח, וְאֶל־פֶּתַח אֹהֶל מוֹעֵד לֹא יְבִיאֶנּוּ לַעֲשׂוֹת אֹתוֹ לַה׳ וְנִכְרַת הָאִישׁ הַהוּא מֵעַמָּיו, *anyone of the House of Israel . . . who will offer an olah or slaughtered offering and will not bring it to the entrance of the Tabernacle to offer it for HASHEM, that man shall be cut off from his people.*

Thus, one who slaughters *and* burns an offering outside of the Temple grounds incurs two *kares* punishments and, if done unintentionally, must bring two *chatas* offerings (*Rav*).[1]

The admonition against burning an offering outside of the Temple is stated in *Deut.* (12:13): הִשָּׁמֶר לְךָ פֶּן־תַּעֲלֶה עֹלֹתֶיךָ בְּכָל־מָקוֹם אֲשֶׁר תִּרְאֶה, *Take heed that you do not offer your olah offerings in any place that you see.*

The admonition against slaughtering an offering outside the Temple is not so clearly stated, but derived exegetically (see *Zevachim* 106a; *Tos. Yom Tov, Makkos* 3:2; *Rashi* ad loc.).

As described above, the *kares* for הַעֲלָאָה, *burning the offering on an altar outside* [the Temple], is applicable to both an offering properly slaughtered within the Temple grounds and one slaughtered unlawfully outside the Temple. This leads the *Gemara* (3a and *Zevachim* 107a) to question [without an answer] the *Tanna's* mention of only one *kares* for the prohibition of הַעֲלָאָה. By right, the *Tanna* should have mentioned one *kares* for burning an offering that was slaughtered within the Temple grounds and another for burning an offering that was slaughtered outside the Temple.

Regarding the prohibitions of *chillul Shabbos* or *avodah zarah,* it suffices for the *Tanna* to list simply the category of prohibition without itemizing all the possible ways of incurring the *kares* because these were itemized elsewhere in their tractates (*Shabbos* 7:1 and *Sanhedrin* 7:6). The distinction of the two forms of the הַעֲלָאָה prohibition, however, are not listed anywhere else (*Tos. Yom Tov* from *Gem.* 3a).[2]

הָאוֹכֵל חָמֵץ בְּפֶסַח; — *[29] one who eats chametz on Pesach;*

Eating any leavened product made from one of the five species of grain is prohibited by the verse (*Ex.* 13:3): וְלֹא יֵאָכֵל חָמֵץ, *and chametz shall not be eaten* (*Tos. Yom Tov, Makkos* 3:2).

Eating *chametz* on Pesach is punishable by *kares* as stated in *Exodus* 12:15: כִּי כָּל אֹכֵל חָמֵץ וְנִכְרְתָה, *for all who eat chametz shall be cut off.*

וְהָאוֹכֵל וְהָעוֹשֶׂה מְלָאכָה בְּיוֹם הַכִּפּוּרִים; — *[30] one who eats [31] or performs work on Yom Kippur;*

1. The mishnah in *Zevachim* (13:1) records a Tannaic dispute on this point. In the view of the Sages, one who slaughters and offers an offering outside the Temple courtyard is liable both for the slaughtering and the offering, as described above. According to R' Yose HaGlili, however, in such a situation only the slaughtering is liable to *kares*; once the animal is slaughtered outside, it is automatically invalidated and burning it on an altar outside of the Temple courtyard is not punishable by *kares*. In R' Yose HaGlili's opinion, then, burning an offering outside the Temple grounds is punishable by *kares* only if it was slaughtered in the Temple courtyard.

2. *Tosafos* (*Zevachim* 107a, s.v. דאיכא) wonder why the *Gemara* doesn't answer that the mishnah in *kereisos* follows the view of R' Yose HaGlili cited in the footnote above.

כְּרִיתוּת הַמְפַטֵּם אֶת־הַשֶּׁמֶן, וְהַמְפַטֵּם אֶת־הַקְּטֹרֶת, וְהַסָּךְ
א/א

Both eating and performing one of the thirty-nine labor categories on Yom Kippur are transgressions punishable by *kares*, as stated in *Lev*. 23:29ff.

The admonition against performing labor on Yom Kippur is stated very clearly in *Lev*. 23:28: וְכָל־מְלָאכָה לֹא תַעֲשׂוּ, *and you shall do no work*. The negative commandment prohibiting eating on Yom Kippur is not so clear. The Rabbis derive it in an exegetical manner (*Tos. Yom Tov*).

שֶׁמֶן הַמִּשְׁחָה, Anointing Oil

At the time of the building of the *Mishkan* (Tabernacle) by the Jewish people in the wilderness, Moses was commanded to produce a special fragrant oil known as שֶׁמֶן הַמִּשְׁחָה, *anointing oil*. With this oil he anointed the *Mishkan*, its vessels and the *Kohanim* to invest them with sanctity.

The ingredients of the anointing oil compound and their quantities are stated in *Exodus* (30:16ff). Basically, the oil consisted of one *hin* (more than a gallon) of olive oil, blended with numerous fragrant spices of varying quantities.[1]

After the building of the Tabernacle, the anointing oil was used to anoint the *Kohen Gadol* and the kings of Judah. According to a tradition of the Rabbis, the first anointing oil manufactured by Moses miraculously remained intact and undiminished despite its repeated use. At the time of King Yoshiyahu (Josiah), the anointing oil was concealed, together

with the Ark and its contents (*Yoma* 52b). The oil was never reproduced subsequently.[2]

The anointing oil is mentioned in our mishnah in connection with two Torah prohibitions: (1) reproducing for personal use an oil compounded in a manner identical with the anointing-oil formula; (2) anointing oneself with the actual anointing oil (which, in practical terms, means the oil manufactured by Moses) for personal reasons. Both of these prohibitions are punishable by *kares* and, with a warning and witnesses, the violator is punished with *malkus* (lashes).

קְטֹרֶת, Incense

An important feature of the daily service in the Temple was the burning of incense twice daily — once in the morning and once in the afternoon. The incense was burnt on the Golden Altar, which stood inside the Temple. The incense was compounded from numerous ingredients in varying quantities, as specified by the Torah (*Exodus* 30:22ff). As explained by the Rabbis, the incense was compounded from eleven ingredients.[3]

Reproducing the incense formula for private use is a violation of Torah law punishable by *kares*.

הַמְפַטֵּם אֶת־הַשֶּׁמֶן, — *[32] one who compounds the [anointing] oil*,

One who, for his own use, compounds an oil according to the formula prescribed

---

1. Actually the prescribed quantities of the spices were much too large to be simply blended into such a small amount of oil. They were therefore cooked in water to allow for the absorption of their fragrance. The water was then added to the oil and slowly boiled off, leaving the oil with the fragrance of the spices (*Rambam, Klei HaMikdash* 1:2) [see *Gem*. 5a for an alternate method].

2. After the concealment of the original anointing oil, the anointing of a king of Judah, when necessary, was done with a valuable oil known as שֶׁמֶן אֲפַרְסְמוֹן, *balsamum oil* (*Gem*. 5b).

3. The segment of Gemara (6a) that details the formula for compounding the incense reads: תָּנוּ רַבָּנָן: פִּטּוּם הַקְּטֹרֶת כֵּיצַד . . . . *The Rabbis taught: How was the compounding of the incense etc.* It is familiar as part of the daily liturgy.

1 [32] one who compounds the [anointing] oil, [33] or one
1 who compounds the incense, [34] or anoints himself

by the Torah (*Exodus* 30:15ff) for the anointing oil in the quantity that it was made by Moses in the Wilderness (*Rav*).

The prohibition against duplicating the anointing oil is stated in *Ex.* 30:32: וּבְמַתְכֻּנְתּוֹ לֹא תַעֲשׂוּ כָּמֹהוּ, *and in its composition you shall not make anything like it* (*Rashi; Tos. Yom Tov*).

The *kares* for duplicating the anointing oil is dependent on two factors: First, the violator must intend to use the oil for his personal use; if he intends merely to learn how to compound it or to ultimately donate it for communal use, he is exempt from *kares*.[1] Second, he must reproduce the oil precisely in the quantity and formula that it was produced in the Wilderness. An increase or decrease in the quantity of any ingredient makes the producer exempt from *kares* (*Gem.* 5a; see *Tos. Yom Tov; Minchas Chinuch* 109).

The *kares* is only for the manufacture of the oil; using the reproduced oil is not liable for *kares*. Only the original oil produced by Moses is excluded from personal use (*Tos. Yom Tov* from *Gem.* 5a).

וְהַמְפַטֵּם אֶת־הַקְּטֹרֶת, — *[33] or one who compounds the incense,*

This refers to one who compounds an incense with the same eleven spices used in the Temple incense, and does so with the intention of making it for his personal use.

However, if his intention is to learn the proper composition of the incense or if he compounds it with the intention of donating it for communal use in the Temple, he is not liable to *kares* (*Rav* from *Gem.* 5a).

In contradistinction to the prohibition regarding the simulation of the anointing oil, one need not produce an incense of the same quantity of the incense prescribed by the Torah to be liable for *kares*. Even if he compounds an amount merely large enough for one offering, using the ingredients in the proportions as in the formula for the incense used in the Temple, he is included in the *kares* for this prohibition (*Rav, Tos. Yom Tov* from *Gem.* ad loc.).

The prohibition of duplicating the incense appears in *Ex.* 30:37: וְהַקְּטֹרֶת אֲשֶׁר תַּעֲשֶׂה בְּמַתְכֻּנְתָּהּ לֹא תַעֲשׂוּ לָכֶם, *And the incense that you shall make, in its proportion you shall not make for yourselves* (*Tos. Yom Tov; Rashi*).

The *kares* punishment is stated in *Ex.* 30:38: אִישׁ אֲשֶׁר־יַעֲשֶׂה כָמוֹהָ לְהָרִיחַ בָּהּ וְנִכְרַת מֵעַמָּיו — *A person who makes [incense] like it, to smell it, shall be cut off from his people.*

The prohibition is only against *duplicating* the incense for the purpose of inhaling its fragrance. Merely smelling the Temple's incense is not liable to *kares*, nor even included in the Biblical prohibition. Unlike the personal use of the anointing oil, which bears a penalty of *kares* as is mentioned in the mishnah below, merely smelling the incense is not considered an action. Therefore, the Torah did not place a prohibition on it. Although he derives benefit from the incense, there is no offering required for benefiting from hallowed objects by smelling them (*Tos. Yom Tov* from *Rashi*).

1. It is noteworthy that either of these intentions is considered an extenuating factor in the *kares* punishment, for actually, there was no need at all to learn how to compound the oil nor to donate it to the community, since the original oil compounded by Moses was preserved for eternity. Furthermore, there was actually an injunction against producing any oil other than that which was manufactured by Moses (see *Rambam Comm.; Tos., Nazir* 47a s.v. וכן). Nevertheless, with the intention of learning how to compound the oil or of donating it for communal use, the one who reproduces it is exempt from *kares* because, in the final analysis, he did not produce it for his own use (*Minchas Chinuch* 109; *Aruch LaNer* 5b).

יד אברהם

וְהַסָּךְ בְּשֶׁמֶן הַמִּשְׁחָה; — *[34] or anoints himself with the anointing oil;*

Using the anointing oil compounded by Moses for any purpose other than the inauguration of a *Kohen Gadol* or a king is a prohibition for which one is liable to *kares* (*Rav*).

This act is prohibited by the negative commandment (*Ex.* 30:32): עַל־בְּשַׂר אָדָם לֹא יִיסָךְ, *It shall not be anointed on the person's flesh.* The *kares* punishment is stated in the following verse: אִישׁ אֲשֶׁר יִרְקַח כָּמֹהוּ וַאֲשֶׁר יִתֵּן מִמֶּנּוּ עַל־זָר וְנִכְרַת מֵעַמָּיו, *Whoever compounds any like it, or whoever puts any of it on a stranger, shall be cut off from his people.* [The term *stranger* in this passage refers to anyone who is not a *Kohen Gadol* or a king (*Rashi*).]

Every *Kohen Gadol* was anointed, even one who inherited his office. By contrast, a king who was the son of a king was not anointed unless his monarchy was contested by others. Thus, any king descended from King David need not be anointed unless there is a pretender to the throne. King Solomon, for example, was anointed because his half-brother Adoniyahu was his rival. Very few kings in history, then, were anointed. Kings of Israel, not of the Davidic dynasty, were never anointed with the anointing oil. A precious balsamum oil was used instead. To anoint a king, the anoint-ing oil was smeared in the form of a crown around the monarch's head. A *Kohen Gadol* was anointed by smearing the oil in the form of the Greek letter *khi* [כ][1] (*Rav; Tos. Yom Tov* from *Gem.* 5b; *Rashi* ad loc.).

הַפֶּסַח וְהַמִּילָה, בְּמִצְוַת עֲשֵׂה. — *[35] [one who neglects the mitzvos of] the Pesach offering [36] or circumcision, which are positive commandments.*

[Intentional failure to fulfill the *mitzvah* of bringing the *Pesach* offering (without the mitigating circumstances of either being *tamei* or at a distance from the Temple) is a violation of Torah law that is punishable by *kares* (*Num.* 9:13). Likewise, intentional failure to fulfill the *mitzvah* of circumcision on oneself[2] is punishable by *kares* (*Gen.* 17:14). However, unlike the previous thirty-four *mitzvos*, all of which were negative precepts (prohibitions stated in the negative — *'Do not ...'*), these last two are positive precepts (commandments stated in the positive — *'Do ...'*), Therefore, there is no obligation to bring a *chatas* offering for their unintentional transgression.] The Torah prescribed a *chatas* offering only for the transgression of negative prohibitions, as it says (*Lev.* 4:27): בַּעֲשֹׂתָהּ אַחַת מִמִּצְוֹת ה׳ אֲשֶׁר לֹא־תֵעָשֶׂינָה, *and he will commit one of the commandments of Hashem that may not be done* (*Rav; Tif. Yis.*).

Others disagree, arguing that the existence of a negative precept is not essential to the obligation to offer a *chatas* for a transgression. Rather, they explain that

1. The exact shape of the letter *khi* is the subject of controversy. Many maintain that it was an x shape (*Rambam, Klei HaMikdash* 1:9; *Musaf HeAruch; Tif. Yis.*). Others identify it with the lower-case Greek upsilon (u) or capital Upsilon (Y) (*Aruch; Tos. Yom Tov Keilim* 20:7); yet others describe it as a capital Pi, which resembles a ח (*Rabbeinu Gershom* 5b; see *Aruch HaShalem* for variant versions of manuscripts of *Aruch*). See also *Menachos* 6:3, and *Yad Avraham*, there.

2. The failure of a father to circumcise his son is likewise a violation of a positive precept, but it does not bear the punishment of *kares*. Only the failure of the adult who had not been circumcised as a child to circumcise himself is punishable by *kares* (*Rashi, Gen.* 17:14).

1 with the anointing oil; [35] [one who neglects the *mitzvos*
1 of] the *pesach* offering [36] or circumcision, which are
positive commandments.

YAD AVRAHAM

the reason there is no offering for violating the *mitzvah* of *Pesach* and *milah* is because these transgressions do not involve an action; they are sins of omission. The Torah compares all transgressions requiring a *chatas* for their commission to that of *avodah zarah* (idolatry) by stating (*Num.* 15:29): תּוֹרָה אַחַת יִהְיֶה לָכֶם לָעֹשֶׂה בִּשְׁגָגָה, *One law shall be for you, for the one who acts in error*: Just as *avodah zarah* involves an action, so must all transgressions for which one must bring a *chatas* involve an action (*Shitah Mekubetzes; Tosafos, Zevachim* 106a s.v. אזהרה; cf. *Tosafos Makkos* 13b s.v. מה).

There is a dispute among the commentators regarding when one is liable for the *kares* punishment for failure to perform *milah* (circumcision). According to *Rambam* (*Hil. Milah* 1:2), one is not liable for *kares* unless one has *finally* not circumcised oneself, i.e., he dies.[1] As long as he is alive, he is not punishable by *kares*, for he still has the ability to do so. In the view of *Ravad* (ibid.), the moment one becomes an adult (*bar mitzvah*) and deliberately fails to circumcise himself, he is under the sentence of *kares*. However, if he circumcises himself at a later date he has extricated himself from the *kares* punishment.

The situation of an inadvertent transgression of the precept of *milah* involves someone who by error failed to circumcise himself until he became maimed in a manner that makes circumcision impossible. Thus, he unintentionally violated the *mitzvah* of *milah* in finality and would bring a sacrifice if the Torah would have phrased this commandment in the negative (*Shitah Mekubetzes*; cf. *Sefer HaMitzvos* of *R' Saadya Gaon* with commentary of R' Y. F. Perla, vol. III, p.66).

As mentioned in the beginning of this mishnah, the *Tanna* specifies that there are thirty-six sins liable to *kares*, to teach us that, if in one lapse of awareness, one transgresses all these commandments, he is liable for thirty-six separate *chatas* offerings. It is, however, technically impossible for one person to actually be liable for thirty-six *chatas* offerings by violating all the prohibitions mentioned in the mishnah, for some apply only to men, e.g., *[4] he who cohabits with a male*, and some only to women, e.g., *[6] a woman who allows herself to be mounted by an animal*. Likewise, the last two *mitzvos* listed — *Pesach* and *milah* — are positive precepts and, as such, do not entail a *chatas* offering for their omission.

1. *Rambam's* view raises a question: If he is not liable to *kares* until he dies, how is he punished? The definition of *kares* is premature death and this violator lived his normal life span *after* which he is liable to *kares*!

Kesef Mishneh explains that *Rambam's* opinion is that *kares* is in effect the *cutting off of the soul from the life in the hereafter*, as he states in *Hil. Teshuvah* (8:1). This holds true even if there are no physical manifestations of the *kares*. Alternatively, the *kares* for failure to circumcise affects the nature of his death, i.e., he lives his normal life span but suffers a sudden death (ibid.).

In the light of the opinions cited in the General Introduction that the punishment of *kares* can bring about the early death of the transgressor's children, even after his lifetime (*Rashi*, *Yevamos* 2a as explained by *Aruch LaNer* there), another answer suggests itself: The effect of the *kares* for not performing *milah* manifests itself in the early death of his children after his own death.

עַל־אֵלּוּ חַיָּבִים עַל זְדוֹנָם כָּרֵת, וְעַל־שִׁגְגָתָם חַטָּאת, וְעַל לֹא הוּדַע

יד אברהם

2.

This mishnah continues its discussion of the prohibitions punishable by *kares*, now focusing on the atonement for their inadvertent transgression (see General Introduction). As prescribed by the Torah (*Lev.* 4:27ff), the unintentional violator of any negative precept that carries the *kares* penalty for willful transgression is the *chatas* offering, which may be either an ewe or a she-goat. Since the Torah's language regarding which transgressions require the atonement of the *chatas* is ambiguous, the mishnah finds it necessary to state that only negative precepts that carry the *kares* punishment are in this category.

The *chatas* offering is only for an unintentional transgression of which one is certain; for example, if one consumed forbidden fat under the mistaken belief that it was permitted meat, or if one performed labor on the Sabbath, not realizing that it was the Sabbath or that the particular act was prohibited. If, however, one is not sure that he did indeed transgress — e.g., he ate one of two pieces of meat and has no definite knowledge that the meat he ate was the prohibited one — he is not liable for the *chatas* offering. Instead, he brings an *asham* offering known as the אָשָׁם תָּלוּי, *the guilt offering of doubt* (*Lev.* 5:17-19). The *asham talui* is effective only as long as there is doubt of the occurrence of a violation; if it subsequently is determined that the violation did indeed take place, the violator must then bring a *chatas*. Hence the name אָשָׁם תָּלוּי, lit., an *asham of suspension*, for the offering *suspends* the heavenly retribution which the violator may incur until the doubts are resolved (*Rambam, Hil. Shegagos* 8:1ff, see below 4:1).

This mishnah also makes the point that the *asham talui* is limited to the doubtful violation of *kares*-bearing prohibitions.

עַל־אֵלּוּ חַיָּבִים עַל זְדוֹנָם כָּרֵת, — *For these, one is liable to kares for a willful transgression,*

I.e., for violating the above-mentioned negative commandments willfully, one is punished by *kares* (*Tif. Yis.*).

וְעַל־שִׁגְגָתָם חַטָּאת, — *and for their inadvertent transgression, a chatas,*

In spelling out the circumstances which necessitate the atonement of the *chatas* offering, the Torah states (*Lev.* 4:27): וְאִם־נֶפֶשׁ אַחַת תֶּחֱטָא בִשְׁגָגָה ... בַּעֲשֹׂתָהּ אַחַת מִמִּצְוֹת ה׳ אֲשֶׁר לֹא־תֵעָשֶׂינָה, *If an individual . . . will sin unintentionally by committing one of the commands of* H*ASHEM that may not be done*. Seemingly, this phrase could include the unintentional transgression of *any* negative prohibition, but in fact, the obligation to bring a *chatas* is limited to those prohibitions which carry the punishment of *kares* for willful transgression. This is derived from *Numbers* 15:27-31 where the Torah specifies that the individual's inadvertent transgression of idolatry must be atoned for by a *chatas* offering. The Torah's concluding statement in that passage (v. 29) — תּוֹרָה אַחַת יִהְיֶה לָכֶם לָעֹשֶׂה בִּשְׁגָגָה, *One law shall be for you, for the one who acts in error* — is understood as a generalization: The *chatas* offering is brought for all prohibitions which are similar to idolatry in the sense that they carry the *kares* punishment for willful transgression (*Tos. Yom Tov* to *Horayos* 2:3, from *Gem.* there 8a; *Shabbos* 68b).

As mentioned earlier (mishnah 1, s.v., הַפֶּסַח וְהַמִּילָה), the phrase אֲשֶׁר לֹא תֵעָשֶׂינָה, *that may not be done*, implies that a

1 **2.** **F**or these, one is liable to *kares* for a willful
2 transgression, and for their inadvertent transgression, a *chatas*, and for their doubtful trans-

YAD AVRAHAM

chatas is brought only for violations of negative precepts. Thus of all the thirty-six *kereisos* mentioned in the previous mishnah, failure to circumcise or to bring the *Pesach* offering are not included in the obligation to bring a *chatas* (*Rav* ad loc.). There are other exceptions as well, as the mishnah goes on to describe.

An inadvertent transgression is one based on an error, not on total ignorance. For example, one did forbidden labor on the Sabbath because he thought that it was a weekday; or one ate forbidden fat thinking that it was the permitted type. Alternatively, one desecrated the Sabbath because he was unaware that the particular act in question was included in the category of forbidden labor; or one prostrated himself before an idol, thinking that only slaughtering and sacrifice are considered idolatry. In all these cases, he was aware of the basic prohibition but was unaware that the act he was committing was prohibited. However, if one was totally ignorant of the basic Torah law that he violated [for example, he was raised as a gentile], he is exempt from a *chatas* offering. Since he had no knowledge of the Torah's prohibition his transgression is judged as an unavoidable accident. Thus, if one was totally unaware that there is a *mitzvah* of *Shabbos* in the Torah or that there is a prohibition against any form of idolatry, he is exempt from a *chatas*. If, however, he once knew of the law of *Shabbos* and subsequently forgot, his transgression makes him liable to a sin offering,[1] as stated in *Shabbos* 7:1 (*Rav; Rashi; Tos. Yom Tov*).

Tos. Yom Tov, citing *Rashi*, elaborates on the prohibitions mentioned in the previous mishnah, explaining how the error in each of the transgressions was caused by a mistake of the circumstances rather than ignorance of the law. The following is a synopsis of his explanation following the order of the previous mishnah:

An inadvertent transgression of any of the eleven incestuous relationships mentioned in the mishnah can be the result of an error of circumstances, i.e., he mistook any of these women for his wife. Likewise, intimacy with a menstruant can be the result of being unaware of her *niddah* status.

A man who cohabited with another man may have intended to engage in unnatural intercourse with his wife [an act which is frowned upon but legally permitted] but, in actuality, cohabited with a male or an animal.

A woman who engaged in bestiality may have intended to engage in intercourse with a male.

The blasphemer may have been aware of the prohibition against blasphemy, but not that the Name that he was blaspheming was subject to the prohibition.

The one who gave his child to the Molech thought he was giving someone else's child.

The necromancer intended to practice a different type of sorcery. [*Rashash* questions these last two illustrations as being examples of the principle of מִתְעַסֵּק, *an unwilling transgression*, which is exempt from a sacrifice, as what he intended to do was actually permitted (see 4:3).]

The Sabbath desecrator thought it was a weekday.

The *tamei* did not realize that he entered the Temple or that he was eating sacrificial foods.

The one who ate *cheilev* fats, blood, leftover, or *piggul* did not realize that he was eating something forbidden (as there are

1. The principle formulated by *Rav* and *Rashi* — that a transgression resulting from total ignorance of a Torah prohibition is exempt from a *chatas* — is actually the subject of dispute in the *Gemara* (*Shabbos* 68b) concerning the status of a תִּינוֹק שֶׁנִּשְׁבָּה בֵּין הַנָּכְרִים, *a [Jewish] infant captured [and raised] among the gentiles.* According to some opinions (*Rambam, Hil. Shegagos* 5:2), a transgression of this nature is also liable for a *chatas* (see *Tif. Yis.*).

שֶׁלָּהֶן אָשָׁם תָּלוּי, חוּץ מִן הַמְטַמֵּא מִקְדָּשׁ וְקָדָשָׁיו, מִפְּנֵי שֶׁהוּא בְעוֹלֶה וְיוֹרֵד; דִּבְרֵי רַבִּי מֵאִיר. וַחֲכָמִים אוֹמְרִים: אַף הַמְגַדֵּף, שֶׁנֶּאֱמַר: ,,תּוֹרָה אַחַת יִהְיֶה לָכֶם לָעֹשֶׂה בִּשְׁגָגָה." יָצָא מְגַדֵּף שֶׁאֵינוֹ עוֹשֶׂה מַעֲשֶׂה.

יד אברהם

permitted types of blood [see 5:1] and fat).

One who slaughtered or offered an offering outside the Temple did not realize that he slaughtered a sacrificial animal or erred in thinking that it is permitted to sacrifice an offering on a בָּמַת צִבּוּר, *communal altar*.

The violator of Pesach or Yom Kippur mistook it for an ordinary weekday.

One who compounded the anointing oil or the incense may have intended to take other ingredients but inadvertently used the ingredients of the anointing oil and of the incense.

One who anointed himself with the anointing oil thought it was ordinary oil.

וְעַל לֹא הוֹדַע שֶׁלָּהֶן — *and for their doubtful transgression,*

If one is uncertain whether he unintentionally transgressed a *kares* prohibition, he does not bring a *chatas*. Instead, he must atone for his suspected transgression by bringing an *asham talui* (guilt offering of doubt), as described in *Lev.* 5:17ff.

Uncertainty is created by a positive element of doubt. For example, one had before him two pieces of fat, one of which was of the permitted variety known as שׁוּמָן and the other was the forbidden type called חֵלֶב. Unwittingly, he ate one of them but was uncertain whether it was the forbidden type (*Rav*; see mishnah 4:1 for elaboration of this concept).

Only an uncertainty regarding a transgression of the *kares*-bearing prohibitions listed above requires an *asham talui*. If the uncertainty concerned a lesser prohibition [such as eating one of two pieces of meat, one of which was forbidden as נְבֵלָה, *ritually unslaughtered meat*], the situation does not call for an *asham talui*, just as the *certain* inadvertent transgression of such a prohibition does not require a *chatas* (*Tif. Yis.*).

אָשָׁם תָּלוּי, — *an asham talui,*

תָּלוּי literally means *suspended*. The *asham* for a doubtful transgression *suspends* any heavenly retribution for as long as one is uncertain that he did indeed commit an inadvertent transgression. The *asham* does not totally expiate his sin for it is effective only for a situation of uncertainty. The moment he determines that a transgression was, in fact, committed, he must bring a *chatas* offering (*Rav* from *Gem.* 26b; see prefatory remarks to 4:1).

חוּץ מִן הַמְטַמֵּא מִקְדָּשׁ וְקָדָשָׁיו, — *with the exception of one who contaminated the Temple or its consecrated foods,*

The doubtful transgression of the person who entered the Temple confines or ate sacrificial flesh while he was *tamei* [prohibitions 21 and 22 of the previous mishnah] is not liable to an *asham talui*, despite the fact that these transgressions are punishable by *kares* (*Rav*).

מִפְּנֵי שֶׁהוּא בְעוֹלֶה וְיוֹרֵד; דִּבְרֵי רַבִּי מֵאִיר. — *because he requires a variable offering; [these are] the words of R' Meir.*

As a rule, the atonement for prohibitions punishable by *kares* is a חַטָּאת קְבוּעָה, *fixed sin offering*. It is fixed in the sense that it does not vary with the financial status of the violator; all violators bring a female sheep or goat, as prescribed in *Lev.* 4:27-35. For the violations of מְטַמֵּא מִקְדָּשׁ וְקָדָשָׁיו, *defiling the*

1
2
gression, an *asham talui*, with the exception of one who contaminated the Temple or its consecrated foods, because he requires a variable offering; [these are] the words of R' Meir. The Sages say: Neither does the one who blasphemes, as it is said (*Num.* 15:29): *One law shall be for you, for the one who acts in error.* This excludes the blasphemer, who does not perform any action.

YAD AVRAHAM

Temple or its consecrated foods [by entering the Temple confines or eating sacrificial foods while *tamei*],[1] however, the prescribed atonement is קָרְבָּן עוֹלֶה וְיוֹרֵד, *the variable [sin] offering*. This is a *chatas* that is adjusted in accordance with the means of the offender: for the wealthy, it is an animal offering [either a female sheep or goat]; for the less prosperous, it is a pair of birds, one as a *chatas* and one as an *olah*; for the very poor, it is a *minchah* (flour offering), as described in *Lev.* 5:11-13.

R' Meir asserts that the violations of מְטַמֵּא מִקְדָּשׁ וְקָדָשָׁיו are exceptions to the Torah's prescribed atonement for a doubtful transgression and require no *asham talui*. R' Meir maintains that the requirement for the *asham talui* applies only to those transgressions for which the sinner would be required to bring a fixed *chatas* if he is aware of his transgression. Transgressions of מְטַמֵּא מִקְדָּשׁ וְקָדָשָׁיו, however, for which one is required to bring a variable *chatas* rather than the fixed *chatas*, do not require the atonement of an *asham talui* for an uncertain transgression (*Rav; Rashi* from *Gem.* 25a).

וַחֲכָמִים אוֹמְרִים: אַף הַמְגַדֵּף, — *The Sages say: Neither does the one who blasphemes,*

[The Sages add that the מְגַדֵּף, *one who blasphemes*, is also exempt from an offering for inadvertent transgression, although his deliberate violation makes him liable to *kares*.] The blasphemer brings neither a *chatas* for a certain inadvertent transgression nor an *asham talui* for a doubtful one [as will be explained].

שֶׁנֶּאֱמַר: ,,תּוֹרָה אַחַת יִהְיֶה לָכֶם לָעֹשֶׂה בִּשְׁגָגָה.'' — *As it is said (Num.* 15:29): *One law shall be for you, for the one who acts in error.*

In the Torah's stated generalization of the requirement for the *chatas* the phrase is for the one who *"acts"* in error, indicating that the obligation to bring a *chatas* is only for one who sins by performing an action (*Rav*).

יָצָא מְגַדֵּף שֶׁאֵינוֹ עוֹשֶׂה מַעֲשֶׂה. — *This excludes the blasphemer, who does not perform any action.*

[Since a mere utterance of speech is not considered action, the blasphemer is not included in the Torah's requirement for a *chatas* offering.] Just as he is exempt from a fixed *chatas* for a transgression of certainty, so he is exempt from an *asham talui* for an uncertain transgression (*Tif. Yis.*).

The Sages' mention of the blasphemer is somewhat incongruous with the prohibition of טֻמְאַת מִקְדָּשׁ וְקָדָשָׁיו cited by R' Meir as exceptions to the rule for *asham talui*: R' Meir's cases are exempt merely from an *asham talui*, but not from the atonement of the variable *chatas*; the transgression of blasphemy, by contrast, is exempt from *both* an *asham talui* and a *chatas*.

The *Gemara* (7a), therefore, explains the Sages' statement in the following manner: It is addressed not to R' Meir but rather to an inference drawn from the *Tanna's* mention

1. As mentioned in the General Introduction the *variable sin offering* is also prescribed for two other violations, which are not punishable by *kares*. See *Lev.* 5:11-13 and *Horayos* 2:5.

כריתות [ג] **יֵשׁ** מְבִיאוֹת קָרְבָּן וְנֶאֱכָל, וְיֵשׁ מְבִיאוֹת
א/ג
וְאֵינוֹ נֶאֱכָל, וְיֵשׁ שֶׁאֵינָן מְבִיאוֹת. אֵלּוּ
מְבִיאוֹת קָרְבָּן וְנֶאֱכָל: הַמַּפֶּלֶת כְּמִין בְּהֵמָה, חַיָּה,
וָעוֹף; דִּבְרֵי רַבִּי מֵאִיר. וַחֲכָמִים אוֹמְרִים: עַד

יד אברהם

of the בַּעַל אוֹב, *the practitioner of the ov*, while omitting the יִדְּעֹנִי, *the practitioner of the yidoni*. In view of one explanation given for this omission, that the *yidoni* does not do any action; he merely places the bone into his mouth and emits a voice.[1] To this the Sages add: *neither does the blasphemer*, i.e., just as the *yidoni* is exempted from a *chatas* because he uses only his voice, so is the blasphemer exempt from a *chatas* (*Tos. Chadoshim*, in explanation of *Gem.* 7a; cf. *Tos. Yom Tov*).

3.

After discussing the *chataos* occasioned by the inadvertent commission of sins punishable by *kares*, the mishnah commences to discuss the laws of *chataos* that are not related to any sin or transgression. The first instance of this category of *chatas* offering discussed by the mishnah is that of a woman in confinement.

As described in the Torah (*Lev.* 12:1ff), as a result of childbirth a woman undergoes a period of *tumah* (ritual impurity) followed by a period of *taharah* (ritual purity), during which she is not *tamei* even if she experiences a menstrual flow. After the birth of a male child a woman is *tamei* for seven days and then *tahor* for thirty-three days. For a female child, the mother is *tamei* for fourteen days and then *tahor* for sixty-six days. Until the end of this *tumah-taharah* period [a total of forty days from birth for a male child and eighty days for a female], a woman may not eat either *kodashim* [sacrificial food] or *terumah*, nor may she enter the Temple grounds. From the eighty-first day on, she may eat *terumah*, but to enable herself to eat *kodashim* and enter the Temple confines, she must first bring an offering. She is in the category of one who is מְחֻסַּר כַּפָּרָה, *lacking atonement* (General Introduction).

The offering required of a woman who has given birth is a *chatas* and an *olah*. If she can afford them, she brings a lamb for an *olah* and a bird for a *chatas;* otherwise, she brings two birds, one for a *chatas* and one for an *olah*.

The discussion in the mishnah centers around miscarriages. If the form of the aborted fetus meets the criteria to be considered a human form, then the woman who miscarries is judged as one who gave birth.

Any miscarriage presents us with three possibilities: (a) It meets the legal criteria of a birth, in which case the woman must bring her offerings just as after a viable birth; (b) it unequivocally does not meet any of the legal criteria of a birth, in which case the woman is exempt from bringing any offerings; or (c) it is of a questionable status. In this last case the woman must bring the offerings to fulfill her possible obligation, but, because of the element of doubt involved, the offering may not be eaten. The mishnah now elaborates on the type of miscarriages that fall under each of these respective categories of offerings.

---

1. This explanation is different from the one mentioned in commentary to mishnah 1, s.v. וּבַעַל אוֹב. According to the view mentioned there, the Sages' incongruous addition of the blasphemer remains unexplained (*Rashi* 7a).

1 **3.** Some [women] bring an offering and it is eaten,
3 and some bring an offering and it is not eaten, and some do not bring [any offering]. The following bring an offering and it is eaten: She who aborts something resembling an animal, beast, or bird; [these are] the words of R' Meir. The Sages, however, say:

YAD AVRAHAM

יֵשׁ מְבִיאוֹת קָרְבָּן וְנֶאֱכָל, — *Some [women] bring an offering and it is eaten,*

[Some women who suffer miscarriages are obligated to bring the offerings required of a יוֹלֶדֶת, *woman who gave birth*, and the *chatas* may be eaten by the *Kohen*, for there is no doubt that the miscarriage is considered as a birth.]

וְיֵשׁ מְבִיאוֹת וְאֵינוֹ נֶאֱכָל, — *and some bring an offering and it is not eaten,*

As detailed in mishnah 4, there are situations of miscarriages for which the mother must bring the offerings, but the *Kohanim* cannot eat them. This occurs when there is a question regarding the status of the aborted substance. Since it *may* be a birth, an offering is brought; on the other hand, since it may *not* be a birth, it is burnt rather than eaten.

Bringing an offering in the event of a doubt is a Torah-ordained obligation, derived exegetically by the Talmud (*Nazir* 29a). As explained there, this offering must consist of birds and it may not be eaten. [In this respect, resolving a doubtful situation of a sin differs from the procedure for resolving a doubtful situation of other *chataos* brought as atonement: The former calls for an *asham talui*, an animal offering which is eaten; the latter offering is a pair of birds which are not eaten. See *Nazir* 29 a-b.] (*Rashi*).

וְיֵשׁ שֶׁאֵינָן מְבִיאוֹת. — *and some do not bring [any offering].*

[In the instances that the aborted substance is definitely not considered a fetus, no offering is required at all.]

אֵלּוּ מְבִיאוֹת קָרְבָּן וְנֶאֱכָל: הַמַּפֶּלֶת כְּמִין בְּהֵמָה, חַיָּה, וָעוֹף; דִּבְרֵי רַבִּי מֵאִיר. — *The following bring an offering and it is eaten: She who aborts something resembling an animal, beast, or bird; [these are] the words of R' Meir.*

R' Meir rules that even if the aborted substance takes the form of an animal, beast,[1] or fowl, rather than that of a human baby, it qualifies as a birth and the mother's obligation to bring an offering is not subject to question. The offering she brings may thus be eaten just as any offering brought by a woman after childbirth.

R' Meir bases his ruling on the fact that in describing Creation, the Torah uses the expression יְצִירָה, *forming*, regarding both animal life and man. This means, R' Meir argues, that in the Torah's view the form of the animal, beast or fowl, may be considered in the same general category as the form of the human. [Fish, for which the Biblical account of Creation does not use the term וַיִּיצֶר, are excluded.] Therefore, a woman who miscarries a fetus resembling one of these creatures is considered as if she bore a fetus with a human form (*Rav; Rashi* from *Niddah* 22b).

1. The term בְּהֵמָה, *animal*, includes all domestic animals, such as cattle, sheep, and goats. The term חַיָּה, *beast*, denotes wild animals, including deer and all those listed in *Deuteronomy* 14:5, see commentary to 5:1.

שֶׁיְּהֵא בוֹ מִצּוּרַת הָאָדָם. הַמַּפֶּלֶת סַנְדָּל, אוֹ שִׁלְיָא, וּשְׁפִיר מְרֻקָּם, וְהַיּוֹצֵא מְחֻתָּךְ. וְכֵן, שִׁפְחָה שֶׁהִפִּילָה מְבִיאָה קָרְבָּן וְנֶאֱכָל.

[ד] **אֵלּוּ** מְבִיאוֹת וְאֵינוֹ נֶאֱכָל: הַמַּפֶּלֶת, וְאֵין יָדוּעַ מַה הִפִּילָה, וְכֵן, שְׁתֵּי נָשִׁים

יד אברהם

וַחֲכָמִים אוֹמְרִים: עַד שֶׁיְּהֵא בוֹ מִצּוּרַת הָאָדָם. — *The Sages, however, say: Unless it has something of human form.*

The Sages disagree with R' Meir and stipulate that a fetus must have some human semblance to qualify as a human birth. Therefore, the basic facial features must have a human quality even if the mouth, or the ears, or the nose, as well as the rest of the body, resemble an animal. If the aborted substance meets these minimum requirements, the mother is *tamei* and must bring an offering.

Some rule that even if only one side of the face resembles a human, it suffices to require the mother to bring an offering.

Others add that in our times, when the fetus' status has no ramifications regarding the sacrificial procedure, the woman is adjudged as *tamei* even if the fetus totally resembles an animal, beast, or fowl (*Tif. Yis.* from *Maggid Mishneh, Hil. Issurei Biah* 10:9).

The halachah is in accordance with the Sages (*Rav; Rambam, Hil. Issurei Biah* 10:9).

הַמַּפֶּלֶת סַנְדָּל, — *She who aborts a sandal,*

A woman aborted a featureless piece of flesh, resembling a large bull's tongue. Such an appendage, called a *sandal* because of its flattened shape, often accompanies a fetus. Although there is no other evidence of a fetus present, this case is unequivocally deemed a birth because the existence of the *sandal* is positive proof that a fetus was once formed (*Rav, Niddah* 3:4[1] from *Gem.* 25b, *Tif. Yis.*).

Alternatively, the *sandal* is actually a misshapen fetus, which resembles a species of fish which has a flat form (*Rav* from *Niddah* 25b). The term סַנְדָּל is explained by some as a portmanteau word consisting of שָׂנאוּי וְדָל, *despicable and lowly* (lit., *poor*), apparently a reflection of the aborted substance's unseemly form (ibid.). Thus the *sandal* is considered a human form, because the substance once contained a fetus, which was flattened out as the result of the impact of a blow to the mother's body or due to the fact that the mother conceived twins and one fetus crushed the other (*Tif. Yis.; Rashi, Niddah* 25a).

אוֹ שִׁלְיָא, — *or an amniotic sac,*

The woman expelled an amnion, i.e., the sac in which the embryo grows. Ordinarily, the fetus ruptures the sac in the course of birth and the remainder is expelled as afterbirth. In our case, the woman bore merely the empty sac without a trace of a fetus (*Tif. Yis.*).

Although there is no presence of a fetus, it is nonetheless considered a birth because of the amniotic sac. This is expressed by the principle אֵין שִׁלְיָא בְּלֹא וָלָד, *there is no amniotic sac without a fetus*, i.e., that the amniotic sac is formed around the embryo. Hence, although at present there is no fetus, there was apparently one originally and it atrophied and liquefied. Therefore, the woman undoubtably must bring an offering, and thus it may be eaten by the

1. *Rav* cites this explanation in the name of his masters, although it is apparently an opinion expressed in the *Gemara* (loc. cit.). See *Tos. Yom Tov*.

1 Unless it has something of human form. She who aborts
4 a sandal, or an amniotic sac, or a fashioned shell, or a fetus that came out in segments. Likewise, a slavewoman who aborted must bring an offering and it is eaten.

4. The following [women] bring [an offering] but it is not eaten: She who aborts, but it is not known what she aborted, and likewise, two women who

Kohen (*Rav; Rashi* from *Niddah* 3:4).

וּשְׁפִיר מְרֻקָּם, — *or a fashioned shell,*

An oval mass of flesh, which is the fetus' skin from which the limbs of the baby are formed. The initial formation of these limbs is already evident. Due to its oval shape, the substance is called a שְׁפִיר, *shefir*, which is derived from the word שְׁפוֹפֶרֶת [*shefoferes*], *[egg]shell* (*Rav; Rashi*).

Rambam in the original version of his *Comm.* renders *shefir* as a coarse covering over the afterbirth. In the final edition, however, he explains it as something contained within the afterbirth (Kafich ed., *Bechoros* 8:1).

וְהַיּוֹצֵא מְחֻתָּךְ. — *or a fetus that came out in segments.*

It was extracted from the womb by dissecting it into segments (*Tif. Yis.*).

וְכֵן, שִׁפְחָה שֶׁהִפִּילָה מְבִיאָה קָרְבָּן וְנֶאֱכָל. — *Likewise, a slavewoman who aborted must bring an offering and it is eaten.*

[A gentile slavewoman owned by a Jew is also subject to the Torah's requirements regarding childbirth. Thus, if she miscarries in any of the above-described fashions, she too must bring the offerings required of a Jewish woman. These offerings may be eaten because they are as valid as those of a full-fledged Jewess.]

It is a general rule that a Canaanite slave [man or woman] is obligated in any Torah law which applies to a Jewish woman. The mishnah, nevertheless, found it necessary to mention this specifically in connection with the laws of childbirth to avoid any error: One may have thought that a slavewoman is not obligated in any *mitzvah* that does not apply to a male slave, a premise which would have, of course, excluded her from the laws of childbirth. The mishnah therefore emphasizes that in this respect, too, she is like a Jewess (*Rav* from *Gem.* 7b).

4.

אֵלּוּ מְבִיאוֹת וְאֵינוֹ נֶאֱכָל: — *The following [women] bring [an offering] but it is not eaten:*

[In the following cases of miscarriages the mother must bring the offering, but, due to the element of doubt involved, the *chatas* offering may not be eaten by the *Kohanim*, as will be explained.]

הַמַּפֶּלֶת, וְאֵין יָדוּעַ מַה הִפִּילָה, — *She who aborts, but it is not known what she aborted,*

It is not known whether what she miscarried had a human form, in which case she would be obligated to bring her offerings, or whether the fetus had the form of fish or locusts, in which case she

שֶׁהִפִּילוּ, אַחַת מִמִּין פְּטוּר וְאַחַת מִמִּין חוֹבָה. אָמַר רַבִּי יוֹסֵי: אֵימָתַי? בִּזְמַן שֶׁהָלְכוּ זוֹ לְמִזְרָח וְזוֹ לְמַעֲרָב, אֲבָל אִם הָיוּ שְׁתֵּיהֶן עוֹמְדוֹת כְּאַחַת, מְבִיאוֹת קָרְבָּן וְנֶאֱכָל.

יד אברהם

would be exempt, as in mishnah 5. To resolve the doubt, therefore, she must bring the required offering of two birds, one for an *olah* and one for a *chatas*.

Regarding the *olah*, she must stipulate as follows: 'If the substance I aborted was indeed a qualified fetus for which I am obligated to bring a sacrifice, then the *olah* bird is designated to fulfill my obligation; if not [i.e., if the aborted substance was not a fetus], then the *olah* shall be a voluntary offering.'

For the *chatas* bird, however, such a stipulation cannot be made since a *chatas* cannot be brought as a voluntary offering. Therefore, she brings the *chatas* because of the possibility of her having aborted a fetus, but, because of the possibility that it may not have been a required offering, the *chatas* cannot be eaten. This is due to the difference between *shechitah*, the slaughtering process of an ordinary bird, and *melikah*, the process required for a sacrificial bird. The former is performed with a knife from the front of the neck; the latter involves nipping the bird from the back of the neck with the *Kohen's* thumbnail. An ordinary bird which is slaughtered by *melikah* is considered a *neveilah*, not ritually slaughtered. Thus, in the event that the bird offered out of doubt is in fact *not* a sacrificial bird, it would have to be judged a *neveilah* since it was not slaughtered according to the rules of שְׁחִיטָה, *ritual slaughter*.

Although there is a possibility that the bird is not a *bona fide* offering, there is no problem of the possibility that *chullin* (non-sacred materials) are being offered on the Altar, a prohibited action, because, in fact, the flesh of the bird is not burnt on the Altar, only the blood is sprinkled on the Altar wall. This does not violate the prohibition against חוּלִין שֶׁנִּשְׁחֲטוּ בָּעֲזָרָה, *chullin slaughtered in the courtyard* (*Rav; Rashi*).

Others object strenuously to the implication of *Rav's* foregoing statement that the *chatas* brought for a doubt is not in question of being in the category of חוּלִין שֶׁנִּשְׁחֲטוּ בָּעֲזָרָה. In their view, this offering must in fact be regarded as a doubtful item of that category for, if in reality, there is no need for this *korban* it will have to be considered as חוּלִין שֶׁנִּשְׁחֲטוּ בָּעֲזָרָה, just as it is considered *neveilah*. It is only because the doubtful *chatas* is ordained by the Torah that it may be offered, as stated in the Talmud (*Nazir* 29a,b). Therefore, this type of *chatas* is not only prohibited from being eaten but also prohibited for any benefit, as is the law for all *chullin* slaughtered in the Temple yard (*Kiddushin* 2:9). This, too, is the view of *Rambam* (*Mechusrei Kapparah* 1:7) (*Tosfos Chaddoshim*; see *Tif. Yis.* and *Tiferes Yaakov* for a defense of *Rav's* view; see also commentary to 6:5). *Aruch LaNer* concludes that whether the bird *chatas* brought for a doubt is subject to the restrictions of חוּלִין שֶׁנִּשְׁחֲטוּ בָּעֲזָרָה, is the subject of Tannaic dispute.

וְכֵן, שְׁתֵּי נָשִׁים שֶׁהִפִּילוּ, — *and likewise, two women who aborted,*

Two women aborted in a dark cave or hiding place [where it could not be clearly determined which woman aborted] (*Rav; Rashi*).

אַחַת מִמִּין פְּטוּר וְאַחַת מִמִּין חוֹבָה. — *one of a category that is exempt and one of a category that is liable.*

One of the women aborted a substance which does not obligate her to bring a sacrifice [e.g., it resembled a fish or a locust] and the other aborted a fetus that does require a sacrifice [e.g., a *sandal*, or an afterbirth]. Now, however, it cannot

1 aborted, one of a category that is exempt and one of a
4 category that is liable. Said R' Yose: When? When this
one went east and this one went west, but if both were
present together, they bring an offering and it is eaten.

YAD AVRAHAM

be determined which woman aborted which substance. [In accordance with the procedure described previously for situations of doubt, each of these women brings an offering of an *olah* and *chatas*, but the *chatas* is not eaten] (*Rav; Rashi*).

Each woman stipulates that her *olah* should be either in fulfillment of her obligation or as a voluntary offering, as described above. As this stipulation cannot be made for the *chatas* [which is valid only as an obligatory offering], neither one's *chatas* may be eaten (*Tif. Yis.*).

אָמַר רַבִּי יוֹסֵי: אֵימָתַי? — *Said R' Yose: When?*

When is it that the two women who are unsure of their obligation for an offering both bring a *chatas* that is not eaten? (*Rav; Rashi*).

בִּזְמַן שֶׁהָלְכוּ זוֹ לְמִזְרָח וְזוֹ לְמַעֲרָב, — *When this one went east and this one went west,*

Both women separately presented their birds to the *Kohen* to be offered up and then went on their separate ways. Since they are not in each other's presence, they cannot arrange to bring one common *chatas* bird [see below] with the stipulation that it be credited to whichever woman is required to bring it (*Rav; Rashi*).

אֲבָל אִם הָיוּ שְׁתֵּיהֶן עוֹמְדוֹת כְּאַחַת, — *but if both were present together,*

Both came together to give their birds to the *Kohen*.

מְבִיאוֹת קָרְבָּן וְנֶאֱכָל. — *they bring an offering and it is eaten.*

They are able to jointly bring one bird for a *chatas*, each stipulating as follows: 'If *I* am the one obligated to bring the offering, let it be mine, and you relinquish your share in the bird to me; if *you* are the one liable for an offering, it is yours, and my share is relinquished to you.' The *chatas* can then be offered and eaten, for now there is no question that it is in fulfillment of an obligation to bring a *chatas* (*Rav; Rashi* on *Gemara* 7b).

It is only in regard to a *chatas* such as the one brought for childbirth that R' Yose advocates a stipulation of this sort so that the offering may be brought without any doubt, since this type of *chatas* simply enables the one who brings it to eat *kodashim* [sacrificial foods] and enter the Temple grounds, but it is not brought to atone for a sin. However, a *chatas* whose function is to atone for a sin cannot be brought and eaten in a situation of doubt even with a stipulation. This is because a *chatas* is contingent on the owner's awareness with a certainty of his transgression, as is stated in the Torah (*Lev.* 4:23): אוֹ־הוֹדַע אֵלָיו חַטָּאתוֹ, *if his sin becomes known to him* (*Rav; Tos. Yom Tov* from *Gem.* 7b, see 5:5).

The halachah does not follow R' Yose. Therefore each woman must bring a separate *chatas* and it may not be eaten (*Rambam Comm.; Hil. Mechusrei Kapparah* 1:7).

It is not clear why the Rabbis disagree with R' Yose. That a *chatas* which does not atone for a sin, such as this one, does not require certainty knowledge of the cause for the offering is a tenet which is apparently undisputed. Why, then, can the stipulation that R' Yose describes not be made? (*Sfas Emes*).

Perhaps it is because any *chatas* brought out of doubt is a novel law, allowed by the Torah despite the possibility of its being *neveilah*. Therefore, it must be brought by each woman individually for it was only in this manner that it was ordained by the Torah.

From *Tosafos* (22b), however, it would appear that there is no dispute between the *Tanna Kamma* and R' Yose: Both agree that a *chatas* can be jointly brought with a stipulation as described by R' Yose (*Rashash*).

כריתות א/ה

[ה] **אֵלּוּ** שֶׁאֵינָן מְבִיאוֹת: הַמַּפֶּלֶת שְׁפִיר מָלֵא מַיִם, מָלֵא דָם, מָלֵא גְנִינִים; הַמַּפֶּלֶת כְּמִין דָּגִים וַחֲגָבִים, שְׁקָצִים וּרְמָשִׂים; הַמַּפֶּלֶת יוֹם אַרְבָּעִים, וְיוֹצֵא דֹפֶן. רַבִּי שִׁמְעוֹן מְחַיֵּב בְּיוֹצֵא דֹפֶן.

יד אברהם

5.

אֵלּוּ שֶׁאֵינָן מְבִיאוֹת: — *The following do not bring [an offering]:*

[The following are the types of miscarriages that do not create even a doubt of a birth. Therefore, there is no requirement at all for an offering.]

הַמַּפֶּלֶת שְׁפִיר מָלֵא מַיִם, מָלֵא דָם, — *She who aborts a shell filled with water, or filled with blood,*

She aborted a shell or oval-shaped sac filled with blood or water — fluids which definitely do not qualify as a fetus (*Tif. Yis.*).

מָלֵא גְנִינִים; — *or filled with a varicolored substance;*

This translation follows *Rav* and *Rashi*. Others render it as fine, wormlike pieces of flesh (*Rambam Comm.; Rav;* see also *Rav* in *Niddah* 3:3 and *Bechoros* 8:1).

הַמַּפֶּלֶת כְּמִין דָּגִים וַחֲגָבִים, שְׁקָצִים וּרְמָשִׂים; — *She who aborts something resembling fish, locusts, abominated creatures, or crawling things;*

The term *abominated creatures* includes all creatures referred to by the Torah or the Rabbis as *abominations*, viz., all prohibited species that reproduce sexually. This includes non-kosher fish; non-kosher sea creatures, such as seals, frogs, and the like; non-kosher birds; flying insects, such as flies, mosquitoes, and bees. It includes also reptiles and rodents.

Crawling things are those that seem to reproduce spontaneously, e.g., from dung, or from rotting carcasses. This includes also those that spawn from fruits and other foods. If they crawl upon the earth, they are prohibited (*Tos. Yom Tov; Tif. Yis.; Makkos* 3:2).

הַמַּפֶּלֶת יוֹם אַרְבָּעִים, — *She who aborts on the fortieth day,*

If a woman aborts a fetus up to and including forty days from the time of conception, she is exempt from the sacrifices of childbirth because up to forty days from conception the embryo is considered merely as a fluid with no resemblance to the human form (*Rav, Rashi* from *Niddah* 30a).

וְיוֹצֵא דֹפֶן. — *or one who delivers by Caesarean section.*

Delivery by Caesarean section is halachically not regarded as a birth and is therefore not subject to the sacrificial rituals attendant to childbirth. This is derived from the verse (*Lev.* 12:2), אִשָּׁה כִּי תַזְרִיעַ וְיָלְדָה, *should a woman take seed and bear*, which, in the *Tanna Kamma's* view, indicates that only a birth from the area through which *she takes seed*, i.e., vaginal birth, is subject to the *tumah* and the requirement of offerings related to childbirth. Therefore, if a woman delivers by Caesarean section, she is not ritually contaminated, nor is she required to bring the offerings (*Rav* from *Gem.* 7b).

רַבִּי שִׁמְעוֹן מְחַיֵּב בְּיוֹצֵא דֹפֶן — *R' Shimon*

1 5. The following do not bring [an offering]: [She who
5 aborts a shell filled with water, or filled with blood, or filled with a varicolored substance; She who aborts something resembling fish, locusts, abominated creatures, or crawling things; She who aborts on the fortieth day, or one who delivers by Caesarean section. R' Shimon declares liable one who delivers by Caesarean section.

YAD AVRAHAM

declares liable one who delivers by Caesarean section.

R' Shimon considers a delivery by Caesarean section as birth. He bases his ruling on the verse (*Lev.* 12:5): וְאִם־נְקֵבָה תֵלֵד, *if she bears a female*. The Torah could have stated simply: וְאִם נְקֵבָה, *And if [it is] a female*. The word תֵלֵד, *she bears*, is superfluous and was inserted to include an additional type of birth, viz., a Caesarean section (*Rav* from *Gem.* 7b).

The halachah does not follow R' Shimon (*Rav* to *Niddah* 5:1).

6.

As already mentioned previously [prefatory remarks to mishnah 3], the laws of a woman in confinement call for an initial period of *tumah* followed by a period of *taharah*. In the case of the birth of a female, the mother is first *tamei* for a period of fourteen days, after which she immerses herself in a *mikveh* (ritual bath), and may resume marital relations. She may not yet, however, eat *kodashim* or enter the Temple grounds. The initial phase of *tumah* is followed by a *tahor* phase of sixty-six days during which the mother is not *tamei* even if she experienced a flow. After the completion of this period, a total of eighty days from birth, the mother brings the offerings required to enable her to eat *kodashim* and enter the Temple grounds. For the birth of a male child, the number of days of the period is different — seven days of *tumah* followed by thirty-three days of *taharah*. In the mishnah's terms, the entire eighty days for a female and forty for a male, from birth until the time she brings her offerings, is called מְלֹאת [*melos*], *completion*, after the Torah's phrase וּבִמְלֹאת יְמֵי טָהֳרָה, *and at the completion of the days of her taharah* (*Lev.* 12:6).

The offerings brought after the *melos* period enable the woman to eat *kodashim* even if she had more than one birth during that period. For example, a woman gives birth to a girl and two weeks later she conceives again. Forty days later, while still within the *melos* period for the first child, she miscarries. Since the miscarriage took place within the time allotted for the first, she is not obligated to bring an additional set of offerings; the offerings brought for the first child are valid for the subsequent miscarriage as well. If, however, the miscarriage took place *after* the *melos* period — i.e., from the eighty-first day on — it requires a new set of offerings, even if she had not yet brought her offerings for the first birth.

Our mishnah records a dispute between Beis Shammai and Beis Hillel regarding an instance of one who miscarried on the *eve* of the eighty-first day, i.e., during the first night after the completion of the eighty-day *melos* period.

[ו] **הַמַּפֶּלֶת** אוֹר לִשְׁמֹנִים וְאֶחָד — בֵּית שַׁמַּאי פּוֹטְרִין מִן הַקָּרְבָּן, וּבֵית הִלֵּל מְחַיְּבִים. אָמְרוּ בֵית הִלֵּל לְבֵית שַׁמַּאי: מַאי שְׁנָא אוֹר לִשְׁמֹנִים וְאֶחָד מִיּוֹם שְׁמֹנִים וְאֶחָד? אִם שָׁוֶה לוֹ לַטֻּמְאָה, לֹא יִשְׁוֶה לוֹ לְקָרְבָּן? אָמְרוּ לָהֶם בֵּית שַׁמַּאי: לֹא, אִם אֲמַרְתֶּם בְּמַפֶּלֶת יוֹם שְׁמֹנִים וְאֶחָד, שֶׁכֵּן יָצְאָה בְשָׁעָה שֶׁהִיא רְאוּיָה לְהָבִיא בָהּ קָרְבָּן; תֹּאמְרוּ בְּמַפֶּלֶת אוֹר

יד אברהם

הַמַּפֶּלֶת אוֹר לִשְׁמֹנִים וְאֶחָד — *She who aborts on the eve of the eighty-first [day]* —

A woman gave birth to a female child, and then during the night preceding the eighty-first day from the birth, which is the day she would be able to bring her offerings, she miscarries (*Rav; Rashi*).

The mishnah discusses a case arising from the birth of a female simply out of practical considerations. For, as explained above, a woman who gives birth to a female is *tamei* for two weeks. She then immerses herself in a *mikveh* and may cohabit with her husband, yet she still may not eat sacrificial foods or enter the Temple until she brings her offerings at the end of an additional sixty-six days. For the birth of a male, the Torah requires a seven-day period of *tumah* followed by a thirty-three-day period of *taharah* after which the sacrifices are offered. Thus, after the birth of a male, a woman cannot conceive and miscarry another legally defined 'birth' in the thirty-three days that elapse before she brings her offerings, since the minimum age for a fetus to be considered a birth is forty days (*Rambam Comm.; Tif. Yis.*; see *Tos. Yom Tov* 2:4).

If the miscarriage took place at anytime other than the eve of the eighty-first day there would be no dispute. All agree that a miscarriage *within* the eighty-day *melos* period does not necessitate a separate offering because whatever occurs during that period is considered as part of the first birth. On the other hand, there is no question that any birth or miscarriage from the eighty-first day on is not included in the offerings for the first birth, even if she miscarried before she actually brought the offerings, because a miscarriage *after* the *melos* period is considered a separate birth. The miscarriage of the *eve* of the eighty-first day, however, is subject to question because, on one hand, it is not during the *melos* period, yet, in a sense, it is still before the beginning of the post-*melos* period, as will be explained (*Rambam Comm.; Rashi, Pesachim* 3a).

בֵּית שַׁמַּאי פּוֹטְרִין מִן הַקָּרְבָּן, וּבֵית הִלֵּל מְחַיְּבִים. — *Beis Shammai exempt [her] from an offering, but Beis Hillel declare [her] liable.*

Beis Shammai hold that although the miscarriage occurred after the completion of the eighty-day *melos* period, the woman is nonetheless not obligated to bring an additional offering. They base their reasoning on the fact that the miscarriage took place during the night after the eightieth day, which is a time when she could not yet have brought her sacrifices for the first birth, as all sacrificial service can be performed only by day. Therefore, a miscarriage occurring this time is considered as if it took place during the *melos* period for, as far as offerings are concerned, the new period has not yet begun. Therefore, it is consid-

6. She who aborts on the eve of the eighty-first [day] — Beis Shammai exempt [her] from an offering, but Beis Hillel declare [her] liable. Said Beis Hillel to Beis Shammai: In what way does the evening preceding the eighty-first day differ from the eighty-first day [itself]? [Furthermore,] if it is the same regarding *tumah*, should it not be the same regarding an offering? Beis Shammai replied to them: No, if you said regarding [a woman] who aborted on the eighty-first day, it is because it came out at a time when she is fit to bring an offering; will you say [it] of one who aborts on the

YAD AVRAHAM

ered just as though she miscarried during the period of her purity, and she is not required to bring a second offering (*Rav; Rashi*).

[Beis Hillel reason that since the miscarriages took place after the completion of the eighty days, it is considered as if it took place on the eighty-first day, which would require a new offering, as will be explained.]

אָמְרוּ בֵית הִלֵּל לְבֵית שַׁמַּאי: מַאי שְׁנָא אוֹר לִשְׁמֹנִים וְאֶחָד מִיּוֹם שְׁמֹנִים וְאֶחָד? — *Said Beis Hillel to Beis Shammai: In what way does the evening preceding the eighty-first day differ from the eighty-first day [itself]?*

Should she abort on the eighty-first day, all agree that she must bring two offerings, since the miscarriage came about after the completion of the eighty days from the first birth. Why, then, should there be any difference if she aborts on the evening preceding the eighty-first day? Is this not also after the *melos* period [as the day begins on the preceding evening]? (*Rav; Rashi*).

אִם שָׁוֶה לוֹ לַטֻּמְאָה, לֹא יִשְׁוֶה לוֹ לְקָרְבָּן? — *[Furthermore,] if it is the same regarding tumah, should it not be the same regarding an offering?*

Based on the laws of the flow of a woman in confinement, Beis Hillel offer an additional proof that the status of the eve of the eighty-first day is considered as the eighty-first day itself (*Tif. Yis.; Rashi, Pesachim* 3a): All agree, Beis Hillel's reasoning runs, that regarding a menstrual flow, the night preceding the eighty-first day is the same as the eighty-first day. In other words, the sixty-six-day period of *taharah* (during which she remains *tahor* although she experienced a flow) comes to an end with the sunset of the eightieth day. If her flow began on the eve of the eighty-first day, she is *tamei*, just as she is if it begins on the eighty-first day itself. This proves, Beis Hillel contend, that the eve of the eighty-first day has the status of the eighty-first day and thus a miscarriage at that time is considered as a birth after the *melos* period (*Rav; Tif. Yis.*).

אָמְרוּ לָהֶם בֵּית שַׁמַּאי: לֹא, — *Beis Shammai replied to them: No,*

[Beis Shammai disputes Beis Hillel's contention that as the beginning of the eighty-first day, the preceding evening is no longer considered in the *melos* period.]

אִם אֲמַרְתֶּם בִּמַפֶּלֶת יוֹם שְׁמֹנִים וְאֶחָד, שֶׁכֵּן יָצְאָה בְשָׁעָה שֶׁהִיא רְאוּיָה לְהָבִיא בָהּ קָרְבָּן; — *if you said regarding [a woman] who aborted on the eighty-first day, it is because it came out at a time when she is fit to bring an offering:*

[Although you say that a miscarriage on the eighty-first day is no longer included in the atonement of the offer-

לִשְׁמֹנִים וְאֶחָד, שֶׁלֹּא יָצְאָה בְּשָׁעָה שֶׁהִיא רְאוּיָה לְהָבִיא בָהּ קָרְבָּן? אָמְרוּ לָהֶן בֵּית הִלֵּל: וַהֲרֵי הַמַּפֶּלֶת יוֹם שְׁמֹנִים וְאֶחָד שֶׁחָל לִהְיוֹת בַּשַּׁבָּת תּוֹכִיחַ, שֶׁלֹּא יָצְאָה בְּשָׁעָה שֶׁהִיא רְאוּיָה לְהָבִיא בָהּ קָרְבָּן, וְחַיֶּבֶת בְּקָרְבָּן. אָמְרוּ לָהֶם בֵּית שַׁמַּאי: לֹא, אִם אֲמַרְתֶּם בְּמַפֶּלֶת יוֹם שְׁמֹנִים וְאֶחָד שֶׁחָל לִהְיוֹת בַּשַּׁבָּת, שֶׁאַף־עַל־פִּי שֶׁאֵינוֹ רָאוּי לְקָרְבַּן יָחִיד, רָאוּי לְקָרְבַּן צִבּוּר; תֹּאמְרוּ בְמַפֶּלֶת אוֹר לִשְׁמֹנִים וְאֶחָד, שֶׁאֵין הַלַּיְלָה רָאוּי לֹא לְקָרְבַּן יָחִיד וְלֹא לְקָרְבַּן צִבּוּר? הַדָּמִים אֵינָן

יד אברהם

ings for the first birth, it is because the miscarriage took place at a time when the mother *could* have brought an offering for the first birth. Therefore, even though the offering had not yet been brought, the miscarriage had not taken place in the *melos* period.]

תֹּאמְרוּ בְמַפֶּלֶת אוֹר לִשְׁמֹנִים וְאֶחָד, שֶׁלֹּא יָצְאָה בְּשָׁעָה שֶׁהִיא רְאוּיָה לְהָבִיא בָהּ קָרְבָּן? — *will you say [it] of one who aborts on the evening preceding the eighty-first day, for it did not come out at a time when she is fit to bring an offering?*

[Will you say that one who aborted on the eve of the eighty-first day must bring an additional offering, although the fetus did not come out in a time that the mother could have brought an offering for the first birth, since no offerings are brought at night?]

Some render the phrase יָצְאָה לְשָׁעָה שֶׁהִיא רְאוּיָה לְקָרְבָּן — *she went out to a time that she could bring an offering,* i.e. the mother, when she miscarried on the eighty-first day, 'went out of her first birth' to a time that she could have brought an offering (*Rashi*, *Pesachim* 3a). The differences in language notwithstanding, the meanings of the readings are the same.

אָמְרוּ לָהֶן בֵּית הִלֵּל: — *Replied Beis Hillel:*

[Beis Hillel responded that the ability to bring an offering is not the critical factor in determining whether the miscarriage still occurred in the same period as the birth.]

וַהֲרֵי הַמַּפֶּלֶת יוֹם שְׁמֹנִים וְאֶחָד שֶׁחָל לִהְיוֹת בַּשַּׁבָּת תּוֹכִיחַ, שֶׁלֹּא יָצְאָה בְּשָׁעָה שֶׁהִיא רְאוּיָה לְהָבִיא בָהּ קָרְבָּן וְחַיֶּבֶת בְּקָרְבָּן — *But she who aborts on the eighty-first day that fell on the Sabbath will prove [our point], for it did not come out at a time when she is fit to bring an offering, yet she is liable to an offering.*

[By citing this case, Beis Hillel prove that the obligation for an additional offering is not determined by the ability to bring the first offering. For even if a woman experienced a miscarriage on the eighty-first day that falls on the Sabbath, when no offering may be brought, she is required to bring an additional offering. So, too, we must conclude that if she miscarried on the eve of the eighty-first day she must bring an additional offering, although the miscarriage took place before she could bring an offering for the first birth.]

אָמְרוּ לָהֶם בֵּית שַׁמַּאי: לֹא, אִם אֲמַרְתֶּם בְּמַפֶּלֶת יוֹם שְׁמֹנִים וְאֶחָד שֶׁחָל לִהְיוֹת בַּשַּׁבָּת, שֶׁאַף־עַל־פִּי שֶׁאֵינוֹ רָאוּי לְקָרְבַּן יָחִיד, רָאוּי לְקָרְבַּן צִבּוּר; — *Replied Beis Shammai:*

1 evening preceding the eighty-first day, for it did not
6 come out at a time when she is fit to bring an offering? Replied Beis Hillel: But she who aborts on the eighty-first day that fell on the Sabbath will prove [our point], for it did not come out at a time when she is fit to bring an offering, yet she is liable to an offering. Replied Beis Shammai: No, if you said of one who aborted on the eighty-first day that fell on the Sabbath, for even though it is unfit for a personal offering, it is fit for a communal offering; will you say of one who aborted on the evening of the eighty-first day, since the night is fit neither for a personal offering nor for a communal offering? [Moreover,] the [law of] the blood is not

YAD AVRAHAM

No, if you said of one who aborted on the eighty-first day that fell on the Sabbath, for even though it is unfit for a personal offering, it is fit for a communal offering;

Although it is true, Beis Shammai respond, that a woman who aborted on the eighty-first day, which fell on the Sabbath, must bring another offering for that miscarriage, this is still no proof that if she aborted on the evening of the eighty-first day, she must also bring another offering. This is because, unlike the eve of the eighty-first day, a time when *no* offerings may be brought, the Sabbath is a time in which *certain* offerings may be brought.

[Although there are no Sabbath offerings permitted for an individual, the communal offerings which are the order of the day (e.g., the daily *tamid* offering and the Sabbath *mussaf* offering) are brought.]

Therefore, in terms of the time, the Sabbath is considered a day fit for sacrificial service. The fact that the woman is enjoined from bringing her offerings then is due to the Torah prohibition to that effect. This is analogous to a woman who did not bring her offerings on the eighty-first day because of illness or lack of funds. Although, in this case, she is personally unable to bring the offerings it is nonetheless adjudged that the *time* for bringing the offerings has arrived. Therefore if she aborts on the eighty-first day, regardless of her particular ability to bring an offering, she is liable to another offering for the miscarriage (*Tif. Yis.*).

The logic of this argument is not entirely clear: Of what relevance is the fact that communal offerings can be brought on the Sabbath? The fact remains that the offerings of this woman cannot be offered. Perhaps what is meant is that if, by error, the woman's offerings were brought on the Sabbath, her obligation is discharged. We do not consider it as if the offerings were brought prematurely. In this sense, the Sabbath is a day that is fit for her offerings and therefore a miscarriage at this point is not considered in the same *melos* period as the first eighty days (*Sfas Emes*).

תֹּאמְרוּ בְּמַפֶּלֶת אוֹר לִשְׁמֹנִים וְאֶחָד, שֶׁאֵין הַלַּיְלָה רָאוּי לֹא לְקָרְבַּן יָחִיד וְלֹא לְקָרְבַּן צִבּוּר? — *will you say of one who aborted on the evening of the eighty-first day, since the night is fit neither for a personal offering nor for a communal offering?*

Can you say of one who aborted on the evening preceding the eighty-first day, that it is counted as though she had

כריתות מוֹכִיחִין שֶׁהַמַּפֶּלֶת בְּתוֹךְ מְלֹאת, דָּמֶיהָ טְמֵאִין,
א/ו וּפְטוּרָה מִן הַקָּרְבָּן.

יד אברהם

already completed the days of purification? On the contrary, since *no* offerings can be brought at that time, it is as though the days of purification were not completed. Therefore, she is liable to only one offering (*Tif. Yis.*).

הַדָּמִים אֵינָן מוֹכִיחִין — *[Moreover,] the [law of] the blood is not conclusive*

[Beis Shammai now respond to Beis Hillel's second argument, which cited proof from the law of a woman who becomes *tamei* because of the onset of a flow on the eve of the eighty-first day.]

In the mishnaic text which appears in the *Gemara* the word appears as וְהַדָּמִים, *and the [law of the] blood* (*Shinuyei Nuschaos*; cf. *Shitah Mekubetzes*). This reflects the independence of the following point of reasoning from the preceding argument.

Beis Shammai reply to Beis Hillel: Moreover, the proof that you bring from the law of the blood — namely, that the law of a woman who perceived a flow on the eve of the eighty-first day and is adjudged *tamei* — is not conclusive proof that the eve of the eighty-first day is considered as after the *melos* period [for the laws of the flow and the laws of birth are not necessarily the same] (*Rav; Rashi*).

שֶׁהַמַּפֶּלֶת בְּתוֹךְ מְלֹאת, דָּמֶיהָ טְמֵאִין, — *since [if a woman] aborts within the melos period, her blood is ritually contaminated,*

[A woman who aborts within the eighty days after bearing a female becomes *tamei* as a result.]

Although a flow does not render her *tamei* during this period, the blood that accompanies a miscarriage does. This is because a miscarriage is accounted as another birth, rather than as blood of purification from the previous one (*Rav; Rashi, Tos. Yom Tov* from *Rambam Comm.*).

וּפְטוּרָה מִן הַקָּרְבָּן. — *yet she is exempt from an offering.*

As long as the miscarriage occurred during the sixty-six-day period of purification it is regarded as an accompaniment to the first birth, and she is therefore exempt from a second offering. Thus, Beis Shammai argue that from this law — to which even Beis Hillel agree — we see that although, as far as the laws of *tumah* are concerned, it is adjudged as a second birth, nonetheless in regard to the laws of offerings, anything that occurs within the eighty days is counted as an accompaniment of the first birth.

The *Gemara* (8a) cites a *Baraisa* [likewise recorded in *Sifra* to *Lev.* 12:6] in which Beis Hillel responded to Beis Shammai's argument by citing a Scriptural source for their ruling: The verse (*Lev.* 12:6) states וּבִמְלֹאת יְמֵי טָהֳרָה לְבֵן אוֹ לְבַת תָּבִיא, *and upon the completion of the days of taharah, for a son or daughter, she shall bring [her offering].* The words אוֹ לְבַת, *or a daughter*, indicate a contrast between the birth of a daughter and that of a son, i.e., the birth of a female can require a separate offering even if it is on the eve of the eighty-first day which is not yet the beginning of the post-*melos* period [something which is not possible by the birth of a male, as explained above].[1]

The dialectic recorded in the mishnah was merely Beis Hillel's attempt to convince Beis

1. *Malbim* makes the following generalization regarding the Torah's choice of words to express differentiation: Whenever the contrast between the two subjects is obvious, a *vav* is sufficient [example (*Lev.* 21:14): אַלְמָנָה וּגְרוּשָׁה וַחֲלָלָה ... לֹא יִקָּח]; whenever the difference is not immediately obvious, the Torah emphasizes it by inserting the word אוֹ (see at length *HaTorah V'HaMitzvah, Kedoshim* #101). Thus, if the Torah meant to say simply *'the completion of the taharah for a son or a daughter,'* it would have sufficed to say לְבֵן וּלְבַת. By

1 conclusive since [if a woman] aborts within the *melos*
6 period, her blood is ritually contaminated, yet she is exempt from an offering.

YAD AVRAHAM

Shammai of the merits of their ruling on the basis of reasoning. In our view, Beis Hillel argued, there is a Scriptural basis for our ruling; but even if you disagree with our exegesis, you must agree with our reasoning. It is to this argument that Beis Shammai responded in our mishnah (*Tos.* cited by *Shitah Mekubetzes*).

7.

This mishnah discusses the law of a woman who gave birth several times but has not brought offerings for any of them, so that she now has several sacrificial obligations. The mishnah distinguishes between the obligation for situations of certainty, i.e., legally qualified births, and those of uncertainty, such as questionable miscarriages or births.

In addition to the obligation for a woman after childbirth to bring offerings, the mishnah discusses the corresponding sacrificial obligations for a *zavah*. As explained elsewhere (see ArtScroll *Pesachim*, Introduction to 8:5; ArtScroll *Arachin*, Introduction to 2:1), a *zavah* is a woman who experienced a menstrual discharge *between* periods. That is to say, with the onset of the regular menstrual flow a woman is called a *niddah*. Her period of *tumah* lasts seven days from the beginning of the flow, regardless of the duration of the actual flow. To become *tahor*, the *niddah* simply immerses herself in a *mikveh* at the end of the seventh day. No counting of 'clean' days is necessary, nor are any offerings, as long as the flow ceased before the end of the seventh day. There are eleven days which mark the end of one *niddah* period to the beginning of the next. Thus, if a woman menstruates during the eleven days after the end of her seven-day *niddah* period, she is deemed a *zavah*. If the menstruation continues for three days or more,[1] she is called a *zavah gedolah* (major *zavah*). The *taharah* process for a *zavah gedolah* is more elaborate than that of *niddah*, involving a counting of seven 'clean' (issue-free) days before her immersion in the *mikveh* and the obligation to bring offerings on the day following her immersion. [It must be noted that already in Talmudic times the halachic distinctions between *niddah* and *zavah* were rendered moot, since any vaginal blood flow is treated as that of a *zavah gedolah* with all the stringencies that status entails.]

Like a woman after childbirth, a woman who was a *zavah* is permitted to cohabit with her husband immediately after her immersion, but may not eat *kodashim* or

---

using the word אוֹ, the Torah indicates that there is a not-so-obvious differentiation intended here. Thus, Beis Hillel reason, there is a difference between the birth of a male and a female concerning a miscarriage on the evening after the *melos*. After the birth of a girl, this miscarriage will necessitate a new *korban* [since it is more than forty days since conception]; after a boy, when only thirty three days elapsed, it will not. Since this distinction between the birth of a male and a female is not so obvious, the Torah states, וּבִמְלֹאת יְמֵי טָהֳרָהּ לְבֵן אוֹ לְבַת [*HaTorah V'HaMitzvah*, *Tazria* #23).

1. If the menstruation is less than three days, she is called a זָבָה קְטַנָּה, *minor zavah*, or שׁוֹמֶרֶת יוֹם כְּנֶגֶד יוֹם, *one who watches a day* [free of discharge] *against a day* [of discharge], whose *taharah* process involves only one day and no offerings and therefore is not related to the discussion of the mishnah.

[ז] הָאִשָּׁה שֶׁיֵּשׁ עָלֶיהָ סְפֵק חֲמִשָּׁה זִיבוֹת, וּסְפֵק חֲמִשָּׁה לֵדוֹת, מְבִיאָה קָרְבָּן אֶחָד, וְאוֹכֶלֶת בַּזְּבָחִים, וְאֵין הַשְּׁאָר עָלֶיהָ חוֹבָה. חָמֵשׁ לֵדוֹת וַדָּאוֹת, חָמֵשׁ זִיבוֹת וַדָּאוֹת, מְבִיאָה קָרְבָּן אֶחָד, וְאוֹכֶלֶת בַּזְּבָחִים, וְהַשְּׁאָר עָלֶיהָ חוֹבָה.

יד אברהם

enter the Temple until she has brought her offerings. She is thus in the category of מְחֻסַּר כַּפָּרָה, *one who is lacking an atonement*. Just as the mishnah distinguishes between the obligation to bring an offering for לֵדָה וַדָּאִית, *a definite birth*, and סָפֵק לֵדָה, *a doubtful birth*, so too, there is a difference between a זָבָה וַדָּאִית, *a definite zavah* — one who is certain that her flow took place during the eleven-day period — and one who is a סָפֵק זָבָה, *a doubtful zavah* — a woman who lost track of her cycle and thus is not sure if her menstruation is subject to the laws of a *niddah* or those of a *zavah*.

הָאִשָּׁה שֶׁיֵּשׁ עָלֶיהָ סְפֵק חֲמִשָּׁה זִיבוֹת, — *A woman, who is liable for five doubtful cases of zivah,*

A woman experienced a menstrual flow for three days but, because she had lost track of the days of her *niddah* cycle, did not know whether these three days were in the seven days of *niddah* or in the eleven days of *zivah* [see prefatory remarks to this mishnah]. Since this doubt can recur each month, the mishnah delineates the procedure required for the accumulated obligation for a number of other doubtful situations (*Rav; Rashi; Tif. Yis.*).

וּסְפֵק חֲמִשָּׁה לֵדוֹת, — *or for five doubtful cases of childbirth,*

She experienced a number of miscarriages and does not know whether she aborted something that is counted as a fetus, for which she must bring the offerings delineated above, or whether it was something that is not counted as a fetus, and she is therefore exempt from offerings.

As explained above in mishnah 4, a situation of doubt calls for an offering which may not be eaten (*Rashi*).

[The question addressed by the mishnah is: How many offerings must be brought to permit the woman to resume eating *kodashim* — must she bring an offering for each of her doubtful obligations or is one enough for all of them?]

מְבִיאָה קָרְבָּן אֶחָד, — *must bring one offering,*

She brings a bird *chatas* known as חַטָּאת הַבָּאָה עַל הַסָּפֵק, *a chatas that comes [to atone] for a doubt* (*Rashi, Rav*).

Some add that she brings two birds — one for an *olah* and one for a *chatas* offering. For the *olah* bird she stipulates: 'If I am liable to bring an offering, let this be for the fulfillment of my obligation; if not, let it be for a voluntary *olah* offering' (*Meleches Shlomo; Beis David*). [The *chatas* offering — for which no such stipulation is possible — is brought but not eaten by the *Kohanim* — as above in mishnah 4.]

וְאוֹכֶלֶת בַּזְּבָחִים, — *and [then] she may partake of offerings,*

[Although there is a question whether or not she is liable to five offerings, only one offering is brought.] Since the purpose of her offerings is to 'purify' her to be able to eat *kodashim*, the offering is

7. A woman, who is liable for five doubtful cases of *zivah*, or for five doubtful cases of childbirth, must bring one offering, and [then] she may partake of offerings, and she is not bound to bring the rest. For five definite cases of childbirth, or for five definite cases of *zivah*, she must bring one offering, and [then] she may partake of offerings, but she is bound to bring the rest.

YAD AVRAHAM

regarded in the same manner as an immersion in a *mikveh* for a person who is *tamei*. Just as one immersion purifies a person from any number of causes of *tumah*, so can one offering 'purify' this woman from all the doubtful cases of *zivah* or childbirth through which she may have become *tamei* (*Rav; Rashi*).

וְאֵין הַשְּׁאָר עָלֶיהָ חוֹבָה. — *and she is not bound to bring the rest.*

The Sages did not require her to bring the remaining four *chatas* offerings as they are not necessary to enable her to eat *kodashim* (*Rav; Rashi;* cf. *Tif. Yis.*).

As a rule, offering a *chatas* bird offering because of an uncertain obligation is not a desirable situation because the slaughtering process for a bird offering involves *melikah* (nipping the back of the neck with the *Kohen's* thumbnail), a procedure which for an ordinary bird is considered *neveilah* (not ritually slaughtered). Thus, offering a *chatas* bird for which the obligation is questionable presents us with the possibility that a *neveilah* is being used for service on the Altar. Consequently, we allow this woman to bring one *chatas* offering because otherwise it would be impossible for her ever to eat *kodashim*. The other offerings, however, which are not essential to her ability to eat *kodashim*, are not brought out of doubt (ibid.).

Meromei Sadeh contends that it cannot be said that the *chatas* of doubt is undesirable; it is, after all, ordained by the Torah. Rather, the reason that only one bird is offered is that the Torah ordained offerings to be brought out of doubt only to serve a purpose — an *asham talui* must suspend punishment for a doubtful transgression and the bird *chatas* of doubt is brought only to enable the owner to partake of *kodashim*. Since even one *korban* is sufficient to serve that purpose, there are no grounds to offer additional offerings of this nature.

חָמֵשׁ לֵדוֹת וַדָּאוֹת, — *For five definite cases of childbirth,*

A woman who gave birth or miscarried five separate times, none of them in the *melos* period of the other, as above (mishnah 6).

חָמֵשׁ זִיבוֹת וַדָּאוֹת, — *or five definite cases of zivah,*

[This is an instance of a woman who experienced a three-day flow in each of five separate *zivah* periods, i.e., on five different occasions, she perceived a three-day flow in between her *niddah* cycle, as explained above (introduction to the mishnah).]

מְבִיאָה קָרְבָּן אֶחָד, וְאוֹכֶלֶת בַּזְּבָחִים, — *she must bring one offering, and [then] she may partake of offerings,*

As explained previously [regarding the obligation for five uncertain cases of *zivah* or childbirth], as far as the ability to eat *kodashim* is concerned, one offering is sufficient for any number of causative factors, just as one immersion in a *mikveh* will remove any number of *tumos* (*Rav*).

וְהַשְּׁאָר עָלֶיהָ חוֹבָה. — *but she is bound to bring the rest.*

This is derived from the Torah's

מַעֲשֶׂה שֶׁעָמְדוּ קִנִּים בִּירוּשָׁלַיִם בְּדִינְרֵי זָהָב. אָמַר רַבָּן שִׁמְעוֹן בֶּן־גַּמְלִיאֵל: ,,הַמָּעוֹן הַזֶּה! לֹא אָלִין הַלַּיְלָה עַד שֶׁיְּהוּ בְדִינָרִין.״ נִכְנַס לְבֵית דִּין וְלִמֵּד: הָאִשָּׁה שֶׁיֵּשׁ עָלֶיהָ חָמֵשׁ לֵדוֹת וַדָּאוֹת, חָמֵשׁ זִיבוֹת וַדָּאוֹת — מְבִיאָה קָרְבָּן אֶחָד, וְאוֹכֶלֶת בַּזְּבָחִים, וְאֵין הַשְּׁאָר עָלֶיהָ חוֹבָה.

יד אברהם

phrase (*Lev.* 12:7): זֹאת תּוֹרַת הַיֹּלֶדֶת, *This is the law of the woman who has given birth.* The word זאת, *this*, is interpreted in a restrictive sense indicating that one offering cannot serve to fulfill her obligation for more than one birth[1] (*Rav, Tos. Yom Tov* from *Gem.* 9b, *Rashi* ad loc.).

Should the woman abort *within* the eighty-day *melos* period, however, she is required to bring only one offering for both the birth and the miscarriage. This is derived from the phrase תּוֹרַת הַיּוֹלֶדֶת, *the law of the woman who has given birth,* which is interpreted in an inclusive manner, indicating that one offering is sufficient for any number of births (*Tos. Yom Tov;* see below 2:4).

מַעֲשֶׂה שֶׁעָמְדוּ קִנִּים בִּירוּשָׁלַיִם בְּדִינְרֵי זָהָב. — *It happened that in Jerusalem the price of pairs [of doves rose until it] settled at golden dinars.*

The great demand by women for birds for offerings caused the price to rise to two golden dinars for two pairs of birds (*Tif. Yis.*). Each pair required for one offering, then, was one golden dinar (*Rav; Rashi*).

One golden dinar is the equivalent of twenty-five silver dinars (*Rav; Rambam Comm.*).

אָמַר רַבָּן שִׁמְעוֹן בֶּן־גַּמְלִיאֵל: — *Said Rabban Shimon ben Gamliel:*

The Rabban Shimon ben Gamliel frequently mentioned in the mishnah was the father of R' Yehudah HaNasi. However, in view of the fact that he lived after the destruction of the Temple, he could not possibly be the one meant in connection with this incident. Perforce the Rabban Shimon ben Gamliel referred to here is the son of Rabban Gamliel the Elder [the grandson of Hillel] who was executed by the Romans at the time of the destruction of the Temple. He was the grandfather of R' Yehudah's father (*Tif. Yis.; Lechem Shamayim*).

,,הַמָּעוֹן הַזֶּה! — *'[By] this Temple!*

This was an expression of oath (*Rav; Rashi*), as it to say, 'I swear by the Temple, God's dwelling place [that I will force the price down]' (*Tif. Yis.*).

The expression הַמָּעוֹן, *by the Temple*, was a customary oath, and is mentioned elsewhere in the mishnah, e.g., 6:3 and *Kesubos* 2:9 (*Rav Zemach Gaon* cited by *Tos. Yom Tov, Kesubos* 2:9).

Others maintain that it was not legally an oath. It is as if one would swear by the Holy Table or by any other of the sacred vessels of the Temple, which is not tantamount to an oath (see *Beis Yosef, Yoreh Deah* 237). The word, then, is meant as an expression of promise, similar to an oath (*Tos. Yom Tov*, loc. cit.).

Rabban Shimon avoided making a real oath because he could not be certain that the

1. The *Brisker Rav* (R' Yitzchak Zev Soloveichik) delineates that the obligation for any of those in the *mechussar kippurim* category to bring their sacrifices is a twofold one: First, to effect atonement to enable them to resume eating *kodashim* and enter the Temple; second, to fulfill a sacrificial obligation. Thus, despite the fact that there is an *obligation* to bring the remaining sacrifices, the atonement factor is accomplished by one set of sacrifices (*Chiddushei Maran R'Y.Z. HaLevi Mechussrei Kapparah* 1:5).

1 It happened that in Jerusalem the price of pairs
7 [of doves rose until it] settled at golden dinars. Said Rabban Shimon ben Gamliel: '[By] this Temple! I will not pass the night until they are sold for [silver] dinars.' He entered the *beis din* and taught: If a woman must bring offerings for five definite cases of childbirth or for five definite cases of *zivah* — she must bring one offering, and [then] she may partake of the offerings, and she is not bound to bring the rest.

price would stay down; even if the smaller demand would force it down, there might be other factors that would raise it again. Moreover, the Sages, as a rule, avoided taking an oath even truthfully (*Tif. Yis.*).

"לֹא אָלִין הַלַּיְלָה עַד שֶׁיְּהוּ בְדִינָרִין." — *I will not pass the night until they are sold for [silver] dinars.'*

Rabban Shimon ben Gamliel feared that, because of the inflated price, poor women would refrain from bringing even the one offering and would perhaps eat *kodashim* or enter the Temple in violation of the law (*Tif. Yis.*).

The word דִּינָרִין denotes silver coins. The word דִּינְרֵי denotes gold ones (*Tos. Yom Tov* from *Aruch*; see *Bava Basra* 166a).

נִכְנַס לְבֵית דִּין וְלִמֵּד: הָאִשָּׁה שֶׁיֵּשׁ עָלֶיהָ חָמֵשׁ לֵדוֹת וַדָּאוֹת, חָמֵשׁ זִיבוֹת וַדָּאוֹת – מְבִיאָה קָרְבָּן אֶחָד, וְאוֹכֶלֶת בַּזְּבָחִים, — *He entered the beis din and taught: If a woman must bring offerings for five definite cases of childbirth or for five definite cases of zivah — she must bring one offering, and [then] she may partake of the offerings,*

[As explained above, as far as her eligibility to eat *kodashim* is concerned, one offering is enough. Rabban Shimon ben Gamliel's new ruling affected the status of the other offerings which, according to what was taught before, were mandatory.]

The following phrase of the mishnah is the subject of controversy among the commentators regarding both its meaning and its wording. Our commentary will discuss the text and explanation according to all views, beginning with that followed by most *Rishonim*.

וְאֵין הַשְּׁאָר עָלֶיהָ חוֹבָה. — *and she is not bound to bring the rest.*

[In order to bring down the price of birds, Rabban Shimon ben Gamliel promulgated a ruling that even a woman who experienced a number of births or was a *zavah* at different times need bring no more than one offering.]

This ruling is apparently in conflict with the uncontested law stated previously (mishnah 6) that each birth in a separate period obligates the mother for a separate offering. Nonetheless, Rabban Shimon ben Gamliel promulgated this decision exempting the woman from additional offerings contrary to the halachah, out of the fear that, because of the prohibitive price of birds, the women would enter the Temple or eat *kodashim* without bringing even one offering [which is a prohibition punishable by *kares*]. To insure that people not commit such a sin, Rabban Shimon implemented the principle of עֵת לַעֲשׂוֹת לַה׳ הֵפֵרוּ תּוֹרָתֶךָ, *For it is a time to act for* H*ASHEM*, *they have voided Your Torah* (*Psalms* 119:126), which enables the Rabbis to suspend Torah law when circumstances warrant such action. Thus, Rabban Gamliel issued an edict exempting the women in question from all additional offerings[1] (*Rav; Rashi*; see *Tif. Yis. Boaz*).

Other *Rishonim* advance a different approach to the mishnah. They explain that Rabban Shimon ben Gamliel does differ with the ruling of Beis Hillel and Beis Shammai in the previous mishnah. Rabban Gamliel holds that, according to Torah Law, the woman is exempt from more than one offering. In Rabban Shimon ben Gamliel's view, the obligation to bring offerings is analogous to the requirement for immersion; just as one immersion is effective to purify a person although he has contracted many types of *tumah*, so too, one offering is sufficient for a woman no matter how many times she became a *zavah* or gave birth. Thus, Rabban Shimon ben Gamliel taught that a woman who gave birth a number of times must bring but one offering and is not bound to bring the rest later (*Tos., Kereisos* 8a; *Perush Ashkenazim*, cited by *Tos. Bava Basra* 166b).

Meleches Shlomo quotes others who reconcile Rabban Shimon's ruling with the previously stated principle that she is liable for a separate offering for each birth. Rabban Gamliel, they explain, did not mean to say that she is not bound to bring the other offerings; he merely intended to emphasize that she is not bound to bring the rest prior to entering the Temple or eating *kodashim*. Thus, Rabban Shimon ben Gamliel was neither suspending nor disputing the previous ruling. He merely *publicized* the fact that even without bringing all her offerings a woman may be 'purified' to eat *kodashim*. This teaching was sufficient to bring down the price of the birds because women were now aware that if they could not afford it, they could bring one offering immediately and the remainder eventually. [This explanation is similar to the one advanced by *Rabbeinu Tam* for a variant reading; see below.]

According to *Rabbeinu Tam* (ad loc.), the text of our mishnah should read: וְהַשְּׁאָר עָלֶיהָ חוֹבָה, *and she is bound to bring the rest*. He explains that the price of birds was high because women thought that *all* their required offerings were necessary to allow them to enter the Temple confines or eat *kodashim*. Accordingly, the poor women would refrain from bringing even one offering since they could not afford to bring them all. Rabban Shimon ben Gamliel therefore taught that one offering sufficed to permit the partaking of *kodashim* and entry to the Temple. The rest are merely חוֹבָה, *a debt*, something which, if need be, can be brought later. Thus they could wait to bring them until birds became cheaper. Consequently, there would not be such a great demand on the birds, and the price would go down (*Tif. Yis.*).[2]

The halachah follows the ruling indicated at the beginning of the mishnah: For the instance of numerous births of questionable status, one offering is sufficient; for those of unquestionable status,

1. Suspending the obligation to do a *mitzvah* as a response to prohibitive prices is a principle applied elsewhere as well. For example, when non-Jewish merchants take advantage of the custom to eat fish at each of the Sabbath meals by raising the price of fish, it is proper for the Rabbis to innovate that the custom be suspended. This is analogous to our mishnah when the Rabbis suspended the *mitzvah* of bringing all the offerings in the face of overpricing (*Magen Avraham, Orach Chaim* 242:1).

2. It is apparent that the *Rishonim* grappled with the understanding of Rabban Gamliel's statement. Our reading וְאֵין הַשְּׁאָר עָלֶיהָ חוֹבָה indicates that Rabban Gamliel either disputed or suspended the earlier ruling that all offerings are mandatory. If so, it should have been mentioned earlier. *Rabbeinu Tam's* explanation, on the other hand, does reconcile Rabban Gamliel's ruling with the earlier mishnah, but it is not consistent with our reading.

Netziv, however, cites with approval a novel interpretation from his son R' Chaim Berlin, that resolves these difficulties with the following keen observation of the Scriptural text:

In citing the sacrificial obligation of the woman after childbirth, the Torah first mentions the obligation for the wealthy woman and concludes with the phrase זֹאת תּוֹרַת הַיֹּלֶדֶת, *this is*

1 And on that day the price of pairs [of doves dropped
7 until it] settled at two quarters of a dinar.

YAD AVRAHAM

one offering is sufficient to allow her to eat *kodashim,* and the remainder remain an obligation [to be brought later, as her resources allow] (*Rambam; Mechusrei Kapparah* 1:10).

Some, however, rule that in all cases one offering is all that must be brought (*Raavad* ad loc.). This view apparently subscribes to the explanation of the mishnah (*Perush Ashkenazim*, cited above) that Rabban Shimon ben Gamliel's ruling disputed the earlier view that an offering must be brought for each birth.

Our version of the *Rambam's Commentary* seems to support this view (which would contradict *Rambam's* own ruling in *Mishneh Torah*), but in the Kafich edition the text appears differently.

וְעָמְדוּ קִנִּים בּוֹ בַּיּוֹם בִּרְבָעָתַיִם — *And on that day the price of pairs [of doves dropped until it] settled at two quarters of a dinar.*

Two pairs of birds cost two quarters of a silver dinar, a quarter dinar a pair (*Rav; Tif. Yis.*).

Each golden dinar is twenty-five silver dinarim (*Rav*). [Thus what previously cost twenty-five silver dinarim now cost a quarter of a silver dinar.]

Chapter 2

1.

In the previous chapter it was explained that a *chatas* (sin) offering is brought to atone for inadvertent transgression and that each transgression incurs the liability for a separate *chatas* offering. This chapter deals with *chataos* that do not conform to

---

the law for the woman who has given birth. The requirements for the woman who cannot afford this, וְאִם־לֹא תִמְצָא יָדָהּ דֵּי שֶׂה, *and if she cannot afford a lamb* (*Lev.* 12:8), are mentioned only *after* this apparently concluding statement. [By contrast, in setting the sacrificial requirements for the *metzora* (*Lev.* 14), the Torah first mentions the requirement for both the rich and the poor and *then* concludes with זֹאת תּוֹרַת אֲשֶׁר־בּוֹ נֶגַע צָרָעַת, *this is the law of the one who has a plague of tzaraas*.]

This observation leads R' Chaim Berlin to the following hypothesis: Since the phrase זֹאת תּוֹרַת הַיֹּלֶדֶת is the one from which we learn that there is a separate obligation for each time that a woman gives birth, the Torah mentions it after stating the sacrificial obligations of the rich woman. This indicates that the obligation to bring a separate offering for each birth *is only for the woman who can afford it;* the poor woman can fulfill her obligations with only one offering. Thus, the Torah concludes its section dealing with the rich woman with the phrase זֹאת תּוֹרַת הַיֹּלֶדֶת, i.e., the one who can afford it must bring a separate offering for each birth. After this the Torah adds: וְאִם־לֹא תִמְצָא יָדָהּ דֵּי שֶׂה, *and if she cannot afford a lamb,* then one pair of birds is sufficient for *all* her obligations.

Rabban Shimon ben Gamliel's statement in our mishnah can be understood in this light. In principle, Rabban Shimon ben Gamliel agreed with the halachah expressed in the previous mishnah that each birth occasions a separate sacrificial obligation. However, that is only if the woman can afford it. When the price of birds became prohibitive though, the halachah changed because it is considered as if all women were in the category of the poor. Under these circumstances, one offering is sufficient for all the births involved. Thus, Rabban Shimon ben Gamliel publicized the ruling that one offering is sufficient; under these circumstances *everyone* was considered impoverished.

In this manner, the text of our mishnah indeed reads וְאֵין הַשְּׁאָר עָלֶיהָ חוֹבָה, *and she is not bound for the rest*, yet it does not differ with the previous ruling (*Meromei Sadeh; Harcheiv Devar* to *Lev.* 12:7).

[א] **אַרְבָּעָה** מְחֻסְּרֵי כִּפּוּרִים, וְאַרְבָּעָה מְבִיאִין עַל הַזָּדוֹן כַּשְּׁגָגָה. אֵלּוּ הֵן מְחֻסְּרֵי כִּפּוּרִים: הַזָּב, וְהַזָּבָה, וְהַיּוֹלֶדֶת, וְהַמְּצֹרָע. רַבִּי אֱלִיעֶזֶר בֶּן־יַעֲקֹב אוֹמֵר: גֵּר מְחֻסַּר

יד אברהם

these generalities: Some (despite the name 'sin offering') are not brought as an atonement for any particular transgression; some are brought even for deliberate transgressions; and some may atone for a number of situations at one time.

The mishnah opens with a listing of the *chataos* that are not brought for atonement. This is a continuation of the discussion in the preceding chapter concerning the *yoledess* (woman who has given birth) and the *zavah*, who are included in the general category of those who are מְחֻסַּר כַּפָּרָה, *lacking atonement*. Although these respective offerings do not atone for a sin, they bring atonement in the sense that they restore the person's ability to eat *kodashim* or to enter the Temple courtyard. In the context of *tumah* (ritual impurity), this means that although the person underwent the rudimentary *taharah* (purification) of immersion, he is not qualified to eat *kodashim* or enter the Temple courtyard before bringing his required offerings, or at least, some of them.

Having mentioned the *woman who has given birth* and the *zavah*, the mishnah proceeds to complete the listing of all situations that fall under the category of the מְחֻסַּר כַּפָּרָה.

אַרְבָּעָה מְחֻסְּרֵי כִפּוּרִים, — *Four lack atonement [offerings],*

There are four categories of people who must bring a *chatas* offering, not as an expiation for sin, but to permit them to eat *kodashim* (*Rav; Rashi*).

In the *Gemara* text, the mishnah reads כַּפָּרָה, *an atonement offering*, in the singular rather than כִּפּוּרִים, *atonement offerings*. [The meaning, however, is the same: *Each* of these needs the atonement of the offering] (*Shinuyei Nuschaos*).

The term כַּפָּרָה, which usually means *atonement*, here actually means *purification* in the sense that the offerings complete his purification process in regards to *kodashim* (*Tif. Yis.*).

וְאַרְבָּעָה מְבִיאִין עַל הַזָּדוֹן כַּשְּׁגָגָה. — *and four bring [offerings] for intentional as well as inadvertent transgression.*

[Although ordinarily a *chatas* is brought for an inadvertent transgression, there are four instances (enumerated in mishnah 2) in which the offering may atone for intentional transgression as well.]

אֵלּוּ הֵן מְחֻסְּרֵי כִפּוּרִים: — *These are the ones who lack atonement [offerings]:*

The following are the four that lack atonement. Although they are all in one category of lacking atonement, the *form* of atonement is not the same for each. The *zav* and the *zavah* each brings a pair of birds, one for an *olah* and one for a *chatas* (*Lev.* 15:14-15, 29-30). The *woman who has given birth* brings a bird *chatas* and an *olah* offering of either a lamb or a bird, depending on her financial circumstances (ibid. 12:6-8). The *metzora* brings the most elaborate offering of all — a male lamb for an *asham*; a second male lamb for an *olah*, and a female lamb for a *chatas*, in addition to a *minchah* offering and a quantity of oil (ibid. 14:10-20). For the *metzora* who is poor, the *olah* and the *chatas* can be birds and the *minchah* contains a lesser quantity of flour (ibid. 14:21-31).

הַזָּב, — *the zav,*

A *zav* is a male who is a *tamei* as the result of experiencing a gonorrheal type

2
1

1. Four who lack atonement [offerings], and four bring [offerings] for intentional as well as inadvertent transgression. These are the ones who lack atonement [offerings]: the *zav*, the *zavah*, the woman who has given birth, and the *metzora*. R' Eliezer ben Yaakov

YAD AVRAHAM

issue (caused by a disorder of the genital mucous membrane). The law of the *zav* is, in brief, as follows: If the issue occurs once, he is *tamei* in the same manner as a *baal keri*, a man who experienced a seminal issue (see *Zavim* 1:1). Should this experience occur on two consecutive days or twice in one day, his *tumah* is more severe. To become *tahor* he must observe seven clean (flow-free) days and then immerse himself in a spring-water *mikveh*. Should the experience occur three times, he must in addition bring an offering before he is rendered *tahor* to eat *kodashim* or enter the Temple. The mishnah refers to this last category of *zav* (*Lev.* 15:1ff; *Rambam, Mechusrei Kapparah* 2:1ff; cf. ArtScroll *Nazir* 9:4, *Pesachim* 8:5, *Megillah* 1:7).

וְהַזָּבָה, — *the zavah,*

As explained above (1:7), a *zavah* is a woman who experiences a menstrual flow for three consecutive days during the eleven days between *niddah* periods. She is required to count seven clean, flow-free days, and then immerse herself in a *mikveh*. To be able to eat *kodashim* or enter the Temple, she must bring an offering identical to that which is required of a *zav*: two birds, one for a *chatas* and one for an *olah* (*Lev.* 15:25ff; *Rambam, Mechusrei Kapparah* 1:6).

וְהַיּוֹלֶדֶת, — *the woman who has given birth,*

As described above (1:3,6), after the birth of a child or a miscarriage, a woman is subject to a period of *tumah* followed by one of *taharah*. The length of these periods vary for a male and female child. At the end of her *taharah* period she must bring an *olah* offering of a lamb and a bird for a *chatas* or, if she cannot afford it, two birds, one for the *olah* and the other for the *chatas*. Before she brings her offerings, she may not eat *kodashim* or enter the Temple.

וְהַמְּצֹרָע. — *and the metzora.*

The *metzora*, usually translated as a leper, is actually an individual who is *tamei* as a result of the appearance of white, leprosy-like spots on his skin.[1] After the disappearance of his *tzaraas* symptoms, the *metzora* undergoes an elaborate purification process, on the eighth day of which he brings his offerings, some of which vary according to his financial status (see above). As long as these offerings are not brought, he may not eat *kodashim* or enter the Temple (*Lev.* 14:1ff; *Rambam, Mechusrei Kapparah* 4:1).

The term *metzora* includes both the male or female *metzora* because the symptoms of the *tumah* and the laws for becoming *tamei* are identical for either sex. The *zav* and the *zavah* [although identical in the *taharah* process] are dissimilar in the laws governing the manner in which the *tumah* takes effect. The *zav* is *tamei* as the result of three emissions even if they occur in one day; the *zavah* must experience her flow on three separate days (*Rav* from *Gem.* 8b). In addition, the *zav* and the *zavah* are distinguished physiologically — the

1. The affliction known in the Torah as צָרַעַת (*tzaraas*) is subject to a spontaneous cure, something unknown for leprosy. For a fuller understanding of the *tzaraas* phenomenon as distinct from leprosy, the reader is directed to the essay entitled נגעים by R' Samson Raphael Hirsch, which appears at the end of his commentary to *Lev.* 13.

כַּפָּרָה עַד שֶׁיִּזָּרֵק עָלָיו הַדָּם, וְנָזִיר לְיֵינוֹ וְתִגְלַחְתּוֹ, וְטֻמְאָתוֹ.

יד אברהם

עַד שֶׁיִּזָּרֵק עָלָיו הַדָּם, — *until the blood is sprinkled for him,*

[As the exact nature of the proselyte's offering is not specified by the Torah, the minimum requirement is simply an offering that involves some form of blood service. This may be either an animal or a pair of birds, but not a *minchah* (*Gem.* 9a).]

The term יִזָּרֵק עָלָיו הַדָּם, *the blood is sprinkled for him*, can refer to either type of offering brought by the proselyte. If he brings an animal for an *olah* offering, he may partake of *kodashim* as soon as the blood is sprinkled on the Altar. Should he bring a pair of birds, he may partake of *kodashim* as soon as the blood of one of them is applied upon the wall of the Altar (*Rav; Rambam Comm.*).

The *Tanna Kamma*, who omits the proselyte from the category of those lacking atonement, disagrees with R' Eliezer ben Yaakov. The requirement of offerings for the conversion process, the *Tanna Kamma* reasons, is not to allow the proselyte to eat *kodashim.* In his view, a proselyte may partake of *kodashim* immediately after his circumcision and immersion. The purpose of the sacrifice is to complete the conversion process and allow him to marry a Jewess.[1] Since, in his view, eating *kodashim* *zav's* emission is white while the *zavah's* is red (*Tos. R' Akiva Eiger* from *Tos.*). Thus, the *Tanna* regarded the *zav* and the *zavah* as separate categories of those who are lacking atonement, but the *metzora* as one.

רַבִּי אֱלִיעֶזֶר בֶּן־יַעֲקֹב אוֹמֵר: גֵּר מְחֻסַּר כַּפָּרָה — *R' Eliezer ben Yaakov says: A proselyte [too] lacks atonement*

The process of the conversion of a proselyte consists of three steps: (a) מִילָה, *circumcision*; (b) טְבִילָה, *immersion in a mikveh*; (c) הַרְצָאַת דָּמִים, *sprinkling of the blood* [on the Altar], i.e., the bringing of offerings. This is derived from the historical experience of the Jewish people at the time of the Exodus from Egypt. Their circumcision took place before they left Egypt and brought the *Pesach* offering (which could be eaten only by the circumcised); the immersion took place at the time of the receiving of the Torah at Sinai, regarding which the Torah specifically mentions both the immersion and the offering of sacrifices (*Gemara* 9a; from *Exodus* 19:10 and 24:5).

R' Eliezer ben Yaakov maintains that the proselyte, too, is considered as one lacking atonement because, without bringing his offering, he cannot eat *kodashim* (*Rav* from *Gem.* 9a; *Rambam Comm.*).

1. As long as there was a Temple, the conversion process was incomplete without the offering of the required offerings. Today, without the Temple, a proselyte's conversion is considered full fledged even though he did not bring his offering. [This is derived from the Torah's phrase וְכִי־יָגוּר אִתְּכֶם גֵּר... לְדֹרֹתֵיכֶם, *a proselyte that dwells among you . . . for your generations* (*Numbers* 15:14), indicating that the conversion process is possible for all generations, even when there is no Temple.]

The obligation to bring an offering, however, is still in force and when the Temple is rebuilt, every proselyte will indeed bring one. In fact, for a while after the destruction of the Temple, every convert would set aside money for his offering. However, seeing that people were not careful to treat this money with the proper *kedushah* (sanctity), the Rabbis put a stop to this practice (*Gem.* 9a).

2 says: A proselyte [too] lacks atonement until the blood is
1 sprinkled for him, and [so does] a *nazir* for his wine, his
haircutting, and his *tumah*.

is permitted even prior to that rite, he does not consider the proselyte in the category of those lacking atonement (*Rav; Rambam Comm.*).

Many others disagree with the explanation advanced by *Rambam* and *Rav*. In their view, the ruling that a proselyte cannot eat *kodashim* before he brings his offering is uncontested by the *Tanna Kamma*. The *Tanna Kamma*, nonetheless, does not list the proselyte in the category of those lacking atonement because his offering serves a different function than those of others in this category. Those lacking atonement cannot eat *kodashim* as long as they do not bring their offering because they are still residually *tamei*; the proselyte cannot eat *kodashim* before bringing his offering simply because he is not yet fully converted. Since it is for want of full conversion rather than for want of atonement or purity that he cannot eat *kodashim*, he cannot be listed in the category of those lacking atonement (*Rambam, Mechusrei Kapparah* 1:2 [in a reversal from his view in the *Comm.*]; *Rashi* 8b; *Tos.* 2b).

According to this explanation, it is difficult to suggest a *practical* difference between the *Tanna Kamma* and R' Eliezer ben Yaakov: Both agree that a proselyte may not eat *kodashim* before he brings his offerings and, presumably, neither *Tanna* disagrees with the ruling that a proselyte may not marry into the Jewish faith prior to bringing his offerings. It must be concluded, therefore, that the point of contention between the two *Tannaim* is simply one of classification and not of practical application. [There are precedents elsewhere for arguments of this nature, see *Bava Kamma* 1:1; *Avodah Zarah* 5:9.] (*Tif. Yis.*).

וְנָזִיר — *and [so does] a nazir*

[A *nazir* is a person who adopts the specific type of vow of abstinence dealt with by the Torah in *Numbers* 6:1ff. During the period of his vow, the *nazir* is subject to three types of restrictions: (a) He may not drink wine or consume any grape derivatives; (b) he may not cut the hair of his head; (c) he must avoid the *tumah* contracted by contact with a corpse. At the close of his period of vow, the *nazir* undergoes a ceremony which concludes with the bringing of three offerings — *chatas, olah* and *shelamim*. After bringing his offerings, the *nazir* is no longer bound by the restrictions of his vow (see General Introduction to ArtScroll *Nazir*).]

Since upon the completion of the term of his *nezirus* vow, a *nazir* must bring three offerings to remove his restrictions, he, too, is considered in R' Eliezer ben Yaakov's view as one lacking atonement.

לְיֵינוֹ, וְתִגְלַחְתּוֹ, וְטֻמְאָתוֹ. — *for his wine, his haircutting, and his tumah.*

Although his period of vow may have passed, the restrictions against his drinking wine, cutting his hair, and coming in contact with a corpse are not lifted until he has brought his offerings. Since the function of the offerings is to permit him that from which he was previously restricted, his obligation to bring these offerings places him in the category of lacking atonement.

The *Tanna Kamma* does not include the *nazir* in the category of lacking atonement because his atonement is not brought to permit him to eat *kodashim* [from which he was never restricted]. The purpose of his offerings is merely to allow him to engage in mundane matters such as drinking wine. As his offering is not related to any restrictions regarding *kodashim* it is not considered in the category of one lacking atonement (*Rav* from *Gem.* 8b).

[ב] אֵלּוּ מְבִיאִים עַל־הַזָּדוֹן כַּשְּׁגָגָה: הַבָּא עַל־הַשִּׁפְחָה, וְנָזִיר שֶׁנִּטְמָא, וְעַל־שְׁבוּעַת הָעֵדוּת, וְעַל־שְׁבוּעַת הַפִּקָּדוֹן.

יד אברהם

2.

אֵלּוּ מְבִיאִין עַל־הַזָּדוֹן כַּשְּׁגָגָה: — *These bring [an offering] for intentional as well as inadvertent transgression:*

[It was stated in the previous mishnah that, in contrast to the conventional *chatas* offering brought for inadvertent transgressions, there are certain categories whose atonement is brought for even intentional transgressions. The mishnah now proceeds to identify them.]

הַבָּא עַל־הַשִּׁפְחָה, — *he who cohabits with a [betrothed] maidservant,*

[The transgression of cohabiting with the type of שִׁפְחָה כְּנַעֲנִית, *gentile slavewoman*, known as the *shifchah charufah*[1] is outlined in the Torah (*Lev.* 19:20ff). It concerns an adulterous relationship with a gentile slavewoman[2] (belonging to a Jewish master), who is 'married,' i.e., betrothed to an עֶבֶד עִבְרִי, *a Jewish servant or indentured bondsman*. By Torah law, marriage cannot legally take effect with a gentile slavewoman. Hence, cohabitation with her by someone other than her 'husband' is technically not adultery. Nonetheless, in view of the semblance of married life maintained when the gentile slavewoman is designated to a Jewish bondsman, cohabitation with her by another man is a more serious transgression than that of cohabiting with an ordinary slavewoman, who is likewise forbidden to a Jewish man.[3]

As prescribed by the Torah (loc. cit.), one who cohabits with a *shifchah charufah* must bring an *asham* offering. This *asham* is brought for both an intentional and an unintentional transgression on the part of the man. The slavewoman, however, must be a deliberate transgressor. Her punishment is *malkus* (lashes) rather than an offering (*Tif. Yis.*).

This is derived from the Torah's repetitious phraseology (*Lev.* 19:22): וְכִפֶּר עָלָיו הַכֹּהֵן בְּאֵיל הָאָשָׁם לִפְנֵי ה׳ עַל־חַטָּאתוֹ אֲשֶׁר חָטָא וְנִסְלַח לוֹ מֵחַטָּאתוֹ אֲשֶׁר חָטָא, *And the Kohen shall atone for him with the ram asham before* HASHEM *for his sin that he sinned, and it shall be forgiven for him from his sin that he sinned*. The repetition is construed to mean that both categories of sin — unintentional and intentional — are atoned for by the *asham* (*Rav* from *Gem.* 9a; see *Tos. Yom Tov*).

וְנָזִיר שֶׁנִּטְמָא, — *a nazir who became tamei,*

[A *nazir* who comes in contact with a corpse interrupts his *nezirus* because of the *tumah* he has contracted. He must purify himself in the manner prescribed by the Torah for this *tumah*, i.e., the procedure calling for the use of the *parah adumah* (Red Cow), which takes a period of seven days. On the seventh day, he shaves his head and immerses himself in a *mikveh*. On the morrow, he brings an offering consisting of a pair of birds, one a *chatas*, the other an *olah*, as well as a

1. See below, mishnah 4 for an elaboration on the origin of the term *shifchah charufah*.

2. Actually there is a Tannaic dispute whether this prohibition involves a full-fledged שִׁפְחָה כְּנַעֲנִית or one who is partially freed. This will be discussed in mishnah 5.

3. Actually, it is not entirely clear whether the prohibition against a *shifchah charufah* is a function of the transgression of cohabiting with a gentile slavewoman or of the prohibition against adultery. See *Rashi, Yevamos* 55a; *Tzofnas Pa'aneach* on *Rambam* (vol. 2, 48a). Likewise there is a question whether the obligation for a sacrifice is in force for a slave who cohabits with a *shifchah charufah* other than his own 'wife.' See R' S.R. Hirsch (*Lev.* 19:20).

2
2

2. These bring [an offering] for intentional as well as inadvertent transgression: he who cohabits with a [betrothed] maidservant, a *nazir* who became *tamei*, for the oath of the testimony, and for the oath of the deposit.

lamb for an *asham*. As soon as he has brought his *chatas* bird, he resumes counting his *nezirus* days anew.]

The *nazir* who becomes *tamei*, too, brings his offerings regardless of whether he became *tamei* intentionally or due to circumstances beyond his control (*Tif. Yis.*).

This is derived from the Torah's phrase וְכִי־יָמוּת מֵת עָלָיו בְּפֶתַע פִּתְאֹם, *If someone dies next to him in unforeseen suddenness* (*Num.* 6:9). פֶּתַע indicates an incident which occurred without intent; פִּתְאֹם indicates an intentional experience (*Rav* from *Gem.* 9a).

וְעַל־שְׁבוּעַת הָעֵדוּת, — *for the oath of the testimony,*

This refers to an oath made by potential witnesses who have been summoned by a claimant in a monetary judgment to testify on his behalf. In response to this demand, the witnesses take an oath to deny any knowledge of the matter. If later they confess that they indeed have knowledge of the testimony that would have enabled the person to win his monetary claim, they are obligated to bring the variable sin-offering (*Lev.* 5:1; see *Shevuos* 4:3ff).

The mishnah now tells us that the obligation for the variable sin-offering applies regardless of whether the witnesses transgressed intentionally or unintentionally.

In the context of the oath of testimony, an unintentional transgression means that the witnesses were unaware of the severity of the prohibition of swearing falsely. In other words, they were conscious of the fact that they were withholding information, but were unaware that an offering must be brought for the false oath to this effect. Should they swear that they have no knowledge of the matter in question because, indeed, they have *forgotten* the testimony, no offering is required (*Tif. Yis.* from *Shevuos* 4:2; see Introduction of *Tif. Yis.* to *Shevuos* ch. 3, par. 3).

Regarding the other transgressions for which the Torah prescribes the variable sin-offering (e.g., entering the Temple in a state of *tumah*), the Torah (*Lev.* 5) uses the word וְנֶעְלַם, *it was concealed*, meaning that the transgression was committed unintentionally. Regarding the transgression of the oath of testimony, however, the word וְנֶעְלַם is omitted. Since the Torah omits it, we conclude that even if the sinners are aware of their transgression (i.e., they intentionally withheld information), they must bring the variable sin-offering (*Rav* from *Gem.* 9a).

וְעַל־שְׁבוּעַת הַפִּקָּדוֹן. — *and for the oath of the deposit.*

This refers to an oath made to deny another person's claim against him for money. This claim may be for any type of obligation, which can be incurred either by stealing, borrowing, accepting a deposit, finding a lost article, or the like. Should the person swear in the denial of any of these and later confess his guilt, he must return the principal [adding an additional fifth to the total sum] and bring an *asham* offering [called אֲשַׁם גְּזֵלוֹת, *asham gezeilos*] (*Tif. Yis.*).

The *asham* requirement mentioned in connection with the oath of deposit is likewise in force regardless of whether or not the transgressor was aware of the sin that he committed. [That is, he was aware of his false denial of monetary obligation but not aware that an oath to that effect must be atoned for by an offering (*Shevuos* 5:1).] This law is derived from a *gezeirah shavah* of the word תֶחֱטָא which appears both concerning the oath of the testimony and con-

חֲמִשָּׁה מְבִיאִין קָרְבָּן אֶחָד עַל־עֲבֵרוֹת הַרְבֵּה, וַחֲמִשָּׁה מְבִיאִים קָרְבָּן עוֹלֶה וְיוֹרֵד. אֵלּוּ מְבִיאִין קָרְבָּן אֶחָד עַל־עֲבֵרוֹת הַרְבֵּה: הַבָּא עַל־הַשִּׁפְחָה בִּיאוֹת הַרְבֵּה, וְנָזִיר שֶׁנִּטְמָא טֻמְאוֹת הַרְבֵּה, וְהַמְקַנֵּא לְאִשְׁתּוֹ עַל־יְדֵי

יד אברהם

cerning the oath of the deposit. This teaches that just as one is liable for the variable sin-offering for both an intentional or unintentional transgression of the oath of the testimony, so too, one is liable for both an intentional or unintentional violation of the oath of the deposit (*Rav* from *Gem.* 9a; see *Tos. Yom Tov*).

3.

As a rule, a *chatas* offering is brought for each time a transgression is repeated. For example, if in one lapse of awareness one eats forbidden *cheilev* fat, and in another lapse of awareness he repeats this transgression, he must bring an atonement for each time he sinned.

Another feature of the conventional *chatas* offering is that it is fixed. That is, it does not vary in accordance with the financial status of the violators.

The mishnah now lists two groups of atonement offerings that do not conform with these rules: Those that are brought singly even for multiple causes and those in the עוֹלֶה וְיוֹרֵד, *variable sin-offering* category.

חֲמִשָּׁה מְבִיאִין קָרְבָּן אֶחָד עַל־עֲבֵרוֹת הַרְבֵּה, — *Five bring a single offering for many transgressions,*

[These are five categories of atonement obligations for which one offering serves to atone even for numerous repeated transgressions.]

וַחֲמִשָּׁה מְבִיאִים קָרְבָּן עוֹלֶה וְיוֹרֵד. — *and five bring a variable sin offering* [lit., *an ascending and descending offering*].

The offering is called עוֹלֶה וְיוֹרֵד, *ascending and descending*, because it fluctuates with the financial status of the transgressor. It 'ascends' — or increases — when the violator is prosperous, and 'descends' — or decreases — when he is poor (*Tif. Yis.*). If he is rich, he brings a she-lamb or a she-kid for a *chatas*. If he cannot afford it, he brings two turtledoves or two young doves, one for a *chatas* and one for an *olah*. For some transgressions, the Torah makes provisions for the poorest category, one who cannot afford even the birds for the *chatas*. In this case, the transgressor brings a *minchah* consisting of a tenth of an *ephah* of fine wheat flour (*Lev.* 5:6-13; see mishnah 4).

אֵלּוּ מְבִיאִין קָרְבָּן אֶחָד עַל־עֲבֵרוֹת הַרְבֵּה: — *These bring a single offering for many transgressions:*

[Four of the five people in this category are listed in this mishnah. The fifth is given in the next mishnah.]

הַבָּא עַל־הַשִּׁפְחָה בִּיאוֹת הַרְבֵּה, — *he who cohabits with a slavewoman many times,*

If one cohabits with a *shifchah charufah* any number of times, he brings but one *asham* to atone for all his transgressions. Thus, if one either deliberately cohabits with the *shifchah charufah* a number of times or unintentionally cohabits with her during two separate lapses of awareness in which he transgressed, he nonetheless brings but one

2
3

3. Five bring a single offering for many transgressions, and five bring a variable sin offering. These bring a single offering for many transgressions: he who cohabits with a slavewoman many times, a *nazir* who became *tamei* many times, he who warned

asham for these multiple transgressions (*Rambam*, *Shegagos* 9:5 cited by *Tosafos Yom Tov*).

It goes without saying that if one unintentionally cohabited with a *shifchah charufah* a number of times during one lapse of awareness, he brings only one *asham*. In the corresponding situation for other transgressions, one *chatas* would likewise suffice, since all the transgressions took place during the same lapse of awareness (see below ch. 3:2). The novelty of the *shifchah charufah* transgression is that even for numerous transgressions committed in *separate* lapses of consciousness, one offering suffices (*Tos. Yom Tov*).

The limitation of one offering for even many transgressions is, in this case, derived from the wording, עַל־חַטָּאתוֹ אֲשֶׁר חָטָא, *for his sin that he sinned*. This apparently superfluous phrase indicates that one is liable to just one offering no matter how many times the sin is repeated. This, however, is true only if he cohabited with one slavewoman many times. In the event that he transgressed by cohabitation with several slavewomen, even in one lapse of awareness, he is liable separately for each one. This is derived from the wording, וְהִוא שִׁפְחָה, *and she is a slavewoman*, indicating that he is liable for each slavewoman (*Rav* from *Gem.* 9a).

וְנָזִיר שֶׁנִּטְמָא טֻמְאוֹת הַרְבֵּה, — *a nazir who became tamei many times*,

As explained above, if a *nazir* becomes *tamei*, the מֵי חַטָּאת, *purification water* [a mixture of the ashes of the *parah adumah* (Red Cow) and מַיִם חַיִּים, *spring water*], must be sprinkled upon him on the third and seventh day from when he became *tamei*. Then, on the seventh day, he shaves off his hair. On the eighth day, he brings a pair of bird offerings [one an *olah* and the other a *chatas*] as well as a lamb for an *asham*. The point of the mishnah is that no matter how many times the *nazir* becomes *tamei*, one set of offerings is sufficient to enable him to resume his *nezirus* period.

Should the second case of *tumah* occur during the first six days of his first *tumah*, it is self-evident that one set is sufficient since the additional *tumah* results in creating simply one extended period of *tumah*. That, then, is not the point of the mishnah. Rather, the mishnah refers to a *nazir* who became *tamei* on the seventh day of his first *tumah* period. Although the *nazir's* offerings are brought on the eighth day, the mishnah holds that the *nazir* commences to count his second period of *nezirus* on the seventh day. Since that is the day of the commencement of his *nezirus* or *taharah*, we would be inclined to believe that if he becomes *tamei*, he would be required to bring a separate set of offerings for each *nezirus* period. The mishnah, therefore, teaches us that since the seventh day is not yet fit for bringing offerings, if he becomes *tamei* on that day, he need not bring individual offerings, but only one set of offerings for both periods (*Rav* from *Gem.* 9b).

The ruling that the *nezirus* of the *nazir tamei* is resumed on the seventh day of his *tumah* period is the view of R' Yose bar Yehudah. In the view of Rabbi (Yehudah HaNasi), however, the second *nezirus* commences only from the eighth day on. The mishnah's ruling that one set of offerings suffices for many causes of *tumah* could not have been formulated according to him: If the *tumah* occurred on the seventh day, that the *nazir* must bring but one set of offerings is self-evident, because he is still in his original

כריתות ב/ג

אֲנָשִׁים הַרְבֵּה, וּמְצֹרָע שֶׁנִּתְנַגַּע נְגָעִים הַרְבֵּה. הֵבִיא צִפּוֹרָיו וְנִתְנַגַּע, לֹא עָלוּ לוֹ, עַד שֶׁיָּבִיא אֶת־חַטָּאתוֹ.

יד אברהם

tumah period; if, on the other hand, the *tumah* occurred on the eighth day, it is obvious that he must bring an individual *asham* sacrifice for each *nezirus* period (*Gem.* ad loc.).

Rambam (*Hil. Nezirus* 6:15) does not rule in accordance with either of the views expressed above. According to his formulation, the *nazir* brings only one set of offerings for all his *tumah* causes, regardless of when they occurred. As long as the second *tumah* occurred before he brought the sacrifice for the first, one set of offerings is sufficient for both. This is the view of the Sages in *Nazir* (18b) (see *Kesef Mishneh* ad loc.; *Tos. Yom Tov; Keren Orah, Nazir* ad loc.).

וְהַמְקַנֵּא לְאִשְׁתּוֹ עַל־יְדֵי אֲנָשִׁים הַרְבֵּה, — *he who warned his wife concerning many men,*

The term *sotah* can refer either to an adulteress or to a woman whose fidelity had been questioned by her husband as a result of her immoral behavior and who has met other criteria making it presumptive that an act of adultery did take place. In the latter case she is known as a סוֹטָה סָפֵק, *presumptive sotah* (see *Yevamos* 11b).

In order for a woman to become a presumptive *sotah,* two events must take place: (1) קִנּוּי — *warning;* her husband must warn her not to seclude herself with a specific man, and (2) סְתִירָה — *seclusion*; the wife then disregards the warning and is observed going into seclusion with that man. Once these two events occur, there is sufficient circumstantial evidence to establish the likelihood that an act of adultery has taken place. She is then forbidden to live with her husband until her innocence is established (*Sotah* 1:2).

The Torah sets forth a procedure through which the *sotah's* innocence or guilt is Divinely determined (see *Numbers* 5:11-31). As part of this procedure, which takes place in the Temple grounds, the *sotah* must bring a *minchah* offering, known as מִנְחַת קְנָאוֹת, *jealousy minchah* [see *Menachos* 1:1].

The *minchah* brought by a man for his *sotah* wife is also one of the offerings which can atone for a number of causes, i.e., if a husband warned his wife not to seclude herself with a number of specific men, and she secluded herself with each of them, he brings but one *minchah* offering for all these instances of uncertain fidelity. This is derived from *Numbers* (5:29): זֹאת תּוֹרַת הַקְּנָאֹת, *This is the law of the warnings,* the singular תּוֹרַת, *law of,* followed by the plural קְנָאֹת, *warnings,* indicates that there is one law for many warnings (*Rav* from *Gem.* 9b).

וּמְצֹרָע שֶׁנִּתְנַגַּע נְגָעִים הַרְבֵּה. — *and a metzora who became afflicted with many lesions.*

[After a *metzora* is cured of his *tzaraas,* he undergoes an elaborate seven-day process of purification. On the first day, he takes two birds — one that is slaughtered and one that is released to fly away into open space. The blood of the slaughtered bird is sprinkled on the *metzora*, who then immerses his clothing in a *mikveh* and shaves all his hair. Neither of these birds is considered an offering and the ceremony does not take place in the Temple. At the end of the seven days, he shaves his hair once again. On the eighth day he brings the following offerings: an *asham,* a *chatas,* an *olah* and a *minchah*. For a person of means the *chatas* and *olah* consist of two lambs; for one who is poor, they are a pair of birds (*Lev.* 14:1ff).

If a *metzora* is healed from his *tzaraas* and, before he brings his offerings, is again afflicted with *tzaraas* and then is healed again, he may bring one set of

2
3 his wife concerning many men, and a *metzora* who became afflicted with many lesions. [If] he brought his birds and was then [again] afflicted, they do not count for him, until he brings his *chatas*. R' Yehudah

YAD AVRAHAM

offerings for all the times that he had the *tzaraas*, regardless how many times this is repeated (*Rav*).

It is not clear when these numerous recurrences of *tzaraas* took place: within the seven-day waiting period before the *metzora* can bring his offerings, or after? It is probable, though, that the law of the *metzora* follows that of the *nazir* who became *tamei* a number of times. Just as, in our *Tanna's* view, a *nazir* who became *tamei* for a second time on the eighth day of his *taharah* period must bring a separate set of offerings for each of the *tumah* causes, so too, the healed *metzora* who became *tamei* on the eighth day of his first *tzaraas* period must bring a separate set of offerings for the second *tumah* (*Tos. Yom Tov*).

Rambam (*Hil. Mechusrei Kapparah* 5:8), however, rules that the *metzora* brings a separate set of offerings only if he became afflicted with the second *tzaraas* after bringing the offerings for the first. Otherwise one set of offerings is sufficient even for numerous *tzaraas* afflictions. This is consistent with his previously cited ruling concerning the *nazir* who became *tamei* more than once (ibid.; cf. *Kesef Mishneh* ad loc.).

הֵבִיא צִפּוֹרָיו וְנִתְנַגַּע, — *[If] he brought his birds and was then [again] afflicted,*

If on the first day of his seven-day purification process a cured *metzora* had already brought the two birds ordained by the Torah — one to be slaughtered and one to be sent away — and then he was stricken with a second *nega* affliction (*Tos. Yom Tov* from *Rashi*).

לֹא עָלוּ לוֹ, עַד שֶׁיָּבִיא אֶת־חַטָּאתוֹ. — *they do not count for him, until he brings his chatas.*

The apparent meaning of this passage is: If he was again stricken with *tzaraas* after bringing his birds, those birds have no validity. In other words, when he is cured from the second *tzaraas* he must bring *two* sets of birds: one for the first affliction and one for the second affliction. This interpretation, however, would be inconsistent with the previous clause of the mishnah, which regards many consecutive afflictions as one as far as the sacrificial obligations are concerned. Accordingly, the birds he brings for the second *nega* would automatically count for the first as well, just as the offerings after the second *tzaraas* atone for the first *tzaraas* as well (*Tif. Yis.* from *Gem.* 9b).

The *Gemara* (9b), therefore, explains this segment of the mishnah in the context of *which* offerings to bring, rather than how many. The mishnah is addressing the issue of the determination of his financial status, which affects the nature of his offerings — the rich person brings lambs for his *olah* and his *chatas;* and the poor person, birds.

Accordingly, the mishnah is to be interpreted in the manner of חַסּוּרֵי מִיחַסְּרָא, *an omission,* which should really read as follows: *If he brought his non-sacrificial birds and was then stricken, he need not bring two sets of offerings after being cured from the second affliction; one set suffices. If he brings his non-sacrificial birds and then his financial status changes, the birds do not count* [to establish his financial status].

In other words, if he became wealthy even after bringing his initial birds — which are in themselves not atonement offerings — he must upgrade his offering to that of the rich man; conversely, if he became poor he may bring a poor man's offering, despite the fact that he had already begun the process as one in the category of the rich. His financial status is not finally determined until he brings the *chatas*. This is derived from

רַבִּי יְהוּדָה אוֹמֵר: עַד שֶׁיָּבִיא אֶת־אֲשָׁמוֹ.

[ד] **הָאִשָּׁה** שֶׁיָּלְדָה וְלָדוֹת הַרְבֵּה: הִפִּילָה בְּתוֹךְ שְׁמֹנִים נְקֵבָה, וְחָזְרָה וְהִפִּילָה בְּתוֹךְ שְׁמֹנִים נְקֵבָה, וְהַמַּפֶּלֶת תְּאוֹמִים.

יד אברהם

אֲשֶׁר לֹא־תַשִּׂיג יָדוֹ בְּטָהֳרָתוֹ, [for him] *who cannot afford [a sacrifice] at his purification,* i.e., it is the day of bringing the offerings for his *taharah* — not the time that he brings his non-sacrificial birds — that is the crucial determining factor in whether to brings the offerings of wealth or of poverty (*Rav*).

Tif. Yis. explains that even with the *Gemara's* emendation, the mishnah is not entirely a matter of omission. The mishnah's phrase *[if] he brought his birds and was then [again] afflicted, they do not count* can be explained to mean that the birds do not count to *separate* the two *tzaraas* incidents, neither to obligate him for separate offerings nor to establish his financial status.

The order of the offerings is *asham*, *chatas*, and *olah*. In the *Tanna Kamma's* view, it is the *chatas* which is crucial in determining the nature of his offerings. Should the *metzora* become poor before bringing his *chatas*, he brings his *chatas* and *olah* as a poor person, viz., two turtledoves or two young doves. Should he become poor after bringing the *chatas*, he must bring the *olah* as a rich person, viz., a lamb. Conversely, if he brings the *chatas* as a poor man and immediately afterwards becomes rich, he need only bring the second bird as an *olah*. The *Tanna's* regard of the *chatas* as the determining factor of his sacrificial status is based on the verse (*Lev.* 14:32): זֹאת תּוֹרַת אֲשֶׁר־בּוֹ נֶגַע צָרָעַת אֲשֶׁר לֹא־תַשִּׂיג יָדוֹ בְּטָהֳרָתוֹ, *This is the law of one who has an affliction of tzaraas, who cannot afford [a sacrifice] at his purification.* The word בְּטָהֳרָתוֹ, *at his purification*, is understood to mean his expiation from the sin for which *tzaraas* is a punishment (see *Arachin* 16a). This is accomplished by the *chatas*. Therefore, the verse is to be understood to mean that the poor man's offerings are brought by one who cannot afford the rich man's offerings at the time he brings his *chatas* (*Rav* from *Gem.* 9b, *Rashi* ad loc.).

רַבִּי יְהוּדָה אוֹמֵר: עַד שֶׁיָּבִיא אֶת־אֲשָׁמוֹ. — *R' Yehudah says: Until he brings his asham.*

R' Yehudah disagrees with the first *Tanna* and holds that the person's financial status is determined at the time that he brings the *asham*. He interprets the verse בְּטָהֳרָתוֹ, *at his purification*, as a reference to the *asham*, the blood of which is sprinkled on the thumbs of the *metzora's* hands and feet. This rite renders him fit to partake of *kodashim*. Thus, he may bring a poor man's offerings even if he becomes rich after bringing his *asham* (*Rav* from *Gem.* ad loc.).

According to some, the halachah is in accordance with the *Tanna Kamma* (*Rav; Rambam Comm.*). Others, however, rule like R' Yehudah (*Rambam, Mechusrei Kapparah* 5:9; Eretz Yisrael version of *Comm.* cited by *Tos. Yom Tov; Rav* and *Rambam Comm., Negaim* 14:11; see *Tos. Yom Tov* and *Lechem Mishneh* ad loc.).

4.

הָאִשָּׁה שֶׁיָּלְדָה וְלָדוֹת הַרְבֵּה: — *A woman who gave birth many times:*

She gave birth and/or miscarried several times in the manner described by the mishnah further (*Rav; Rashi*).

Other versions of the mishnah read: הָאִשָּׁה

says: Until he brings his *asham*.

4. A woman who gave birth many times: if she aborted a female within the eighty days, and then again aborted a female within the eighty days, or if she aborted a multiple birth. R' Yehudah says: She

YAD AVRAHAM

שֶׁהִפִּילָה, *a woman who miscarried*. [The reference to miscarriages rather than births apparently reflects the subsequent sections of the mishnah which refer to numerous miscarriages in succession] (*Rav* as cited by *Tos. Yom Tov; Shinuyei Nuschaos*).

הִפִּילָה בְּתוֹךְ שְׁמוֹנִים נְקֵבָה, וְחָזְרָה וְהִפִּילָה בְּתוֹךְ שְׁמוֹנִים נְקֵבָה, — *if she aborted a female within the eighty days, and then again aborted a female within the eighty days,*

A woman bore a female child and immersed herself immediately after the two-week period of *tumah*. She immediately conceived another female child, which she aborted after the first forty days of gestation, a total of fifty-four days after the initial birth. She then repeated the process, aborting fifty-four days later. Since the first miscarriage took place within the eighty days of the first birth, and the second miscarriage took place within the eighty days of the first miscarriage, all are counted as one, and she brings only one offering.

The mishnah discusses the situation only for a female child, because the circumstances in question cannot be created by the birth of a male. Since the entire *melos* period for a male child is forty days from birth of which the first seven are *tamei*, it is impossible to again abort a minimum-age fetus, forty days, within the *melos* period of the first birth. In other words, if the woman immersed herself after seven days and then aborted within forty days of the initial birth of a female, this miscarriage would not count as a birth, since before forty days of conception, an aborted fetus is considered as merely a liquefied substance (*Rav; Rashi*).

Actually, the above-described scenario is impossible only from the standpoint of Torah law, which forbids relations for the first week after birth. Technically speaking, however, it *is* possible to conceive a child immediately after birth, in which case the mishnah's law would apply to a male child as well. The *Tanna* does not discuss such a case, though, since it presupposes a violation of Torah law. As a rule the *Tanna* does not deal with situations created by deliberate Torah violators, in this case those who do not keep the laws of marital purity (*Tos. Yom Tov*).

וְהַמַּפֶּלֶת תְּאוֹמִים. — *or if she aborted a multiple birth.*

She aborted a multiple birth one fetus at a time, with a forty-day period separating the abortions. This case could be even if she aborted males, e.g., if she conceived male triplets, aborted one forty days after conception, and the second one within the *melos* period, and the third within the *melos* period of the second.[1] In both of the cases mentioned by the mishnah, the woman brings but one set of offerings, since the second miscarriage occurred within the *melos* period of the first and the third miscarriage came about within the *melos* period of the second.

This law is derived from the words זֹאת תּוֹרַת הַיֹּלֶדֶת לַזָּכָר אוֹ לַנְּקֵבָה, *This is the law of the woman who has given birth to a male or to a female* (*Lev.* 12:7). The implication is that the woman who gave birth brings these offerings even if she bore or aborted a number of fetuses.

1. Strictly speaking, the mishnah's law includes regular births as well as miscarriages. I.e., if she bore a male child and within forty days bore one of its triplets and within the next forty days the other. The *Tanna* refers to miscarriages because it is uncommon for full-term births to take place with interruptions of so long a period (*Tif. Yis., Boaz*).

רַבִּי יְהוּדָה אוֹמֵר: מְבִיאָה עַל הָרִאשׁוֹן, וְאֵינָהּ מְבִיאָה עַל הַשֵּׁנִי, מְבִיאָה עַל הַשְּׁלִישִׁי, וְאֵינָהּ מְבִיאָה עַל הָרְבִיעִי.

אֵלּוּ מְבִיאִין קָרְבָּן עוֹלֶה וְיוֹרֵד: עַל שְׁמִיעַת הַקּוֹל, וְעַל בִּטּוּי שְׂפָתַיִם, וְעַל טֻמְאַת מִקְדָּשׁ וְקָדָשָׁיו,

יד אברהם

However, this law applies only if each birth or miscarriage took place in the *melos* period of the preceding birth. If the second birth was after the *melos* period, it requires a separate offering. This is indicated from the words זֹאת תּוֹרַת, *This is the law*, a restrictive phrase that teaches that only in certain cases is this so, not in the case of the third that took place after the purification days of the second (*Rav* from *Gem.* 9b).

רַבִּי יְהוּדָה אוֹמֵר: מְבִיאָה עַל הָרִאשׁוֹן, וְאֵינָהּ מְבִיאָה עַל הַשֵּׁנִי, — *R' Yehudah says: She brings [an offering] for the first, but she does not bring for the second,*

[In either of the two cases — either in the case that she conceived after her first birth or in the case that she aborted triplets — she brings an offering for the first but does not bring an offering for the second.]

Since it was aborted within the *melos* period of the first, one offering suffices for two births or miscarriages that occurred within one *melos* period (*Rav*).

מְבִיאָה עַל הַשְּׁלִישִׁי, — *she brings for the third,*

R' Yehudah differs with the *Tanna Kamma* and rules that in both the abovementioned cases, the woman must bring an offering for the third fetus since the time it was aborted coincided only with the *melos* period of the second miscarriage, not with that of the first. Since that miscarriage does not mandate an offering, its *melos* period does not count. Even the case of the triplets is, according to R' Yehudah, not considered as one long birth, thereby giving the second the same status as the first. As long as the third miscarriage took place after the *melos* period of the first, it requires its own offering (*Rav; Rashi*).

וְאֵינָהּ מְבִיאָה עַל הָרְבִיעִי. — *but she does not bring for the fourth.*

Since she does bring an offering for the third miscarriage, the fourth does not require a separate offering, if it occurred within the *melos* period of the third.

Although R' Yehudah rules that the second fetus does not count, that is only insofar as it does not exempt the third from an offering. As regards the postpartum days of *tumah* and *taharah*, the second miscarriage *is* counted as a birth. Thus, if she aborts a male, she must wait seven days of *tumah* and thirty-three days of *taharah*, and if a female, she must wait fourteen days of *tumah* and sixty-six days of *taharah* (*Rav* from *Gem.* 10a).

The halachah is not in accordance with R' Yehudah (*Rav; Rambam Comm.*).

[Although all standard editions of the Mishnah use the numbering system that we follow, a marginal gloss in the Vilna edition notes that all of mishnah 4 until this point logically belongs to mishnah 3. Indeed, an earlier edition of Mishnah with *Rav* sets the number 4 at this point.]

אֵלּוּ מְבִיאִין קָרְבָּן עוֹלֶה וְיוֹרֵד: — *These bring a variable offering* [lit., *ascending and descending*]:

[This is a *chatas* offering which varies according to a person's financial situation:] For the rich it 'ascends' [i.e., increases to a she-lamb or a she-goat]; for the poorer it 'descends' [i.e., diminishes to a pair of birds]; and for some transgressions it can descend even further to an *issaron* [a tenth of an *ephah* measure] of flour for a

2 brings [an offering] for the first, but she does not bring
4 for the second, she brings for the third, but she does not bring for the fourth.

These bring a variable offering: for [the sin of] hearing the voice [of adjuration], for uttering [an oath], for contaminating the Temple or its consecrated foods,

minchah (*Rav* from *Lev.* 5:1-13).

עַל שְׁמִיעַת הַקּוֹל, — *for [the sin of] hearing the voice [of adjuration],*

The sin of שְׁמִיעַת הַקּוֹל, *hearing the voice* [of adjuration], is a reference to what is called earlier (mishnah 2) שְׁבוּעַת הָעֵדוּת, *the oath of testimony*. The expression is based on the verse (*Lev.* 5:1): וְנֶפֶשׁ כִּי־תֶחֱטָא וְשָׁמְעָה קוֹל אָלָה וְהוּא עֵד ... אִם־לוֹא יַגִּיד וְנָשָׂא עֲוֹנוֹ, *should a person sin and hear the voice of adjuration and he is a witness . . . if he does not testify, he shall bear his iniquity* (see *Horayos* 2:5). As described above, it refers to witnesses who have information that could win the financial claim of a litigant but, when summoned to testify, deny with a false oath having this information (*Tif. Yis.*).

It is possible that this mishnah uses the phrase שְׁמִיעַת הַקּוֹל, *hearing the voice*, because it appears in *Lev.* 5:1 in the same section that discusses the obligation of the variable sin-offering for this sin, as well as for the next two — בִּטּוּי שְׂפָתַיִם, *uttering an oath* (5:4), and טֻמְאַת מִקְדָּשׁ, *contaminating the Temple* (5:2-3) — discussed by the mishnah (*Aruch LaNer*).

וְעַל בִּטּוּי שְׂפָתַיִם, — *for uttering [an oath]* [lit., *with the lips*],

This is a sin of swearing falsely. A false oath can be in reference to the future — to perform a deed at some future time or to refrain from performing one. It can also be a false oath regarding a past incident, e.g., swearing that one did or did not perform a certain act in the past.

The term *uttering of the lips* is derived from the verse stated in connection with the variable sin-offering (*Lev.* 5:4): אוֹ נֶפֶשׁ כִּי תִשָּׁבַע לְבַטֵּא בִשְׂפָתַיִם לְהָרַע אוֹ לְהֵיטִיב, *if a person swears, uttering with his lips, to do evil or to do good* (*Tif. Yis.*; *Rav*, *Horayos* 2:5; see *Shevuos* 3:1).

וְעַל טֻמְאַת מִקְדָּשׁ וְקָדָשָׁיו, — *for contaminating the Temple or its consecrated foods,*

[This sin is that of entering the Temple courtyard or consuming sacrificial food while in a state of *tumah*. This applies if he either forgot his status of *tumah* or if he forgot that the place he entered was the Temple or that the food was sacrificial. See *Shevuos* 2:1.]

In our mishnah, the sins of entering the Temple or eating *kodashim* in a state of *tumah* is counted as one sin [or else there would be *six* sins for which the variable sin-offering is brought]; in the listing of the thirty-six *kereisos* at the beginning of the tractate, these sins are listed as two. The explanation for this distinction is that as far as *kereisos* are concerned, entering the Temple and eating *kodashim* in a state of *tumah* are two separate categories, the *kares* for each being mentioned separately. As far as the variable sin-offering is concerned, however, both sins are mentioned together in one verse[1] [although each sin mandates its own offering] (*Tos.*).

The mishnah's first three cases are those mentioned by the Torah in connection with the variable sin-offering (*Lev.* 5:1ff). In these instances the variable sin offering consists of three levels: a *chatas* lamb for the rich, a pair of birds [one an *olah*, one a *chatas*] for the poor, and a

1. *Rambam* (*Shegagos* 10:1), by contrast, lists *six* obligations for the variable sin-offering. This is because *Rambam* categorizes by the *actions* themselves rather than their Biblical sources. In this context, טֻמְאַת מִקְדָּשׁ וְקָדָשָׁיו is counted as two sins, for it refers to two distinct actions. [Fittingly enough, *Rambam* uses the phrase וְהַנִּשְׁבָּע שְׁבוּעַת הָעֵדוּת, *one who swears the oath of*

כריתות ב/ד

וְהַיּוֹלֶדֶת, וְהַמְּצֹרָע.

ומַה בֵּין הַשִּׁפְחָה לְבֵין כָּל־הָעֲרָיוֹת? שֶׁלֹּא שָׁוְתָה לָהֶן לֹא בָעֹנֶשׁ וְלֹא בַקָּרְבָּן: שֶׁכָּל הָעֲרָיוֹת בְּחַטָּאת — וְהַשִּׁפְחָה בְאָשָׁם; כָּל הָעֲרָיוֹת בִּנְקֵבָה, וְשִׁפְחָה — בְּזָכָר; כָּל־הָעֲרָיוֹת, אֶחָד הָאִישׁ וְאֶחָד

יד אברהם

minchah for the very poor. Regarding the next two circumstances for which the variable sin-offering is brought, it consists of only two levels: an animal offering for the rich and a pair of birds for the poor.

וְהַיּוֹלֶדֶת, — *the woman who has given birth,*

If she is rich, she brings a lamb for an *olah* and a turtledove or a young dove for a *chatas*. If she is poor, she brings two turtledoves or two young doves; one for an *olah*, one for a *chatas*. Since in this case the Torah makes no mention of a lesser offering for the very poor woman, the halachah is that even the poorest must bring two turtledoves or two young doves (*Rav* from *Gem.* 10b).

וְהַמְּצֹרָע. — *and the metzora.*

As has been mentioned, the *metzora* brings sacrifices as part of his *taharah* process. A rich person brings two lambs, one for an *olah* and one for a *chatas*, and a poor person brings two turtledoves or two young doves. As above, only the offering of the rich and the poor are mentioned. Even the very poor must bring the two bird offerings (*Rav* from *Gem.* 10b).

שִׁפְחָה חֲרוּפָה, Betrothed Slavewoman

The following segment of the mishnah is not related to the previous discussion of the variable sin-offering. Instead, it returns to the subject of the *shifchah charufah* mentioned earlier, in mishnah 2. [Indeed, in the *Gemara* text the following appears as a separate mishnah beginning with (מַה (בֵּין שִׁפְחָה, *what (is the difference between a slavewoman etc.)*, without the conjunction *and*.]

As mentioned already in mishnah 2, the prohibition of the *shifchah charufah* involves cohabitation with a specific category of שִׁפְחָה כְּנַעֲנִית, *a gentile slavewoman* owned by a Jew. The *shifchah charufah* is in some way betrothed [the word חֲרוּפָה meaning *betrothed*].[1] The prohibition of *shifchah charufah* resembles other sexual offenses [listed in mishnah 1] in the sense that it, too, is atoned for by an offering. However, the *shifchah charufah* transgression differs significantly from those sexual transgressions known as עֲרָיוֹת. Those differences are the subject of the following discussion.

The Torah's description of the *shifchah charufah* is couched in ambiguous terms

testimony, in contrast to the mishnah's phrase וְעַל שְׁמִיעַת הַקּוֹל, *and hearing the voice*, for the mishnah's expression is based on Biblical usage while *Rambam's* language is couched in practical terms] (*Aruch LaNer*).

1. The actual term חֲרוּפָה is an unusual one. It is based on the Torah's description of the slavewoman in question with the words וְהוּא שִׁפְחָה נֶחֱרֶפֶת לְאִישׁ, *and she was a slavewoman who has been designated for another man* (*Lev.* 19:20). Simply, it means a *betrothed maidservant*, a slavewoman married in the sense that she is assigned to live with one man exclusively.

Rashi (ad loc.) notes that there is no parallel for the usage of the word חֲרוּפָה to mean married or betrothed. *Ramban* (ad loc.) renders חֲרוּפָה as a synonym for the word נַעֲרָה, *youth* (as the word חֹרֶף means *winter*, i.e., the beginning of life). This term is used in the sense of *personal attendant*. She is, *Ramban* explains, *a maidservant assigned as a personal attendant* of a man, i.e., to live with him as a *de facto* wife. See also R' Hirsch for an elaboration of this theme and *Ibn Ezra* for an alternate approach.

2 the woman who has given birth, and the *metzora*.
4 And what is the difference between the slavewoman and all [other] forbidden intimacies? She is similar to them neither regarding the punishment nor regarding the offering: For all forbidden intimacies require a *chatas*, but the slavewoman — an *asham;* all forbidden intimacies require a female [animal], but the slavewoman — a male; regarding all forbidden intimacies both the man and the woman are the same regarding

that lend themselves to a number of interpretations. The verse reads (*Lev.* 19:20ff): וְאִישׁ כִּי־יִשְׁכַּב אֶת־אִשָּׁה שִׁכְבַת־זֶרַע וְהִוא שִׁפְחָה נֶחֱרֶפֶת לְאִישׁ וְהָפְדֵּה לֹא נִפְדָּתָה אוֹ חֻפְשָׁה לֹא נִתַּן־לָהּ בִּקֹּרֶת תִּהְיֶה לֹא יוּמְתוּ כִּי־לֹא חֻפָּשָׁה. וְהֵבִיא אֶת־אֲשָׁמוֹ לַה׳..., *If a man lies carnally with a woman, and she is a slavewoman who has been designated for another man, and who has not been redeemed, or whose freedom has not been granted her; there shall be an investigation — they shall not be put to death, for she has not been freed. He shall brings his asham to* HASHEM . . .

The details of the *shifchah charufah* transgression are set forth in the following segment; *shifchah charufah* is defined and discussed in the next mishnah.

וּמַה בֵּין הַשִּׁפְחָה לְבֵין כָּל־הָעֲרָיוֹת? — *And what is the difference between the slavewoman and all [other] forbidden intimacies?*

What are the differences between the sin of cohabiting with the slavewoman, i.e., the *shifchah charufah* (betrothed slavewoman), and the sins of cohabitation known as עֲרָיוֹת, *forbidden intimacies?* (*Tif. Yis.*).

שֶׁלֹּא שָׁוְתָה לָהֶן לֹא בָעֹנֶשׁ וְלֹא בַקָּרְבָּן: — *She is similar to them neither regarding the punishment nor regarding the offering:*

The *Tanna* replies that the difference is that the *shifchah charufah* is unlike other forbidden intimacies regarding both the offering and the punishment, as the *Tanna* proceeds to delineate (*Tif. Yis.*).

שֶׁכָּל הָעֲרָיוֹת בְּחַטָּאת — וְהַשִּׁפְחָה בְּאָשָׁם; — *For all forbidden intimacies require a chatas, but the slavewoman — an asham;*

[As explained in chapter 1, mishnah 2, all forbidden unions punishable by *kares* require a *chatas* if the sin was unintentional, but if one is intimate with a slavewoman, he must bring an *asham*, as in *Lev.* 19:21.][1]

כָּל־הָעֲרָיוֹת בִּנְקֵבָה, וְשִׁפְחָה — בְּזָכָר; — *all forbidden intimacies require a female [animal], but the slavewoman — a male;*

[The animal brought for the offering to atone for any forbidden intimacy is female — a she-lamb or a she-goat; the offering for the sin of intimacy with the *shifchah charufah* is male — a ram.]

כָּל־הָעֲרָיוֹת אֶחָד הָאִישׁ וְאֶחָד הָאִשָּׁה שָׁוִין בְּמַכּוֹת וּבְקָרְבָּן, — *regarding all forbidden intimacies, both the man and the woman are the same regarding lashes or an offering,*

If a sexual offense is committed inten-

1. *Ibn Ezra* (ad loc.) suggests that the reason for the *asham* sacrifice requirement is that the *shifchah charufah* transgression represents a *theft* of the maidservant from her rightful owner. Thus the Torah sets forth an *asham* sacrifice requirement for this transgression, just as it does for a conventional theft. Interestingly, *Ibn Ezra* offers an interpretation of the *shifchah charufah* passage according to which the reference is to a *Jewish* maidservant. This approach, of course, is consistent with neither of the views expressed in the following mishnah.

הָאִשָּׁה שָׁוִין בְּמַכּוֹת וּבְקָרְבָּן, וּבַשִּׁפְחָה, לֹא הִשְׁוָה אֶת־הָאִישׁ לָאִשָּׁה בְּמַכּוֹת, וְלֹא אֶת־הָאִשָּׁה לָאִישׁ בְּקָרְבָּן; כָּל־הָעֲרָיוֹת, עָשָׂה בָהֶן אֶת־הַמַּעֲרֶה כַּגּוֹמֵר, וְחַיָּב עַל כָּל־בִּיאָה וּבִיאָה. זֶה חֹמֶר, הֶחֱמִיר בַּשִּׁפְחָה: שֶׁעָשָׂה בָהּ אֶת־הַמֵּזִיד כַּשּׁוֹגֵג.

יד אברהם

tionally, both the male and female partner are subject to the punishment of *malkus* (lashes). This is derived from the Torah's statement (*Num.* 5:6): אִישׁ אוֹ־אִשָּׁה כִּי יַעֲשׂוּ מִכָּל־חַטֹּאת הָאָדָם, *If a man or woman shall commit any of the sins of a person* — which indicates that men and women are equal in regard to all punishments in the Torah. Likewise, both male and female violators are liable to *kares* for an intentional transgression, as the Torah states (*Lev.* 18:29): וְנִכְרְתוּ הַנְּפָשׁוֹת הָעֹשֹׂת, *the persons doing so will be cut off*. For an unintentional transgression, then, both are liable for a *chatas* because anyone liable for *kares* brings a *chatas* to atone for an unintentional transgression (*Rav; Rashi*).

וּבַשִּׁפְחָה, לֹא הִשְׁוָה אֶת־הָאִישׁ לָאִשָּׁה בְּמַכּוֹת, — *[whereas] regarding the slavewoman, [the Torah] did not equate the man to the woman concerning lashes,*

[The sin of cohabiting with the *shifchah charufah* carries with it the liability for the *malkus* (lashes) punishment.] It is only the woman who is punishable by *malkus*, not the man (*Tif. Yis.*).

The *malkus* punishment is derived from the Torah's expression (*Lev.* 19:20): בִּקֹּרֶת תִּהְיֶה, *there shall be an investigation*, which means the corporal punishment of *malkus*.

Literally, the word בִּקֹּרֶת means *distinction* or *critical examination*, which in our context means the courts shall *distinguish* between the capital punishment normally applied in the instance of a deliberate sexual offense with a married woman and the punishment for cohabiting with the *shifchah charufah* [i.e., she is subject to corporal punishment, but not death] (*Rashi, Lev.* ad loc.).

The association of the word בִּקֹּרֶת with the *malkus* punishment is based on the exegetic interpretation of the word as בִּקְרִיאָה תְּהֵא, *she shall be subject to the reading*, referring to the reading of verses which accompany the administration of *malkus* (see *Makkos* 3:14).

Alternatively, the word בִּקֹּרֶת means *an examination*, an allusion to the physical examination given prior to the administration of *malkus* to determine how many lashes the violator's body can tolerate without danger to his or her life (see *Makkos* 3:11)[1] (*Rav* from *Gem.* 11a).

That the woman receives *malkus* and not the man is derived from the words בִּקֹּרֶת תִּהְיֶה, which can also be translated, *she shall be subject to disciplinary judgment: she* but not he (*Rav* from *Gem.* 11a).

וְלֹא אֶת־הָאִשָּׁה לָאִישׁ בְּקָרְבָּן; — *nor the woman to the man regarding an offering;*

It is only the man for whom the Torah prescribes the *asham* offering, not the woman (*Tif. Yis.*).

This is derived from the Torah's statement וְהֵבִיא אֶת־אֲשָׁמוֹ לַה׳, *and he shall*

1. Both the *Gemara's* explanations, *Malbim* explains, stem from the same root word: בִּקֹּרֶת, *critical analysis*. The purpose of reading the verses as the accompaniment to the *malkus* is intended as a chastisement, a critical analysis of the spiritual factors that brought the violator to sin and that must now be rectified. In this sense it is a *spiritual* examination. The examination prior to the *malkus* is of course an examination of his physical condition (*HaTorah V'haMitzvah* on *Toras Kohanim, Lev.* 19:54).

2 lashes or an offering, [whereas] regarding the slave-
4 woman, [the Torah] did not equate the man to the woman concerning lashes, nor the woman to the man regarding an offering; in all forbidden intimacies, [the Torah] considers a partial union as a complete one, and he is liable for every act of intimacy. [With] the following stringency, [the Torah] dealt more stringently with the slavewoman: Regarding her case, [the Torah] equated the willful transgression with the inadvertent one.

YAD AVRAHAM

bring his asham to HASHEM (*Lev.* 19:21), which indicates that *he* shall bring the *asham* but not she (*Rav* from *Gem.* 11a).

כָּל־הָעֲרָיוֹת, עָשָׂה בָהֶן אֶת־הַמְּעָרֶה כַּגּוֹמֵר, — *in all forbidden intimacies, [the Torah] considers a partial union as a complete one,*

[In the eyes of the Torah the act of sexual union is usually distinguished into two categories: הַעֲרָאָה (lit., *exposure*), *initial contact*, of the sexual organs[1] and גְּמַר בִּיאָה, *consummated coitus*. The mishnah compares the halachic standards of cohabitation for the *shifchah charufah* vis-a-vis those of the sexual offenses known as *arayos*.]

Regarding the sin of *arayos* listed in the beginning of the tractate, the unconsummated sex act is just as severe as the consummated one. For either, one is liable for a *chatas*, or the respective punishments of *malkus*, *kares*, or the death penalty, depending on the circumstances. Furthermore, one is also liable for בִּיאָה שֶׁלֹּא כְדַרְכָּהּ, *intimacy in an unnatural way* (or sodomy). This is derived from the expression (*Lev.* 18:22): מִשְׁכְּבֵי אִשָּׁה, lit., *the lyings of a woman*, the plural form denoting that both natural and unnatural sex acts are regarded as coitus. Regarding the *shifchah charufah*, by contrast, one is liable only for a natural sex act. This is derived from שִׁכְבַת זֶרַע, *lying carnally* [lit., *lying of seed*] (ibid. 19:20), meaning only in a manner through which she can conceive (*Rav*, *Rashi* from *Yevamos* 54b).

וְחַיָּב עַל כָּל־בִּיאָה וּבִיאָה. — *and he is liable for every act of intimacy.*

Likewise, the *arayos* sins are more stringent in the respect that each incidence of coitus is separately liable for a *chatas* or *malkus*. Regarding the *shifchah charufah*, however, we learned above (mishnah 3) that one is liable for only one offering for many acts of coitus (*Rav; Rashi*).

Rambam (*Comm.*) explains the phrase — עַל כָּל־בִּיאָה וּבִיאָה, *for every act of intimacy*, as a reference to the unnatural as well as the natural sex act. The mishnah contrasts the *shifchah charufah* prohibition to that of *arayos*, by stating that as far as *arayos* is concerned, both the natural and unnatural acts are included in the prohibition, as explained in *Yevamos* (6:2); regarding the *shifchah charufah* prohibition, only the natural sex act is included in the prohibition. This, too, is derived from the phrase שִׁכְבַת זֶרַע, which indicates the natural carnal act.

However, *Sifra* (*Kedoshim* ch. 5) supports the explanation of the mishnah advanced by *Rashi* and *Rav*.

זֶה חֹמֶר, הֶחֱמִיר בַּשִּׁפְחָה: שֶׁעָשָׂה בָהּ אֶת־הַמֵּזִיד כַּשּׁוֹגֵג. — *[With] the following stringency, [the Torah] dealt more stringently with the slavewoman: Regarding her case, [the Torah] equated the willful transgression with the inadvertent one.*

[Although as a rule the Torah was

1. There is actually a Talmudic dispute regarding the extent of contact required to qualify as הַעֲרָאָה. See *Yevamos* 54a,b.

כריתות [ה] **אֵיזוֹ** הִיא שִׁפְחָה? כָּל שֶׁחֶצְיָהּ שִׁפְחָה
ב/ה וְחֶצְיָהּ בַּת־חוֹרִין, שֶׁנֶּאֱמַר: ,,וְהָפְדֵּה
לֹא נִפְדָּתָה" — דִּבְרֵי רַבִּי עֲקִיבָא. רַבִּי יִשְׁמָעֵאל
אוֹמֵר: זוֹ הִיא שִׁפְחָה וַדָּאִית. רַבִּי אֶלְעָזָר בֶּן־

יד אברהם

more lenient regarding the *shifchah charufah* prohibition than with other forbidden intimacies, in this one respect, it was more stringent: Unlike other forbidden intimacies, for which case he brings a *chatas* only for an unintentional transgression, regarding the *shifchah charufah*, the guilty man is liable to an *asham* even if he committed the sin intentionally.

This applies, however, only if they both sinned intentionally, or if he did so unintentionally but she did so intentionally. Should *she* commit the sin unintentionally,[1] however, neither party is liable. The *Gemara* derives this ruling from the sequence of the chapter. Since the entire chapter deals with the man involved in the affair, it should first state that he must bring an *asham* and then that she is liable to *malkus*. Since the clause בִּקֹּרֶת תִּהְיֶה, construed as a reference to her penalty of *malkus*, is stated first, and the clause, *And he shall bring his asham to* HASHEM, follows that, we deduce that his *asham* is contingent upon her *malkus*. Only if she is liable to *malkus* is he liable to an *asham* (*Rav*).

5.

Having addressed numerous details of the *shifchah charufah* transgression, the mishnah now directs its attention to the very basic question of exactly what the *shifchah charufah* is.

The concept of a betrothed *shifchah* presents a halachic dilemma of sorts, for in regards to issues of marriage and divorce the שִׁפְחָה כְּנַעֲנִית, *gentile slavewoman*, is the same as a gentile. Thus, by Torah law, marriage cannot legally take effect with the gentile slavewoman. Even if someone should formally betroth her, the act is of no legal consequence. Additionally, it is prohibited for any Jew to cohabit with — much less live in marriage with — a *shifchah*. She is permitted only to either her male counterpart, the עֶבֶד כְּנַעֲנִי, *gentile slave*, whose marital status, too, is that of a gentile, or to the עֶבֶד עִבְרִי, *Jewish bondsman*, who is a fully qualified Jew indentured for a period of time. The fact that the Torah describes the slavewoman as נֶחֱרֶפֶת לְאִישׁ, *designated for a man*, indicates a relationship with the Jewish עֶבֶד עִבְרִי. However, even then the concept of betrothal is at odds with the laws of the gentile slavewoman. This gives rise to one view in the following mishnah that the *shifchah charufah* is not a full-fledged slave. On the other hand, the Torah cannot be referring simply to an emancipated slave, for she would have the status of a Jewish woman, just as a convert would. Her betrothal to a Jew would be binding and both she and her partner would be subject to capital punishment for adultery.

The mishnah presents two views on the resolution of these difficulties.

1. This can occur in two ways: (1) She is unaware that she is forbidden to have relations with any man other than her betrothed. (2) She thought her partner was her betrothed. These are the same circumstances that create the *chatas* obligations of a married woman in 1:1.

2
5

5. Which is the slavewoman? Anyone who is half slave and half free, as it is stated (*Lev.* 19:20): 'And redeemed she was not redeemed' — [these are] the words of R' Akiva. R' Yishmael says: This is she who is a real slavewoman. R' Elazar ben Azariah

YAD AVRAHAM

אֵיזוֹ הִיא שִׁפְחָה? — *Which is the slavewoman?*

Who is the *shifchah charufah* mentioned in the Torah, which has been the subject of discussion since the beginning of this chapter? (*Tif. Yis.*).

כָּל שֶׁחֶצְיָהּ שִׁפְחָה וְחֶצְיָהּ בַּת־חוֹרִין, — *Anyone who is half slave and half free,*

In R' Akiva's view, the *shifchah charufah* of the Torah does not refer to a woman who is totally enslaved; *she* cannot be legally betrothed. Rather, the *shifchah charufah* is a woman who is half slave and half emancipated. This is possible if a slave belonged to two partners and one owner freed his half, leaving the slave as a half a free person. Similarly, it is possible that a master received payment for half of her value and freed her halfway in exchange for that money [since one of the ways a slave is freed is by the payment of his value (*Kiddushin* 1:3) (*Gittin* 41b)]. If this woman is then betrothed, the betrothal is thereby valid for the half of her that is free.

Accordingly, the *shifchah charufah* can be betrothed only to an עֶבֶד עִבְרִי, *a Jewish bondman*.[1] A gentile-born slave would be prohibited to her as a result of her free part; an ordinary Jew would be prohibited because of her 'slave part.' A Jewish bondsman, however, is permitted to marry either a Canaanite slavewoman or a free woman [see *Exodus* 21:3-4]. In this manner, her betrothal has a binding effect, for her 'free part' is subject to the laws of marriage. In fact, were she not half slave, the betrothal would be completely binding, and the act of intimacy would be a capital sin. Now, however, the betrothal is only partially binding since she is half slave. This is the meaning of the Torah's statement: לֹא יוּמְתוּ כִּי־לֹא חֻפָּשָׁה, *they shall not be put to death for she has not been freed* — i.e., she is a woman who, if she were completely emancipated, would be liable to death for an adulterous relationship (*Rav* from *Gem.* 11a, *Rashi* ad loc.).

שֶׁנֶּאֱמַר: ,,וְהָפְדֵּה לֹא נִפְדָּתָה" — דִּבְרֵי רַבִּי עֲקִיבָא. — *as it is stated (Lev. 19:20): 'And redeemed she was not redeemed' — [these are] the words of R' Akiva.*

The double expression: *and redeemed she was not redeemed*, means she was redeemed but she was not redeemed fully, i.e., she was partially redeemed (*Rav* from *Gem.* 11a, *Rashi* ad loc.).

רַבִּי יִשְׁמָעֵאל אוֹמֵר: זוֹ הִיא שִׁפְחָה וַדָּאִית. — *R' Yishmael says: This is she who is a real slavewoman.*

R' Yishmael is of the view that the *shifchah charufah* is an ordinary full-fledged slavewoman, one who was not emancipated at all. As far as the repetitive phrase וְהָפְדֵּה לֹא נִפְדָּתָה is concerned, R' Yishmael subscribes to the principle of דִּבְּרָה תוֹרָה כִּלְשׁוֹן בְּנֵי אָדָם, *The Torah speaks in the people's language*. Accordingly, the expression is a colloquial phrase meaning simply: *and she was not redeemed* (*Rav* from *Gem.* 11a).

1. Although it is the Jewish bondsman that is always mentioned in connection with the *shifchah charufah*, she actually can be betrothed to any Jew, as far as the *asham* is concerned. The *Gemara* mentions the Jewish bondsman only because a free Jew may not cohabit with a woman who is even partially slave. From a legal point of view, betrothal to any Jew is binding, although he may not consummate the marriage (*Rashi, Gittin* 39a, s.v. ואם לחשך).

כריתות ב/ו

עֲזַרְיָה אוֹמֵר: כָּל־הָעֲרָיוֹת מְפֹרָשׁוֹת, וּמַה שִּׁיּוּר? אֵין לָנוּ אֶלָּא שֶׁחֶצְיָהּ שִׁפְחָה וְחֶצְיָהּ בַּת־חוֹרִין.

[ו] **כָּל** הָעֲרָיוֹת, אֶחָד גָּדוֹל וְאֶחָד קָטָן, הַקָּטָן

יד אברהם

R' Yishmael agrees with R' Akiva that the *shifchah charufah* is betrothed to a Jewish bondsman.[1] This is obvious from the phrase לֹא יוּמְתוּ כִּי־לֹא חֻפָּשָׁה, *they shall not be put to death because she had not been freed*. Were she not betrothed, there would be no point in saying that because she was not freed, there is no capital punishment as there is no capital punishment elsewhere for relations with an unmarried woman (*Tos. Yom Tov*).

רַבִּי אֶלְעָזָר בֶּן־עֲזַרְיָה אוֹמֵר: כָּל־הָעֲרָיוֹת מְפֹרָשׁוֹת, — *R' Elazar ben Azariah says: All forbidden intimacies are stated explicitly,*

All the forbidden intimacies included in the *arayos* categories are explicitly described; without exception they all concern women who are free (*Rav; Rashi*).

וּמַה שִּׁיּוּר? — *and what is the exception?*

Why is the *shifchah charufah* the exception? It is not included in the Torah's passage of *arayos* nor does it say that she is a free woman. Apparently, then, the *shifchah charufah* is distinct from the other type of forbidden intimacies. In what way, then, is it different?[2] (*Rav; Chafetz Chaim* on *Toras Kohanim, Kedoshim* ch. 5).

In *Toras Kohanim*, R' Elazar ben Azariah's words appear as a declarative statement rather than a question: כָּל הָעֲרָיוֹת מְפוֹרָשׁוֹת וְזוֹ

1. As a result of their different views regarding the definition of *shifchah charufah*, though, there is a major conceptual difference between R' Yishmael and R' Akiva regarding the nature of the 'betrothal' under discussion. According to R' Akiva, who holds that the *shifchah charufah* is a half-free slave, her betrothal to the Jewish bondsman has at least the semblance of a betrothal, because it is binding for the 'free part' of the slavewoman. It is only because the other half is in the slave category that this betrothal is less stringent than that of a free woman.

According to R' Yishmael, who holds that it is a full-fledged slavewoman under discussion, her relationship with the Jewish bondsman is not at all in the betrothal category; she is simply 'designated' to him (*Rashi, Kiddushin* 6a; *Tos.* ibid.).

This leads the *Gemara* (11a) to question why, according to R' Yishmael, is it necessary to say that she is betrothed to an Jewish bondsman? The relationship of the *shifchah* to the Jewish bondsman can be enjoyed by a gentile slave as well. The *Gemara* answers that since the verse states כִּי־לֹא חֻפָּשָׁה, *she has not been freed*, it leaves us to understand that *he* was not a slave; i.e., the man to whom she was betrothed was in the category of a freeman, which is possible only if she was betrothed to a Jewish bondsman, who is essentially a free man (*Gemara* 11a as explained by *Aruch LaNer*).

2. The Bible commentators point out that the *shifchah charufah* prohibition is not mentioned in the Torah's section dealing with sexual transgressions (*Lev:* 18:6ff; ibid. 20:8ff). Instead it is mentioned in connection with the verses dealing with the prohibition of *kilayim* (prohibited *mixtures*), such as wearing a mixture of wool and linen or plowing with an ox and a donkey (ibid 19:19). The implication is that the cohabitation with a slavewoman constitutes a *mixture*, the mixed marriage of the free and the slave (*Ibn Ezra; Haamek Davar*; R' Hirsch, et al.).

Perhaps this is the thrust of R' Elazar ben Azariah's query: 'All other *arayos* are mentioned in the section dealing with forbidden relations; *shifchah charufah* is in the section of *kilayim* (prohibited mixtures). This indicates that the *shifchah charufah* is herself a mixture — a woman half free and half slave.'

2 says: All forbidden intimacies are stated explicitly, and
6 what is the exception? We must conclude that it is she who is half slave and half free.

6. In all forbidden intimacies, if one was of age and one was a minor, the minor is exempt; if one was awake

YAD AVRAHAM

מְשֻׁיָּר, *all the arayos are explicit and this is omitted*. R' Elazar ben Azariah observes that all the women forbidden by the Torah are explained clearly; some outright and others by exegetical means. Regarding the *shifchah charufah*, however, the Torah is ambiguous about the nature of the slavewoman under discussion. We must resort to our own means to determine the Torah's intention (*Rabbeinu Shimshon*, ad loc.).

אֵין לָנוּ אֶלָּא שֶׁחֶצְיָהּ שִׁפְחָה וְחֶצְיָהּ בַּת־חוֹרִין. — *We must conclude that* [lit. *we have only*] *it is she who is half slave and half free.*

The *shifchah charufah* is different from the other *arayos* in the sense that she is half free and half slave (*Rav*).

Others explain R' Elazar ben Azariah's statement as an argument to support the view that the *shifchah charufah* is half free, unlike R' Yishmael's view that she is a full-fledged slavewoman. R' Elazar ben Azariah reasons that since all *arayos* deal with women who are completely free, but this one was excepted, it is more likely that it deals with one slightly different from all the others rather than radically different, viz., a half-free half slave, rather than a slavewoman who was not emancipated at all (*Tif. Yis.*; *Beur HaGra* on *Sifra* ad loc., *Korban Aharon* ibid.).

The *Gemara* (11a) questions the difference between the views of R' Akiva and R' Elazar ben Azariah, since they both concur that the Torah is referring to a half-slave rather than a full slave. The *Gemara* explains that in principle R' Elazar ben Azariah concurs with R' Yishmael that *the Torah speaks in the people's language*. In this case, however, he reasons that the phrase וְהָפְדֵּה לֹא נִפְדָּתָה cannot mean simply that she is an unredeemed slave. Since the Torah later states: כִּי־לֹא חֻפָּשָׁה, *for she has not been freed*, the clause *and redeemed she was not redeemed* is superfluous. The duplicate phrase in question must therefore be construed to mean that the Torah's *shifchah charufah* is someone who is only partially redeemed (*Rav*).

The halachah is in accordance with R' Akiva (*Rav; Rambam Comm.; Hil. Isurei Biah* 3:13).

6.

The mishnah now lists two additional differences between the *shifchah charufah* prohibition and that of those in the *arayos* category. [Why this mishnah was not placed after mishnah 4 — where the other differences between the *shifchah charufah* and other forbidden intimacies are mentioned — will be explained at the end of the mishnah.]

כָּל הָעֲרָיוֹת, אֶחָד גָּדוֹל וְאֶחָד קָטָן, הַקָּטָן פָּטוּר; — *In all forbidden intimacies, if one was of age and one was a minor, the minor is exempt;*

If either of the partners was of age of culpability — thirteen for the man, and twelve for the woman — and the other one was a minor, the minor is exempt from any punishment.

However, the partner who is of age is liable for the appropriate punishment, provided that the minor was old enough

פָּטוּר; אֶחָד עֵר וְאֶחָד יָשֵׁן, הַיָּשֵׁן פָּטוּר; אֶחָד שׁוֹגֵג וְאֶחָד מֵזִיד, הַשּׁוֹגֵג בְּחַטָּאת וְהַמֵּזִיד בְּהִכָּרֵת.

יד אברהם

to be considered in the eyes of the halachah to be sexually active. For the male the minimum age is nine years old and for the female it is three (*Rambam Comm.; Tif. Yis.*).

In contrast, the halachah regarding the *shifchah charufah* is that if she is a minor,[1] who cannot be punished, the man is likewise exempt from bringing an *asham*, even if he is of age (*Rav* from *Gem.* 11a). This is based on the principle (previously mentioned in mishnah 4) that the juxtaposition of the verse indicates that the man is compared to the woman: Only when she is liable for her punishment of *malkus* is the man obligated to bring his *asham*.

There is a three-sided dispute amongst the *Rishonim* concerning the opposite case — if the male partner was a minor but the *shifchah charufah* was of age.

In one view, the *Gemara's* comparison between the man and the woman is mutual: Just as he is exempt if she is a minor, so is she exempt from *malkus* if he is not obligated for an offering. Thus, they are both exempt if he is a minor (*Raavad, Issurei Biah* 3:17).

Tosafos, however, cite *Toras Kohanim* (*Kedoshim* ch. 5) that derives from the word וְאִישׁ, *and a man* [the prefix ו, *and*, being extra], that even a minor may cause the *shifchah charufah* to be punished. Reasoning that a minor is certainly exempt from bringing an offering, this view concludes that the *shifchah* is punished by *malkus*, although the minor is exempt. The comparison of the man to the woman is only to say that the man is exempt when she is, but not vice versa (*Tos.* 11a; *Rabbeinu Hillel* to *Toras Kohanim* ibid.; this view is also mentioned by *Raavad, Shegagos* 9:3).

Rambam (*Issurei Biah* 3:17) rules that both the man and the woman are liable for their respective punishments even if he is a minor [adding elsewhere (*Shegagos* 9:13), that it is logical that the minor must at least become of age before he brings the offering].

אֶחָד עֵר וְאֶחָד יָשֵׁן, הַיָּשֵׁן פָּטוּר; — *if one was awake and one was asleep, the one who was asleep is exempt;*

Regarding the *arayos* prohibition, if one of the partners was asleep, the party who was awake is nonetheless liable to punishment. Regarding the *shifchah charufah*, by contrast, if the *shifchah* was asleep, the man is also exempt. As explained above, he is likened to her and shares her exemption (*Rav*). If *she* was awake, however, she is liable even if her partner was asleep (*Tif. Yis.* from *Rambam, Hil. Issurei Biah* 3:16; *Maggid Mishneh* ad loc.).

אֶחָד שׁוֹגֵג וְאֶחָד מֵזִיד, — *if one was unintentional and one was intentional,*

[Regarding the *arayos* prohibitions, there is culpability even if only one of the parties was aware that there was a sin involved in this union, e.g., if the man was unaware that the woman had menstruated, but the woman knew it, or if the man thought that the woman was his wife, but she knew that the man was her brother.]

1. The *Acharonim* pose an interesting question: According to the view in the previous mishnah, accepted by halachah, that a *shifchah charufah* is a woman who is half free and half slave and betrothed to a Jewish bondsman, how is it possible for her to be a minor? If she was under twelve years old, she can be betrothed only by her father, which, in the case of the gentile slavewoman is, of course, not possible. Some answer that it is possible, in the following manner: A Jewish man had a daughter by a woman who is half free and half slave. The child will have the mother's status and likewise be half free and half slave. However, as far as the 'free part' of her is concerned, she has a Jewish father who has the authority to betroth her, whereupon she would achieve the status of a *shifchah charufah* who is a minor (*Rashash*, citing an anonymous scholar; *R' Akiva Eiger*, glosses on *Rambam*, Frankel ed., in the name of his son R' Shlomo Eiger).

2 and one was asleep, the one who was asleep is exempt; if
6 one was unintentional and one was intentional, the
unintentional one is liable for a *chatas*, and the
intentional one is liable to *kares*.

YAD AVRAHAM

.הַשּׁוֹגֵג בְּחַטָּאת וְהַמֵּזִיד בְּהִכָּרֵת — *the unintentional one is liable for a chatas, and the intentional one is liable to kares.*

Regarding the *shifchah charufah*, by contrast, if he acted intentionally, and she unintentionally, both are exempt. The axiom is that the man is not liable for an *asham* unless the woman is liable to *malkus*. If his action was unintentional and hers was intentional, she is punished with *malkus*, and he brings an *asham*, as in mishnah 2 (*Rav; Rashi*).

It has already been mentioned [in the prefatory remarks to this mishnah] that the position of this mishnah poses a problem: Why are these three distinctions between the *shifchah charufah* prohibition and the *arayos* prohibitions not mentioned in the mishnah's earlier comparison of the prohibitions (mishnah 4)? Furthermore, why is it that the earlier mishnah spells out clearly the contrast between *arayos* and the *shifchah charufah*, whereas our mishnah mentions just the features of the *arayos* prohibitions, leaving the contrast to the *shifchah charufah* to implication?

The *Acharonim* explain the difference in the two mishnayos in the following manner: The distinctions drawn in the past mishnah are unequivocal; those in the last mishnah are not. For example, when the first mishnah states that for *arayos* one brings a *chatas* and for the *shifchah charufah* one brings an *asham*, it is a rule that has no exception. By contrast, when this mishnah states that concerning the *arayos* prohibitions if one is a minor and the other is of age, the one of age is liable and the other is not, this rule *could* apply to a *shifchah* as well — in the event that *he* was a minor and she was of age.[1] Thus the mishnah cannot make the unqualified distinction between *arayos* and the *shifchah charufah*, leaving it instead to the implication that in *some cases* there is a distinction between the two (*Rashash; Aruch LaNer*).

Chapter 3

At the outset of the tractate, it was stated in general terms that the atonement for an inadvertent transgression of a prohibition punishable by *kares* is a *chatas* offering. Chapter three deals with some of the specifics of that law: How is an inadvertent transgression determined? When does one *chatas* atone for many transgressions? When is each transgression counted separately?

1.

This mishnah clarifies what evidence is acceptable to make a person liable to a *chatas*. The chosen example of the *kares*-punishable transgression is the prohibition of eating חֵלֶב, *cheilev fat. Cheilev* refers to forbidden fat, as distinct from שׁוּמָן, *shumman*, permitted fat. The forbidden category includes only the fat on the innards, the fat on the kidneys, and the fat on the flanks (see *Rambam, Hil. Maachalos Assuros* 7:5; see also 1:1 above).

---

1. This supports the view (cited above) that if he was a minor, she is not exempt (*Tos.* and *Raavad*); according to the dissenting view (*Rambam*) that they are both liable or the view of *Raavad* that they are both exempt, the *shifchah charufah* prohibition never resembles *arayos* in this respect (*Aruch LaNer*; cf. *Rashash*).

כריתות [א] **אָמְרוּ** לוֹ: ,,אָכַלְתָּ חֵלֶב,״ מֵבִיא חַטָּאת.
ג/א עֵד אוֹמֵר: ,,אָכַל,״ וְעֵד אוֹמֵר: ,,לֹא
אָכַל,״ אִשָּׁה אוֹמֶרֶת: ,,אָכַל,״ וְאִשָּׁה אוֹמֶרֶת: ,,לֹא
אָכַל,״ מֵבִיא אָשָׁם תָּלוּי. עֵד אוֹמֵר: ,,אָכַל,״

יד אברהם

אָמְרוּ לוֹ: ,,אָכַלְתָּ חֵלֶב,״ — *[If] they said to him: 'You ate forbidden fat,'*

Although the mishnah uses the plural form *they said*, according to the *Gemara* (11b) it means that even if only one witness tells him, 'You ate forbidden fat,' he is liable to a *chatas* (*Rav*).

A rationale for the mishnah's use of the plural form may be to indicate that it is possible for more than one person to be involved in determining the transgression, even though, in fact, only one testified. For example, even if one witness relates merely what he heard from another witness (עֵד מִפִּי עֵד), it is also acceptable as testimony to create the obligation for a *chatas*. Although, as a rule, where the testimony is required by Torah law, it must be direct — not second-hand — information, the testimony required in our case is not governed by the formal guidelines of court procedure. In fact, even a woman's testimony is acceptable. Similarly, even if the witness merely related the fact [instead of making a deposition in court], it is considered valid. It is not important how the information is imparted; as long as the 'accused' person acquiesces by his silence, he is liable to a *chatas* (*Tif. Yis.*).

מֵבִיא חַטָּאת. — *he brings a chatas.*

As long as he does not contradict the witness, the testimony is accepted to make the alleged sinner liable to a *chatas*. Should he contradict the witness, however, the testimony is ineffective. The rule is that the testimony of a solitary witness has no validity except in monetary disputes, in which case it creates an obligation for the litigant to take an oath (*Tos. Yom Tov* from *Tos.* 11b).

עֵד אוֹמֵר: ,,אָכַל,״ וְעֵד אוֹמֵר: ,,לֹא אָכַל,״ — *[If] a witness says: 'He ate,' and [another] witness says: 'He did not eat,'*

A person ate a piece of fat, and one witness says to him, 'What you ate was *cheilev*,' and another witness says, 'You did not eat *cheilev*' (*Rambam, Hil. Shegagos* 8:3).

אִשָּׁה אוֹמֶרֶת: ,,אָכַל,״ וְאִשָּׁה אוֹמֶרֶת: ,,לֹא אָכַל,״ — *[or if] a woman says: 'He ate,' and [another] woman says: 'He did not eat,'*

[The same ruling applies if the two contradicting witnesses were women, who ordinarily are not acceptable as witnesses in court cases. Although in this instance a woman's testimony is acceptable regarding the obligation to bring a *chatas*, the conflicting statements of the two women create a situation of doubt.]

מֵבִיא אָשָׁם תָּלוּי. — *he must bring an asham talui.*

As already explained elsewhere (see above 1:2 and below 4:1), the *asham talui* is the guilt offering brought in case of doubt. As illustrated by the mishnah later, a situation of doubt is one in which two pieces of fat were lying before a person, one was permissible *shumman* and the other was prohibited *cheilev*.[1] Unaware

1. As mentioned earlier (1:1) and explained at length elsewhere (4:1), the prevailing opinion in the *Gemara* is that the presence of the two pieces of fat is critical to *asham talui* obligation. Should there be but one piece which later was *suspected* of being *cheilev*, there is no need for the *asham talui*.

In our case, too, there are commentaries that mention explicitly that the conflicting testimony involved two pieces of fat. In other words, a person had two pieces of fat in front of him, one prohibited and one permitted. According to the testimony of one witness he ate

3
1 **1.** [If] they said to him: 'You ate forbidden fat,' he brings a *chatas*. [If] a witness says: 'He ate,' and [another] witness says: 'He did not eat,' [or if] a woman says: 'He ate,' and [another] woman says: 'He did not eat:' he must bring an *asham talui*. [If] a witness says:

YAD AVRAHAM

that one of the two pieces of meat was forbidden, he ate one. Since he is now uncertain whether the piece he ate was *cheilev*, he must bring the *asham talui* (literally, *suspended asham*) to suspend Divine retribution for as long as the doubt remains unresolved.

Since, in the case of our mishnah, we have a conflict of testimony[1] regarding whether or not he ate the prohibited fat, a situation of doubt is created, and he must bring an *asham talui*.

As has already been mentioned, the testimony of the solitary witness is effective only if the accused does not contradict him. If he disagrees, or even expresses doubt, he is not liable for a *chatas*.

Therefore, it must be presumed that in the situation of conflicting testimony described by the mishnah, the accused remains entirely silent. If he sides with either of the witnesses or even simply states that he, too, does not know, he would be exempt from the *asham talui* (*Tos.* cited by *Tos. Yom Tov*).

the prohibited piece; according to the other witness it was the permitted piece that he ate. Therefore he must bring the *asham talui* (*Raavad; Hil. Shegagos* 8:3).

Others indicate that in the case of conflicting testimony, sufficient doubt is created to bring an *asham talui* even if the question focused on only one piece of fat [i.e., one witness said that it was permitted and the other claims that it was not] (*Rambam* ibid., according to one interpretation of *Kesef Mishneh;* cf. *Lechem Mishneh;* ad loc.; *Shev Shmaatsa* 1:8).

1. Generally there is a principle that כָּל מָקוֹם שֶׁהֶאֱמִינָה הַתּוֹרָה עֵד אֶחָד הֲרֵי הוּא כִּשְׁנַיִם, *whenever the Torah* [makes an exception to its general rules of evidence and] *accepts the testimony of one witness, he is as* [believed as are] *two* [witnesses]. Accordingly, once a solitary witness' testimony is accepted in court it takes on the force of the testimony of two witnesses and can no longer be contradicted by the testimony of another solitary witness (*Yevamos* 117b; *Kesubos* 22b; *Sotah* 31a et al.). It is only when the two conflicting witnesses testify at the same time that a situation of doubt is created. Since at that point the court has not yet accepted the validity of the testimony of the first witness, it has not yet taken on the force of testimony by two witnesses, and is thus no stronger than the testimony with which it conflicts (see *Yad Avraham* comm. to *Sotah* 6:4).

Therefore, *Tosafos* (11b) comment that regarding our case, too, the witnesses testified simultaneously in *beis din*. Should the one who testifies that he ate *cheilev* testify first, his testimony is accepted as that of two witnesses, and the testimony of the second witness is of no value. In that case, too, he would be required to bring a *chatas*.

Rambam (*Hil. Shegagos* 8:13), however, does not explicitly make a distinction between simultaneous conflicting testimony and otherwise; he states simply that if two witnesses contradict each other, he brings an *asham talui*. Some explain that he disagrees with *Tosafos*, reasoning that in *Rambam's* opinion, even if the second witness testifies after the first one said that the alleged violator ate *cheilev*, his testimony can render the first indecisive. The logic for this view is that the Torah actually never believed a solitary witness to create the obligation for a *chatas*. Rather, it is the person's *silence* which is construed as acquiescence, according to the principle שְׁתִיקָה כְּהוֹדָאָה, *silence is tantamount to confession*. Since it is the silence of the accused, rather than the testimony of the witness which brings about the *chatas* obligation, if the subsequent contradicting testimony shakes the person's original conviction that he sinned, he is no longer liable to the *chatas* and must bring an *asham talui* instead (*Aruch LaNer*; cf. *Lechem Mishneh* ad loc.).

כריתות ג/א

וְהוּא אוֹמֵר: ,,לֹא אָכַלְתִּי,'' פָּטוּר. שְׁנַיִם אוֹמְרִים: ,,אָכַל,'' וְהוּא אוֹמֵר: ,,לֹא אָכַלְתִּי,'' רַבִּי מֵאִיר מְחַיֵּב. אָמַר רַבִּי מֵאִיר: אִם הֱבִיאוּהוּ שְׁנַיִם לְמִיתָה חֲמוּרָה, לֹא יְבִיאוּהוּ לְקָרְבָּן הַקַּל? אָמְרוּ לוֹ: מָה אִם יִרְצֶה לוֹמַר: ,,מֵזִיד הָיִיתִי!''?

יד אברהם

עֵד אוֹמֵר: ,,אָכַל,'' וְהוּא אוֹמֵר: ,,לֹא אָכַלְתִּי,'' פָּטוּר. — *[If] a witness says: 'He ate,' and he says: 'I did not eat,' he is exempt.*

As mentioned before, concerning the obligation to bring a *chatas* the Torah states (*Lev.* 4:28): אוֹ הוֹדַע אֵלָיו חַטָּאתוֹ, *if his sin becomes known to him*. Thus, even if a witness testified that he ate *cheilev*, if he denies it, he is exempt. This is true even if he says, 'I don't know,' for in the final analysis he is not convinced of his transgression (*Tos. Yom Tov* from *Tos.* 11b).

שְׁנַיִם אוֹמְרִים: ,,אָכַל,'' וְהוּא אוֹמֵר: ,,לֹא אָכַלְתִּי,'' — *[If] two say: 'He ate,' and he says: 'I did not eat,'*

Even if a hundred witnesses testify that he ate *cheilev*, and he insists, 'I am certain that I did not eat it,' the witnesses are not believed to require him to bring a *chatas*. This, too, is based on the Torah's phrase אוֹ הוֹדַע אֵלָיו חַטָּאתוֹ, *if his sin becomes known to him*, which is interpreted by the Sages to mean וְלֹא שֶׁיּוֹדִיעוּהוּ, *but not that others make it known to him* [i.e., knowledge of a transgression must be predicated on his own conviction rather than the mere testimony of witnesses] (*Rav; Rambam Comm.*).

רַבִּי מֵאִיר מְחַיֵּב. — *R' Meir declares him liable.*

[R' Meir holds that the testimony of two witnesses is sufficient to make him liable to a *chatas* — even if he contests their testimony — for the reason that he provides below.]

There are minor textual variations to this clause. In some editions, we find the word פָּטוּר, *he is exempt*, before 'R' Meir declares him liable.' This reading is cited in *Yevamos* (87b) (*Tos. Yom Tov*). Alternatively, *Bach* emends it to read: רַבִּי מֵאִיר מְחַיֵּב וַחֲכָמִים פּוֹטְרִין, *R' Meir declares him liable, and the Sages exempt him*. The *Gemara* in *Bava Metzia* (3b) quotes the mishnah in this manner. Either way the meaning is clear: If a person contests the testimony of two witnesses, he is liable for a *chatas* according to R' Meir and exempt according to the Sages.

אָמַר רַבִּי מֵאִיר: אִם הֱבִיאוּהוּ שְׁנַיִם לְמִיתָה חֲמוּרָה, לֹא יְבִיאוּהוּ לְקָרְבָּן הַקַּל? — *Said R' Meir: If two can bring him to the more severe death penalty, can they not bring him to the lighter penalty of an offering?*

R' Meir reasoned: When two witnesses testify that someone murdered, he is guilty, although he denies the crime. The testimony of witnesses is considered the supreme proof even regarding cases of capital punishment. [Is it not logical, then, that the testimony of two witnesses is strong enough to obligate him for a mere sacrifice, despite his contention to the contrary?] (*Rav; Rashi*).

The commentators question R' Meir's view on the basis of the ruling articulated by the mishnah in *Arachin* 5:6: חַיָּבֵי חַטָּאוֹת וַאֲשָׁמוֹת אֵין מְמַשְׁכְּנִין אוֹתָן, *no pledge is exacted from those required to bring chataos or ashamos*. In other words, the *beis din* does not enforce the obligation to bring a *chatas* or an *asham*; it is left to the sinner himself to do so. In that case, why does R' Meir rule that we believe the witnesses instead of the alleged sinner? The entire discussion seems to address a moot issue: Since the alleged violator denies the witnesses' assertion, he will certainly not agree to bring an offering; since we cannot force him to do so, what is the point of discussing whether or not he is obligated? *Tosafos* conclude that apparently in the case of our mishnah we *do* enforce the

3 'He ate,' and he says: 'I did not eat,' he is exempt. [If] two
1 say: 'He ate,' and he says: 'I did not eat,' R' Meir declares him liable. Said R' Meir: If two can bring him to the more severe death penalty, can they not bring him to the lighter penalty of an offering? They said to him: What if he would want to say: 'I was an intentional transgressor!'?

obligation to bring the *chatas*. The reasoning is that ordinarily the obligation to bring a *chatas* or *asham* need not be enforced, since the person will be anxious on his own to attain atonement. In our case, where the person denies ever having sinned, he will not bring the offering on his own accord and must therefore be forced to do so (*Tos. Yevamos* 87b; *Tif. Yis.*; cf. *Tos.* cited by *Tos. Yom Tov*; *Or Chadash, Kiddushin* 65; *Ner Tamid*; *Chasam Sofer, Responsa, Choshen Mishpat* 22).

אָמְרוּ לוֹ: — *They said to him:*

[The Sages responded to R' Meir's reasoning with the following argument.]

מָה אִם יִרְצֶה לוֹמַר: ,,מֵזִיד הָיִיתִי!״? — *What if he would want to say: 'I was an intentional transgressor!'?*

Had he wished to resort to lying to exempt himself from bringing an offering, he could easily have said that he *intentionally* ate the *cheilev*, an assertion that the witnesses cannot refute [as they cannot determine his state of mind] (*Rav*; *Rashi*).

The implication of the above explanation is that we must believe the person's contention that he did not eat the *cheilev*, because if he had wanted to lie mainly to exempt himself from an offering he could have offered a better lie, viz., that he was an intentional violator, who is exempt from an offering. This seems to be based on the מִגּוֹ, *miggo*, principle, by which a person's claim is believed in a situation that he could have fabricated a better lie had he wished to do so [see ArtScroll *Kesubos* 1:6, 2:2, *Bava Metzia* 1:1 et al.]. *Tos.*, however, reject this rationale because of the known principle מִגּוֹ בְּמָקוֹם עֵדִים לֹא אַמְרִינַן, *a miggo is not said against witnesses*. This means that a person's claim is never believed to contradict the testimony of witnesses, even if his claim is backed up by a *miggo*. Thus, how can the Sages reason that a person is believed to assert he did not eat, against the testimony of witnesses, merely because he could have produced a better lie?[1] *Tosafos* therefore submit the explanation given below.

Others explain the Sages' reasoning in a slightly different vein. The Sages do not contend that we *believe* the alleged violator's assertion that he did not eat the *cheilev*. They agree merely that since he could exempt himself from an offering by pleading guilty to eating the *cheilev* intentionally, we *interpret* his words to mean just that: 'I did not eat unintentionally, [but I did eat *intentionally*].' This is a statement, of course, which cannot be refuted by the witnesses and therefore he is exempt from an offering.

R' Meir, in fact, agrees that if the

1. *Ramban* (*Bava Metzia* 3b) resolves the difficulties raised by *Tosafos*. He explains that the reasoning of the Sages is actually based on the premise that regarding the *chatas* obligation the critical factor is the person's own conviction that he sinned. This is derived from the verse אוֹ הוֹדַע אֵלָיו חַטָּאתוֹ, *if his sin becomes known to him* (as indeed cited by *Rashi* and *Rav* earlier in the mishnah). Thus, regarding this case, a *miggo* is effective against the testimony of witnesses because, in the final analysis, the person still has a claim that he is exempt and the requirement for his own conviction remains unfulfilled. However, were a person to dispute the testimony of witnesses *without* the benefit of a *miggo*, he would not be believed, for we would assume that the testimony, in fact, constitutes his knowledge of the sin; and his own contention to the contrary is simply an attempt to exempt himself from his obligation.

[ב] **אָכַל** חֵלֶב וְחֵלֶב בְּהֶעְלֵם אֶחָד, אֵינוֹ חַיָּב אֶלָּא חַטָּאת אַחַת. אָכַל חֵלֶב וְדָם וְנוֹתָר וּפִגּוּל בְּהֶעְלֵם אֶחָד, חַיָּב עַל כָּל אֶחָד וְאֶחָד. זֶה חֹמֶר בְּמִינִין הַרְבֵּה מִמִּין אֶחָד. וְחֹמֶר בְּמִין אֶחָד מִמִּינִין הַרְבֵּה: שֶׁאִם אָכַל כַּחֲצִי זַיִת, וְחָזַר וְאָכַל כַּחֲצִי זַיִת — מִמִּין אֶחָד, חַיָּב; מִשְּׁנֵי מִינִין, פָּטוּר.

יד אברהם

accused actually said immediately that he ate it intentionally, he would be exempt. He disagrees with the Sages' view, however, that we *interpret* his words to mean that. Moreover, once he did not respond in this manner immediately, he is no longer believed afterward to say that he meant it originally (*Tos. Yom Tov* from *Tos.*).

The *Gemara* (12a), in fact, offers two explanations for the Sages' reasoning. The first is based on the principle of מְתָרְצִינָן דִּיבּוּרֵיהּ, *we reconcile his words*, that is, we interpret his statement in the above-described manner so as not to conflict with the witnesses' testimony. The other approach is that the Sages disagree with R' Meir in principle. They hold that אָדָם נֶאֱמָן עַל עַצְמוֹ יוֹתֵר מִמֵּאָה עֵדִים, *a person is believed regarding himself more than [even] a hundred witnesses*. In other words, in matters that concern himself (such as *his* obligation to bring an offering), a person is his own final authority. Therefore, if he insists that he did not eat the *cheilev*, we must believe him regarding his personal affairs.[1]

According to the latter explanation, the Sages hold that the alleged violator who claims that he did not eat is exempt not merely because he could have said — or meant — that he did not eat unintentionally, but because, regarding himself, his statement must be taken at face value, i.e., he did not eat at all. The Sages cite the fact that he could have said that his action was intentional only to refute R' Meir's view. Their argument is as if to say: "In our opinion, regarding himself, a person is believed more than witnesses are. You, however, who do not subscribe to this principle, should at least admit that he is believed because he can say, 'I did not eat it unintentionally but intentionally.' "

2.

The following mishnah begins a discussion of the rules governing the number of *chataos* required for repeated or varied transgressions. In some situations one *chatas* is sufficient for more than one measure of a forbidden substance, but at other times multiple offenses each require a separate *chatas*.

The basic rule postulated by the mishnah is as follows: A repetition of the same transgression — such as eating *cheilev* twice — calls for only one *chatas*, provided he did not become aware of his sin between the two eatings. Different transgressions such as eating *cheilev* and eating blood call for a separate *chatas* for each.

1. The difference between the two explanations arises when the man's statement cannot be reconciled with the witnesses' testimony. For example, if someone entered the Temple and witnesses testify that he became *tamei* just prior to entering; the man denies the allegation by saying, 'I did not enter.' Whether the man is believed to contest the witnesses' testimony by saying, 'I did not enter,' depends on which of the interpretations of the mishnah we accept. If it is that a person is believed concerning himself even against witnesses, then, of course, even in this case he is exempt. If, however, we must reconcile his words so that they not conflict with the witnesses' testimony, then he is not believed. For even if we were to interpret his

3
2 **2.** [If] he ate two portions of *cheilev* in one lapse of awareness, he is liable to only one *chatas*. [But] if he ate *cheilev*, blood, leftover offerings, and *piggul* in one lapse of awareness, he is liable for each one. In this, many kinds are more stringent than one kind. But [in the following], one kind is more stringent than many kinds: If he ate half an olive's bulk, and again ate half an olive's bulk — [if they were] of one kind, he is liable; of two kinds, he is exempt.

YAD AVRAHAM

אָכַל חֵלֶב וְחֵלֶב בְּהֶעְלֵם אֶחָד, — *[If] he ate two portions of cheilev* [lit., *cheilev and cheilev*] *in one lapse of awareness,*

The minimum amount that one must eat in order to be liable to a *chatas* is a כְּזַיִת [*kezayis*], *an olive's bulk*. The mishnah, then, deals with a person who twice ate a *kezayis* of *cheilev* (*Rav; Rashi*).

He was either unaware that the fat before him was *cheilev*, or he was unaware that *cheilev* is prohibited. Without gaining awareness of his sin, he ate a second *kezayis* of the forbidden substance (*Tif. Yis.*).

אֵינוֹ חַיָּב אֶלָּא חַטָּאת אַחַת. — *he is liable to only one chatas.*

Although each *kezayis*-measure constitutes a separate transgression, they are still deemed as one sin for atonement purposes, since there was no awareness between the eating of the two *kezayis*-measures of *cheilev*. He is therefore liable to only one *chatas*. However, should he become aware of the prohibition after eating the first portion and then forget it again and eat the second portion, the rule is that יְדִיעוֹת מְחַלְּקוֹת, *periods of awareness effect separate sacrifices*. Therefore, he is liable to two *chataos* (*Rav; Tif. Yis.* from *Gem.* 12b).

אָכַל חֵלֶב וְדָם וְנוֹתָר וּפִגּוּל בְּהֶעְלֵם אֶחָד, חַיָּב עַל כָּל אֶחָד וְאֶחָד. — *[But] if he ate cheilev, blood, leftover offerings, and piggul in one lapse of awareness, he is liable for each one.*

[Each of the four prohibitions mentioned by the mishnah are punishable by *kares*, as explained in 1:1. Hence each *kezayis* consumed represents a distinct obligation for a *chatas* even if eaten in a single lapse of awareness.]

זֶה חֹמֶר בְּמִינִין הַרְבֵּה מִמִּין אֶחָד. — *In this, many kinds are more stringent than one kind.*

[The stringency is that since each is a separate category of prohibition, they call for a separate *chatas* for a multiple violation even if not separated by a lapse of awareness. Had these number of *kezayis*-measures been of one prohibition, there would have been only one *chatas* for the repeated transgression.]

וְחֹמֶר בְּמִין אֶחָד מִמִּינִין הַרְבֵּה: — *But [in the following], one kind is more stringent than many kinds:*

[In the following respect, however, there is a greater stringency in one kind over many kinds.]

שֶׁאִם אָכַל כַּחֲצִי זַיִת, וְחָזַר וְאָכַל כַּחֲצִי זַיִת — מִמִּין אֶחָד, חַיָּב; מִשְּׁנֵי מִינִין, פָּטוּר. — *If he ate half an olive's bulk, and again ate half an olive's bulk — [if they were] of one kind, he is liable; of two kinds, he is exempt.*

He ate two half-*kezayis* measures of one prohibited substance at separate

words to mean, 'I did not enter *tamei* [but I immersed in a *mikveh* first],' it would be of no avail, because someone who became *tamei* cannot enter the Temple on that day even if he immersed himself in a *mikveh* first (ibid.).

כריתות [ג] **וְכַמָּה** יִשְׁהֶה הָאוֹכְלָן? כְּאִלּוּ אֲכָלָן קְלָיוֹת; דִּבְרֵי רַבִּי מֵאִיר. וַחֲכָמִים אוֹמְרִים: עַד שֶׁיִּשְׁהֶה מִתְּחִלָּה וְעַד סוֹף כְּדֵי אֲכִילַת פְּרָס.

יד אברהם

times but did not gain awareness of the prohibition between the eatings (*Tos. Yom Tov* from *Gem.* 12b).

Had he gained awareness of the prohibition between the eatings, that realization would separate the two acts of eating and he would in fact be exempt from a *chatas* altogether because each eating would be less than the minimum-required amount of a *kezayis*.

This follows the prevailing view of the Sages in *Shabbos* 12:6, יֵשׁ יְדִיעָה לַחֲצִי שִׁיעוּר, *there is an awareness [factor] for [even] less than the required amount.* In other words, awareness of the transgression committed is a separating factor even if the amount consumed was less than a *kezayis* and cannot in itself create the obligation for a *chatas*.

Rabban Gamliel in the mishnah there disagrees and postulates that אֵין יְדִיעָה לַחֲצִי שִׁיעוּר, *there is no awareness for less than the required amount*. In his view, our mishnah's law requiring one *chatas* for the separate eating of two half-*kezayis* measures would apply even if there was an awareness between the eatings (ibid.).

If the two half-*kezayis* measures were of one kind of prohibited substance he is liable to a *chatas*, for the substances can be combined to form one *kezayis*. If, however, the two half-*kezayis* measures are not of the same substance, e.g., *cheilev* and blood, they cannot, of course, be combined and he is exempt from a *chatas*.

It would seem that these last statements are superfluous. It is self-evident that half measures of the same substance can be combined to make one measure but half measures of different substances cannot.

The *Gemara* (12b) therefore reads a novelty into the statement that half measures of the same substance can be combined.

The mishnah means that he is liable to a *chatas* even if the same forbidden substances were prepared in two dishes, e.g., one was cooked and one was roasted. This is a reference to the view of R' Yehoshua in mishnah 9 who rules that תַּמְחוּיין מְחַלְּקִין, *[different] dishes effect separate offerings*, i.e., one is obligated for a separate *chatas* for each *kezayis* if each was prepared in a different manner (e.g. one was cooked and one was baked). What our mishnah teaches is that R' Yehoshua's principle applies only to effect a more stringent ruling, not to serve as a basis for exemption. Thus, regarding the case in which he consumed two whole *kezayis*-measures prepared in different manners, he rules that each act is considered separate because in that way he is obligated for two *chataos* instead of one. Regarding our case, where he consumed two half-*kezayis* measures, separating the substances on the basis of the difference in their preparation would *exempt* him from a *chatas*. Thus, even according to R' Yehoshua, the rule 'different dishes effect separate offerings' does not apply.

This, then, is the meaning of our mishnah's statement that one substance is more stringent than many: If he ate half a *kezayis* and ate again half a *kezayis*, he is liable to a *chatas* even if they were prepared in different manners. See mishnah 9 where the halachah is discussed (*Rav* from *Gem.* 12b, *Rabbeinu Gershom* ad loc.).

The last clause (that two *kezayis*-measures of dissimilar substances do not combine), however, still remains self-evident. It was stated to teach that two unlike substances do not combine even in one lapse of awareness (*Tos.*).

3.

After stating that if one eats two half-*kezayis* measures of one kind of prohibited substance he is liable to one *chatas*, the *Tanna* proceeds to delineate how long it may take for the entire act of eating to still be counted as one act of eating.

3 **3.** And how much time may it take for him to eat
3 them? As if he would eat them as parched grains of corn; [these are] the words of R' Meir. But the Sages say: Until it takes no more from the beginning to the end than it would take to eat a *peras*.

YAD AVRAHAM

וְכַמָּה יִשְׁהֶה הָאוֹכְלָן? — *And how much time may it take for him to eat them?*

How much time may it take for him to eat the two half-*kezayis* measures that he should still be liable? (*Rav; Rashi*).

כְּאִלּוּ אֲכָלָן קְלָיוֹת; דִּבְרֵי רַבִּי מֵאִיר. — *As if he would eat them as parched grains of corn; [these are] the words of R' Meir.*

Although he ate the *kezayis* in small increments, with pauses between the eatings, we figure how long it would have taken him to eat the *kezayis* without interruptions if he had crumbled it into pieces as small as parched grains of corn. Since these grains must be eaten singly, it takes longer to eat the quantity in question. If it took him longer than that period of time to eat the *kezayis* of the forbidden foods, he is exempt from a *chatas*. Otherwise, he is liable.

If, in fact, he did not interrupt his eating, but simply took a long time to chew and swallow, he is liable even if it took him all day to finish eating the *kezayis* (*Rav* from conclusion of *Gem.* 12b, 13a, *Rashi* ad loc.; cf. *Rambam Comm.; Aruch LaNer*).

There are, then, two points implicit in R' Meir's statement: (1) If there were pauses in his eating, he is nonetheless liable if the entire act took no longer than it takes the equivalent amount of parched-grain granules. (2) If there were no pauses in his eatings, he is liable no matter how long it took to eat the *kezayis*. The Sages in the following statement dispute both of these contentions (*Aruch LaNer*).

Others explain that there were no pauses in his eating. He merely ate the *kezayis* slowly, as if he were eating granules of parched grain. As long as he is continually involved in chewing and swallowing it is considered, in R' Meir's view, as one continuous act of eating (*Rambam Comm.*).

וַחֲכָמִים אוֹמְרִים: עַד שֶׁיִּשְׁהֶה מִתְּחִלָּה וְעַד סוֹף כְּדֵי אֲכִילַת פְּרָס. — *But the Sages say: Until it takes no more from the beginning to the end than it would take to eat a peras.*

The Sages hold that the required time span for the eating of one *kezayis*, even if there were no pauses between bites, is כְּדֵי אֲכִילַת פְּרָס [*k'dei achilas peras*], *the amount of time that it takes to eat a peras.* [The definition of *peras* is given below.] If the two half-*kezayis* measures were eaten in the time that it takes to eat the *peras*, they are combined[1] and he is liable; if it took longer than that, he is exempt[2] (*Rav*).

1. The above reflects the conventional understanding of the *k'dei achilas peras* requirement, viz., that the entire eating not exceed that time frame. This means that the measure of time begins with the commencement of the eating of the *kezayis* and ends with its conclusion.

There are indications elsewhere that the *k'dei achilas peras* requirement refers solely to the *pause* between the eatings, i.e., when eating two halves of *kezayis*, the pause between them must not exceed the *k'dei achilas peras* or else the two acts of eating are regarded as separate (*Ran, Yoma* 73b [s.v. ולענין]; *Chinuch, Mitzvah* 313; see *Tos. Yom Kippurim, Yoma* 80b, *Minchas Chinuch* loc. cit.).

2. The requirement that fractions of a *kezayis* — to be combined — must be eaten within the כְּדֵי אֲכִילַת פְּרָס time frame, has numerous ramifications in the area of practical halachah. Two notable examples:

(a) Eating on Yom Kippur carries the penalty of *kares* if one ate the equivalent of a כּוֹתֶבֶת, *a date*. This amount must have been eaten within a *k'dei achilas peras* in order for the penalty

אָכַל אֳכָלִין טְמֵאִין וְשָׁתָה מַשְׁקִין טְמֵאִין, שָׁתָה רְבִיעִית יַיִן וְנִכְנַס לַמִּקְדָּשׁ וְשָׁהָה כְּדֵי אֲכִילַת פְּרָס.

יד אברהם

As stated in the mishnah elsewhere (*Eruvin* 8:2), the *peras* is a half of a bread loaf, the size of which is given as one third of a *kav*. As a *kav* is the equivalent of the volume of twenty-four eggs, the loaf used as the standard measure is the volume of eight eggs. The *peras* therefore contains the volume of four eggs (*Rav*, citing his Masters). Others hold that the *peras* is the equivalent of three eggs (*Rambam* cited by *Rav*; see *Eruvin* 8:2; *Shulchan Aruch, Orach Chaim* 612:4).

The authorities differ regarding the time frame required for liquids. According to *Rambam* (*Maachalos Assuros* 14:8), separate drinkings can be combined only if they occur within the amount of time that it takes to drink a *reviis* (a quarter of a *log*), which is the minimum-required amount of liquid to be halachically considered a drink. According to *Raavad* (ad loc.), the *reviis* of liquid like solids, must be consumed in the *k'dei achilas peras* time frame. This view is supported by the simple reading of our *Gemara* (13a,b)[1] [see *Kesef Mishneh* ad loc.] (*Tif. Yis.*; see *Shulchan Aruch, Orach Chaim* 612:10).

As a rule, *tumah*-contaminated foods cannot render a person *tamei* on contact. By Rabbinic decree, however, if a person eats a minimum amount of *tamei* food or drinks *tamei* fluids he becomes *pasul*, a lesser degree of *tumah* in which the person himself is considered as if he is *tamei*, but does not transmit *tumah* to any object with which he comes in contact. As a result of his *pasul* condition, the person may not eat *terumah* until he immerses himself in a *mikveh* (*Yoma* 80b).

The minimum amount of *tamei* food required to render a person *pasul* is half a *peras* [i.e., a quarter of the standard loaf], which is either two- or one-and-a-half-eggs volume [depending on the respective views cited above for the volume of a *peras*] (*Eruvin* 8:2).

The mishnah now proceeds to specify that a person becomes *pasul* only if he ate or drank the required amount of food or beverage within a *k'dei achilas peras*.

אָכַל אֳכָלִין טְמֵאִין וְשָׁתָה מַשְׁקִין טְמֵאִין, — *[If] he ate tamei foodstuffs or drank tamei beverages,*

If one ate or drank a minimum amount of *tamei* food — which for solids is half of a *peras* (two-eggs volume according to some and one-and-a-half-eggs volume according to others; see above) and for liquids is a *reviis* (see below) — he becomes *pasul*, i.e., he is in a lesser state of *tumah* as a result of

to apply (*Orach Chaim* 612:3,4). Under the circumstances which allow for a sick person to eat on Yom Kippur, care is taken that less than the *shiur* (minimum amount) is eaten in intervals of more than *k'dei achilas peras* (ibid. 618:7). *Mishnah Berurah* (ad loc.) cites *Chasam Sofer* who rules that the *k'dei achilas peras* time frame is nine minutes.

(b) The *mitzvah* of eating matzah on the first night of Pesach must be fulfilled with the minimum amount of a *kezayis*. This measure must be eaten without a pause greater than *k'dei achilas peras* (*Orach Chaim* 475; see *Magen Avraham* ibid. 15).

1. There is a question in the later authorities concerning the time frame required when drinking hot beverages which must be sipped slowly. Some say that if the drinking takes longer than *k'dei achilas peras*, it is not viewed as one continuous act. Therefore, when drinking a *reviis* quantity of hot coffee or tea, for example, a *berachah acharonah* (the blessing after eating) cannot be made if the time that it takes to drink it exceeds the required time to be considered as one consumption. Others reason that since it is the usual fashion to drink a hot liquid slowly, the *k'dei achilas peras* requirement does not apply (*Tos. Yom HaKippurim*, *Yoma* 80b).

3 [If] he ate *tamei* foodstuffs or drank *tamei* beverages,
3 or if he drank a *reviis* of wine and entered the Temple and tarried [in their consumption] for as long as it takes to eat a *peras* [he is liable]. R' Eliezer says: If

which he may not eat *terumah* until he immerses himself in a *mikveh*, although he cannot transmit the *tumah*. These *tamei* foodstuffs, too, the mishnah teaches, must be consumed in the *k'dei achilas peras* time span in order to render the person *pasul* (*Rav*).

שָׁתָה רְבִיעִית יַיִן וְנִכְנַס לַמִּקְדָּשׁ — *or if he drank a reviis of wine and entered the Temple*

One who drinks a *reviis*[1] measure of wine and afterwards enters the Temple courtyard is punished by מִיתָה בִידֵי שָׁמַיִם (death at the hands of Heaven) and disqualifies the service that he performs (*Rav*).

[Merely entering the Temple grounds after drinking wine, without performing *avodah*, is not subject to the מִיתָה בִידֵי שָׁמַיִם punishment. There is, however, a prohibition on entering the area between the Altar and the Temple while in such a condition (*Tos.* 13b citing *Toras Kohanim; Tos. Yom Tov*, cf. *Kesef Mishneh, Bias Mikdash* 1:1).]

Our commentary follows the view of *Rashi* who asserts that the clause *and he entered the Temple* can refer only to the prohibition of entering the Temple after drinking intoxicating beverages. The prohibition of entering the Temple after drinking *tamei* beverages is not Torah mandated because the level of *tumah* created by eating or drinking *tamei* foods is in fact only Rabbinical.

Tosafos (13b) however, point out that there are instances when a person becomes *tamei* on the Torah level by eating or drinking: if he eats the meat of an unslaughtered kosher bird or if he drinks the blood of reptiles. The mishnah, then, means that if this eating or drinking took place within the *k'dei achilas peras* time frame, he is *tamei* and if he subsequently enters the Temple he is liable to the punishment for that prohibition (*Tif. Yis.*; see *Aruch LaNer*).

וְשָׁהָה כְּדֵי אֲכִילַת פְּרָס. — *and tarried [in their consumption] for as long as it takes to eat a peras [he is liable].*

The consequences described above — becoming *pasul* by eating or drinking *tamei* foods or the punishment for entering the Temple after drinking wine — apply only if the eating or drinking took place within the *k'dei achilas peras* period (*Rav* from *Gemara*).

It was mentioned earlier that according to some authorities, the limitation of *k'dei achilas peras* apply only to solids; for liquids the time frame is כְּדֵי שְׁתִיַּת רְבִיעִית, *the amount of time it takes to drink a reviis* (*Rambam*). *Raavad* (*Hasagos* to *Hilchos Terumos*) cites this mishnah, which obviously refers to both food and drink, as proof that the *k'dei achilas peras* time frame applies to beverages as well as food (although he concedes that a *Tosefta* does support *Rambam's* view).

Aruch LaNer resolves the difficulties of *Rambam's* view by suggesting the following: Whenever the required amount of liquid is a *reviis*, the time span is *k'dei achilas peras*, otherwise he would have to drink a *reviis* without interruptions; when the required amount of liquid is less than a *reviis* (as on Yom Kippur when the forbidden amount is מְלֹא לוּגְמָיו, *a cheekful*), it must be drunk within the amount of time it takes to drink a *reviis*.

1. A *reviis* [lit., one-quarter] is a fourth of a *log*, the amount of liquid displaced by 1.5 eggs. (It is, in other words, the liquid equivalent of half a *peras*.) Its conversion into contemporary measures is the subject of dispute among latter-day authorities: The amounts range from approximately 3 fluid ounces to approximately 5.3 fl. oz.

רַבִּי אֱלִיעֶזֶר אוֹמֵר: אִם הִפְסִיק בָּהּ, אוֹ שֶׁנָּתַן לְתוֹכוֹ מַיִם כָּל־שֶׁהוּא, פָּטוּר.

[ד] יֵשׁ אוֹכֵל אֲכִילָה אַחַת, וְחַיָּב עָלֶיהָ אַרְבַּע חַטָּאוֹת וְאָשָׁם אֶחָד: טָמֵא שֶׁאָכַל אֶת־הַחֵלֶב, וְהָיָה נוֹתָר מִן־מֻקְדָּשִׁים, וּבְיוֹם הַכִּפּוּרִים.

יד אברהם

רַבִּי אֱלִיעֶזֶר אוֹמֵר: אִם הִפְסִיק בָּהּ, — *R' Eliezer*[1] *says: If he interrupted,*

He did not drink the entire *reviis* at once, but paused during the drinking (*Rav; Rashi*).

אוֹ שֶׁנָּתַן לְתוֹכוֹ מַיִם כָּל־שֶׁהוּא, — *or if he diluted it with the least bit of water,*

He drank the wine at one time but diluted it with even a small bit of water (*Rambam Comm.; Tif. Yis.*).

פָּטוּר. — *he is exempt.*

If he drinks the *reviis* wine either with a pause or in diluted form and then enters the Temple, he is exempt from the punishment of death by the hands of Heaven.

This exemption is derived from the Torah's expression (*Lev.* 10:9): יַיִן וְשֵׁכָר אַל־תֵּשְׁתְּ, *Wine and intoxicating drink you shall not drink ...,* which is construed to mean 'do not drink wine in the manner of intoxication [and then enter the Temple].' Pausing during drinking of the *reviis* or diluting it with any amount of water is not considered the manner of intoxication, and he is therefore exempt (*Rav; Rambam Comm.* from *Gem.* 13b).

The halachah is in accordance with R' Eliezer (*Rav; Rambam Comm.* from *Gem.* 13b; *Bias Mikdash* 1:1).

R' Eliezer's ruling of exemption applies only to someone who drank exactly one *reviis*; someone who drank more than a *reviis* is liable for entering the Temple even if he pauses in the drinking or dilutes it with water (*Rav; Rambam* ibid.; see *Raavad, Hasagos* ad loc.).

Just as a *Kohen* may not perform the *avodah* after drinking a *reviis* of wine, so may a rabbi not render a halachic decision after consuming that amount of intoxicating beverage. This is derived from the Torah's phrase (*Lev.* 10:11): וּלְהוֹרֹת אֶת־בְּנֵי יִשְׂרָאֵל, *to rule for the Jewish people*. Thus, should a rabbi drink a *reviis* of undiluted wine at one time, he may not rule on a matter of Torah law. However, if he paused while drinking or if he diluted the wine, he may issue a ruling (*Rambam Comm.*).

4.

In continuation of the ongoing discussion of circumstances that create multiple obligations for a *chatas*, the following two mishnayos cite illustrations where one action can occasion the obligation for a number of *chataos*. This occurs when the forbidden act represents the coincidence of several distinct prohibitions, so that with one action the person actually commits a number of transgressions, each

1. Although the mishnah text reads R' Eliezer, it seems clear from the *Gemara* (13b) that R' Elazar (Ben Shammua) is meant (*Shitah Mekubetzes; Tos. Chadashim; Meleches Shlomo*). [Nevertheless, we will follow the text as it stands.]

he interrupted, or if he diluted it with the least bit of water, he is exempt.

4. There is [an instance of] one who performs one act of eating and is liable for it to four *chataos* and one *asham*: a *tamei* [person] who ate *cheilev*, which was leftover from consecrated food, and [it was] on Yom Kip-

YAD AVRAHAM

of which is liable to a separate *kares*.

As a general rule, multiple-coinciding transgressions are restricted by the Talmudic dictum אֵין אִיסוּר חָל עַל אִיסוּר, *a prohibition cannot take effect on another [pre-existing] prohibition*. For example, eating *neveilah* [ritually unslaughtered meat] is a violation of a negative precept. Eating *neveilah* of a non-kosher animal, however, does not make one liable for both the prohibition against non-kosher animals and the prohibition against *neveilah*. Since the prohibition against non-kosher animals was already in effect before the animal was killed, the *neveilah* prohibition cannot take effect afterwards.

There are, however, a number of exceptions to this rule:

(a) אִיסוּר בַּת אַחַת, *simultaneous prohibition*, i.e., when the prohibitions occur at the same time. Since neither prohibition precedes the other, both can take effect.

(b) אִיסוּר כּוֹלֵל, *more inclusive prohibition*, which is when the second prohibition includes more people than the first.

(c) אִיסוּר מוֹסִיף, *an additive prohibition,* which adds more dimensions to the original prohibition (see *Yad Avraham* commentary in ArtScroll *Yevamos* 3:10 footnote 2).

These principles will be clarified by the illustrations which are cited by the following mishnayos.

יֵשׁ אוֹכֵל אֲכִילָה אַחַת, וְחַיָּב עָלֶיהָ אַרְבַּע חַטָּאוֹת וְאָשָׁם אֶחָד: — *There is [an instance of] one who performs one act of eating and is liable for it to four chataos and one asham:*

[He ate but one food item but thereby transgressed a number of coinciding prohibitions, resulting in the liability to four *chatas* offerings and one *asham* offering, as will be explained.]

The point of the mishnah is to demonstrate how a number of prohibitions can take effect on the same object despite the rule that אֵין אִיסוּר חָל עַל אִיסוּר, *a prohibition cannot take effect on another [pre-existing] prohibition*. The prohibitions listed by the mishnah either take effect simultaneously or are more comprehensive than the original prohibition [as will be explained] (*Tif. Yis.*).

טָמֵא שֶׁאָכַל אֶת־הַחֵלֶב, וְהָיָה נוֹתָר מִן־מֻקְדָּשִׁים, וּבְיוֹם הַכִּפּוּרִים. — *a tamei [person] who ate cheilev, which was leftover from consecrated food, and [it was] on Yom Kippur.*

This one act of eating obligates him to a *chatas* for each of the following four transgressions: (1) eating *cheilev*, (2) eating *kodashim* (consecrated food) while in a state of *tumah*, (3) eating the leftover of a sacrifice, and (4) eating on Yom Kippur. Each of these prohibitions is separately punishable by *kares* if done willfully and calls for a *chatas* to atone for its inadvertent transgression, as mentioned in the first mishnah of this tractate. When they coincide in one piece of food, they each account for a separate

יד אברהם

chatas obligation. [The *asham* obligation will be explained shortly.]

The coincidence of these prohibitions does not fall under the category of אֵין אִיסוּר חָל עַל אִיסוּר, *a prohibition cannot take effect on another [pre-existing] prohibition*, because each is, in a way, more comprehensive than the first. Initially this meat is prohibited simply as *cheilev*, a prohibition which applies to sacrificial as well as ordinary meat. When the man becomes *tamei* he is enjoined from eating all sacrificial meat, not just the *cheilev* of the sacrifice. As an אִיסוּר כּוֹלֵל, *a more inclusive prohibition*, the prohibition of eating *kodashim* while *tamei* includes the already forbidden *cheilev* as well. When the piece of *cheilev* is not eaten within its allotted time, it becomes *nossar* (leftover). A third *chatas* obligation is thus created because the *nossar* prohibition is more extensive in that it *adds* the prohibition of burning the *cheilev* on the Altar, something which was heretofore permitted. This is an illustration of אִיסוּר מוֹסִיף, the *additive prohibition* principle: Just as the *cheilev* now becomes prohibited to the Altar, it also becomes additionally prohibited for human consumption. If all this happened on Yom Kippur, a new prohibition — eating on Yom Kippur — is introduced. This, too, is a more inclusive prohibition [אִיסוּר כּוֹלֵל] because on Yom Kippur *all* foods become prohibited. Therefore, just as other foods became prohibited, so does this *cheilev* which was already prohibited for other reasons, and as a result the person becomes liable to a fourth *chatas* for eating on Yom Kippur (*Rav* from *Gem.* 14a).

Eating on Yom Kippur is a prohibition that requires a larger than usual amount — the size of a כּוֹתֶבֶת הַגַּסָּה, *a large date*, which is roughly the equivalent of two *kezayis* measures (*Yoma* 8:2; see *Yad Avraham* comm. there). So, while the first three prohibitions take effect simultaneously on one *kezayis*, he is obligated for the fourth *chatas* only if he ate an additional quantity of the food. Nonetheless, it can be considered one eating if it involved one food item. For example, he ate a kidney with its surrounding fat or a piece of fat filled with dates. Since the food item as a whole is the equivalent of a large date, he is liable for the prohibition of eating on Yom Kippur as well as the other prohibitions (*Tos. Yom Tov* from *Gemara* 14a).

The fifth sacrifice is the *asham me'ilos*, the sacrifice brought for misappropriation of sacred property. As will be explained in Tractate *Me'ilah*, one who unintentionally derives benefit from *kodashim* must repay the value of the principal plus a fifth to the Temple and bring an *asham*. In our case, the *me'ilah* prohibition is in force notwithstanding that the *cheilev* was already prohibited before its consecration. The fact that it was consecrated creates a more comprehensive prohibition in the respect that it adds a prohibition against deriving benefit, whereas previously it was forbidden only to be eaten. Therefore, this is in the category of אִיסוּר מוֹסִיף, *additive prohibition*, since an additional prohibition takes effect on the *cheilev* itself. Thus, just as the prohibition of benefits takes effect on the *cheilev*, the prohibition of eating does so as well (*Rav* from *Gemara* 14a).

Apart from the principle of אֵין אִיסוּר חָל עַל אִיסוּר, the idea of being liable for the *asham me'ilos* for the consumption of *nossar* is subject to question because of another consideration: the absence of monetary value of the *nossar*. Since one must burn *nossar* and derive no benefit from it, it is essentially worthless and as such should not occasion the *asham*, for *me'ilah* is the *monetary* misappropriation of sacred property. [This principle is set forth in *Pesachim* (29a), where the *Gemara* states that one who on Pesach ate *chametz* that was sacred property is exempt from the *asham* because the *chametz* is worthless.]

pur. R' Meir says: If it was the Sabbath and he carried it out in his mouth, he is [additionally] liable. They said to

One answer to this question is that when benefiting from sacrificial *kodashim*, such as the *nossar* under discussion, the monetary factor is not an issue. The Torah regarded the misappropriation of a *korban* as *me'ilah* regardless of its monetary value. It is only regarding the misappropriation of sacred *property*, objects which belong to the Temple treasury, that the monetary value of the object is an issue. In this context, the *me'ilah* which constitutes the prohibition is fundamentally a *theft* and therefore the fact the object is without value renders the theft as meaningless (*Nesivos HaMishpat*, 28:2).

Another approach is that the value of an object must be determined by reckoning what it *would be* worth if it were non-*kodesh* property. Thus, this *cheilev* is only valueless as a result of restrictions imposed because of its sacred status. *Chametz* on Pesach, by contrast, is valueless because of laws that have no relationship to the laws of *kodashim*, and therefore the object is considered valueless even in the context of the laws of *me'ilah* (*Tif. Yis.*).

רַבִּי מֵאִיר אוֹמֵר: אִם הָיְתָה שַׁבָּת וְהוֹצִיאוֹ בְּפִיו, חַיָּב. — *R' Meir says: If it was the Sabbath and he carried it out in his mouth, he is [additionally] liable.*

[R' Meir adds that it is possible through the act of eating to be liable for yet additional *chataos*, in the following manner:]

If the Yom Kippur on which he ate the *cheilev* was also a Shabbos, and he walked from a private domain to a public domain (or vice versa) while he was eating the *cheilev*, he was thereby guilty of transgressing the work category of הוֹצָאָה, *transporting*, from one domain to another. Thus, he is liable to one additional *chatas* for desecrating the Sabbath and another one for desecrating Yom Kippur.[1]

There is discussion in the *Gemara* whether there is the same prohibition against transporting on Yom Kippur that there is on Shabbos. According to the prevailing view that יֵשׁ עֵרוּב וְהוֹצָאָה לְיוֹם הַכִּפּוּרִים, *the concepts of eruv and transporting do apply on Yom Kippur*, it was not necessary to create a situation of Yom Kippur which is on the Sabbath to add the prohibition of transporting; that prohibition is in force on an ordinary Yom Kippur as well. R' Meir chose a case of the Sabbath coinciding with Yom Kippur only to increase the *chatas* obligation to two [one for the Sabbath and one for Yom Kippur] (*Rav* from *Gem.* 14a).

The principle of אֵין אִיסוּר חָל עַל אִיסוּר, *a prohibition cannot take effect on another prohibition*, does not apply here since the Sabbath and Yom Kippur occur simultaneously and whenever two prohibitions occur simultaneously, both take effect. [This exception is known as

1. *Ketzos HaChoshen* (28:1) poses the following incisive question on R' Meir's statement: There is a well-known dictum that קִים לֵיהּ בִּדְרַבָּה מִינֵּיהּ, *one is punished with the more severe of two offenses*. That is, if at one time, one commits a capital offense [even unintentionally] and an offense with monetary liability, he is exempt from the monetary liability. Applied to our situation, this means that when he desecrates the Sabbath, he commits a capital offense and should be exempt for the monetary payment of the resulting *me'ilah*, which in turn exempts him from the *me'ilah* offering. Therefore, when R' Meir added a case of *chillul Shabbos* to create another *chatas* obligation he eliminated the previously stated obligation for *me'ilah*. How, then, did R' Meir add another sacrifice obligation to that which the Sages stated? By creating an illustration of an additional *chatas* he also subtracted the *asham*, thereby precluding a net increase in the amount of offerings, as listed by the Sages!

Nesivos HaMishpat (ad loc.) responds by postulating that *me'ilah* caused by misappropriation of offerings is independent of any financial considerations; even if no restitution is to be made, the *asham* must be brought. It is only for the misappropriation of sacred property that the financial obligation is a factor in the *asham* obligation.

חַיָּב. אָמְרוּ לוֹ: אֵינוֹ מִן־הַשֵּׁם.

[ה] **יֵשׁ** בָּא בִּיאָה אַחַת וְחַיָּב עָלֶיהָ שֵׁשׁ חַטָּאוֹת. הַבָּא עַל בִּתּוֹ חַיָּב עָלֶיהָ מִשּׁוּם בִּתּוֹ, וַאֲחוֹתוֹ, וְאֵשֶׁת אָחִיו, וְאֵשֶׁת אֲחִי אָבִיו, וְאֵשֶׁת אִישׁ, וְנִדָּה.

יד אברהם

[אִיסּוּר בַּת אַחַת] (*Rav* from *Gem.* 14a).

Although the mishnah (*Shabbos* 10:3) considers carrying by mouth as an act performed in an unusual manner (כִּלְאַחַר יָד), this does not include eating. Eating while walking from one domain to another is considered a normal manner of transporting food and when one swallows the food it is as if he placed the object in the domain where he now finds himself (*Tif. Yis.* from *Shabbos* 102a).

אָמְרוּ לוֹ: אֵינוֹ מִן־הַשֵּׁם. — *They said to him: That is not in the [same] category.*

[The Sages replied to R' Meir that while it is true that it is possible to be liable for additional *chataos* in the manner he described, the *Tanna* is nonetheless justified in not using this as an illustration of the maximum amount of *chataos* for which one act of eating can create an obligation, for the following reason:]

The *Tanna* counts only those *chataos* that are occasioned by transgressions committed by *eating*; the *chataos* added by R' Meir are required because of transgressions of *transferring* from one domain to another (*Rav; Rashi*).

The Sages' objection to the *chataos* added by R' Meir is that the *Tanna* does not count the two additional *chataos* occasioned by his transporting any more than he would count the *chatas* of any other sin performed concomitantly with the eating of the *cheilev* (e.g., he transgressed any other *kares*-punishable prohibition while eating *cheilev*).

R' Meir's reasoning, though, is that since the transporting was done with the fat while he was eating, the additional *chataos* are to be considered as resulting from the same action as are the others. Moreover, all the *chataos* are the result of *eating*, for if he were not eating the *cheilev* he would not be liable for transporting it either, as transporting by mouth without eating is considered an unusual manner of labor, as explained previously. Thus, the eating is a causative factor for all the *chataos* (*Tif. Yis.*; addendum of author's son R' Boruch Yitzchok).

5.

The following two Mishnayos provide other illustrations of multiple *chataos* obligations stemming from a solitary action, these in the area of אִיסּוּר בִּיאָה, *prohibitions of cohabitation*. The illustrations involve a man who inadvertently commits an act of incest with a woman to whom he is related in a number of ways. Each of these relations becomes the cause of a separate *chatas* obligation. As in the previous mishnah, the *Tanna's* point is that the following cases are exceptions to the principle of אֵין אִיסּוּר חָל עַל אִיסּוּר, *a prohibition cannot take effect on another [pre-existing] prohibition.*

יֵשׁ בָּא בִּיאָה אַחַת וְחַיָּב עָלֶיהָ שֵׁשׁ חַטָּאוֹת. — *There is one who performs one act of cohabitation and is liable for it to six chataos.*

[It is possible that a person cohabits with a woman but once, yet is liable for up to six *chataos*. This occurs when the woman in question is related to him in numerous ways, so as to occasion six separate *chatas* obligations. The mishnah now proceeds to explain how cohabitation with one woman can be the violation

him: That is not in the [same] category.

5. There is one who performs one act of cohabitation and is liable for it to six *chataos*. He who cohabits with his daughter may be liable for her as his daughter, his sister, his brother's wife, his father's brother's wife, a married woman, and a menstruant.

of six separate prohibitions.]

הַבָּא עַל בִּתּוֹ חַיָּב עָלֶיהָ מִשּׁוּם בִּתּוֹ, וַאֲחוֹתוֹ,
וְאֵשֶׁת אָחִיו, וְאֵשֶׁת אֲחִי אָבִיו, וְאֵשֶׁת אִישׁ, וְנִדָּה.
— *He who cohabits with his daughter may be liable for her as his daughter, his sister, his brother's wife, his father's brother's wife, a married woman, and a menstruant.*

One was intimate with a woman who is at the same time his daughter, his sister, his brother's wife, his father's brother's wife, a married woman, and a menstruant. Since each of these relationships is independently liable to a *chatas*, he is obligated to bring a total of six *chataos*.

It is possible for one woman to be related in so many ways in the following manner [these relationships are delineated in diagram 1]: Reuven fathered a daughter, Dinah, by an incestuous union with his mother, Leah. This child is forbidden to Reuven both as a daughter and a half-sister, as they share a common mother. Since these two prohibitions take effect simultaneously — at the time of the child's birth — they each occasion a separate *chatas* obligation. If this woman then was married to Reuven's brother Shimon, the prohibition of *brother's wife* is added. This is an אִיסוּר כּוֹלֵל, *more inclusive prohibition*, as it includes Reuven's other brothers as well as Reuven. Therefore, just as the marriage prohibits her to Shimon's other brothers, it prohibits her to Reuven as well. If, upon Shimon's death or in the event of a divorce, the woman was married to Reuven's father's brother Esav, the prohibition of *father's brother's wife* adds a fourth *chatas*. This, too, is an אִיסוּר כּוֹלֵל, because, as a result of this marriage, she now also becomes prohibited to Reuven's other uncles as a brother's wife [see diagram 2]. Thus, she also becomes prohibited to Reuven as his father's brother's wife[1] (*Rav; Rambam; Rashi*).

Although the reason she is prohibited to the father's brothers is because of the relationship of אֵשֶׁת אָח, *brother's wife*, it is still sufficient reason for the prohibition of אֵשֶׁת אֲחִי אָב, *father's brother's wife* (which per-

---

1. *Rashi* also cites a reading of the Gemara according to which the new people included in the prohibition as a result of this marriage are the *children* of Reuven's father's brother [rather than the *brothers* of Reuven's father]. The prohibition to them is אֵשֶׁת אָב, *father's wife*, i.e., Reuven's cousins to whom this woman was previously permitted now are prohibited to marry her because she is their father's wife. This too is an אִיסוּר כּוֹלֵל.

It is difficult, though, to see what it is that this reading really changes. The prohibition in question is אֵשֶׁת אָב, which in principle is no different than the אֵשֶׁת אֲחִי אָב prohibition referred to by our reading. *Aruch LaNer*, therefore, suggests that this reading means that she becomes prohibited to Reuven's *other* cousins, i.e., the children of his father's other brothers, not of the one who married the woman [see diagram 2]. The prohibition *to them*, of course, is אֵשֶׁת אֲחִי אָב, *father's brother's wife*, which is the same prohibition that applies to Reuven. Just as she becomes prohibited to Reuven's cousins after marrying their uncle, as the wife of their father's brother, she becomes prohibited to Reuven, too, as the wife of his father's brother. Accordingly, the prohibition to the cousins is the same as the prohibition to Reuven, unlike the other explanations, in which the additional prohibition is distinct from the one that affects Reuven.

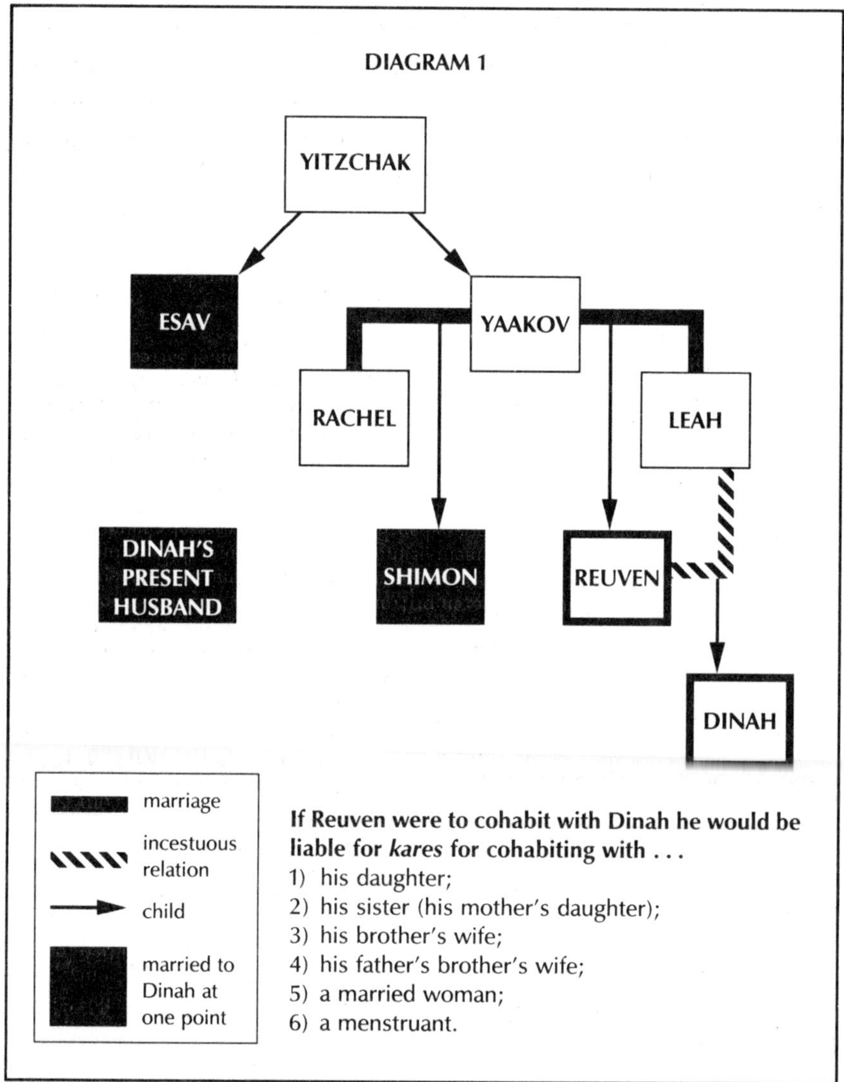
DIAGRAM 1
YITZCHAK
ESAV
YAAKOV
RACHEL
LEAH
DINAH'S PRESENT HUSBAND
SHIMON
REUVEN
DINAH
marriage
incestuous relation
child
married to Dinah at one point
If Reuven were to cohabit with Dinah he would be liable for *kares* for cohabiting with . . .
1) his daughter;
2) his sister (his mother's daughter);
3) his brother's wife;
4) his father's brother's wife;
5) a married woman;
6) a menstruant.

tains to Reuven), to take effect. To be in the category of אִיסוּר כּוֹלֵל, a prohibition must merely include more people than the previous prohibition did, but it need not be necessarily for the same reason. Thus, since the father's brothers are now prohibited because of the new marriage, it is sufficient reason to say that the prohibition which pertains to the son takes effect as well. This principle is equally evident from the following mishnah, as will be explained there (*Aruch LaNer* from *Tos. Yevamos* 32b).

The prohibition of אֵשֶׁת אִישׁ, *a married woman*, is also in effect because, as a result of her marriage,[1] she becomes prohibited to everyone but her husband and as a

1. *Rambam Comm.* explains that the אֵשֶׁת אִישׁ is the result of a subsequent marriage, i.e., her husband (Reuven's uncle) died and she married someone else. This detail, however, is

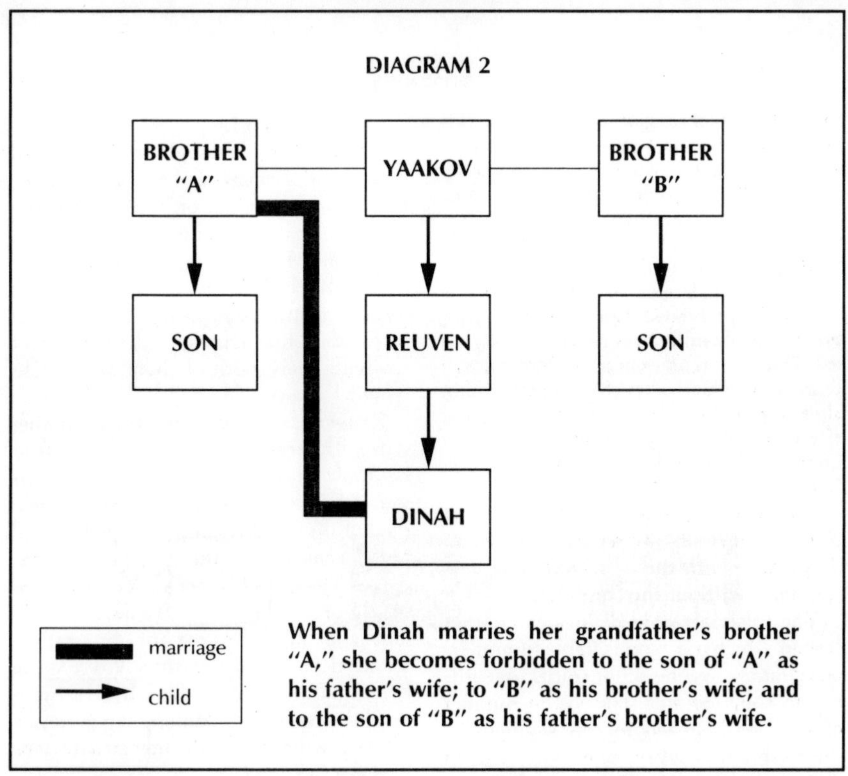

When Dinah marries her grandfather's brother "A," she becomes forbidden to the son of "A" as his father's wife; to "B" as his brother's wife; and to the son of "B" as his father's brother's wife.

result of this inclusive factor the prohibition takes effect even to those for whom she was already prohibited. This brings us to a total of five *chataos* for the numerous relations through which the woman is prohibited to Reuven. Upon her becoming a menstruant, a sixth *chatas* is added because now she is prohibited to everyone including her husband to whom she was heretofore permitted. Thus, she again becomes prohibited to Reuven as well (*Rav*).

As is stated elsewhere (*Yevamos* 4:13; *Kiddushin* 3:12), a child of an incestuous union is known as a *mamzer* and is by Torah law forbidden to 'enter the congregation of Hashem,' i.e., to marry a legitimate Jew. Accordingly, the woman under discussion here — as the daughter born of a union of mother and son — is a *mamzeres* and is prohibited to marry any legitimate Jew. Thus, it may be asked, why do her subsequent marriages to Reuven's brother or uncle increase the prohibitions to other people as she was already forbidden to everyone as a *mamzeres*?

Tosafos concludes that a stringent prohibition, punishable by *kares*, can take effect upon a less stringent prohibition, punishable only by *malkus* (lashes). Therefore, when she is married to Reuven's brother, the marriage — although contrary to Torah law — is valid (as the prohibition of *mamzeres* does not involve *kares*) and as a result the prohibition of אֵשֶׁת אָח, *brother's wife*, can take effect upon the prohibition of taking a *mamzeres*, resulting in an additional prohibition.

Others (apparently unwilling to subscribe

apparently unnecessary because the moment she is married to Reuven's uncle she is at once a father's brother's wife and a married woman. As they occur simultaneously, both prohibitions take effect (*Tos. Yom Tov*; cf. *Aruch LaNer*).

וְהַבָּא עַל בַּת בִּתּוֹ חַיָּב עָלֶיהָ מִשּׁוּם בַּת בִּתּוֹ,

to this principle) suggest ways in which this marriage can create a prohibition for someone to whom the woman was previously permitted. For example, if all — or even one — of Reuven's brothers were themselves *mamzerim*, then, as a result of the legally binding marriage to Reuven's brother (even if he himself is not a *mamzer*), she is henceforth prohibited even to this *mamzer* brother to whom she was previously permitted. Thus, this is an example of איסור כולל, a prohibition which takes effect on something already prohibited in the course of taking effect on something permitted (*Rambam Comm.* as explained by *Tos. Yom Tov*; cf. *Rav; Tos.; Aruch LaNer*).

The following segment appears in the *Gemara* text as a separate mishnah [beginning with the word הַבָּא, *one who cohabits*, without the conjunctive *and*.

The mishnah now delineates another case in which a person is liable to numerous *chataos* for one act of coitus. According to some commentators, the number of *chataos* itemized in this segment of the mishnah is seven, one more than in the previous case (*Rambam Comm.*); according to others, there are six *chatas* obligations in this segment just as there were in the previous one (*Tos.*). Our commentary will at first detail the numerous *chatas* obligations according to the former approach (followed by *Rav*) and then explain where *Tosafos* differ and why.

וְהַבָּא עַל בַּת בִּתּוֹ — *And he who cohabits with his daughter's daughter*

A person who cohabits with his daughter's daughter may be liable for up to seven *chataos*, if she is related in more ways than the simple granddaughter-grandfather relationship. This is possible in the following manner [see diagram 3, opposite page]:

Yaakov had a daughter Dinah, and Lavan had a daughter Leah. Lavan married Dinah, daughter of Yaakov; Yaakov married Leah, daughter of Lavan. To Lavan and Dinah was born a daughter, named Rachel. Rachel is, therefore, both Yaakov's granddaughter (the daughter of his daughter Dinah) and the sister of his wife Leah (both of them are daughters of Lavan).

Reuven, Yaakov's son (from another wife), then married Rachel, who thus became Yaakov's daughter-in-law (the wife of his son Reuven). Then Reuven died or divorced Rachel, and she married Esav, Yaakov's brother. Rachel now becomes Yaakov's brother's wife. Esav died or divorced her, and Yaakov's uncle Yishmael (the brother of his father, Yitzchak) married her, thus also making her Yaakov's aunt, as her father's brother's wife. In addition, she is now a married woman.[1] If she menstruates, she is also a *niddah* (*Tif. Yis.*).

If Yaakov is intimate with Rachel, he is liable to seven *chataos*. The mishnah will now proceed to explain the prohibitions for which he is liable for a *chatas* and we will explain why these respective prohibitions take effect despite the principle of אֵין אִיסוּר חָל עַל אִיסוּר.

חַיָּב עָלֶיהָ מִשּׁוּם — *may be liable for her as*

[If he inadvertently cohabited with this granddaughter, he is liable for a separate *chatas* for the respective prohibitions, as follows:]

בַּת בִּתּוֹ, — *his daughter's daughter,*

[Because she is the daughter of his daughter Dinah, Yaakov is liable for the prohibition against a granddaughter.]

1. Here, too, *Rambam* (*Comm.*) mentions that Yishmael dies or divorces her, and she remarries another party, thus making her a married woman. Again, it is puzzling why this detail is necessary; one would be equally liable for her as an אֵשֶׁת אִישׁ, *married woman*, if she were still married to Yishmael, Yaakov's relative. As both the prohibition for אֵשֶׁת אֲחִי אָבִיו, *father's brother's wife*, and אֵשֶׁת אִישׁ occur simultaneously, both can take effect (*Tif. Yis.*).

3
5 And he who cohabits with his daughter's daughter may be liable for her as his daughter's daughter, his

YAD AVRAHAM

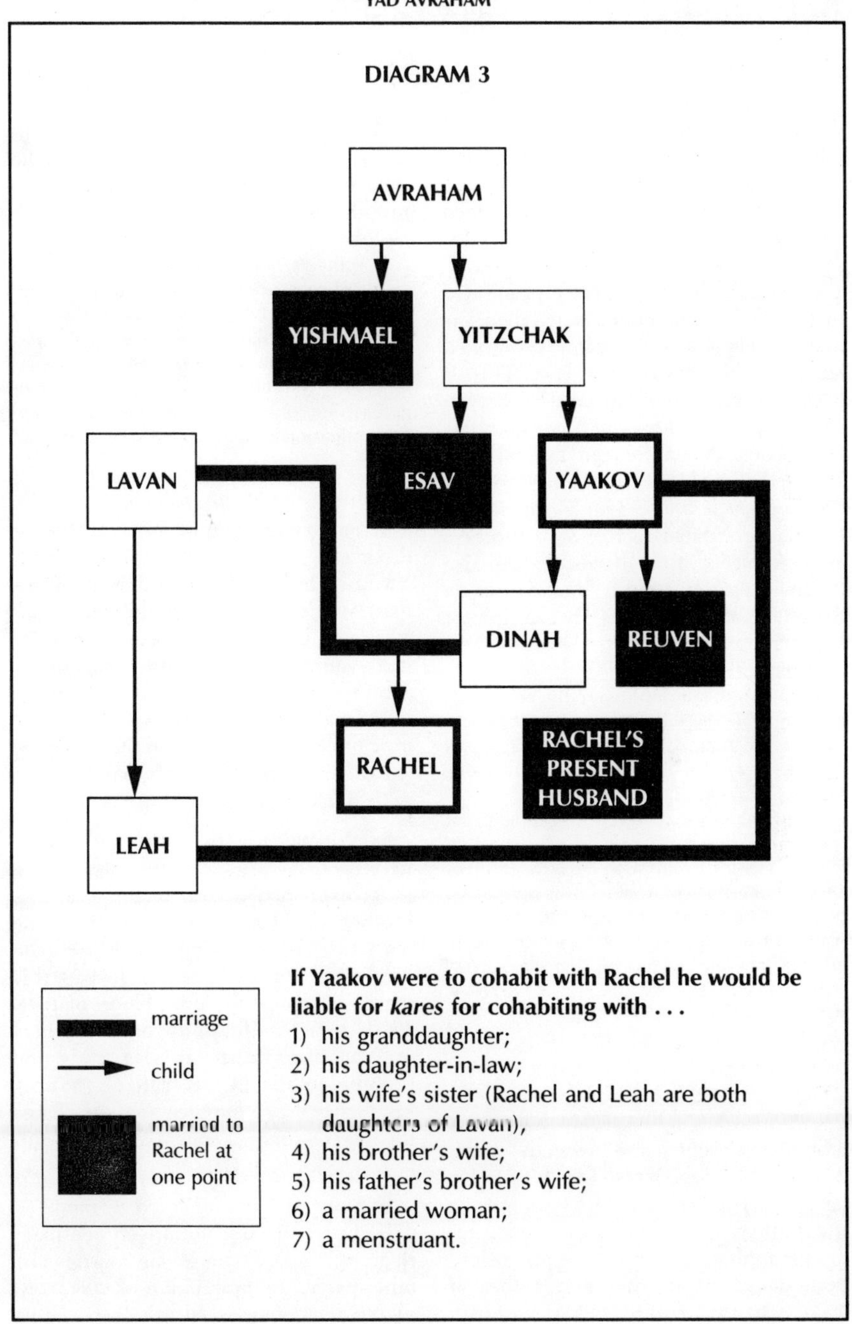

If Yaakov were to cohabit with Rachel he would be liable for *kares* for cohabiting with . . .

1) his granddaughter;
2) his daughter-in-law;
3) his wife's sister (Rachel and Leah are both daughters of Lavan),
4) his brother's wife;
5) his father's brother's wife;
6) a married woman;
7) a menstruant.

כריתות ג/ה

וְכַלָּתוֹ, וַאֲחוֹת אִשְׁתּוֹ, וְאֵשֶׁת אָחִיו, וְאֵשֶׁת אֲחִי אָבִיו, וְאֵשֶׁת אִישׁ, וְנִדָּה. רַבִּי יוֹסֵי אוֹמֵר: אִם עָבַר הַזָּקֵן וּנְשָׂאָהּ, חַיָּב עָלֶיהָ מִשּׁוּם אֵשֶׁת אָב, וְכֵן הַבָּא

יד אברהם

וְכַלָּתוֹ, — *his daughter-in-law,*

Since she was married to his son [Reuven in the diagram], she is prohibited as a daughter-in-law (*Rav*). Even when Reuven dies or divorces her, she remains prohibited to her father-in-law Yaakov.

Although she was already prohibited to him as his granddaughter, when she married his son she became prohibited again as his daughter-in-law. This is because prior to her marriage to Reuven she was permitted to any of her grandfather's sons. When Reuven married her, she became prohibited to them as an אֵשֶׁת אָח, *brother's wife*. Thus, just as she became prohibited to Reuven's brothers as a result of this marriage, she also became prohibited to Yaakov as a daughter-in-law. This is an example of an אִיסּוּר כּוֹלֵל, *more inclusive prohibition* (*Rambam Comm.*).

Although the prohibition to the brothers is אֵשֶׁת אָח, *brother's wife*, and the prohibition to Yaakov as כַּלָּתוֹ, *daughter-in-law*, it is still considered a valid אִיסּוּר כּוֹלֵל, *more inclusive prohibition* (as explained above).

This mishnah is cited by *Tosafos* as proof that a prohibition can take effect on a previously existing prohibition if it is the result of an act that affects that which was previously permitted, even though not for the same reason. [This is termed אִיסּוּר מוֹסִיף מִשְּׁנֵי שֵׁמוֹת, *an additive prohibition of two categories*] (*Tos. Yeshanim* 14b, s.v. מגו, *Yevamos* 32b s.v. איסור).

וַאֲחוֹת אִשְׁתּוֹ, — *his wife's sister,*

Since Yaakov is married to his son-in-law's (Lavan) daughter (Leah), his granddaughter (Rachel, the woman under discussion) — who is also Lavan's daughter — is further prohibited to him as אֲחוֹת אִשְׁתּוֹ, *his wife's sister*, since his granddaughter and his wife are sisters, both daughters of the same father. If Yaakov had married his wife (Leah) first, when his granddaughter was born to his daughter (and her husband Lavan, who is already Yaakov's father-in-law), she is prohibited at birth to him both as granddaughter and sister-in-law.

In some versions of the mishnah, mention of the obligation of the *chatas* for the prohibition of אֲחוֹת אִשְׁתּוֹ, *wife's sister*, does not appear. This follows the view of *Tosafos* mentioned at the outset, that this case represents only the coincidence of six *chatas* obligations, not seven. Why this particular *chatas* obligation is omitted will be explained below.

וְאֵשֶׁת אָחִיו, — *his brother's wife,*

After Reuven, son of Yaakov, died or divorced her, Rachel married Esav, Yaakov's brother. Since, as a result of this marriage, she became prohibited to *all* Yaakov's brothers, she became prohibited again to her grandfather Yaakov, as a brother's wife. This is an אִיסּוּר כּוֹלֵל, *more inclusive prohibition*. Thus, we now have listed four *chataos* to which he is liable if he inadvertently has relations with Rachel (*Rambam Comm.*).

וְאֵשֶׁת אֲחִי אָבִיו, — *his father's brother's wife,*

As explained above, when Yaakov's brother died or divorced Rachel, she married Yishmael, his uncle — the brother of Yaakov's father. Just as this marriage creates the prohibition of אֵשֶׁת אָח, *brother's wife*, to the other brothers of Yaakov's father, it also adds the prohibition of אֵשֶׁת אֲחִי אָבִיו, *the wife of his father's brother*, to Yaakov. Thus, the total of *chataos* obligations is now up to five (*Rambam Comm.*).

וְאֵשֶׁת אִישׁ, — *and a married woman,*

If, upon the dissolution of her marriage to Yaakov's uncle she marries another party, the prohibition of אֵשֶׁת אִישׁ, *married woman*, is added. Just as this

3 daughter-in-law, his wife's sister, his brother's wife, his
5 father's brother's wife, a married woman, and a
menstruant. R' Yose says: If the [great-]grandfather transgressed and married her, he is liable for her as his

marriage creates a prohibition for all men to whom she was permitted, it takes effect regarding Yaakov as well. The total of *chataos* is now six (*Rambam Comm.*).

Here again, it is not clear why a *new* marriage is necessary to add the prohibition of אֵשֶׁת אִישׁ; that prohibition can just as well take effect as a result of her marriage to Yaakov's uncle, as both the prohibition of אֵשֶׁת אֲחִי אָבִיו and אֵשֶׁת אִישׁ take effect simultaneously (*Tif. Yis.*).

.וְנִדָּה — *and a menstruant.*

As a result of her menstruation, a seventh *chatas* obligation is created, for just as she is now prohibited to her husband, she becomes prohibited to others as well.

Accordingly, the mishnah's three illustrations follow a sequence: the previous case of one who is liable to six *chataos*, the present case of one who is liable to seven, and the next case cited by R' Yose which involves eight *chataos* (*Rambam Comm.*).

As already mentioned, *Tosafos* disagree, maintaining that the previous introductory clause to the beginning of the mishnah — *There is one who performs one act of habitation and is liable for it to six chataos* — applies to this segment of the mishnah as well. They therefore delete the words וַאֲחוֹת אִשְׁתּוֹ, *his wife's sister*, from this segment, thereby reducing the number of *chatas* obligations to six.

Tosafos explain that the אֲחוֹת אִשְׁתּוֹ prohibition is not listed since it can come about only in one of two ways: (a) if he marries the sister *before* his granddaughter was born, so that his granddaughter was at birth both a granddaughter and sister-in-law; (b) he married the sister *after* his granddaughter was born, in which event the marriage to his granddaughter's sister adds a prohibition to his already prohibited granddaughter. For each of these possibilities there is a reason why this prohibition should be omitted. Regarding the first possibility that the sister-in-law prohibition occurred at birth, *Tosafos* postulate that this prohibition is not mentioned because the mishnah lists only instances of more comprehensive prohibitions that occur sequentially, not prohibitions that take effect because they occur simultaneously (אִיסוּר בַּת אַחַת). Alternatively, the mishnah does not list relations by marriage unless they occurred at the time of marriage [e.g., daughter-in-law]. Regarding the case under discussion, however, the prohibition took effect upon the birth of the granddaughter, not at the time that he married his wife.

Regarding the other possibility — that his granddaughter is born before he marries her sister [in which case the sister-in-law prohibition takes effect after the granddaughter prohibition] — *Tosafos* maintain that it is omitted from the mishnah because the mishnah lists additional prohibitions only if they are at least as stringent as the preceding ones. The prohibition of a wife's sister, however, is punishable only by *kares*, whereas the existing prohibition is punishable by death. [This premise is consistent with the view of R' Yose in the next segment of the mishnah, as will be explained.]

,רַבִּי יוֹסֵי אוֹמֵר: אִם עָבַר הַזָּקֵן וּנְשָׂאָהּ — *R' Yose says: If the [great-]grandfather transgressed and married her,*

The father (Yitzchak) of the man in question (Yaakov) married the woman in question (Rachel) mentioned above (*Rav; Tif. Yis.*).

Marrying a great-granddaughter is forbidden only by Rabbinic decree. Thus, although this marriage is considered a transgression, it nevertheless does take effect, as explained below (*Tif. Yis.*).

As a result of this marriage between the woman and her great-grandfather, an additional *chatas* obligation is created for the situation described above, which involved the cohabitation of the woman and her grandfather. In addition to all the prohibitions mentioned previously, the prohibition of אֵשֶׁת אָב, *father's wife*, is now added, see below (*Rashi; Rav*).

Tos. Yeshanim, however, explain that R' Yose does not agree that all the prohibitions enumerated by the earlier *Tanna* are in force. They postulate that in R' Yose's view the principle of אִיסוּר מוֹסִיף does not apply if the new prohibition is less severe than the original one. In the specific case under discussion — one who transgressed with a granddaughter — only two of the additional prohibitions involved are as severe as (or more severe than) the original prohibition of בַּת בִּתּוֹ, *a daughter's daughter*, which is punishable by שְׂרֵפָה, *death by burning:* that of כַּלָּתוֹ, *daughter-in-law*, punishable by סְקִילָה, *death by stoning*, and אֵשֶׁת אָב, *father's wife*, likewise punishable by שְׂרֵפָה. The other prohibitions mentioned by the earlier *Tanna* are less severe than that of בַּת בִּתּוֹ: that of אֵשֶׁת אִישׁ, *a married woman*, punishable only by חֶנֶק, *death by choking* (considered not as severe as שְׂרֵפָה; see *Sanhedrin* 7:1), and certainly those of אֵשֶׁת אָח (*brother's wife*), אֵשֶׁת אֲחִי אָבִיו (*father's brother's wife*), and a *niddah* (menstruant) punishable only by *kares*, are less severe. Thus, in R' Yose's view, one who cohabits with a granddaughter can be liable for two additional transgressions — כַּלָּתוֹ and אֵשֶׁת אָבִיו.

חַיָּב עָלֶיהָ מִשּׁוּם אֵשֶׁת אָב, — *he is liable for her as his father's wife,*

If Yaakov cohabits with that woman he is liable to another *chatas*, because she is now also prohibited as אֵשֶׁת אָבִיו, *father's wife* (*Rav*).

The *Gemara* (14b) questions the validity of the marriage, inasmuch that it was mentioned previously that the man is liable for *chatas* for the prohibition of אֵשֶׁת אֲחִי אָבִיו, *father's brother's wife* [by virtue of her marriage to Yishmael, Yaakov's uncle]. Once she is married to Yaakov's father's brother, she is automatically forbidden to Yaakov's father [the great-grandfather] because she is his own brother's wife! [A marriage to a woman who is prohibited by a *kares*-punishable offense is not valid.] Therefore, the prohibition of a father's wife should not take effect. The *Gemara* explains that the great-grandfather married her in a situation of *yibum* (levirate marriage), i.e., his brother, to whom she was previously married, died without children [see diagram 4]. Although this woman is in the category of עֲרָיוֹת שְׁנִיּוֹת, *secondary* [Rabbinically prohibited] *arayos*, [both one's great-granddaughter and one's son's daughter-in-law] for whom *yibum* is Rabbinically proscribed (*Yevamos* 2:4, 21b), the transgression of performing such *yibum* is not reason enough to invalidate the marriage[1] (*Rav*).

The prohibition of *father's wife* is considered more comprehensive because it affects more people: If the great-grandfather had another son (besides Yaakov), the prohibition of *father's wife* would now be in force for him as a result of this *yibum* marriage. Hence, just as the prohibition of *father's wife* takes effect regarding the other son, it takes effect regarding Yaakov as well (*Rav* from *Gem.* 14b).

According to some versions, the *Gemara* actually reads כְּגוֹן דְּאִיתְיְלִיד בֶּן קָטָן לְסָבָא, *a young son was born to the great-grandfather.* The significance of the fact that the son in question was young is that he was a minor prior to the marriage of the great-grandfather with the woman under discussion. Otherwise, the woman would have already been prohibited to the son because she had been married to his father's brother (Yishmael) and, as a result, the new marriage to the great-grandfather would not create a prohibition for something previously permitted. However, since the son in question was a minor at the time of the marriage, when he becomes of age, the prohibitions of אֵשֶׁת אֲחִי אָבִיו and אֵשֶׁת אָבִיו will take effect simultaneously (*Rambam Comm.; Tif. Yis.;* cf. *Tos. Yom Tov*).

Nonetheless, *Rambam* (ibid.) expresses amazement that the *Gemara* finds it necessary altogether to explain the additional prohibition with the hypothetical existence of a *son* of the great-grandfather. A simpler solution would have been to state merely that the marriage of the great-grandfather prohibits the woman to his[2] [maternal half-] brothers to whom she was previously permitted. This

1. The marriage should also be invalidated because she is the great-grandfather's daughter-in-law, inasmuch as she was married to Yaakov's brother, as described previously, s.v. ואשת אחיו. However, it may be simply explained that she was married to Yaakov's *maternal* brother, who is not related to Yaakov's father (*Rav* from *Gemara* 14b).

2. Maternal half-brothers are mentioned because only they were permitted previously to

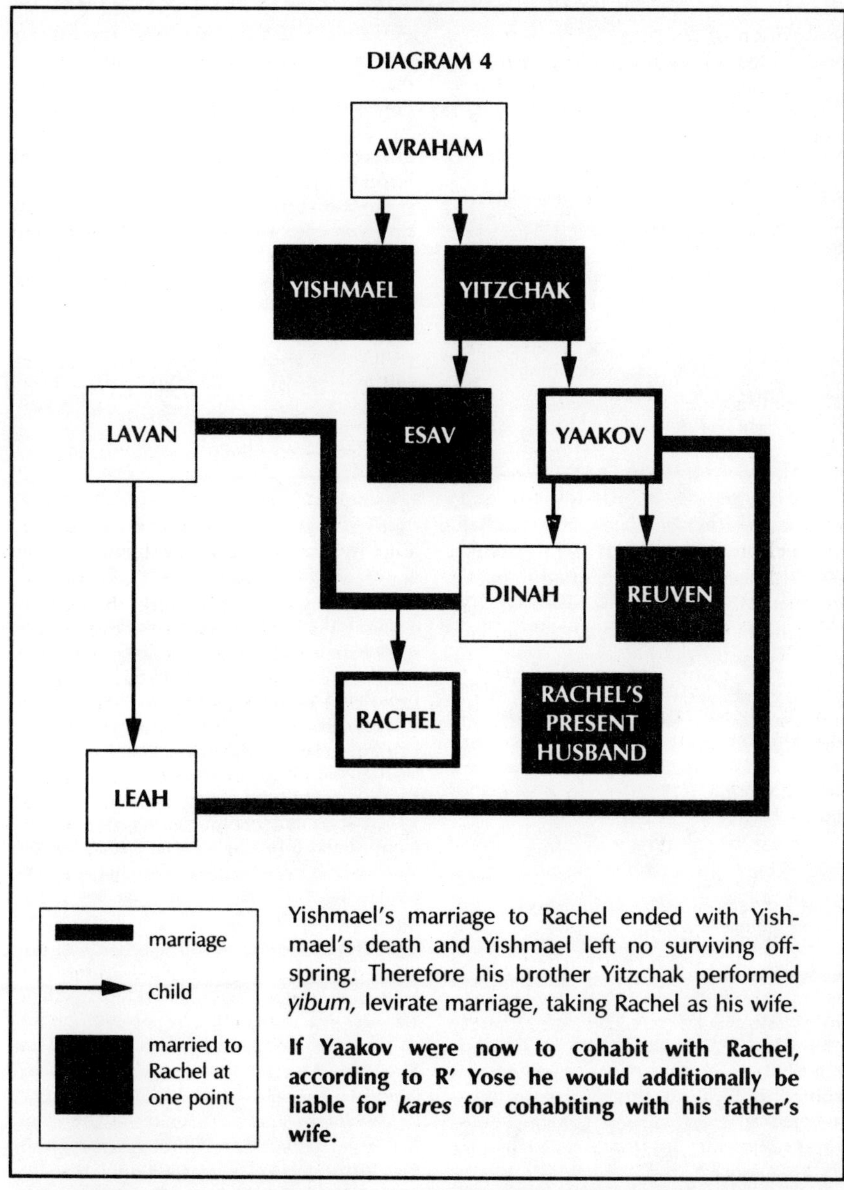
DIAGRAM 4
AVRAHAM
YISHMAEL
YITZCHAK
LAVAN
ESAV
YAAKOV
DINAH
REUVEN
RACHEL
RACHEL'S PRESENT HUSBAND
LEAH
marriage
child
married to Rachel at one point
Yishmael's marriage to Rachel ended with Yishmael's death and Yishmael left no surviving offspring. Therefore his brother Yitzchak performed *yibum,* levirate marriage, taking Rachel as his wife.
If Yaakov were now to cohabit with Rachel, according to R' Yose he would additionally be liable for *kares* for cohabiting with his father's wife.

marry this woman. If she was the wife of the great-grandfather's *paternal* half-brother she was prohibited to the other brothers prior to the great-grandfather's marriage (see *Birkas Hazevach*).

It can be argued, though, that it is not only for maternal half-brothers for whom a new prohibition was created. Since the brother who died left no children, his wife was permitted to all his paternal brothers in fulfillment of the *mitzvah* of *yibum*; when she is married to one of the brothers, the prohibition of אֵשֶׁת אָח is in effect anew. Thus the marriage to the great-grandfather did create a new prohibition, even to the paternal half-brothers. Indeed, this

כְּרִיתוּת עַל בַּת־אִשְׁתּוֹ וְעַל־בַּת בַּת־אִשְׁתּוֹ. ג/ה

יד אברהם

explanation would be consistent with the one offered by the *Gemara* for the previous case. In the Eretz Yisrael versions of the commentary, *Rambam* concludes that this segment of the *Gemara* must have been the addition of the Rabbanan Savurai of the post-Talmudic period. Indeed, in his *Mishneh Torah* (*Hil. Shegagos* 4:2), *Rambam* does not cite the *Gemara's* solution, preferring the other alternative of an additional prohibition to the great-grandfather's brothers, as explained below (*Tos. Yom Tov; Tif. Yis.;* cf. *Aruch LaNer; Likkutim*).

Alternatively, it can be explained that this marriage creates an additional prohibition to the *brothers* of Yitzchak, who — upon the death of the childless Yishmael — were permitted to marry her. Just as because of this new marriage the prohibition of אֵשֶׁת אָח, *brother's wife*, is now in force regarding the brothers of the great-grandfather [Yitzchak], so too does it create the additional prohibition on the grandfather [Yaakov] because of אֵשֶׁת אָב, *father's wife* (*Rambam, Hil. Shegagos* 4:2; cf. *Tos. Yom Tov* and *Tif. Yis.*).

וְכֵן הַבָּא עַל בַּת־אִשְׁתּוֹ — *and so is he who cohabits with his wife's daughter*

If one is intimate with his wife's daughter, he also can be liable to the same number of *chataos* mentioned previously regarding one who is intimate with his own daughter. Just as the result of a combination of circumstances a woman who is his own daughter can be prohibited for a total of six reasons (viz., daughter, sister, brother's wife, uncle's wife, married woman, menstruant), a wife's daughter too can be prohibited for the same six reasons. She can simultaneously be related to him as his wife's daughter, his sister, his brother's wife, his uncle's wife, as well as being prohibited as

a married woman and a menstruant (*Rav; Rambam Comm.*).

The difficulty with this explanation arises: How can one's wife's daughter be his sister? One's *own* daughter can be his sister if he fathered a daughter from an incestuous relationship with his mother, making the child his maternal half-sister. In this circumstance, though, the child can never be his wife's daughter, as he obviously cannot marry the mother of this child, who is his own mother as well.

It is possible in the following manner [see diagram 5]:

Yaakov's father (Yitzchak) had a child (Rachel) from a woman (Leah) out of wedlock. Yaakov then married Leah who, although she is the mother of his father's child, was nonetheless never married to his father. Rachel is thus his wife's daughter and his own paternal half-sister. If Yaakov's maternal half-brother married Rachel, she became prohibited also as his brother's wife. If his brother died or divorced her and then she married Yaakov's father's brother, she is further prohibited as the wife of Yaakov's father's brother and also as a married woman. When she menstruates, she is prohibited to her husband, effecting another prohibition on Yaakov. If Yaakov cohabits with her inadvertently, he is liable to six *chataos* (*Rav; Rambam; Tif. Yis.*).

Although in the case described there is a possibility of a seventh *chatas*, for this woman (Rachel) could be married to Yaakov's son as well (creating the prohibition of daughter-in-law), the Mishnah wanted to keep the cases similar to each other: The *chataos* for which one can be liable as a result of cohabitation with his own daughter can also apply to his wife's daughter; those which may possibly arise from cohabitation with his own granddaughter may also apply to his wife's granddaughter. Thus, just as one's own daughter can never be his daughter-in-law this prohibition is not mentioned in connection with his wife's daughter (*Tif. Yis.*). [This explanation, however, is disputed by the one

is indicated by the absence of any mention of maternal half-brother in the citation of this case by *Rambam* (*Hil. Shegagos* 4:2), as below (*Aruch LaNer*).

3 father's wife, and so is he who cohabits with his wife's
5 daughter or with his wife's daughter's daughter.

YAD AVRAHAM

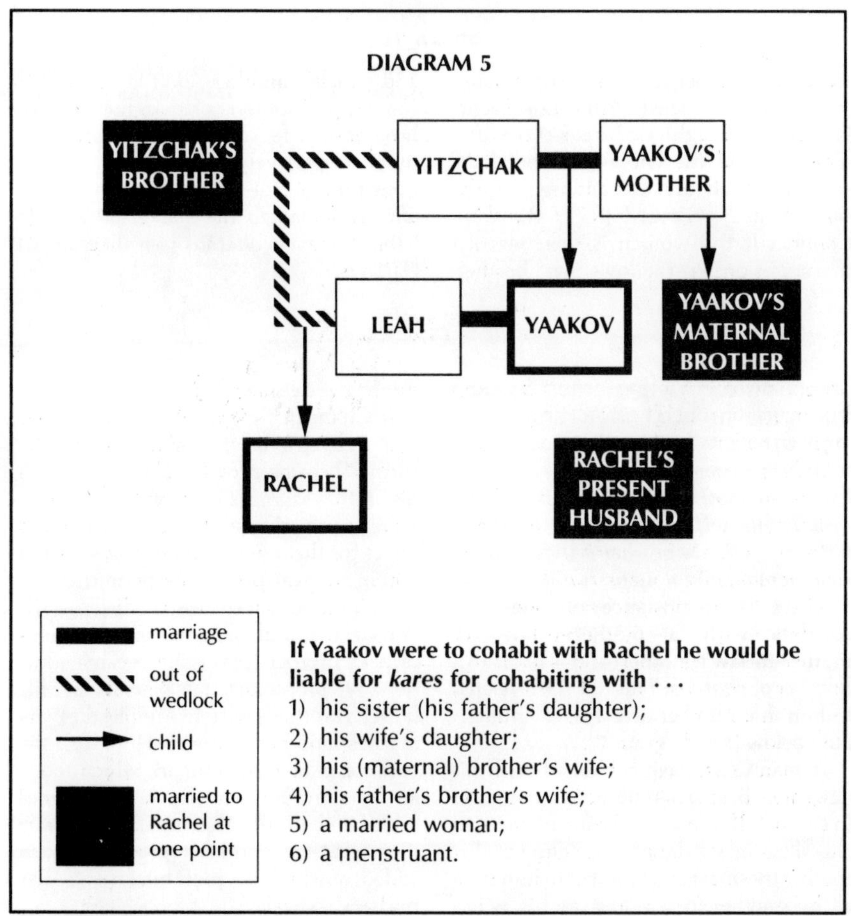

DIAGRAM 5
YITZCHAK'S BROTHER
YITZCHAK
YAAKOV'S MOTHER
LEAH
YAAKOV
YAAKOV'S MATERNAL BROTHER
RACHEL
RACHEL'S PRESENT HUSBAND
marriage
out of wedlock
child
married to Rachel at one point
If Yaakov were to cohabit with Rachel he would be liable for *kares* for cohabiting with . . .
1) his sister (his father's daughter);
2) his wife's daughter;
3) his (maternal) brother's wife;
4) his father's brother's wife;
5) a married woman;
6) a menstruant.

cited in the next paragraph.]

According to others, the mishnah means that for one's wife's daughter [and granddaughter], one can be liable for the seven *chataos* mentioned previously in connection with his granddaughter, i.e., daughter-in-law, brother's wife, etc. (*Rashi*).

וְעַל־בַּת בַּת־אִשְׁתּוֹ. — *or with his wife's daughter's daughter.*

Someone who cohabits with his wife's granddaughter can be liable to the same number of *chataos* mentioned previously in connection with someone who cohabits with his own daughter's daughter [viz. she can be his daughter-in-law, wife's sister, brother's wife, father's brother's wife, married woman, menstruant] (*Rav*).

It is possible for a woman to be both his wife's sister and his wife's granddaughter in the following manner. Lavan was intimate with the daughter of his daugh-

הַבָּא עַל־חֲמוֹתוֹ חַיָּב עָלֶיהָ מִשּׁוּם חֲמוֹתוֹ, וְכַלָּתוֹ, וַאֲחוֹת אִשְׁתּוֹ, וְאֵשֶׁת אָחִיו, וְאֵשֶׁת אֲחִי אָבִיו, וְאֵשֶׁת אִישׁ, וְנִדָּה. וְכֵן הַבָּא

יד אברהם

ter Leah and begot a daughter Rachel. Yaakov then married Leah. Thus Rachel is both the daughter of Yaakov's wife's daughter and his wife's [paternal half] sister [as both are the children of the same man — Lavan] (*Rav; Rambam Comm.*). If the woman is then married in succession to Yaakov's son, brother, and uncle, another *chatas* is added for the prohibitions of daughter-in-law, brother's wife, and father's brother's wife, respectively. When the obligations for a married woman and menstruant are added to the above, he will be liable to seven *chataos* [see diagram 6] (*Tif. Yis.*).

6.

הַבָּא עַל־חֲמוֹתוֹ חַיָּב עָלֶיהָ מִשּׁוּם חֲמוֹתוֹ, וְכַלָּתוֹ, וַאֲחוֹת אִשְׁתּוֹ, וְאֵשֶׁת אָחִיו, וְאֵשֶׁת אֲחִי אָבִיו, וְאֵשֶׁת אִישׁ, וְנִדָּה. — *He who cohabits with his mother-in-law may be liable for her as his mother-in-law, his daughter-in-law, his wife's sister, his brother's wife, his father's brother's wife, a married woman, and a menstruant.*

There is an instance of one who cohabits with a mother-in-law (or mother-in-law's mother) and is liable to a number of *chataos*. This is if she is related to him in a number of ways, as enumerated below [see diagram 7].

A man (Yishmael) cohabited with his daughter (Bosmas), who bore a daughter (Yehudis). If someone (Reuven) married this illegitimate daughter (Yehudis), her mother (Bosmas) is prohibited to him both as his mother-in-law and as his wife's (paternal) half-sister, since both mother and daughter are children of the same father (Yishmael). Both prohibitions — against his mother-in-law and his wife's sister — apply, since they took effect simultaneously (at the time of the marriage). If Reuven's son (Chanoch) subsequently married Bosmas, she became further prohibited to Reuven as his daughter-in-law. [This is an אִיסוּר כּוֹלֵל, *more inclusive prohibition*, because this marriage creates the additional prohibition of *brother's wife* to Chanoch's brother, if he has one.]

If Chanoch then died or divorced her and Reuven's brother married her, she further became prohibited to Reuven as his brother's wife. [This prohibition, too, is more comprehensive because it takes effect for the other brothers of Reuven to whom she was previously permitted.]

If Shimon subsequently died or divorced her and she married Reuven's father's brother (Esav), she became additionally prohibited to Reuven as his father's brother's wife. If, after he dies, she marries another [unrelated] party, she becomes a married woman, which too is an אִיסוּר כּוֹלֵל since she now becomes prohibited to all other men. When she menstruates, another prohibition is added, one which prohibits her to her husband as well.

In summary, then, Bosmas is now prohibited to Reuven as (1) his mother-in-law, since she is the mother of his wife, Yehudis; (2) his daughter-in-law, because she was married to his son Chanoch; (3) his wife's sister, since both she and her mother (Bosmas) are the daughters of Yishmael; (4) his brother's wife, since she was married to Shimon; (5) his aunt, since she was married to Esav, his father's brother. In addition, she is also (6) a married woman and (7) a menstruant (*Rav; Rambam Comm.*).

3 6. He who cohabits with his mother-in-law may be
6 liable for her as his mother-in-law, his daughter-in-law, his wife's sister, his brother's wife, his father's brother's wife, a married woman, and a menstruant.

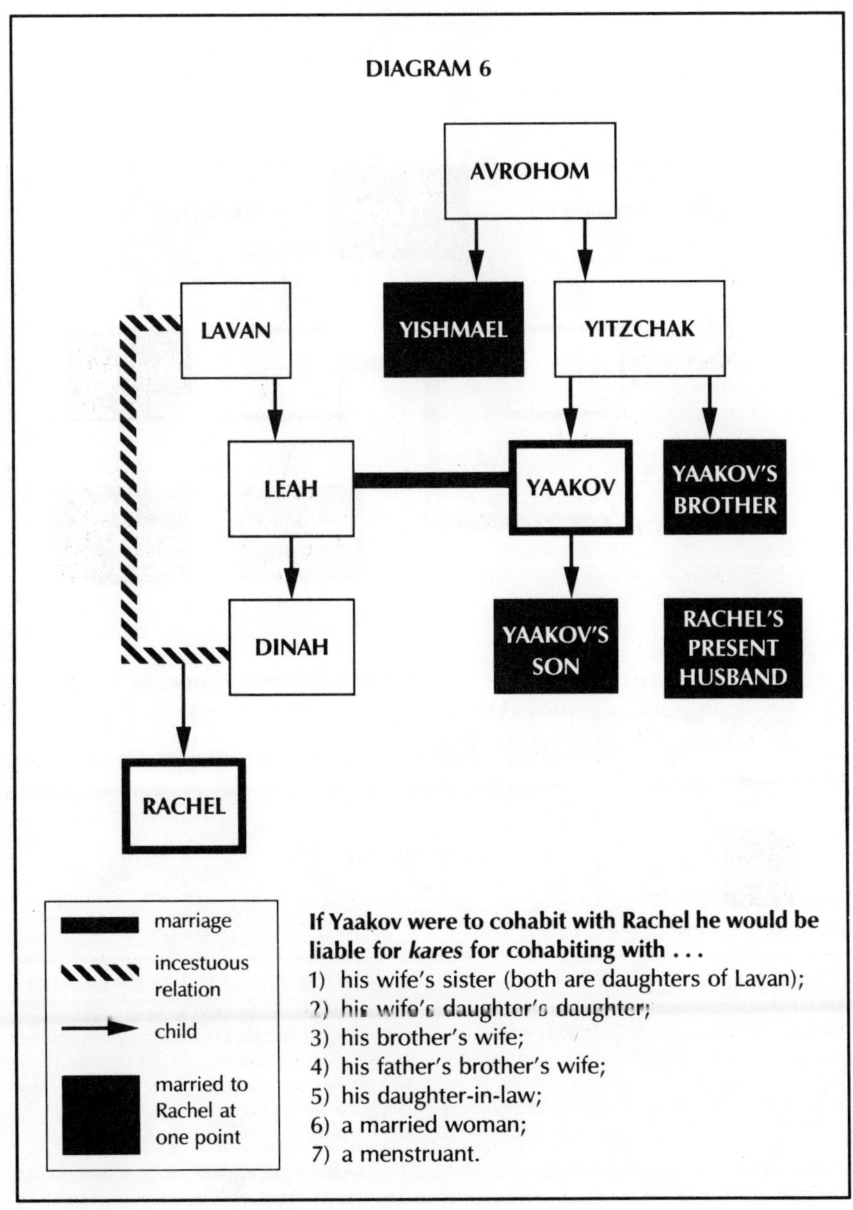
DIAGRAM 6
AVROHOM
LAVAN
YISHMAEL
YITZCHAK
LEAH
YAAKOV
YAAKOV'S BROTHER
DINAH
YAAKOV'S SON
RACHEL'S PRESENT HUSBAND
RACHEL
marriage
incestuous relation
child
married to Rachel at one point
If Yaakov were to cohabit with Rachel he would be liable for *kares* for cohabiting with . . .
1) his wife's sister (both are daughters of Lavan);
2) his wife's daughter's daughter;
3) his brother's wife;
4) his father's brother's wife;
5) his daughter-in-law;
6) a married woman;
7) a menstruant.

עַל־אֵם חֲמוֹתוֹ וְעַל־אֵם חָמִיו. רַבִּי יוֹחָנָן בֶּן נוּרִי

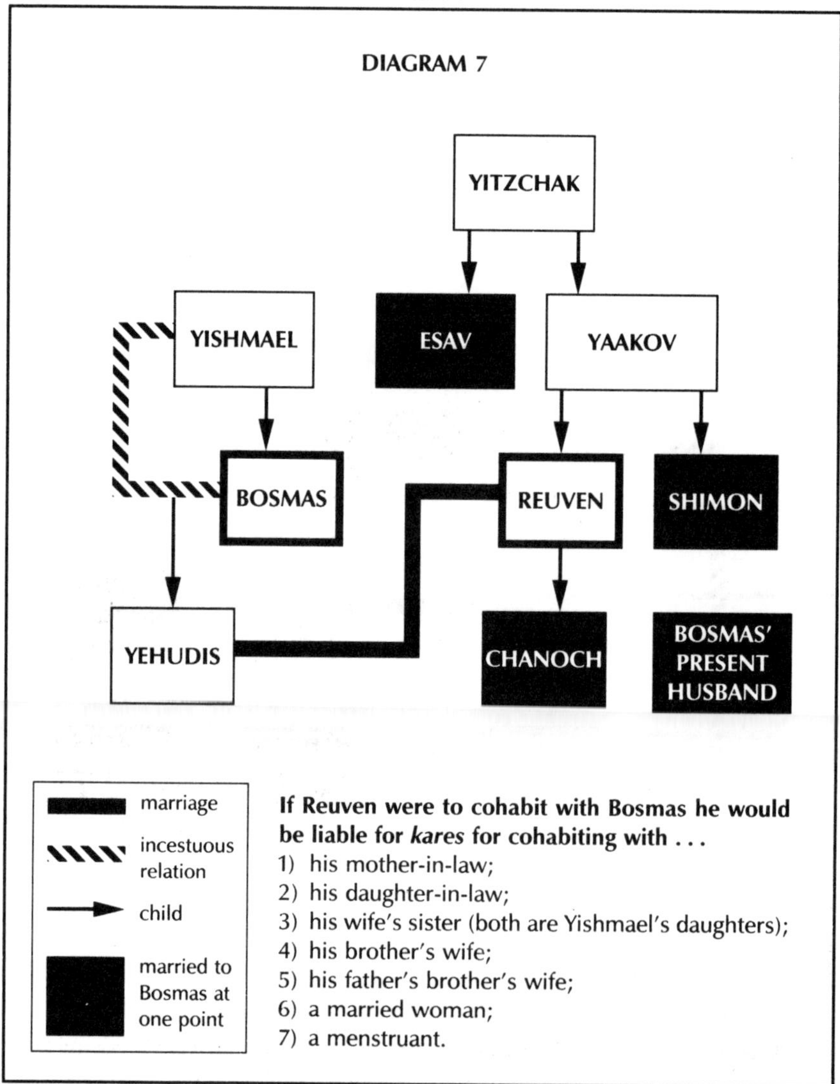
DIAGRAM 7
YITZCHAK
YISHMAEL
ESAV
YAAKOV
BOSMAS
REUVEN
SHIMON
YEHUDIS
CHANOCH
BOSMAS' PRESENT HUSBAND
marriage
incestuous relation
child
married to Bosmas at one point
If Reuven were to cohabit with Bosmas he would be liable for kares for cohabiting with . . .
1) his mother-in-law;
2) his daughter-in-law;
3) his wife's sister (both are Yishmael's daughters);
4) his brother's wife;
5) his father's brother's wife;
6) a married woman;
7) a menstruant.

Instead of using an illustration of a woman who is the offspring of an incestuous union between a father and a daughter, others explain that a man's mother-in-law can be his sister-in-law also through permissible marriages in the following manner [see diagram 8]: Leah and Rachel were sisters. Leah had a daughter named Dinah. Yaakov married Dinah, and his son Reuven married her mother Leah. Leah became prohibited to Yaakov as his mother-in-law and his daughter-in-law. Then Dinah, Yaakov's wife, died[1] and he

1. [It is not clear why this detail is necessary; Yaakov would be permitted to marry Rachel even if Dinah was still alive for she is not his wife's sister (cf. *Rashi, Kesubos* 77a s.v. ליתני).]

3 And so is he who cohabits with his mother-in-law's
6 mother or his father-in-law's mother. R' Yochanan ben

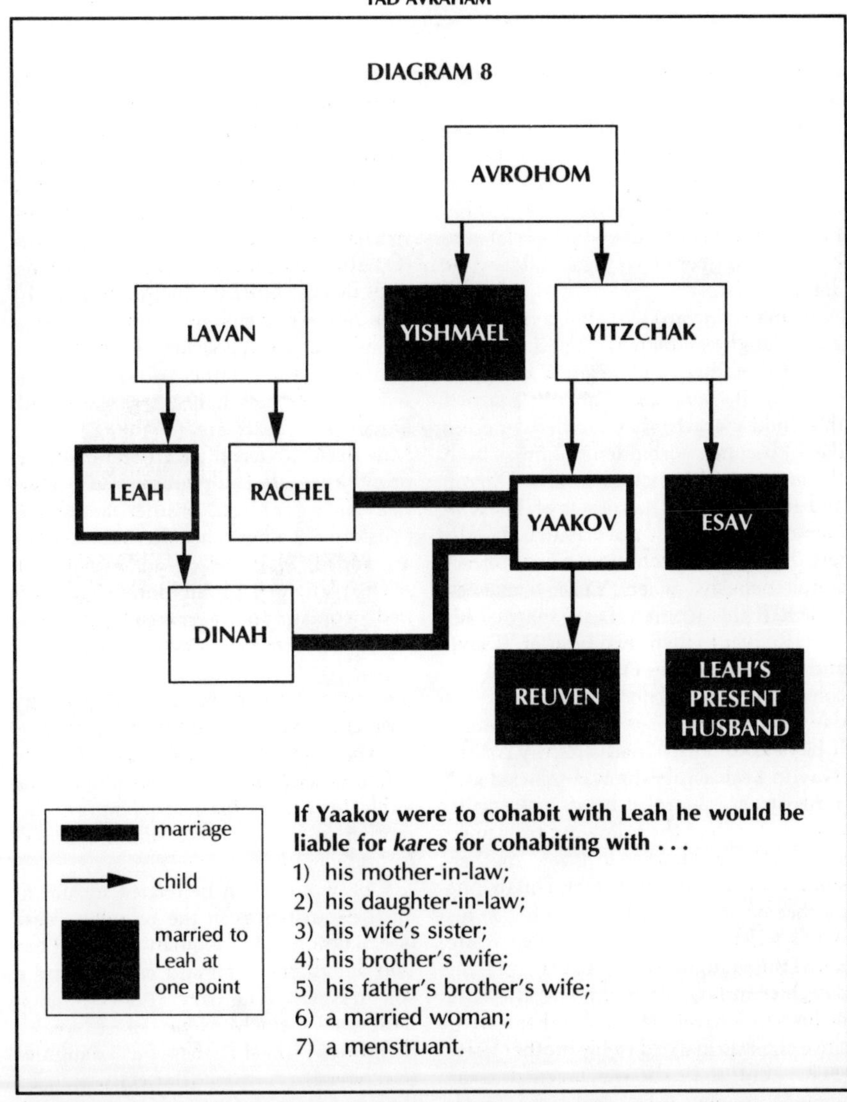
DIAGRAM 8
AVROHOM
LAVAN
YISHMAEL
YITZCHAK
LEAH
RACHEL
YAAKOV
ESAV
DINAH
REUVEN
LEAH'S PRESENT HUSBAND
marriage
child
married to Leah at one point
If Yaakov were to cohabit with Leah he would be liable for *kares* for cohabiting with . . .
1) his mother-in-law;
2) his daughter-in-law;
3) his wife's sister;
4) his brother's wife;
5) his father's brother's wife;
6) a married woman;
7) a menstruant.

married Rachel, Leah's sister. Leah then became further prohibited to Yaakov as his wife's sister. [This is an אִיסוּר כּוֹלֵל if there were other sisters who also became prohibited to him.] If Reuven died and Leah married in succession Esav, the brother of Yaakov, and Yishmael, Yaakov's uncle, the prohibitions of his brother's wife and his father's brother's wife apply, as well as those of married woman, and menstruant, as explained above (*Tif. Yis.*; *Reshash*, see *Aruch LaNer*).

וְכֵן הַבָּא עַל־אֵם חֲמוֹתוֹ וְעַל־אֵם חָמִיו. — *And so is he who cohabits with his mother-in-*

אוֹמֵר: הַבָּא עַל־חֲמוֹתוֹ חַיָּב עָלֶיהָ מִשּׁוּם חֲמוֹתוֹ, וְאֵם חֲמוֹתוֹ, וְאֵם חָמִיו. אָמְרוּ לוֹ:

יד אברהם

law's mother or his father-in-law's mother.

One can also be liable to all the *chataos* mentioned previously if he cohabits with his mother-in-law's mother or his father-in-law's mother. A mother in-law's mother can likewise be related to him in a number of ways, as follows [see diagram 9].

A man (Lavan) cohabited with his granddaughter (Dinah), his daughter's (Leah) daughter, and begot a daughter (Serach). If someone (Yaakov) married this child (Serach), her mother's mother (Leah) becomes forbidden to him as both the mother of his mother-in-law (Dinah), and the (paternal) half-sister of his wife (Serach), since both are Lavan's daughters. Both these prohibitions took effect simultaneously, when Yaakov married Serach. If this woman (Leah) married his son (Reuven), then his brother (Esav), and then his uncle (Yishmael), she becomes further related to him as his daughter-in-law, sister-in-law and aunt. If he (Yaakov) then inadvertently cohabits with Leah while she was married and a menstruant, he must bring a *chatas* to atone for each of the following transgressions: (1) his mother-in-law's mother, since Leah is the mother of Dinah, the mother of Serach, Yaakov's wife, (2) his wife's sister, since Leah and Serach are both the daughters of Lavan, (3) his daughter-in-law, since she was the wife of his son Reuven, (4) his brother's wife, since she was married to his brother Esav, (5) his aunt, since she was married to his uncle Yishmael, (6) a married woman and (7) a menstruant, which are self-explanatory. Each of these succeeding prohibitions are more comprehensive than the previous ones (אִיסוּר כּוֹלֵל) for the reasons explained above (*Rav; Rambam, Comm.; Tif. Yis.*).

The manner in which he can be obligated for these *chataos* by cohabiting with his father-in-law's mother is as follows [see diagram 10]. Someone (Reuven) cohabited with his grandmother (Milkah), his mother's (Leah) mother, and she bore him a daughter (Dinah). Someone else (Yissachar) married this illegitimate daughter (Dinah). Her father's (Reuven) mother (Leah) is prohibited to Yissachar both as the mother of his father-in-law and his wife's (maternal) half-sister, since both Dinah and Leah are the daughters of Milkah. As above, these are simultaneous prohibitions. If Leah subsequently marries Yissachar's son, brother, and uncle (Yaakov's brother), the other prohibitions are added, as above, in addition to the self-explanatory prohibitions of a married woman and a menstruant (*Rav; Rambam, Comm.*).

רַבִּי יוֹחָנָן בֶּן נוּרִי אוֹמֵר: הַבָּא עַל־חֲמוֹתוֹ חַיָּב עָלֶיהָ מִשּׁוּם חֲמוֹתוֹ, וְאֵם חֲמוֹתוֹ, וְאֵם חָמִיו. — *R' Yochanan ben Nuri says: He who cohabits with his mother-in-law can be liable for her as his mother-in-law, his mother-in-law's mother, and his father-in-law's mother.*

One woman can be related to him in all these instances in the following case [see diagram 11]: A woman (Chavah) has two daughters (Leah and Rachel), and a son (Asher). The son (Asher) has a daughter (Serach). One of Chavah's daughters (Leah) has a daughter (Yocheved). A man (Reuven) married both of Chavah's granddaughters Serach and Yocheved, as well as her daughter Rachel. Consequently, Chavah is at one time his mother-in-law, since she is the mother of his wife, Rachel; his mother-in-law's mother, since she is the mother of Leah, the mother of his wife

3
6 Nuri says: He who cohabits with his mother-in-law can be liable for her as his mother-in-law, mother-in-law's mother, and father-in-law's mother. They said to him:

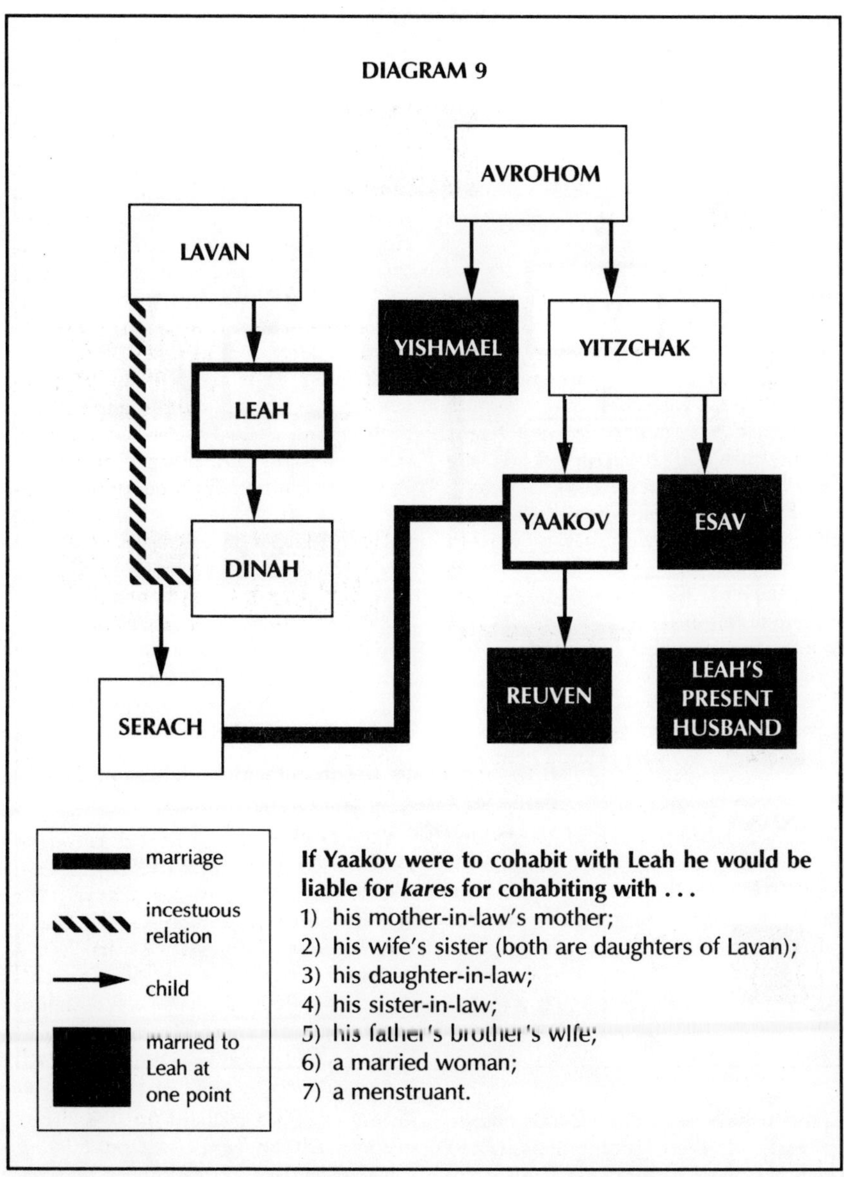
DIAGRAM 9
AVROHOM
LAVAN
YISHMAEL
YITZCHAK
LEAH
YAAKOV
ESAV
DINAH
SERACH
REUVEN
LEAH'S PRESENT HUSBAND
marriage
incestuous relation
child
married to Leah at one point
If Yaakov were to cohabit with Leah he would be liable for *kares* for cohabiting with . . .
1) his mother-in-law's mother;
2) his wife's sister (both are daughters of Lavan);
3) his daughter-in-law;
4) his sister-in-law;
5) his father's brother's wife;
6) a married woman;
7) a menstruant.

Yocheved; and his father-in-law's mother, since she is the mother of Asher, the father of his wife Serach. Therefore, if Reuven cohabits with this woman

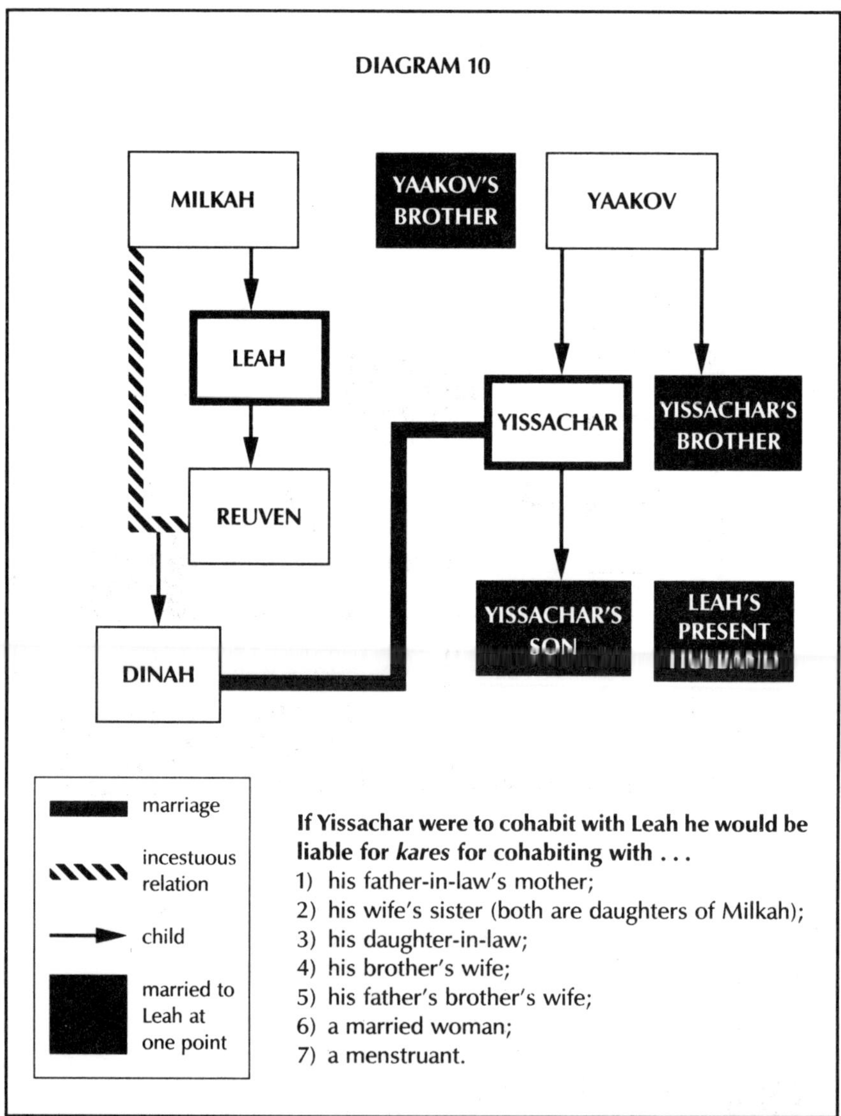
DIAGRAM 10
MILKAH
YAAKOV'S BROTHER
YAAKOV
LEAH
YISSACHAR
YISSACHAR'S BROTHER
REUVEN
YISSACHAR'S SON
LEAH'S PRESENT
DINAH
marriage
incestuous relation
child
married to Leah at one point
If Yissachar were to cohabit with Leah he would be liable for kares for cohabiting with . . .
1) his father-in-law's mother;
2) his wife's sister (both are daughters of Milkah);
3) his daughter-in-law;
4) his brother's wife;
5) his father's brother's wife;
6) a married woman;
7) a menstruant.

(Chavah), he is liable to a separate *chatas* for each of these prohibitions (*Rav; Rashi; Rambam Comm.; Tif. Yis.*).

Presumably, Reuven married each of these three women in successive marriages. Then it must be concluded that the successive marriages are each considered creating a more comprehensive prohibition than the preceding one, because each time the woman's other relatives become prohibited

The three of them are of one denomination.

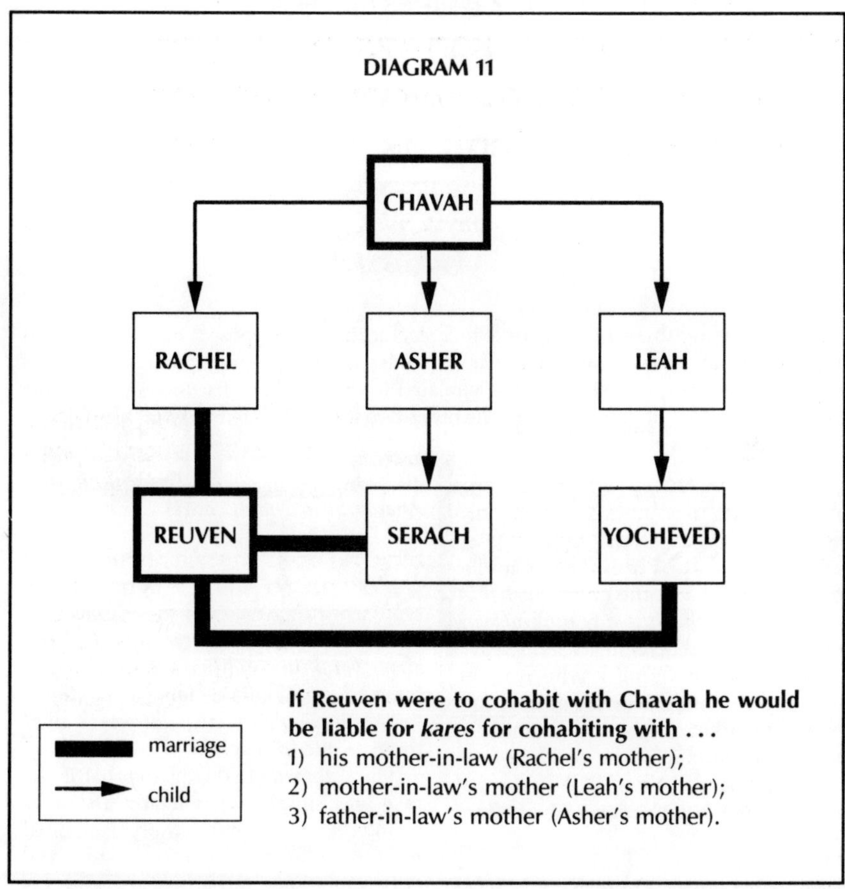
DIAGRAM 11
CHAVAH
RACHEL
ASHER
LEAH
REUVEN
SERACH
YOCHEVED
marriage
child
If Reuven were to cohabit with Chavah he would be liable for *kares* for cohabiting with . . .
1) his mother-in-law (Rachel's mother);
2) mother-in-law's mother (Leah's mother);
3) father-in-law's mother (Asher's mother).

as a result. Therefore, just as the prohibition of his wife's sister, for example, takes effect, so does the prohibition of his wife's mother's mother take effect, even though she was already prohibited as his wife's mother (*Rashash*; see there for alternate explanations).

אָמְרוּ לוֹ: שְׁלָשְׁתָּן שֵׁם אֶחָד הֵן. — *They said to him: The three of them are of one denomination.*

[The Sages said to R' Yochanan ben Nuri:] All of these prohibitions are derived from one verse and included in one negative commandment: עֶרְוַת אִשָּׁה וּבִתָּהּ לֹא תְגַלֵּה אֶת־בַּת־בְּנָהּ וְאֶת־בַּת־בִּתָּהּ לֹא תִקַּח לְגַלּוֹת עֶרְוָתָהּ שַׁאֲרָה הֵנָּה זִמָּה הִוא, *Do not uncover the nakedness of a woman and her daughter; do not take her son's daughter or her daughter's daughter to uncover her nakedness — they are close relatives, it is a depraved plot* (*Lev.* 18:17). Therefore, there is no separation effected regarding *chatas* [because it is considered as if he repeated the same transgression three times, rather than transgressed three distinct prohibitions] (*Rav; Rashi,* cf. *Rambam Comm.*).

The halachah is in accordance with the Sages (*Rav; Rambam Comm.*).

[ז] **אָמַר** רַבִּי עֲקִיבָא: שָׁאַלְתִּי אֶת־רַבָּן גַּמְלִיאֵל וְאֶת־רַבִּי יְהוֹשֻׁעַ בְּאִטְלִיס שֶׁל־אֶמָּאוּם שֶׁהָלְכוּ לִקַּח בְּהֵמָה לְמִשְׁתֵּה בְנוֹ שֶׁל־רַבָּן גַּמְלִיאֵל: הַבָּא עַל־אֲחוֹתוֹ, וְעַל־אֲחוֹת אָבִיו, וְעַל־אֲחוֹת אִמּוֹ, בְּהֶעְלֵם אֶחָד — מַהוּ? חַיָּב אַחַת עַל־כֻּלָּן אוֹ אַחַת עַל־כָּל־אַחַת וְאַחַת?

יד אברהם

7.

The following three mishnayos cite halachic questions posed by R' Akiva to Rabban Gamliel when the latter was in midst of the preparations for his son's wedding. The first of these questions is related to the previous discussion of multiple *chataos* for one act of cohabitation. The other two are mentioned only incidentally as they were asked at the same time.

אָמַר רַבִּי עֲקִיבָא: שָׁאַלְתִּי אֶת־רַבָּן גַּמְלִיאֵל וְאֶת־רַבִּי יְהוֹשֻׁעַ בְּאִטְלִיס שֶׁל־אֶמָּאוּם שֶׁהָלְכוּ לִקַּח בְּהֵמָה לְמִשְׁתֵּה בְנוֹ שֶׁל־רַבָּן גַּמְלִיאֵל: — *Said R' Akiva: I asked Rabban Gamliel and R' Yehoshua in the meat market of Emmaus when they went to purchase an animal for Rabban Gamliel's son's feast:*

While Rabban Gamliel who was the *Nasi*, and R' Yehoshua were in the cattle and meat market of the town Emmaus to purchase an animal for the wedding feast of Rabban Gamliel's son [R' Akiva posed the following halachic questions] (*Rav; Tif. Yis.*).

The mishnah mentions that this exchange took place in the marketplace in the course of wedding-feast preparations to teach that the Sages were neither too preoccupied with their own affairs to answer any question nor were they ashamed to admit their ignorance in the presence of the multitude milling in the meat market (*Shoshannim LeDavid; Tif. Yis.*).

[Others explain that the mishnah mentions that Rabban Gamliel and R' Yehoshua went to the marketplace to prepare for a wedding feast to teach us that, as a rule, the Sages went into the marketplace only for matters of *mitzvos*, such as a wedding preparation,[1] and even then, they did not refrain from discussing Torah matters (*Tos.* 15a; *Korban Aharon, Sifra Chatas* ch. 1).]

הַבָּא עַל־אֲחוֹתוֹ, וְעַל־אֲחוֹת אָבִיו, וְעַל־אֲחוֹת אִמּוֹ, בְּהֶעְלֵם אֶחָד — מַהוּ? חַיָּב אַחַת עַל־כֻּלָּן אוֹ אַחַת עַל־כָּל־אַחַת וְאַחַת? — *One who cohabits with his sister, his father's sister, and his mother's sister, in one lapse of awareness — what is he [liable for]? Is he liable to one [chatas] for all of them or one for each?*

The *Gemara* (15a) explains that if the case was simply what it appears to be *prima facie*, i.e., one simply cohabited with these three women — his sister and two aunts (his father's sister and his mother's sister) — there would be no question: He transgressed three distinct prohibitions with three separate people and is certainly liable to three *chataos*. The question, rather, involves cohabitation with one woman who is prohibited by three prohibitions, i.e., she is at the same time his sister, his father's sister, and his mother's sister. This is possible in the following case [see diagram 12]: A man (Reuven) fathered daughters

1. In *Kiddushin* (32b), the *Gemara* relates that at the wedding feast of Rabban Gamliel's son, Rabban Gamliel personally attended to the needs of his guests. This conduct was challenged at the time by R' Eliezer, who felt that it was unfitting to the position of Rabban Gamliel, the

3 7. **S**aid R′ Akiva: I asked Rabban Gamliel and R′
7 Yehoshua in the meat market of Emmaus when they went to purchase an animal for Rabban Gamliel's son's feast: One who cohabits with his sister, his father's sister, and his mother's sister, in one lapse of awareness — what is he [liable for]? Is he liable to one [*chatas*] for all of them or one for each? And they

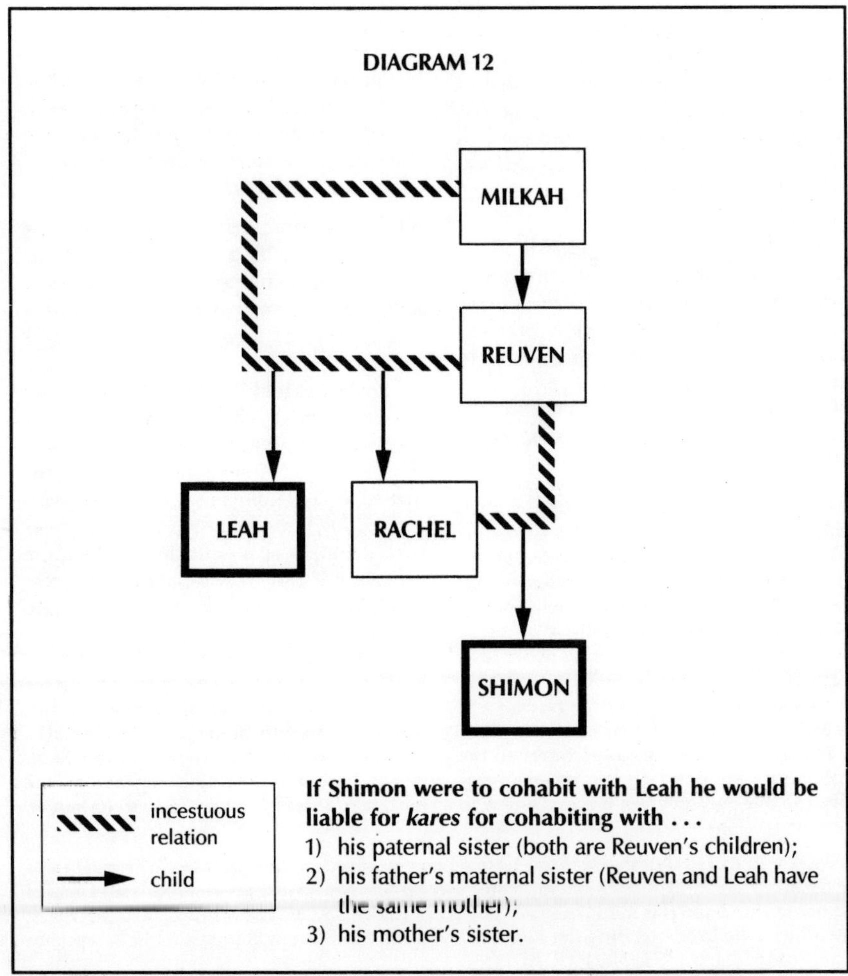
DIAGRAM 12
MILKAH
REUVEN
LEAH
RACHEL
SHIMON
incestuous relation
child
If Shimon were to cohabit with Leah he would be liable for *kares* for cohabiting with . . .
1) his paternal sister (both are Reuven's children);
2) his father's maternal sister (Reuven and Leah have the same mother);
3) his mother's sister.

Nasi, to lower himself in this manner. R′ Yehoshua then defended Rabban Gamliel's actions by articulating the dictum נָשִׂיא שֶׁמָּחַל עַל כְּבוֹדוֹ, כְּבוֹדוֹ מָחוּל, *[when] a Nasi forgoes his honor, his honor may be overlooked.*

Although this story is not related anywhere in a mishnah, our mishnah can be taken as an

וְאָמְרוּ לִי: לֹא שָׁמַעְנוּ, אֲבָל שָׁמַעְנוּ, הַבָּא עַל־חָמֵשׁ נָשָׁיו נִדּוֹת, בְּהֶעְלֵם אֶחָד, שֶׁהוּא חַיָּב עַל־כָּל־אַחַת וְאַחַת, וְרוֹאִין אָנוּ שֶׁהַדְּבָרִים קַל וָחֹמֶר.

יד אברהם

(Rachel and Leah) from an incestuous relationship with his mother. He later fathered a son (Shimon) by an incestuous relationship with one of his daughters (Rachel). If this son (Shimon) cohabits with the other daughter (Leah), he has transgressed three negative precepts, as she is at once his own (paternal) half-sister, his father's (maternal) half-sister and his mother's (full) sister.

What R' Akiva meant to ask, then, was: Do we say that since the sin is committed with one person,[1] he is liable to only one *chatas*, or since it involves three distinct prohibitions, he is liable to three *chataos*? (*Gem.* 15a).

One may well ask that in the course of the preceding mishnayos it was made amply clear that cohabitation with a woman to whom one is related in a number of ways is sufficient cause for multiple *chataos*, as long as each prohibition took effect. Since this woman is obviously prohibited by three distinct prohibitions (which take effect simultaneously, viz., at the moment of his birth), why should there be any question of multiple *chataos*? We must conclude, therefore, that in our case, the prohibitions are really similar, i.e., all three are a form of sister — his own, his father's and his mother's [a situation that was not present in any of the preceding cases]. Since all the prohibitions are based on her being a sister (albeit to different people), it is analogous to one prohibition (*Shitah Mekubetzes* from *Rosh*).

וְאָמְרוּ לִי: לֹא שָׁמַעְנוּ, — *And they replied to me: [This] we have not heard,*

The Sages replied: We have received no teaching regarding a sin committed with one person by which one transgresses three negative commandments (*Chafetz Chayim* on *Sifra*, ch. 1 of *Chatas*).

אֲבָל שָׁמַעְנוּ הַבָּא עַל־חָמֵשׁ נָשָׁיו נִדּוֹת, בְּהֶעְלֵם אֶחָד, שֶׁהוּא חַיָּב עַל־כָּל־אַחַת וְאַחַת, — *but we have heard that one who cohabits with his five menstruous wives, in a single lapse of awareness, is liable for each one,*

[The Sages told R' Akiva: Although we have no explicit teaching regarding your case, we do have a ruling of a similar case. If, in one lapse of awareness, a person cohabits with a number of his wives who are *niddos* (menstruants), we do not regard it simply as a repetition of the same offense but rather as separate transgressions, each of which occasion a separate *chatas*.]

The phrase in the mishnah חָמֵשׁ נָשָׁיו נִדּוֹת, *his five menstruous wives*, is misleading for the prohibition of *niddah* applies to any woman — his wife or not, as is clearly stated by *Rama* in *Shulchan Aruch* (*Yoreh Deah* 183:1). Indeed in alternate versions of the mishnah (*Makkos* 14a; *Toras Kohanim*,

allusion to it. By relating that Rabban Gamliel was involved in the purchase of the meat to be served at the wedding, the *Tanna* intimates that despite his exalted position, Rabban Gamliel did not refrain from this mundane task. It was for this reason that he was accompanied by R' Yehoshua, who later — during the course of the wedding — brought proofs to the acceptance of this conduct (*Aruch LaNer*).

1. According to this explanation, the words בְּהֶעְלֵם אֶחָד, *in one lapse of awareness*, are totally inappropriate; since it was, in fact, only one act that was performed, it goes without saying that it was done in one *he'elam*. Indeed, in the mishnah printed with the *Gemara*, these words do not appear. In some manuscripts, the wording is simply בְּהֶעְלֵם, *in a state of forgetfulness* (see *Shinuyei Nuschaos* and *Rashash*).

3 replied to me: [This] we have not heard, but we have
7 heard that one who cohabits with his five menstruous
wives, in a single lapse of awareness, is liable for each
one, and we believe that the matter is a *kal vachomer*.

YAD AVRAHAM

Chataos 1), the text reads חָמֵשׁ נָשִׁים נִדּוֹת, *five menstruous women* (*Kol Sofer*; cf. *Hon Ashir*).

.וְרוֹאִין אָנוּ שֶׁהַדְּבָרִים קַל וָחֹמֶר — *and we believe that the matter is a kal vachomer.*

The Sages (Rabban Gamliel and R' Yehoshua) concluded their answer to R' Akiva's question by means of a *kal vachomer* (a fortiori reasoning): If one who cohabits with five *niddos,* who are all prohibited by the same negative commandment, is liable to five *chataos*, then one who transgresses by cohabiting with his sister who is also his father's sister and his mother's sister — an act prohibited by three separate negative commandments — should surely be liable to a *chatas* for each one (*Rav* from *Gem.* 15a).

The *Gemara* (ibid.) notes that this *kal vachomer* is actually inconclusive; it can be refuted by arguing that the case of the five *niddos* is different since each woman is regarded separately, as she is a distinct person. [This principle is referred to as גּוּפִין מְחֻלָּקִים, *distinct persons* (lit., *bodies*), a factor which creates a separate *chatas* obligation.] Our case, by contrast, involves a woman who is triply prohibited, but only one person. [This is called שֵׁמוֹת מְחֻלָּקִים, *distinct categories*, which according to R' Akiva's question may not be sufficient grounds to create a separate *chatas* obligation.]

The *Gemara* concludes, therefore, that in actuality the ruling calling for separate *chataos* in our case is Scripturally derived from the Torah's superfluous phrase עֶרְוַת אֲחֹתוֹ גִּלָּה, *he exposed his sister's nakedness* (*Lev.* 20:17). This teaches that there is a separate *chatas* obligation for each type of sister [his, his father's and his mother's] even though they coincide in one person (*Rav; Rambam Comm.;* see *Tos.* 15a).

Rabban Gamliel and R' Yehoshua, who state the *kal vachomer* and do not consider its refutation, apparently believe that the fact of שֵׁמוֹת מְחֻלָּקִים, *distinct categories*, is a stronger distinguishing factor than the fact of גּוּפִין מְחֻלָּקִים, *distinct people*. Therefore, they reason that if the Torah required separate *chataos* for cohabitation with five *niddos* only by virtue of the fact that they are distinct people, then certainly the Torah requires separate *chataos* from one who cohabits with his sister, who is his father's sister and his mother's sister, which are distinct categories (*Korban Aharon; Tif. Yis.*).

8.

This mishnah deals with the subject of *tumah* regarding limbs which are [about to be] removed from a living animal [or person].

A limb removed from a living animal is called אֵבֶר מִן הַחַי, *limb [removed] from the living*, which is forbidden to be eaten and has the status of *neveilah* [ritually unslaughtered carcass] as far as *tumah* is concerned. Thus, this severed limb can transmit *tumah* to other people or utensils through מַגָּע וּמַשָּׂא, *contact and lifting*. Likewise, the severed limb of a living person has the status of a corpse as far as these forms of *tumah* are concerned. The question of the mishnah concerns a limb which is almost severed, i.e., it is attached to the body with only a small strand of skin.

[ח] **וְעוֹד** שְׁאָלָן רַבִּי עֲקִיבָא: אֵבֶר הַמְדֻלְדָּל בַּבְּהֵמָה — מַהוּ? אָמְרוּ לוֹ: לֹא שָׁמַעְנוּ, אֲבָל שָׁמַעְנוּ בְּאֵבֶר הַמְדֻלְדָּל בָּאָדָם שֶׁהוּא טָהוֹר, שֶׁכַּךְ הָיוּ מֻכֵּי שְׁחִין בִּירוּשָׁלַיִם עוֹשִׂין: הוֹלֵךְ לוֹ עֶרֶב פֶּסַח אֵצֶל הָרוֹפֵא, וְחוֹתְכוֹ עַד שֶׁהוּא מַנִּיחַ בּוֹ כִּשְׂעוֹרָה וְתוֹחֲבוֹ בְּסִירָה, וְהוּא נִמְשָׁךְ מִמֶּנּוּ. וְהַלָּה עוֹשֶׂה פִסְחוֹ וְהָרוֹפֵא עוֹשֶׂה פִסְחוֹ,

יד אברהם

וְעוֹד שְׁאָלָן רַבִּי עֲקִיבָא: אֵבֶר הַמְדֻלְדָּל בַּבְּהֵמָה — *R' Akiva asked them further: A dangling limb of an animal —*

The limb is not completely severed but is dangling from the body of a living animal. Most of it is detached [and will not grow back] but it is still connected by a small portion of meat or skin. Were it to be completely severed it would be considered *tamei* as אֵבֶר מִן הַחַי [see above and ArtScroll *Chullin* 9:7 with prefatory remarks in *Yad Avraham*] (*Rav; Tif. Yis.*).

מַהוּ? — *what is it [considered]?*

What is [the law regarding this situation]? Is it considered as if it were severed and hence subject to the laws of *tumah* as an אֵבֶר מִן הַחַי or not (*Rav; Tif. Yis.*)?

אָמְרוּ לוֹ: לֹא שָׁמַעְנוּ, אֲבָל שָׁמַעְנוּ בְּאֵבֶר הַמְדֻלְדָּל בָּאָדָם שֶׁהוּא טָהוֹר, — *They replied to him: [This] we have not heard, but we have heard that a dangling limb of a human is tahor,*

Rabban Gamliel and R' Yehoshua replied: We did not hear of any ruling regarding this specific law, but we did hear of one regarding a similar situation, a dangling human limb, even one partially attached to a person is *tahor* (*Rav*). Were it completely severed, it would be *tamei* as a corpse [see *Chullin* 9:8] (*Tif. Yis.*).

שֶׁכַּךְ הָיוּ מֻכֵּי שְׁחִין בִּירוּשָׁלַיִם עוֹשִׂין: — *for so were the lepers in Jerusalem wont to do:*

Victims of a malady which caused their limbs to disintegrate and fall off their bodies would do the following when they wished to have their dangling limbs surgically removed (*Rav; Tif. Yis.*).

The term מֻכֵּי שְׁחִין [*sing.* מֻכֵּה], *lepers* [lit. *victims of boils*], is not to be confused with the *metzora* [victim of the skin affliction called *tzaraas*] a word which is also commonly — albeit inaccurately — described as a *leper*. *Tzaraas* is a form of *tumah*, for which discoloration of the skin is the physical symptom. The מֻכֵּה שְׁחִין, however, is not *tamei* at all. He is simply a leper, one who suffers from a malady which causes the loss of a limb as a result of disintegration. See *Yad Avraham* commentary, *Kesubos* 3:5.

הוֹלֵךְ לוֹ עֶרֶב פֶּסַח אֵצֶל הָרוֹפֵא, — *He would go to a surgeon on the eve of Pesach,*

On the eve of Pesach (when they wanted to fulfill their sacrificial obligations in Jerusalem) these lepers would have their dangling limbs removed. It was not a matter of becoming *tahor*, as even without the amputation they were not *tamei*. It was simply a matter of esthetics: They did not want to appear repulsive on the festival. They therefore went to a surgeon to have these limbs amputated [in a manner that would allow both the leper and the surgeon to eat of the *korban pesach*] (*Rav; Rashi*).

Rashash, arguing that an amputee is just as repulsive as one with one dangling limbs, suggests that the surgical removal of the limbs was dictated by considerations of halachah rather than esthetics: As it was an

3
8

8. R' Akiva asked them further: A dangling limb of an animal — what is it [considered]? They replied to him: [This] we have not heard, but we have heard that a dangling limb of a human is *tahor*, for so were the lepers in Jerusalem wont to do: He would go to a surgeon on the eve of Pesach, and [the latter would] sever it until he would leave over a barleycorn's breadth and impale it on a thorn, and he would pull away from it. Then, that person would make his Pesach [offering] and the surgeon would make his Pesach [offering],

YAD AVRAHAM

obligation to purify oneself before the festival to be able to eat of the *korban Pesach*, it was necessary to amputate the dangling limb lest it be a חֲצִיצָה, *an obstruction*, that would invalidate the immersion in a *mikveh*.[1]

וְחוֹתְכוֹ עַד שֶׁהוּא מַנִּיחַ בּוֹ כִּשְׂעוֹרָה — *and [the latter would] sever it until he would leave over a barleycorn's breadth*

Were he to sever it completely, the surgeon would become *tamei* when he touches the limb at the time of its separation from the body. [Therefore, he leaves it attached by the minutest amount to insure his remaining *tahor*] (*Rav; Rashi; Tif. Yis.*).

The reading of the mishnah in the *Gemara* text is כִּשַׂעֲרָה, *a hairsbreadth*. This is the reading which seems to have been followed by *Rav* and *Rashi* and also appears in numerous comparative sources (*Sifra; Yalkut Shimoni; Midrash HaGadol*). In fact, *Shoshannim LeDavid* considers the standard version of the mishnah an error. Regardless of semantics, the meaning is the same: The surgeon left the limb dangling by a minute amount.

וְתוֹחֲבוֹ בְסִירָה, — *and impale it on a thorn,*

The patient himself would impale the dangling limb on a thorn attached to the wall or secured on the ground (*Rav; Rashi; Korban Aharon* on *Sifra*).

Rambam Comm. renders סִירָה as a *strap* or *thong*. This seems incongruous, however, with the context, since one cannot impale anything on a thong (*Tif. Yis.*). Indeed, *Kafich* deems our printed version an error.

וְהוּא נִמְשָׁךְ מִמֶּנּוּ. — *and he would pull away from it.*

The patient would abruptly pull himself away from the thorn, and the limb would detach itself by the force of his movement. Since he would pull away with all his might, the limb would be torn away and not touch his body as it became detached (*Rambam Comm., Rav* from *Gem.* 15b).

וְהַלָּה עוֹשֶׂה פִסְחוֹ — *Then, that person would make his Pesach [offering]*

Since the limb did not touch his body when it separated, the leper did not become *tamei*, and may therefore make his Pesach sacrifice (*Korban Aharon*).

וְהָרוֹפֵא עוֹשֶׂה פִסְחוֹ, — *and the surgeon would make his Pesach offering,*

The surgeon remains *tahor* because he, too, did not touch the limb after it became completely detached.

From the fact that they exercised caution not to touch the limb only after it became detached, the Sages concluded

1. Actually, the ruling that a dangling limb constitutes a חֲצִיצָה is the subject of controversy. According to one version of *Tosefta* (*Mikvaos* ch. 6) cited by *Rosh* (ibid. #26) and *Tur* (Y.D. 198), it is a חֲצִיצָה; according to others (*Rash* ibid.; *Beis Yosef* ad loc.), it is not. The ruling of the *Shulchan Aruch* (Y.D. 198:22) follows the former view.

וְרוֹאִין אָנוּ שֶׁהַדְּבָרִים קַל וָחֹמֶר.

[ט] **וְעוֹד** שְׁאָלָן רַבִּי עֲקִיבָא: הַשּׁוֹחֵט חֲמִשָּׁה זְבָחִים בַּחוּץ בְּהֶעְלֵם אֶחָד — מַהוּ? חַיָּב אַחַת עַל־כֻּלָּם אוֹ אַחַת עַל־כָּל־אַחַת וְאַחַת?

יד אברהם

that it did not convey *tumah* while it was still attached (*Korban Aharon*).

In fact, it was for this reason that the limb was impaled on a thorn attached to the wall or the ground, rather than being held by the surgeon, for an amputated limb has the *tumah* status of a corpse, which can convey *tumah* by means of מַשָּׂא, *carrying*. Thus, if the surgeon were left holding the limb, even by means of a thorn or the like, he would become *tamei* by virtue of carrying [i.e., supporting the weight of] the amputated limb (*Tif. Yis.*).

וְרוֹאִין אָנוּ שֶׁהַדְּבָרִים קַל וָחֹמֶר. — *and we believe that the matter is a kal vachomer.*

[The law of the *tumah* status of an animal's dangling limb can be derived by means of a *kal vachomer* from the law of the dangling human limb:] If the dangling limb of a human who is susceptible to contracting *tumah* while still alive does not convey *tumah*, that of an animal — which is not susceptible to contracting *tumah* while alive — surely does not convey *tumah* (*Rashi*, *Rav* from *Gem.* 15b [see *Shitah Mekubetzes*]).

The reason that, as far as *tumah* is concerned, the laws governing a human are more stringent than those governing animals is that even a live person is susceptible to *tumah*, as explained above. According to some, this refers to the fact that a living person can become *tamei* on contact from others, something which has no parallel in live animals (*Rashi*). According to others, the contrast is that a live human can become a source of *tumah* (e.g., a *zav*, a *metzora*, etc.), whereas an animal creates *tumah* only as a *neveilah*, which comes after the animal dies or through the *tumah* of a detached limb, which comes about only when the limb no longer is sustained from the body of the animal (*Rambam Comm.*).

9.

The following mishnah, which cites a third question of R' Akiva, is related to the subject matter of the previous mishnayos, including the first question of R' Akiva: It discusses the law governing the number of *chataos* brought for a repetition of one offense in one *he'elam* or *lapse of awareness.*

It is axiomatic that the repeated violation of the prohibition in one *he'elam* is viewed as a continuum and is atoned for by one *chatas*. For example, as we learned in mishnah 2, if one eats a *kezayis* of *cheilev* (forbidden fat) and then, in the same lapse of awareness, eats another *kezayis*, he is liable to only one *chatas*, although technically he committed two distinct offenses. On the other hand, as we learned in mishnah 7, if one cohabits with five menstruous women in one *he'elam*, he is liable to a separate *chatas* for each one. This is because the acts are distinguished by virtue of the principle of גּוּפִין מְחֻלָּקִים, *distinct persons;* i.e., since each woman is a distinct entity, the five acts are considered as five distinct offenses as far as the *chatas* obligation is concerned.

and we believe that the matter is a *kal vachomer*.

9. R' Akiva asked them further: [If] one slaughters five offerings outside [the Temple] in one lapse of awareness — what is the ruling? Is he liable to one [*chatas*] for all of them or one for each? They replied to

YAD AVRAHAM

The following question posed by R' Akiva involves the prohibition of הַשּׁוֹחֵט בַּחוּץ, *someone who slaughters [an offering] outside* [*the Temple grounds*], which is punishable by *kares* and therefore requires a *chatas* atonement for inadvertent transgression, as we learned in 1:1.

וְעוֹד שְׁאָלָן רַבִּי עֲקִיבָא: — *R' Akiva asked them further:*

It is not clear when all these questions were posed. According to some commentators, these apparently unrelated questions are listed together because they were asked at the same time (*Shoshannim LeDavid*). According to others they were asked on different occasions, but were arranged together in a listing of all the questions that R' Akiva asked of Rabban Gamliel and his mentor R' Yehoshua[1] (*Beis David*).

הַשּׁוֹחֵט חֲמִשָּׁה זְבָחִים בַּחוּץ בְּהֶעְלֵם אֶחָד — מַהוּ? חַיָּב אַחַת עַל־כֻּלָּם אוֹ אַחַת עַל־כָּל־אַחַת וְאַחַת? — *[If] one slaughters five offerings outside [the Temple] in one lapse of awareness — what is the ruling? Is he liable to one [chatas] for all of them or one for each?*

[Shall we say that since the slaughter of all five animals is a repetition of the same offense, one *chatas* is sufficient for all of them?] Or shall we say that since each of the five animals is a distinct offering, their multiple slaughter calls for separate *chataos*? (*Korban Aharon*).

The question is raised by the commentators: Why should slaughtering five separate animals be less distinct than the transgressions of cohabitation with five menstruous women? Just as we learned in mishnah 7 that the repetition of the identical transgression with five separate people is considered as if each was a separate transgression due to the principle of גּוּפִין מְחֻלָּקִים, *distinct persons*, so too the separate bodies of the sacrificial animals should create a distinction between the prohibitions.

There are various approaches to resolve this difficulty. Some suggest that the principle of גּוּפִין מְחֻלָּקִים applies only to a distinct person, but not to animals (*Tif. Yis.*).

Alternatively, the fact that each woman is considered a separate entity is due to the fact that each of the women involved in this transgression is herself separately liable to a *chatas*. The additional *chatas* for each woman is enough reason to separate them in regard to their male partner's offering as well (*Korban Aharon*).

Shoshannim LeDavid reasons: Five women are physically five distinct bodies that can never be combined. The meat of animals, by contrast, can become indistinguishable.

1. *Tif. Yis.* (on mishnah 7) suggests that the pattern to R' Akiva's apparently unrelated questions is based on their relationship to the circumstances surrounding the wedding which was about to be celebrated (as in mishnah 7). The first question, which dealt with the subject of *arayos* (incestuous relations), is related to a wedding (as indicated by the blessing recited under the *chupah:* אֲשֶׁר קִדְּשָׁנוּ בְּמִצְוֹתָיו וְצִוָּנוּ עַל הָעֲרָיוֹת, *Who commanded us regarding arayos*). The second question, about אֵבֶר הַמְדֻלְדָּל, *a dangling limb* of a slaughtered animal, was occasioned by the slaughtering done for the wedding meal. The third question, regarding the subject of offerings, was prompted by the custom to offer *shelamim* to mark a momentous joyous occasion.

אָמְרוּ לוֹ: לֹא שָׁמַעְנוּ. אָמַר רַבִּי יְהוֹשֻׁעַ: שָׁמַעְתִּי בְּאוֹכֵל מִזֶּבַח אֶחָד בַּחֲמִשָּׁה תַמְחוּיִים בְּהֶעְלֵם אֶחָד שֶׁהוּא חַיָּב עַל־כָּל־אֶחָד וְאֶחָד מִשּׁוּם מְעִילָה, וְרוֹאֶה אֲנִי שֶׁהַדְּבָרִים קַל וָחֹמֶר.

אָמַר רַבִּי שִׁמְעוֹן: לֹא כָךְ שְׁאָלָן רַבִּי עֲקִיבָא, אֶלָּא בְּאוֹכֵל נוֹתָר מֵחֲמִשָּׁה זְבָחִים בְּהֶעְלֵם אֶחָד — מַהוּ? חַיָּב אַחַת עַל־כֻּלָּן אוֹ אַחַת עַל־כָּל־אֶחָד וְאֶחָד? אָמְרוּ לוֹ: לֹא שָׁמַעְנוּ. אָמַר רַבִּי יְהוֹשֻׁעַ: שָׁמַעְתִּי בְּאוֹכֵל מִזֶּבַח אֶחָד בַּחֲמִשָּׁה תַמְחוּיִים בְּהֶעְלֵם אֶחָד, שֶׁהוּא חַיָּב עַל־כָּל־אַחַת וְאַחַת מִשּׁוּם מְעִילָה, וְרוֹאֶה אֲנִי שֶׁהַדְּבָרִים קַל וָחֹמֶר.

יד אברהם

Thus, after the slaughter of the five offerings, when they have been flayed and butchered, they may become mixed together, and no longer remain five distinct bodies.

אָמְרוּ לוֹ: לֹא שָׁמַעְנוּ. — *They replied to him: [This] we have not heard.*

We have no teaching regarding this specific case, where the repetition of the offense, in itself, does not in any way affect the violator's experience. He experiences no increased personal benefit from the slaughter of five animals — it is a cut-and-dry action. We do, however, have a teaching regarding someone who eats from five sacrifices and is liable for each one separately, as follows (*Tif. Yis.*).

אָמַר רַבִּי יְהוֹשֻׁעַ: שָׁמַעְתִּי בְּאוֹכֵל מִזֶּבַח אֶחָד בַּחֲמִשָּׁה תַמְחוּיִים בְּהֶעְלֵם אֶחָד שֶׁהוּא חַיָּב עַל־כָּל־אֶחָד וְאֶחָד מִשּׁוּם מְעִילָה, — *Said R' Yehoshua: I have heard that one who eats of one offering in five dishes in one lapse of awareness is liable for a me'ilah offering for each one,*

One who eats from a *korban* of קֹדֶשׁ קָדָשִׁים, *the most-holy category* (e.g., a *chatas* or an *asham*), prior to the זְרִיקַת הַדָּם, *sprinkling of the blood* [on the altar], is guilty of *me'ilah*. As a consequence, he is liable to pay the Temple treasury the principal plus a fifth and to bring an *asham* as an atonement. Should he eat five *kezayis* measures of one offering which were distinguished simply by their manner of preparation (for example, one piece was cooked, one was roasted and one was stewed), he is liable to five *ashamos* although he ate them all in one lapse of awareness, i.e., he was unaware that he was eating sacrificial meat (*Rav; Rashi*).

וְרוֹאֶה אֲנִי שֶׁהַדְּבָרִים קַל וָחֹמֶר. — *and I believe that the matter is a kal vachomer.*

If one is liable to five *ashamos* for eating from one offering simply because the five portions were prepared in different manners, surely one should be liable to five *chataos* for the slaughtering of five offerings, which are essentially five separate bodies (*Rav* from *Gem.* 15b).

אָמַר רַבִּי שִׁמְעוֹן: לֹא כָךְ שְׁאָלָן רַבִּי עֲקִיבָא, — *Said R' Shimon: R' Akiva did not ask them about such a case,*

Had R' Akiva asked them a question concerning the slaughter of five offer-

3 him: [This] we have not heard. Said R′ Yehoshua: I have
9 heard that one who eats of one offering in five dishes in one lapse of awareness is liable for a *me′ilah* offering for each one, and I believe that the matter is a *kal vachomer*.

Said R′ Shimon: R′ Akiva did not ask them about such a case, rather if one ate leftover of five offerings in one lapse of awareness — what is [he liable for]? Is he liable to one for all of them or to one for each one? They replied to him: We have not heard. Said R′ Yehoshua: I have heard that if one eats from one offering in five dishes, he is liable for a *me′ilah* offering for each one, and I believe that the matter is a *kal vachomer*. Said R′

YAD AVRAHAM

ings, the answer they had given him would not have been valid, as it is possible to refute their *kal vachomer* from one who ate five differently prepared portions of an offering by arguing that the reason the Torah is stringent with one who eats [of one offering in five dishes] is because by eating he derives benefit from eating the offering. One who slaughters five offerings outside, however, derives no benefit from his slaughter. Therefore, regarding this case, it is possible that the Torah did not make him liable to five *chataos* (*Rav* from *Gem.* 15b).

Korban Aharon explains that the significance of experiencing benefit as a separating factor is that with each *kezayis* he receives renewed pleasure. Therefore, with each bite it is as though he becomes aware of his sin and then forgets again. He is, therefore, liable to five separate *chataos*. One who slaughters five offerings outside the Temple, however, experiences no benefit or pleasure. Therefore, he is possibly liable to only one *chatas*.

[The question R′ Akiva posed, R′ Shimon reasons, must have concerned something more analogous to the answer he received, as he explains below.]

אֶלָּא בְּאוֹכֵל נוֹתָר מֵחֲמִשָּׁה זְבָחִים בְּהֶעְלֵם אֶחָד — מַהוּ? חַיָּב אַחַת עַל־כֻּלָּן אוֹ אַחַת עַל־כָּל־אַחַת וְאַחַת? — *rather if one ate leftover of five offerings in one lapse of awareness — what is [he liable for]? Is he liable to one for all of them or one for each one?*

[As we learned above (1:1), if one eats *nossar*, the meat of an offering left over after the time allowed for eating it, he is liable to *kares*. Should he do so inadvertently, he is liable to a *chatas*. R′ Akiva asks whether there is a separate obligation for the *nossar* of each offering or are they all viewed as one category: *nossar*.]

אָמְרוּ לוֹ: לֹא שָׁמַעְנוּ. אָמַר רַבִּי יְהוֹשֻׁעַ: שָׁמַעְתִּי בְּאוֹכֵל מִזֶּבַח אֶחָד בַּחֲמִשָּׁה תַמְחוּיִים בְּהֶעְלֵם אֶחָד, שֶׁהוּא חַיָּב עַל־כָּל־אֶחָד וְאֶחָד מִשּׁוּם מְעִילָה, וְרוֹאֶה אֲנִי שֶׁהַדְּבָרִים קַל וָחֹמֶר. — *They replied to him: We have not heard. Said R′ Yehoshua: I have heard that if one eats from one offering in five dishes, he is liable for a me′ilah offering for each one, and I believe that the matter is a kal vachomer.*

If one is liable to five *ashamos* for eating five *kezayis* measures of one offering simply because they were prepared in five dishes, surely he is liable to five *chataos* for eating the leftover of five offerings which are entirely separate entities (*Rambam Comm.*).

[To this question, which deals with the *chatas* obligation of eating *nossar*, the proof cited from the law of eating an offering before the blood has been placed on the Altar is appropriate.]

אָמַר רַבִּי עֲקִיבָא: אִם הֲלָכָה, נְקַבֵּל, וְאִם לָדִין, יֵשׁ תְּשׁוּבָה. אָמַר לוֹ: הָשֵׁב. אָמַר לוֹ: לֹא, אִם אָמַרְתָּ בִּמְעִילָה, שֶׁעָשָׂה בָהּ אֶת הַמַּאֲכִיל כְּאוֹכֵל, וְאֶת־הַמַּהֲנֶה כְּנֶהֱנֶה, צֵרַף הַמְּעִילָה לִזְמַן מְרֻבֶּה, תֹּאמַר בְּנוֹתָר שֶׁאֵין בּוֹ אֶחָד מִכָּל־אֵלּוּ?

יד אברהם

Since both cases deal with eating, R' Shimon's objection [based on the benefit factor] does not apply (*Rav; Rambam Comm.*).

אָמַר רַבִּי עֲקִיבָא: אִם הֲלָכָה, נְקַבֵּל, — *Said R' Akiva: If [this is] an accepted halachah, we will accept [it],*

If you heard from your Masters that one who eats the *nossar* of five offerings in one lapse of awareness is liable to five *chataos*, we will accept this ruling (*Rav; Rashi*). If your Masters ruled this way they surely knew the reason for it (*Korban Aharon*).

וְאִם לָדִין, יֵשׁ תְּשׁוּבָה. — *but if [it is] a logical deduction, there is a refutation.*

But if you did not hear it from your teacher, but merely deduced it on your own from the law of *me'ilah* with a *kal vachomer*, the comparison can be refuted (*Rav; Rashi, Korban Aharon*).

אָמַר לוֹ: הָשֵׁב. — *He said to him: Refute [it].*

[R' Yehoshua said to R' Akiva: If you say that it can be refuted, let me hear your refutation.]

אָמַר לוֹ: לֹא, — *He replied to him: No,* [the cases cannot be compared]

[R' Akiva then replied to R' Yehoshua: We cannot compare the case of *me'ilah* to that of *nossar* for we find numerous details of the laws of *me'ilah* that have no parallel in the laws of *nossar*, as follows:]

אִם אָמַרְתָּ בִּמְעִילָה, — *if you say [that] in the case of me'ilah,*

[If you say that in the case of *me'ilah* he is liable to a separate *asham* for each dish he eats, it is because *me'ilah* has other stringencies as well.]

שֶׁעָשָׂה בָהּ אֶת־הַמַּאֲכִיל כְּאוֹכֵל, — *in which [the Torah] made the one who gives to eat as though he were eating,*

The halachah is if one takes something out of the domain of the Temple treasury and gives it to another, it is the one who removed the article who is liable for *me'ilah*, not the one to whom it is given (*Rav; Rashi*). Thus, one who gives another *kodashim* to eat is liable as though he had eaten it himself.

וְאֶת־הַמַּהֲנֶה כְּנֶהֱנֶה, — *and the one who bestows benefit as though he were receiving benefit,*

And similarly with non-edibles, one who gives consecrated articles to another is guilty of *me'ilah* just as though he had misappropriated them himself (*Rav; Rashi*).

צֵרַף הַמְּעִילָה לִזְמַן מְרֻבֶּה, — *[and the Torah] reckoned together the me'ilah over a long period of time,*

The laws of *me'ilah* have yet another stringency, this one regarding the minimum amount required to be guilty for *me'ilah*, which is one *perutah* [roughly the equivalent of a penny]: One who took half a *perutah* from the Temple treasury and then, even years later, took a second half-*perutah*, the two half-*perutos* are reckoned together to total a *perutah*. We derive this ruling from the double expression תִמְעֹל מַעַל, *commits treachery* (*Lev.* 5:15), which the Torah uses in connection with the liability for *me'ilah* (*Rav; Rashi* from *Gem.* 18b).

תֹּאמַר בְּנוֹתָר שֶׁאֵין בּוֹ אֶחָד מִכָּל־אֵלּוּ? — *can you say [the same] regarding the case of*

3 Akiva: If [this is] an accepted halachah, we will accept
9 [it], but if [it is] a logical deduction, there is a refutation. He said to him: Refute [it]. He replied to him: No, if you say [that] in the case of *me'ilah*, in which [the Torah] made the one who gives to eat as though he were eating, and the one who bestows benefit as though he were receiving benefit, [and the Torah] reckoned together the *me'ilah* over a long period of time, can you say [the same] regarding the case of the leftover offering, which has none of these [stringencies]?

YAD AVRAHAM

the leftover offering, which has none of these [stringencies]?

You cannot compare the case of eating *nossar* to the case of *me'ilah* since the Torah added many stringencies in the case of *me'ilah*, which it did not add in the case of eating leftover sacrificial flesh. Therefore, it may be that the Torah is also more stringent regarding separate *ashamos* for *me'ilah* than it is regarding separate *chataos* for eating *nossar*.

The *Gemara* (16a) does not clarify whether or not R' Yehoshua accepted R' Akiva's refutation.[1]

The halachah, however, is that he is liable to one *chatas*, and that different dishes do not effect a separation either to cause leniency or stringency, i.e., if one eats two half-*kezayis* measures of a forbidden substance in two dishes, he is liable to a *chatas*, and the fact that it was prepared in two different ways does not prevent it from being combined to the amount of a *kezayis*. Should he eat two *kezayis* measures of a forbidden substance, he is liable to one *chatas* even if these two amounts were prepared in two different manners. The two dishes do not separate it into two to require two *chataos* (*Rav; Rambam Comm.*).

10.

The following mishnah cites another question that R' Akiva asked his mentor R' Eliezer concerning the subject of *shegagos* (inadvertent transgression of *kares*-punishable prohibitions). This question centers on the laws determining the number of *chataos* brought for multiple acts of *chillul Shabbos* (desecration of the Sabbath) in one lapse of awareness.

The laws of *shegagos* relating to *chillul Shabbos* hinge on two factors: (a) The *melachah*, the actual act performed (e.g., planting, reaping, cooking, etc.); (b) the *shegagah* (שְׁגָגָה), the error or unawareness which caused him to desecrate the Sabbath. The understanding of both of these factors is critical to the following discussion and some preliminary remarks will be useful.

(a) מְלֶאכֶת שַׁבָּת, *labor categories of the Shabbos*: As listed in *Shabbos* (7:2), there are thirty-nine אֲבוֹת מְלָאכוֹת, *primary* [lit., *fathers*] *labors*, prohibited on the Sabbath.

---

1. *Tos. R' Akiva* points out that, from the *Gemara* 12b cited in the commentary on mishnah 2, it appears that R' Yehoshua did not accept R' Akiva's refutation, but adhered to his original view that if he ate the leftover in different dishes, he is liable to separate *chataos*, and surely if he ate the *nossar* of many offerings.

כריתות [י] **אָמַר** רַבִּי עֲקִיבָא: שָׁאַלְתִּי אֶת רַבִּי
ג/י אֱלִיעֶזֶר: הָעוֹשֶׂה מְלָאכוֹת הַרְבֵּה
בְּשַׁבָּתוֹת הַרְבֵּה מֵעֵין מְלָאכָה אַחַת בְּהֶעְלֵם
אַחַת — מַה הוּא? חַיָּב אַחַת עַל־כֻּלָּן אוֹ
אַחַת עַל־כָּל אַחַת וְאַחַת? אָמַר לִי: חַיָּב עַל־

יד אברהם

These are the labors that were performed in the course of the construction of the *Mishkan* (Tabernacle of Biblical times) and its components. Actually, these thirty-nine are merely the headings of categories of labor; activities similar to these thirty-nine activities either in method or function are equally prohibited. Since, however, these other labors were not employed in the construction of the *Mishkan*, they are known as תולדות (*tolados*), *secondary labors* [lit., *offspring*]. In terms of origin, they are derivatives of the *avos melachos* (see General Introduction to ArtScroll Tractate *Shabbos*, section I, at length). In terms of the severity of the offense, the *avos* and *tolados* are alike: Each is a violation of the negative commandment לֹא־תַעֲשֶׂה כָל־מְלָאכָה, *Do not perform any labor [on the Sabbath day*] (*Exodus* 20:10). Each *toladah* is punishable by either *sekilah* (stoning), *kares*, or a *chatas* depending on the circumstances under which it was committed.

The primary function of the *avos-tolados* classification is to distinguish between these labors in terms of the number of *chataos* for which one is liable in the event of inadvertent Sabbath desecration. This means that each of the *avos melachos* constitutes a distinct entity as far as the *chatas* obligation. For example, if one inadvertently plows and reaps on the Sabbath he is liable to two *chataos*, as *plowing* and *reaping* are each considered an *av melachah*. In this sense the laws of the Sabbath are an exception to the general laws of *shegagos*: Whereas when dealing with other prohibitions, a repetition of the same offense in one lapse of awareness (e.g., he twice eats *cheilev*) is liable to only one *chatas* (as above mishnah 2), performing a number of forbidden labor categories on the Sabbath — although a repetition of the same negative precept (לֹא־תַעֲשֶׂה כָל־מְלָאכָה) — is liable to separate *chataos* for each of them. [This is derived exegetically by the Talmud, *Shabbos* 69b.] The status of performing various *tolados* of the same *av* [e.g., planting trees, grafting and pruning — all *tolados* of the *av*, *planting*] is discussed in this mishnah.

(b) The שְׁגָגָה (*shegagah*), *error:* Inadvertent desecration of the Sabbath can occur as the result of one of three errors:

(1) שׁוֹכֵחַ עִיקַּר שַׁבָּת, *forgetting the essence of the Sabbath* — one who forgot the entire *mitzvah* of the Sabbath. He was unaware of the concept of the day of Sabbath in terms of forbidden labor categories, i.e., he thought all labor was permitted.

(2) שִׁגְגַת שַׁבָּת וּזְדוֹן מְלָאכָה, *unawareness of the Sabbath but awareness of melachah* — he knew that the deed was prohibited on the Sabbath but he was unaware of the date; he thought it was a weekday.

(3) זְדוֹן שַׁבָּת וְשִׁגְגַת מְלָאכָה, *awareness of the Sabbath but unawareness of the melachah* — he knew it was the Sabbath and labor may not be performed but was unaware that this particular act was included in the category of forbidden labor.

Each of these cases has a different status regarding the number of *chataos* brought for multiple violations. This is discussed at length in *Shabbos* (7:1) and is mentioned in the mishnah here.

The case in the mishnah involves a repetition of an act of *chillul Shabbos* on a

3 **10. Said** R′ Akiva: I asked R′ Eliezer: [If] one performs
10 many labors on many Sabbaths of the same type of work in one lapse of awareness — what is the ruling? Is he liable to one for all of them or to one for each one?

YAD AVRAHAM

number of Sabbaths. The question is: Is one *chatas* enough to cover all the Sabbaths that were desecrated or does each Sabbath require a separate *chatas*?

אָמַר רַבִּי עֲקִיבָא: שָׁאַלְתִּי אֶת רַבִּי אֱלִיעֶזֶר: הָעוֹשֶׂה מְלָאכוֹת הַרְבֵּה בְּשַׁבָּתוֹת הַרְבֵּה מֵעֵין מְלָאכָה אַחַת בְּהֶעְלֵם אַחַת — מַה הוּא? חַיָּב — אַחַת עַל־כֻּלָּן אוֹ אַחַת עַל־כָּל אַחַת וְאַחַת? *Said R′ Akiva: I asked R′ Eliezer: [If] one performs many labors on many Sabbaths of the same type of work in one lapse of awareness — what is the ruling? Is he liable to one for all of them or to one for each one?*

[The case in the mishnah involves someone who, on a number of Sabbaths, performed more than one *toladah* of the same *av* (see prefatory remarks to this mishnah). For example, if someone inadvertently watered plants and pruned — both actions which are the *toladah* of the same *av* (זוֹרֵעַ, *planting*) — on one Sabbath and then repeated his error on the subsequent Sabbath.]

R′ Akiva relates that he asked his mentor R′ Eliezer the following question:

If one performed many *tolados* of the same *av*, performing these labors on several Sabbaths in one lapse of awareness, i.e., without becoming aware of his error in the interim, what is his status as far as *chatas* obligations are concerned? Do we say that since, in the end result, he repeated the same transgression of *chillul Shabbos*, one *chatas* is enough or are there distinguishing factors which create separate *chatas* obligations?

The *Gemara* (16a) explains that R′ Akiva's expressed query actually comprises two distinct questions:

(a) What is the law regarding one who performs two separate labors which are both *tolados* of the same *av*?[1] Is he liable to a separate *chatas* for each of them, just as he would be if they were two *avos melachos* or do we consider them repetitions of the same act as they are both derivatives of the same primary labor?

(b) What is the law concerning one who performs the same labor[2] on two

1. The phrase מְלָאכוֹת הַרְבֵּה מֵעֵין מְלָאכָה אַחַת, *many labors of the same type of work*, also appears in *Shabbos* 7:1. Our explanation that it means numerous *tolados* of one *av* is based on the understanding of the major commentaries (*Rashi; Rav; Rambam Comm.*).

Rambam (*Shegagos* 7:7), however, seems to render the phrase as *variant forms of one labor* rather then *tolados*. As explained by *Rambam* (*Shabbos* 7:2ff) there can be more than one form of the same *av melachah*, e.g., *planting* and *grafting* are two variant forms of the same *av* — זוֹרֵעַ, *planting*. Neither is a *toladah* of the other; each is simply the *identical* act with different materials. [Another example: *Cooking* and *baking* are considered alternate forms of מְבַשֵּׁל, *cooking* (*Rambam*, ibid. 9:1).]

Accordingly, the question in the mishnah involved the performance of similar *av* categories (e.g., planting and grafting) in one lapse of awareness. While this explanation [an apparent reversal of *Rambam's* own commentary] would fit well into the words of the mishnah, it does not seem to be supported by the *Gemara* text which makes specific reference to *tolados*. See *Lechem Mishneh* ad loc.

2. The conventional explanation of this question is that he did the exact same *melachah* on two or more Sabbaths, e.g., he planted twice or twice made a fire (*Rashi; Rav; Rambam Comm.*).

Rambam (*Shegagos* 7:8), however, indicates the case concerns one who performed *similar* labor categories on two or more Sabbaths. For example, he planted a seed on one Sabbath

כָּל־אַחַת וְאַחַת מִקַּל וָחֹמֶר. וּמָה אִם הַנִּדָּה, שֶׁאֵין בָּהּ תּוֹצָאוֹת הַרְבֵּה וְחַטָּאוֹת הַרְבֵּה, חַיָּב עַל־כָּל־אַחַת וְאַחַת, שַׁבָּת, שֶׁיֶּשׁ־בָּהּ תּוֹצָאוֹת

יד אברהם

Sabbaths, being unaware that the said labor was prohibited on the Sabbath? Ordinarily one who repeats the same *av melachah* on one Sabbath in a single lapse of awareness is liable to one *chatas* [just as one who eats *cheilev* twice in one lapse of awareness, as above mishnah 2] but this case involves two Sabbaths. Is the fact that the transgressions took place at different dates a separating factor that creates separate *chataos* obligations?

As explained by the mishnah in *Shabbos* (7:1), there are two types of errors that can cause inadvertent *chillul Shabbos*, beyond not being aware of the entire concept of forbidden labor on the Sabbath. One can be aware that it is Sabbath but not aware that the labor in question is a prohibited activity (זְדוֹן שַׁבָּת וְשִׁגְגַת מְלָאכָה) — in this case he is liable to a *chatas* for each *melachah* performed. Alternatively, one can be aware that the labor is prohibited but not aware that it is the Sabbath (זְדוֹן מְלָאכָה וְשִׁגְגַת שַׁבָּת) — in this case he is liable to one *chatas* for all labor performed on that Sabbath.

Accordingly, it must be clarified on which of the two errors is R' Akiva's question regarding repeated *chillul Shabbos* based.

The *Gemara* (16a) records a dispute on this issue. According to one opinion (Rabbah), R' Akiva's question involved a repetition of *melachos* because of the error that the labor was permitted. In other words, someone was not aware that planting, for example, was forbidden on the Sabbath. He planted on two or more Sabbaths, although each time he was aware that it was the Sabbath. R' Akiva's question, then, is do we say that the fact that the *melachah* was repeated on separate Sabbaths sufficient reason to distinguish between the *chatas* obligations. If the error were of the other variety (זְדוֹן מְלָאכָה וְשִׁגְגַת שַׁבָּת, *he was aware that the labor was prohibited but unaware that it was the Sabbath*), there would be no question — each time he mistook the Sabbath for a weekday it is regarded as a separate error. This concept is expressed with the principle of יָמִים שֶׁבֵּינְתַיִם הַוְיָין יְדִיעָה לְחַלֵּק, *the interim days effect an awareness to distinguish between* [*chatas obligations of one week to the next*]. In other words, the fact that a week passed between transgressions is in itself sufficient reason to distinguish between them. It is considered likely that he became aware of his error with the passing of time and his subsequent transgression is the result of a new lapse of awareness. This opinion is followed by *Rav* in his commentary and is the basis of our explanation to the mishnah as well.

According to the other opinion in the Gemara (Rav Chisda), precisely the opposite is true. R' Akiva's question was only regarding an error of date (זְדוֹן מְלָאכָה וְשִׁגְגַת שַׁבָּת; *he knew the melachah* was forbidden but did not realize that the day was the Sabbath). R' Akiva questioned whether a repetition of this error is regarded as two errors or one. However, regarding the other case — when he was aware that it was the Sabbath but repeated the performance of a *melachah* because he thought it was permitted — he is liable to a separate *chatas* for each Sabbath the error was repeated. The fact that the desecration of the Sabbath took place on two successive weeks serves to distinguish between the two *chatas* obligations because the fact that the *melachos* were repeated on separate Sabbaths makes it considered as if each *melachah* were a separate entity. Performing the same *av* on two Sabbaths is the halachic equivalent of performing two different *avos* on one Sabbath (*Tif. Yis.*; cf *Rashi* 15a s.v. או דילמא). This opinion is followed by *Rambam* in his commentary. At the end of the mishnah, we will point out the differences in the explanation of the mish-

(זוֹרֵעַ), planted a tree on another Sabbath (נוֹטֵעַ) and grafted on a third Sabbath (מַבְרִיךְ). None of these labors are *tolados* (as explained in previous footnote). It is difficult, though, to reconcile this explanation with our reading of the *Gemara* (*Lechem Mishneh* loc. cit., *Aruch LaNer*).

3
10 He replied to me: He is liable for each one from a *kal vachomer*. Now, if [for] a menstruous woman, [a prohibition] which has no numerous classifications or many ways of being liable to a *chatas*, he is liable for each one, [does it not follow that for] the Sabbath,

nah which stem from this approach.

אָמַר לִי: חַיָּב עַל־כָּל־אַחַת וְאַחַת — *He replied to me: He is liable for each one*

R' Eliezer replied that in both cases, the ruling is stringent: He is liable to separate *chataos*. This means that if one performed many *tolados* of one *av*, he is liable for each one, just as if he had performed different *avos*. Additionally, if by error one presumed a type of labor to be permitted and repeated his desecration of the Sabbath on more than one Sabbath, he is liable to a *chatas* for each Sabbath that he desecrated. Each Sabbath is sufficient cause to regard each *toladah* as a separate entity [along the principle of גּוּפִין מְחַלְּקִין, *distinct persons*] (*Tif. Yis.*; *Rav* from *Gem.* 16 according to Rabbah).

מִקַּל וָחֹמֶר. — *from a kal vachomer.*

[R' Eliezer proceeded to prove the reasoning of his reply by means of a *kal vachomer* based on the laws of *chatas* as related to the transgression of the *niddah* prohibition. Since it is known that a repeated violation of *niddah* can occasion separate *chataos*, it stands to reason that a repeated violation of the Sabbath can certainly obligate him to separate *chataos*, for the Sabbath is considered a more stringent prohibition than *niddah*, as follows.]

From the context of R' Eliezer's reasoning it is clear that he was bringing a proof only to one of his replies — that each Sabbath is a separate entity [just as each *niddah* is separate]. His other reply that each *toladah* is like a separate *av* remained unsupported. The *niddah* prohibition, which has no *tolados*, certainly provides no parallel for this (*Tos. Yom Tov* from *Rashi*).

וּמָה אִם הַנִּדָּה, — *Now, if [for] a menstruous woman,*

As was taught previously (mishnah 7), one who cohabited with five menstruous women during one lapse of awareness is liable to five *chataos* (*Rav* from *Gem.* 17a).

Although the mishnah uses the singular form (הַנִּדָּה), the reference is to someone who transgressed with many *niddos*. The mishnah actually should read הַנִּדּוֹת (ibid.).

According to the other explanation of the mishnah (Rav Chisda), however [that the question involved one who was unaware that it was the Sabbath], the above emendation need not be made. The mishnah discusses one who transgressed repeatedly with the same *niddah*. This will be explained further below (ibid.).

שֶׁאֵין בָּהּ תּוֹצָאוֹת הַרְבֵּה — *[a prohibition] which has no numerous classifications*

The prohibition of *niddah*, unlike that of the Sabbath, has no *avos* and *tolados* categories. The only sin for which one is liable to a *chatas* is cohabitation (*Rav*; *Rashi*; *Tif. Yis.*).

וְחַטָּאוֹת הַרְבֵּה, — *or many ways of being liable to a chatas,*

The *niddah* prohibition does not feature a variety of errors that can create the *chatas* obligation. The only way a person can become liable to a *chatas* through cohabitation with a *niddah* is if he thinks that she is permitted to him. The Sabbath, by contrast, has more than one way by which one can be liable to a *chatas*: *avos* and *tolados*; numerous *avos*; forgetting that the day is the Sabbath; being unaware that this type of work is prohibited on the Sabbath (*Tif. Yis.*).

חַיָּב עַל־כָּל־אַחַת וְאַחַת, — *he is liable for each one,*

He is liable for cohabitation with each

הַרְבֵּה וְחַטָּאוֹת הַרְבֵּה, אֵינוֹ דִין שֶׁיְּהֵא חַיָּב עַל־כָּל־אַחַת וְאַחַת? אָמַרְתִּי לוֹ: לֹא, אִם אָמַרְתָּ בַּנִּדָּה, שֶׁיֵּשׁ־בָּהּ שְׁתֵּי אַזְהָרוֹת – שֶׁהוּא מֻזְהָר עַל הַנִּדָּה, וְהַנִּדָּה מֻזְהֶרֶת עָלָיו – תֹּאמַר בַּשַּׁבָּת שֶׁאֵין בָּהּ אֶלָּא אַזְהָרָה אַחַת? אָמַר לִי: הַבָּא עַל־הַקְּטַנּוֹת יוֹכִיחַ, שֶׁאֵין בָּהֶם אֶלָּא אַזְהָרָה אַחַת, וְחַיָּב עַל־כָּל־אַחַת וְאַחַת. אָמַרְתִּי לוֹ: לֹא, אִם אָמַרְתָּ בַבָּא עַל־הַקְּטַנּוֹת, שֶׁאַף־עַל־פִּי שֶׁאֵין בָּהֶן עַכְשָׁיו, יֵשׁ בָּהֶן לְאַחַר זְמַן, תֹּאמַר בַּשַּׁבָּת, שֶׁאֵין

niddah although he does not become aware of the prohibition between one act of cohabitation and the next (*Rav* from *Gem.* 17a).

שַׁבָּת, שֶׁיֵּשׁ־בָּהּ תּוֹצָאוֹת הַרְבֵּה וְחַטָּאוֹת הַרְבֵּה, *— [does it not follow that for] the Sabbath, which has numerous classifications and many ways of being liable to a chatas,*

The transgressions of desecrating the Sabbath creates numerous circumstances which lead to a *chatas* obligation. This is because the prohibitions of work on the Sabbath involve a variety of work categories, each with a number of *tolados*. In addition, there are a number of inadvertencies through which one is liable to a *chatas* (*Tif. Yis.*).

אֵינוֹ דִין שֶׁיְּהֵא חַיָּב עַל־כָּל־אַחַת וְאַחַת? *— that he should be liable for each one?*

Does it not follow that if he performed a *melachah* on more than one Sabbath that he is liable for a *chatas* for each one, just as he is liable for a separate *chatas* for each *niddah* (*Tif. Yis.*)?

His ruling, though — that a separate *chatas* for each *toladah* — is based on logic, not on the foregoing *kal vachomer* [as explained above] (ibid.).

אָמַרְתִּי לוֹ: לֹא, *— I replied to him: No,*

[This is not a valid *kal vachomer*, since it can be refuted.]

אִם אָמַרְתָּ בַּנִּדָּה, *— if you say this in regard to the menstruant,*

[Just because in regard to the *niddah* prohibition you say that the man who cohabits with five menstruous women is liable to five *chataos*, it does not necessarily follow that the Sabbath prohibition is regarded the same way. It may be that there are factors which influence the laws of *niddah* that do not apply to the Sabbath prohibition, as follows:]

שֶׁיֵּשׁ־בָּהּ שְׁתֵּי אַזְהָרוֹת – שֶׁהוּא מֻזְהָר עַל הַנִּדָּה, וְהַנִּדָּה מֻזְהֶרֶת עָלָיו – *— it is because two prohibitions are involved — for he is prohibited from being intimate with the menstruant, and the menstruant is prohibited from being intimate with him —*

Regarding sexual offenses the Torah states: וְנִכְרְתוּ הַנְּפָשׁוֹת הָעֹשֹׂת מִקֶּרֶב עַמָּם, *the persons doing so will be cut off from among their people* (*Lev.* 18:29). From the plural usage we learn that both the male and the female are punished by *kares* (*Rav; Rashi*). The prohibition is also stated in the plural (ibid. 18:6): אִישׁ אִישׁ אֶל־כָּל־שְׁאֵר בְּשָׂרוֹ לֹא תִקְרְבוּ, *Any man shall not approach his close relative to uncover nakedness.* Since the punishment includes the female partner, we interpret the plural form of the prohibi-

3 which has numerous classifications and many ways of
10 being liable to a *chatas*, that he should be liable for each one? I replied to him: No, if you say this in regard to the menstruant, it is because two prohibitions are involved — for he is prohibited from being intimate with the menstruant, and the menstruant is prohibited from being intimate with him — can you say the same regarding the Sabbath, in which only one prohibition is involved? He replied: The case of one who cohabits with minors will prove [this ruling], for they have only one prohibition, yet he is liable for each one. I replied to him: No, if you state this ruling regarding one who cohabits with minors, which, although there is no prohibition now, there is one later, can you state it regarding the

tion wording to include the female as well (*Shoshannim LeDavid*).

As explained above, since each of the women is liable for her own sin, the man is also liable to a separate *chatas* for each one (*Korban Aharon*).

תֹּאמַר בַּשַּׁבָּת שֶׁאֵין בָּהּ אֶלָּא אַזְהָרָה אַחַת? — *can you say the same regarding the Sabbath, in which only one prohibition is involved?*

[The Sabbath involves only one prohibition for the desecrator. If he repeats the same *melachah* in a number of Sabbath days there is nothing to distinguish between the acts and obligate him for separate *chataos*.]

אָמַר לִי: הַבָּא עַל־הַקְּטַנּוֹת יוֹכִיחַ, — *He replied: The case of one who cohabits with minors will prove [this ruling],*

The case of one who cohabits with five menstruant minors will prove that this is a *kal vachomer* (*Rav*).

שֶׁאֵין בָּהֶם אֶלָּא אַזְהָרָה אַחַת, וְחַיָּב עַל־כָּל־אַחַת וְאַחַת. — *for they have only one prohibition, yet he is liable for each one.*

Although the *chatas* obligation is not in force for the female partners because they are minors, yet the man who is intimate with them is liable to five *chataos*. [This demonstrates that the separate *chataos* for the women is not the critical factor for his separate *chatas* obligations.] The same can therefore apply to the Sabbaths: One who repeats a *melachah* on several Sabbaths is liable for each Sabbath (*Rav*).

אָמַרְתִּי לוֹ: לֹא, — *I replied to him: No,*

[The case of one who is intimate with five minors who are *niddos* is inconclusive support for the validity of the *kal vachomer*.]

אִם אָמַרְתָּ בַּבָּא עַל־הַקְּטַנּוֹת, — *if you state this ruling regarding one who cohabits with minors,*

[Just because you state this ruling concerning minor girls that the man who is intimate with them is liable for each one, it is still not analogous to doing one *melachah* on several Sabbath days.]

שֶׁאַף־עַל־פִּי שֶׁאֵין בָּהֶן עַכְשָׁיו, יֵשׁ בָּהֶן לְאַחַר זְמַן, — *which, although there is no prohibition now, there is one later,*

[Although they are not now liable to separate *chataos* they are still each a distinct entity, for when they reach their majority, they will be liable for such an act.]

בָּהּ לֹא עַכְשָׁיו וְלֹא לְאַחַר־זְמַן? אָמַר לִי: הַבָּא־עַל־הַבְּהֵמָה יוֹכִיחַ. אָמַרְתִּי לוֹ: בְּהֵמָה כַּשַּׁבָּת.

יד אברהם

תֹּאמַר בַּשַּׁבָּת, שֶׁאֵין בָּהּ לֹא עַכְשָׁיו וְלֹא לְאַחַר־זְמַן? — *can you state it regarding the Sabbath, which neither now nor later has [separate chataos]?*

Can you say the same regarding the Sabbath [that the transgressor should be liable to a *chatas* for each Sabbath]? The Sabbath has only one prohibition at all times and there is no reason for it to be considered separate entities.

אָמַר לִי: הַבָּא־עַל־הַבְּהֵמָה יוֹכִיחַ. — *He replied to me: The case of one intimate with an animal will prove [it].*

One who was intimate with five animals during one lapse of awareness is liable to five *chataos* (*Shoshannim LeDavid*).

[The fact that someone who engages in sexual acts with five animals is liable to five *chataos* is proof that it is not the distinct liability of each of the partners that is the distinguishing factor, as it is obvious that an animal is not included in the prohibition. The reason that he is liable to separate *chataos* can only be because each act is by nature distinguished from the other, as each animal represents a distinct entity. It follows, then, that the same should apply to the case of the one who performs labor on several Sabbaths: He should be liable to a *chatas* for each Sabbath.]

Actually, there is a punishment factor for the animals as well, for by Torah law the animal with whom the man engaged in sexual acts is put to death (*Lev.* 20:15). Nevertheless, this is not a distinguishing factor as far as the *chatas* obligation is concerned because, in the final analysis, there is no separate *prohibition* on the part of the animals (*Tos. Yom Tov*). Furthermore, the death to the animals is not intended as a punishment. It was ordained to protect the dignity of the sinner [so that no one should later say, 'This is the animal with which so-and-so transgressed'], as in *Sanhedrin* 7:4 (*Tif. Yis.*).

אָמַרְתִּי לוֹ: בְּהֵמָה כַּשַּׁבָּת. — *I replied to him: [Indeed, the case concerning] the animal is like [the case of the] Sabbath.*

R' Akiva concluded: Indeed, the cases are analogous. Therefore, just as I am in doubt concerning the status of one who desecrates several Sabbaths in one lapse of awareness, so am I in doubt concerning one who is intimate with several animals in one lapse of awareness.

Neither of R' Eliezer's decisions was accepted by R' Akiva. Thus in either question that he raised — viz., regarding one who repeated a *melachah* on more than one Sabbath, and one who performed several *tolados* of one *av* in a single lapse of awareness — R' Akiva did not accept R' Eliezer's ruling that each transgression is liable for a separate *chatas*. The halachah in neither case follows R' Eliezer. Therefore, in both cases, the transgressor is liable to only one *chatas* (*Rav; Rashi*).

As mentioned earlier, our commentary on the mishnah follows *Rav*, who explained the mishnah according to the view of Rabbah in the *Gemara*. According to this explanation, R' Akiva's question involved זְדוֹן שַׁבָּת וְשִׁגְגַת מְלָאכָה, *an awareness of the Sabbath [day] but an unawareness of [the prohibition of] the labor*. Accordingly, the principle in question was whether the fact that each *av* was performed on a separate Sabbath is a distinguishing factor that gives each *av* performance the status of a separate *av*. Since this is similar to the reasoning of גּוּפִין מְחֻלָּקִין, *distinct persons*, employed in the repetition of the *niddah* prohibition, hence R' Eliezer's proofs all focused on the same prohibition being repeated with separate people as in the case of numerous menstruous women or numerous animals.

According to Rav Chisda, the question was quite different. R' Akiva asked about a case of שִׁגְגַת שַׁבָּת וּזְדוֹן מְלָאכָה, *an unaware-*

3 Sabbath, which neither now nor later has [separate
10 *chataos*]? He replied to me: The case of one intimate with an animal will prove [it]. I replied to him: [Indeed, the case concerning] the animal is like [the case of the] Sabbath.

ness of the Sabbath day but an awareness of [the prohibition of] the labor. In other words, one was aware that the labor in question was prohibited but repeatedly thought that the Sabbath was a weekday. R' Akiva's question, then, centered on the principle of יָמִים שֶׁבֵּינְתַּיִם הַוְיָין יְדִיעָה לְחַלֵּק או לא, *whether or not the interim days effect an awareness to distinguish between [chatas obligations]*. R' Eliezer's proof from a *niddah* was not from an instance in which one transgressed with five separate women. Rather, he refers to a case where someone repeatedly transgressed with one *niddah* [thus the phrase הַנִּדָּה in the singular] — although there was a period of *taharah* in the interim. In other words, one cohabited with a *niddah* who subsequently completed her *tumah* and immersed in a *mikveh*. He repeated the transgression the next time she became a *niddah*. R' Eliezer uses the fact that he is obligated to a separate *chatas* for each *niddah* period as proof that the interim days effect a distinction. R' Akiva rejects R' Eliezer's proofs until, finally, R' Eliezer cites the case of one who was repeatedly intimate with an animal[1] to which R' Akiva replies in agreement: *The [case concerning the] animal is like [the case of the] Sabbath*. Thus he accepted R' Eliezer's ruling that he is liable to a separate *chatas* for each Sabbath.

[The major difference between the two explanations as far as the halachah is concerned is someone who repeats a *melachah* on two Sabbaths, being unaware that the *melachah* is forbidden (זְדוֹן שַׁבָּת וְשִׁגְגַת מְלָאכָה): according to the first explanation, this was R' Akiva's question and he rejected R' Eliezer's ruling and held that he is not liable to a separate *chatas* for each Sabbath. According to the second explanation, R' Akiva presumed that he is liable to a separate *chatas* for each Sabbath and questioned only a case regarding one who repeatedly erred and mistook the Sabbath for a weekday.]

Rambam (*Shegagos* 7:8,9) rules that one who repeats a similar *melachah* on two or more Sabbaths — either because he thought that the *melachah* was permitted or because he thought that each Sabbath was a weekday — is liable to a separate *chatas* for each Sabbath on which the labor was performed.

This is consistent with *Rambam's* explanation of the mishnah according to Rav Chisda. According to this explanation, R' Akiva presumed that each Sabbath is considered as a separate entity regarding an error of the *melachah* (זְדוֹן שַׁבָּת וְשִׁגְגַת מְלָאכָה) and questioned only the effect of the interim days creating a separate *chatas* obligation in the event he forgot it was the Sabbath (שִׁגְגַת שַׁבָּת וּזְדוֹן מְלָאכָה). Regarding this question he accepted R' Eliezer's ruling that there is a separate *chatas* for each Sabbath.

If one performed many subcategories of one *melachah* on one Sabbath he is liable to only one *chatas* (ibid. 7). [This was R' Akiva's other question to which he did not accept R' Eliezer's reply and held that there is only one *chatas* obligation for all *tolados* of one *melachah* (see Sabbath 7:1).]

1. The proof R' Eliezer cited from the case of repeated transgressions of cohabitation with an animal is difficult to comprehend according to this explanation: If R' Eliezer was referring to a case in which a person repeatedly cohabited with one animal, the analogy to the repetition of Sabbath desecration is faulty: An animal has no 'periods' and there is therefore no basis for the principle of יָמִים שֶׁבֵּינְתַּיִם הַוְיָין יְדִיעָה לְחַלֵּק. If, on the other hand, R' Eliezer meant to cite a case of someone who engaged in sexual acts with five different animals, the analogy to Sabbath desecration is certainly difficult to understand, for R' Akiva agreed to the principle of גּוּפִין מְחֻלָּקִין and questioned only if time effects a division (*Shitah Mekubetzes* in the name of *Rosh*).

[א] **סָפֵק** אָכַל חֵלֶב, סָפֵק לֹא אָכַל; וַאֲפִלּוּ אָכַל, סָפֵק יֵשׁ בּוֹ כַּשִּׁעוּר, סָפֵק שֶׁאֵין בּוֹ; חֵלֶב וְשֻׁמָּן לְפָנָיו, אָכַל אֶת־אֶחָד מֵהֶן, וְאֵין

יד אברהם

Chapter 4

The following chapter deals with the obligation to bring an אָשָׁם תָּלוּי, *guilt offering of doubt*. As stated previously (1:2), for any situation in which a definite unintentional transgression occasions a *chatas*, a doubtful transgression calls for an *asham talui* (1:2). As already explained, the *asham talui* does not *atone* for the sin. It merely suspends Divine retribution until the person in question ascertains if he has erred and if so, brings a *chatas* (*Gem.* 26b). The term אָשָׁם תָּלוּי literally means *a suspended asham*, for it is an *asham* which suspends retribution but provides no expiation or atonement.[1] [Moreover, the term תָּלוּי is used in mishnayos to connote doubt and uncertainty; see e.g., *Pesachim* 1:5,7 (*Tif. Yis.*).]

1.

סָפֵק אָכַל חֵלֶב, סָפֵק לֹא אָכַל; — *[If there is] a doubt whether one ate cheilev fat or did not eat [it];*

[This is a general statement: If there exists a doubt whether or not a sin was committed, he is liable for an *asham talui*.]

What the circumstances are that create the doubts will be explained by the mishnah shortly (*Rav*, following one opinion in the *Gem.* 17b).

וַאֲפִלּוּ אָכַל, — *or even if he ate [it],*

He now is certain that what he ate was *cheilev* (forbidden fat). When he ate it, however, he thought it was *shumman*[2] (permitted fat) (*Rav; Rashi*).

סָפֵק יֵשׁ בּוֹ כַּשִּׁעוּר, סָפֵק שֶׁאֵין בּוֹ; — *[if] there is [still] a doubt whether it contained the amount [required for a chatas], or whether it did not;*

He does not know whether it contained a *kezayis* (olive's bulk) (*Rav*).

In light of the subsequently articulated stipulation that for the obligation of *asham talui* to take effect there must be a doubt created by the presence of two items, one permitted and one prohibited, it must be explained that here, too, there were *two* pieces of fat lying before him, one *cheilev* and one *shumman*, each of which contained a *kezayis*. Being unaware that one was *cheilev*, he ate one of them, but it is not known whether he ate exactly the amount required for a *chatas* or less. As a result of this doubt, he is liable to an

1. *Iyyun Tefillah* (R' Tzvi Hirsch Meklenberg) explains that the word תָּלוּי denotes any doubt that will probably be clarified in the future by the revelation of facts heretofore unknown. In this case, the *person* involved is in suspense, not knowing whether the future will reveal that he sinned and must bring a *chatas*, or that he did not sin and need not bring a *chatas*. According to this definition the term is possessive, meaning *the asham of the suspended one*. Accordingly, *Iyyun Tefillah* maintains that the vowelization should be אֲשַׁם תָּלוּי, *the guilt offering of the person held in suspense* (*Siddur Derech HaChayim*, pp. 56, 445). [However, from 5:2 וְהָאָשָׁם תָּלוּי, it does not appear so.]

2. From the fact that the above commentators emphasize that he ate the fat thinking that it was *shumman*, we can deduce that were he to have known that it was *cheilev* at the time of his eating (even if he thought it was less than a *kezayis*), he brings no *asham*, for his sin would be considered deliberate, not unintentional.

Apparently, the intention to eat a prohibited substance, even in less than the required amount, is deemed sufficient intent to consider him a מֵזִיד, *an intentional violator*. However, the reason for this premise is not entirely clear [see *Shabbos* 69b] (*Rashash*).

4
1

1. [If there is] a doubt whether one ate *cheilev* fat or did not eat [it]; or even if he ate [it], [if] there is [still] a doubt whether it contained the amount [required for a *chatas*], or whether it did not; if *cheilev* fat and permissible fat were before him, and he ate one of them,

YAD AVRAHAM

asham talui. Actually, there is now a סְפֵק סְפֵיקָא, *double doubt*, concerning his committing a sin: Perhaps what he ate was the permitted piece and even if it was the prohibited piece perhaps he ate less than the required *shiur*. [Generally, a single doubt regarding a Torah-ordained prohibition is treated stringently, and a double doubt is treated leniently. Hence, we would expect him not to be liable to an *asham talui* in our case.] Nonetheless he is obligated to bring an *asham talui*, for an *asham talui* is required to atone for *any* doubt, even one classified as a סְפֵק סְפֵיקָא (*Tos.*).

Rambam (*Shegagos* 8:2), however, apparently does not subscribe to this principle. He indicates that the mishnah refers to one who had but one piece of *cheilev* before him, which he ate unintentionally. Subsequently, when he learned that he had indeed eaten *cheilev*, he was still in doubt whether or not he had eaten a *kezayis*. This doubt in itself is sufficient to create an *asham talui* obligation (*Tos. Yom Tov*; *Lechem Shamayim* ad loc.; cf. *Rashash*).

חֵלֶב וְשֻׁמָּן לְפָנָיו, — *if cheilev fat and permissible fat were before him,*

This is the qualifying clause for the beginning of the mishnah, i.e., after making the generalizations to the effect that one brings an *asham talui* for a doubtful transgression, the *Tanna* specifies in which case a person is liable to an *asham talui* if there is a doubt whether he ate *cheilev*. The *Tanna* states that the doubt is created if two pieces of fat were before him, one of *cheilev* and one of *shumman*, and he is now uncertain which he ate. The presence of the one prohibited piece means that the prohibition has been established. If, however, there was only one piece of meat lying before a person, and he ate it, thinking that it was *shumman*, only to learn afterwards that it might have been *cheilev*, he is not liable to an *asham talui* (*Rav* from *Gem.* 17b, 18a).

The above reflects the view expressed in the *Gemara* (loc. cit.) that the *asham talui* obligation depends on the presence of two pieces, one permitted and one prohibited. The doubt for which the Torah prescribes the atonement of the *asham talui* must be one which involves חֲתִיכָה אַחַת מִשְּׁתֵּי חֲתִיכוֹת, *one of two pieces*, as explained previously.

There is another view, though, that even one piece of doubtful status is sufficient to create an obligation for *asham talui*. Thus, if one ate a piece of meat about the status of which a doubt was later created, he is liable to an *asham talui*. According to this view, the opening statement of the mishnah stands unqualified: If one ate a piece of meat and later was in doubt whether it was *cheilev*, he must bring an *asham talui*. And it goes without saying, the mishnah continues, that if there were two pieces of meat, one certainly prohibited, that he is liable to an *asham talui*.

The *Gemara* notes various distinctions between a doubt created by one piece of meat and a doubt created by two pieces. The distinction cited by *Rambam* (*Shegagos* 8:2) is the one alluded to by *Rav*, namely that a doubt created by two pieces is classified as אִיקְבַע אִסּוּרָא, *the prohibition was established* [for one piece is certainly forbidden]. However, in a doubt involving only one piece of meat there is no established prohibition. The presence of a prohibited piece of meat changes the nature of the doubt. It is no longer simply a question of *whether* a prohibition existed; it is a question of whether he ate the piece that was prohibited. It is for this type of doubtful transgression that the Torah prescribed an *asham talui*.[1] [For the other two reasons advanced by the *Gemara* and the differences

1. The requirement for the אִיקְבַע אִסּוּרָא factor must be viewed in the larger context of the status of questionable prohibitions.

There is a well-known rule that סָפֵק דְּאוֹרַיְיתָא לְחוּמְרָא, *a doubt regarding a Torah prohibition must be dealt with stringently*. For example, if one is in doubt regarding the permissibility of

יָדוּעַ אֵיזוֹ מֵהֶן אָכַל; אִשְׁתּוֹ וַאֲחוֹתוֹ עִמּוֹ בַבַּיִת, שָׁגַג בְּאַחַת מֵהֶן, וְאֵין יָדוּעַ בְּאֵיזוֹ מֵהֶן שָׁגַג; שַׁבָּת וְיוֹם חוֹל וְעָשָׂה מְלָאכָה בְּאַחַת מֵהֶן, וְאֵין יָדוּעַ בְּאֵיזוֹ מֵהֶם עָשָׂה — מֵבִיא אָשָׁם תָּלוּי.

[ב] **כְּשֵׁם** שֶׁאִם אָכַל חֵלֶב וְחֵלֶב בְּהֶעְלֵם אַחַת אֵינוֹ חַיָּב אֶלָּא חַטָּאת אַחַת, כָּךְ עַל לֹא הוֹדַע שֶׁלָּהֶן אֵינוֹ מֵבִיא אֶלָּא אָשָׁם אֶחָד. אִם

יד אברהם

between them, see the *Gemara's* discussion (17b-18a); *Rambam, Shegagos* 8:24 and *Lechem Mishnah* ad loc.]

אָכַל אֶת־אֶחָד מֵהֶן, וְאֵין יָדוּעַ אֵיזוֹ מֵהֶן אָכַל; — *and he ate one of them, but it is not known which of them he ate;*

At the time he ate one of the pieces, he thought they were both *shumman*. Later, though, he learned that one of them was *cheilev*. Now he is uncertain which piece he ate, the *cheilev* or the *shumman*. If, however, he knew from the outset that one of the pieces of fat lying before him was *cheilev*, and he nevertheless ate one of them, it is deemed a deliberate, rather than unintentional, sin. He cannot, therefore, bring an *asham talui*[1] for he *deliberately* entered into a situation of doubt (*Rav; Rashi*). [Others disagree. See *Shitah Mekubetzes, Kesubos* 22b s.v. וז״ל תלמידי ר״י; *Kovetz Shiurim* ad loc.]

אִשְׁתּוֹ וַאֲחוֹתוֹ עִמּוֹ בַבַּיִת, שָׁגַג בְּאַחַת מֵהֶן, וְאֵין יָדוּעַ בְּאֵיזוֹ מֵהֶן שָׁגַג; — *[or] if his wife and his sister were with him in the house, and he inadvertently cohabited with one of them, but it was not known with which one of them he inadvertently cohabited;*

Another instance of an *asham talui* obligation is if his wife and his sister were together with him, and he was intimate

any food, he must act stringently and not eat it. In the opinion of *Rambam* (*Issurei Biah* 18:17, *Avos Hatumah* 16:1, *Kilayim* 10:27 et al., cf. *Hil. Tumas Hames* 9:12), this law is only Rabbinic in nature. As far as the Torah is concerned, one may consume any food or commit any act which is not certainly prohibited. *Rashba, Kiddushin* 73a, *Toras Habayis* (*Shaar Hataaruvos* p. 22), disagrees, arguing that even a doubt of a prohibition is sufficient grounds for a Torah prohibition. The requirement of an *asham talui* for the transgression of a doubtful nature indicates that a sin *was* committed. This is apparently at variance with *Rambam's* view: If the act was permitted by Torah standards, an atonement is unnecessary. It must therefore be concluded that a doubt of the אִיקְבַע אִסּוּרָא category is regarded more severely and is prohibited by the Torah. It is only regarding an ordinary doubt (involving only one piece) that *Rambam* makes his statement that all doubtful prohibitions are prohibited only מִדְּרַבָּנָן, *by the Rabbis.*

Others explain the question of the status of doubtful prohibitions as the basis of the dispute in the *Gemara* regarding whether the *asham talui* obligation requires two pieces of meat or if one is sufficient. The opinion that an *asham talui* calls for חֲתִיכָה אַחַת מִשְּׁתֵּי חֲתִיכוֹת, *one of two pieces,* is based on the view that an ordinary doubt is not prohibited by the Torah (as is the view of *Rambam*). The opinion that one doubtful piece is sufficient grounds for an *asham talui* regards all doubtful prohibitions as prohibited by the Torah (as is the view of *Rashba*) (*Responsa* of *Maharit, Yoreh Deah* 1, cited by *Shev Shmaatsa* 1:1).

1. If he later learns that he did, indeed, eat the *cheilev* piece, it is not clear whether he is liable to bring a *chatas*. One can reason that he was deliberate merely regarding an uncertain prohibition; he did not intentionally eat a definitely prohibited item (*Rashash*).

but it is not known which of them he ate; [or] if his wife and his sister were with him in the house, and he inadvertently cohabited with one of them, but it was not known with which one of them he inadvertently cohabited; [or] if it was either the Sabbath or a weekday and he performed labor on one of them, but it is not known on which day he did it — he must bring an *asham talui*.

2. Just as if he ate two portions of *cheilev* fat in one lapse of awareness he is liable to only one *chatas*, so when the transgression is not known he brings only one

YAD AVRAHAM

with one of them, thinking she was his wife. When he later discovers that his sister was also present, and that he may have been intimate with her, he must bring an *asham talui* (*Rav; Rashi*).

שַׁבָּת וְיוֹם חוֹל וְעָשָׂה מְלָאכָה בְּאַחַת מֵהֶן, וְאֵין יָדוּעַ בְּאֵיזוֹ מֵהֶם עָשָׂה, — *[or] if it was either the Sabbath or a weekday and he performed labor on one of them, but it is not known on which day he did it,*

He performed labor at twilight, a time that there is a doubt whether it is day or night.[1]

In view of the previously articulated stipulation that an *asham talui* is occasioned only by a doubt created by the presence of an unquestionable prohibition, which creates the status of אִיקְבַע אִסּוּרָא, the *asham talui* for labor performed during the twilight must be for the twilight between the Sabbath and Sunday. Since we are sure that the Sabbath had already been in effect but we are in doubt whether or not it had come to an end, this is tantamount to the אִיקְבַע אִסּוּרָא effect created by the presence of a prohibition. Labor performed on the twilight between Friday and the Sabbath does not occasion an *asham talui* for the prohibition was never clearly established (*Tos.* 17b).

Rambam (*Shegagos* 8:2), however, makes no such distinction, indicating that one is equally liable for labor performed on the twilight of Friday as he is for that performed on the twilight of the Sabbath. His reasoning apparently is that the twilight period is by its very nature a doubt of the אִיקְבַע אִסּוּרָא variety, for the fact that the time is part day and part night in itself establishes the prohibition (*Lechem Mishneh* ad loc.).

מֵבִיא אָשָׁם תָּלוּי. — *he must bring an asham talui.*

[In each of the above-mentioned cases, he brings an *asham talui*.]

The *Tanna* mentions these three cases to illustrate the principle of the *asham talui* obligation in the three main categories of *shegagos*: (1) forbidden food, (2) forbidden sexual relations, (3) forbidden actions (*Rambam Comm.*; cf. *Aruch LaNer*).

2.

כְּשֵׁם שֶׁאִם אָכַל חֵלֶב וְחֵלֶב בְּהֶעְלֵם אַחַת אֵינוֹ חַיָּב אֶלָּא חַטָּאת אַחַת, כָּךְ עַל לֹא הוֹדַע שֶׁלָּהֶן אֵינוֹ מֵבִיא אֶלָּא אָשָׁם אֶחָד. — *Just as if he ate two portions of cheilev fat in one*

1. The twilight period is known as בֵּין הַשְּׁמָשׁוֹת (lit., *between the suns*), the time between sundown and nightfall. There is considerable discussion in Rabbinic literature regarding what constitutes this questionable period and its ramifications in halachah. See ArtScroll *Shabbos* 2:7.

הָיְתָה יְדִיעָה בֵּינְתַּיִם, כְּשֵׁם שֶׁהוּא מֵבִיא חַטָּאת עַל־כָּל־אַחַת וְאַחַת, כָּךְ הוּא מֵבִיא אָשָׁם תָּלוּי עַל־כָּל־אַחַת וְאַחַת. כְּשֵׁם שֶׁאִם אָכַל חֵלֶב, וְדָם, נוֹתָר, וּפִגּוּל בְּהֶעְלֵם אַחַת, חַיָּב עַל־כָּל־אַחַת וְאַחַת, כָּךְ עַל לֹא הוֹדַע שֶׁלָּהֶן, מֵבִיא אָשָׁם תָּלוּי עַל־כָּל־אֶחָד וְאֶחָד.

חֵלֶב וְנוֹתָר לְפָנָיו, אָכַל אֶחָד מֵהֶם, וְאֵין יָדוּעַ אֵיזֶה מֵהֶם אָכַל; אִשְׁתּוֹ נִדָּה וַאֲחוֹתוֹ עִמּוֹ בַבַּיִת, שָׁגַג בְּאַחַת מֵהֶן, וְאֵין יָדוּעַ בְּאֵיזֶה מֵהֶן שָׁגַג; שַׁבָּת וְיוֹם הַכִּפּוּרִים, וְעָשָׂה מְלָאכָה בֵּין הַשְּׁמָשׁוֹת, וְאֵין יָדוּעַ בְּאֵיזֶה מֵהֶם עָשָׂה — רַבִּי אֱלִיעֶזֶר מְחַיֵּב חַטָּאת,

יד אברהם

lapse of awareness he is liable to only one chatas, so when the transgression is not known he brings only one asham talui.

Just as we have learned above (3:2) that a repetition of the *cheilev* prohibition in one lapse of awareness occasions only one *chatas*, so too does the repetition of a questionable prohibition occasion only one *asham talui*.

For example, a person ate two of numerous pieces of meat, all of which he supposed were *shumman*, and later learns that both pieces he ate may have been *cheilev*. [Thus he has a situation of uncertainty regarding *two* possible transgressions.] Since he did not gain awareness of their doubtful state between eating the two pieces, he is liable to one *asham talui* for eating both (*Rav; Rashi; Tif. Yis.*).

אִם הָיְתָה יְדִיעָה בֵּינְתַּיִם, — *[But] if there was awareness in the interim,*

If between eating the first *kezayis* and the second *kezayis*, he became aware that there was a possibility that he ate *cheilev*, and then he forgot again and ate the second piece (*Rav; Rashi; Tif. Yis.*).

כְּשֵׁם שֶׁהוּא מֵבִיא חַטָּאת עַל־כָּל־אַחַת וְאַחַת, כָּךְ הוּא מֵבִיא אָשָׁם תָּלוּי עַל־כָּל־אַחַת וְאַחַת. *— just as he brings a chatas for each one, so does he bring an asham talui for each one.*

Just as he would bring a chatas for each *kezayis* that he ate if he became aware between eating them that they were definitely *cheilev*, so if he became aware of the doubt between eating the first piece and the second piece, he must bring a separate *asham talui* for each piece (*Rav; Rashi*).

כְּשֵׁם שֶׁאִם אָכַל חֵלֶב, וְדָם, נוֹתָר, וּפִגּוּל בְּהֶעְלֵם אַחַת, חַיָּב עַל־כָּל־אַחַת וְאַחַת, כָּךְ עַל לֹא הוֹדַע שֶׁלָּהֶן, מֵבִיא אָשָׁם תָּלוּי עַל־כָּל־אֶחָד וְאֶחָד. — *Just as if he ate cheilev, blood, nossar, and piggul in one period of forgetfulness, he is liable for each one, so when the transgression is not known, he must bring an asham talui for each one.*

Just as if he is liable for a separate *chatas* for all these distinctly prohibited substances if he ate them consecutively without reminding himself of their prohibitions, as we learned above (3:2), so does each distinct category of prohibition occasion a separate *asham talui* (*Tif. Yis.*).

חֵלֶב וְנוֹתָר לְפָנָיו, אָכַל אֶחָד מֵהֶם, וְאֵין יָדוּעַ אֵיזֶה מֵהֶם אָכַל; — *[If] cheilev and nossar were before him, and he ate one of them, but it is not known which of them he ate;*

4 *asham talui.* [But] if there was awareness in the interim,
2 just as he brings a *chatas* for each one, so does he bring an *asham talui* for each one. Just as if he ate *cheilev*, blood, *nossar*, and *piggul* in one period of forgetfulness, he is liable for each one, so when the transgression is not known, he must bring an *asham talui* for each one.

[If] *cheilev* and *nossar* were before him, and he ate one of them, but it is not known which of them he ate; [or if] his menstruous wife and his sister were with him in the house, and he inadvertently cohabited with one of them, but it is not known with which one of them he inadvertently cohabited; [or if] the Sabbath and Yom Kippur [followed one another], and he performed labor at twilight, but it is not known on which of them he performed [labor] — R' Eliezer holds [him] liable to a *chatas*,

YAD AVRAHAM

He thought that they were both pieces of permissible *shumman* meat (*Rav; Rashi*).

[It later became apparent that one of the pieces of fat was *cheilev* and the other was *nossar* [sacrificial meat left over beyond its allotted eating time]. Although there no longer is any question that he inadvertently transgressed a *kares* prohibition, for either piece is prohibited, it is still a matter of doubt as to *which* prohibition he violated.]

אִשְׁתּוֹ נִדָּה וַאֲחוֹתוֹ עִמּוֹ בַבַּיִת, שָׁגַג בְּאַחַת מֵהֶן, וְאֵין יָדוּעַ בְּאֵיזֶה מֵהֶן שָׁגַג; — *[or if] his menstruous wife and his sister were with him in the house, and he inadvertently cohabited with one of them, but it is not known with which one of them he inadvertently cohabited;*

He thought that the woman with whom he was intimate was his wife, and he did not know that she was a *niddah*. He later discovered that his wife was a *niddah* and, in addition, the woman with whom he was intimate may have been his sister (*Rav; Rashi*).

שַׁבָּת וְיוֹם הַכִּפּוּרִים, וְעָשָׂה מְלָאכָה בֵּין הַשְּׁמָשׁוֹת, — *[or if] the Sabbath and Yom Kippur [followed one another], and he performed labor at twilight,*

Yom Kippur and the Sabbath fell consecutively and he performed labor at twilight between the two holy days, thinking that it was a weekday (*Rav*).

Yom Kippur could fall on Friday or Sunday only when the *beis din* sanctified the month based on sighting the moon. After the adoption of the calendar [formulated in 4118 (358 c.e.) by R' Hillel HaSheini, the son of R' Yehudah Nesia (*Seder HaDoros*)], Yom Kippur cannot fall on Sunday, Tuesday, or Friday. See *Rambam Comm., Rosh Hashanah* 2:3 and *Menachos* 11:7 and ArtScroll *Menachos*, p. 242, footnote 1.

וְאֵין יָדוּעַ בְּאֵיזֶה מֵהֶם עָשָׂה — *but it is not known on which of them he performed [labor]* —

[Since *bein hashemashos* is regarded as the doubtful period, it is uncertain whether the labor took place during the day or night.]

רַבִּי אֱלִיעֶזֶר מְחַיֵּב חַטָּאת, — *R' Eliezer holds [him] liable to a chatas,*

Since, in any of the aforementioned events, he certainly committed a transgression. For example, in the case of *cheilev* and *nossar*, whatever he ate was a prohibited substance, and so on regarding the other cases (*Rav* from *Gem.* 19a).

וְרַבִּי יְהוֹשֻׁעַ פּוֹטֵר.

אָמַר רַבִּי יוֹסֵי: לֹא נֶחֱלְקוּ עַל־הָעוֹשֶׂה מְלָאכָה בֵּין־הַשְּׁמָשׁוֹת שֶׁהוּא פָּטוּר, שֶׁאֲנִי אוֹמֵר מִקְצַת מְלָאכָה עָשָׂה מֵהַיּוֹם וּמִקְצָתָהּ לְמָחָר. וְעַל־מַה נֶחֱלְקוּ? עַל הָעוֹשֶׂה בְּתוֹךְ הַיּוֹם, וְאֵין יָדוּעַ אִם בַּשַּׁבָּת עָשָׂה וְאִם בְּיוֹם הַכִּפּוּרִים עָשָׂה, אוֹ עַל הָעוֹשֶׂה, וְאֵין יָדוּעַ מֵעֵין אֵיזוֹ מְלָאכָה עָשָׂה. רַבִּי אֱלִיעֶזֶר מְחַיֵּב חַטָּאת, וְרַבִּי יְהוֹשֻׁעַ פּוֹטֵר. אָמַר רַבִּי יְהוּדָה: פּוֹטְרוֹ הָיָה רַבִּי יְהוֹשֻׁעַ אַף מֵאָשָׁם תָּלוּי.

יד אברהם

וְרַבִּי יְהוֹשֻׁעַ פּוֹטֵר. — *but R' Yehoshua exempts [him].*

[Although regardless of what scenario transpired a sin was inadvertently committed, R' Yehoshua considers him exempt from a *chatas* because, in the final analysis, it is still unknown precisely which prohibition was violated.]

R' Yehoshua derives this exemption from the Torah's phrase regarding the *chatas* obligation (*Lev.* 4:23): חַטָּאתוֹ אֲשֶׁר חָטָא בָּהּ, *his sin in which he sinned*. This denotes that in order to be liable to a *chatas*, the sinner must know which transgression he committed. R' Eliezer, for his part, claims that this superfluous expression was written to exclude מִתְעַסֵּק, *an unwitting act*, from a *chatas*. This will be discussed at the end of mishnah 3 (*Rav* from *Gem.* 19).

אָמַר רַבִּי יוֹסֵי: לֹא נֶחֱלְקוּ עַל־הָעוֹשֶׂה מְלָאכָה בֵּין־הַשְּׁמָשׁוֹת שֶׁהוּא פָּטוּר, — *Said R' Yose: They did not disagree that one who performed labor at twilight is exempt,*

R' Yose says that the previously mentioned dispute between R' Eliezer and R' Yehoshua — regarding someone who is uncertain which prohibition he transgressed — does not concern someone who performed a labor during *bein hashemashos* between the Sabbath and Yom Kippur. In that case, even R' Eliezer — who rules that the sinner is liable to a *chatas* although he does not know which sin he committed — does not differ with R' Yehoshua. Both agree that he is exempt (*Rav; Rashi*).

שֶׁאֲנִי אוֹמֵר מִקְצַת מְלָאכָה עָשָׂה מֵהַיּוֹם וּמִקְצָתָהּ לְמָחָר. — *for I may say that he did part of the labor today and part of it tomorrow.*

It is possible that, in doing the forbidden labor in the twilight period between the two holy days, less than the minimum amount of labor required for a *chatas* obligation was done on the Sabbath, and less than the minimum amount was done on Yom Kippur. Thus, even though the labor in its totality was prohibited, neither of its portions are sufficient to create a *chatas* obligation (*Rav*).

[Therefore, R' Yose argues, everyone would agree that performing labor in the twilight between the Sabbath and Yom Kippur would not call for a *chatas*.]

Actually, in R' Yose's opinion — recorded elsewhere, (*Shabbos* 34b) — the entire *bein hashemashos* interval is only כְּהֶרֶף עַיִן, *as the blink of an eye*, a period much too short to be divided into two parts. R' Yose's argument is tenable nonetheless, for it is still possible that part of the labor was done on one day and the remainder during *bein hashemashos* and beyond (*Tif. Yis.*)

וְעַל־מַה נֶחֱלְקוּ? — *Concerning what did they differ?*

[Concerning which case does R' Eliezer

4 but R′ Yehoshua exempts [him].
2 Said R′ Yose: They did not disagree that one who performed labor at twilight is exempt, for I may say that he did part of the labor today and part of it tomorrow. Concerning what did they differ? Concerning one who performed [labor] in the middle of the day, but it is not known whether he did it on the Sabbath or on Yom Kippur, or concerning one who performed [labor], but it is not known what type of labor he did. R′ Eliezer holds [him] liable to a *chatas*, but R′ Yehoshua exempts [him]. Said R′ Yehudah: R′ Yehoshua exempted him even from an *asham talui*.

YAD AVRAHAM

consider him obligated for a *chatas* and R′ Yehoshua exempt him?]

עַל הָעוֹשֶׂה בְּתוֹךְ הַיּוֹם, וְאֵין יָדוּעַ אִם בַּשַּׁבָּת עָשָׂה וְאִם בְּיוֹם הַכִּפּוּרִים עָשָׂה, — *Concerning one who performed [labor] in the middle of the day, but it is not known whether he did it on the Sabbath or on Yom Kippur,*

[In this situation, of course, a transgression undoubtably took place, although it is not known which day was desecrated. Thus R′ Eliezer holds him liable for a *chatas*. R′ Yehoshua exempts him.]

אוֹ עַל הָעוֹשֶׂה, וְאֵין יָדוּעַ מֵעֵין אֵיזוֹ מְלָאכָה עָשָׂה. — *or concerning one who performed [labor], but it is not known what type of labor he did.*

He knows definitely that he performed labor on the Sabbath, but is uncertain which. For example, he doesn't recall whether he plowed or he sowed (*Rav; Rashi*).

רַבִּי אֱלִיעֶזֶר מְחַיֵּב חַטָּאת, — *R′ Eliezer holds [him] liable to a chatas,*

[R′ Eliezer holds him liable since he certainly committed a sin.]

וְרַבִּי יְהוֹשֻׁעַ פּוֹטֵר. — *but R′ Yehoshua exempts [him].*

[As explained above, R′ Yehoshua requires definite knowledge of which sin the person committed in order to make him liable to a *chatas*, a principle he derives from the phrase אֲשֶׁר חָטָא בָּהּ, *in which he sinned*.]

אָמַר רַבִּי יְהוּדָה: פּוֹטְרוֹ הָיָה רַבִּי יְהוֹשֻׁעַ אַף מֵאָשָׁם תָּלוּי. — *Said R′ Yehudah: R′ Yehoshua exempted him even from an asham talui.*

[Not only is he exempt from bringing a *chatas* — as it remains uncertain which prohibition he violated — but he is also exempt from bringing an *asham talui*, despite the fact that there is an uncertainty about his transgression.]

R′ Yehudah bases his ruling on the Torah's phrase (*Lev.* 5:17): וְאִם־נֶפֶשׁ כִּי תֶחֱטָא... וְלֹא־יָדַע, *And if a person sins ... and he did not know*. He is obligated to bring an *asham talui* only if he was uncertain whether he sinned. In the above-described situation, however, he knows that he sinned; only the nature of the sin is not known. At the same time, though, he is not liable to a *chatas* since the nature of the sin is not certain (*Rav*).

In other words, he knows too much to bring an *asham talui* but not enough to bring a *chatas* (*Tif. Yis.*).

The halachah does not follow R′ Yehudah. He is liable for an *asham talui* whether it is a doubt that can be resolved [such as eating a piece of meat which was either *cheilev* or *nossar*] or it is a doubt that cannot be resolved [such as doing labor in the twilight between the

[ג] רַבִּי שִׁמְעוֹן שְׁזוּרִי וְרַבִּי שִׁמְעוֹן אוֹמְרִים: לֹא נֶחֱלְקוּ עַל־דָּבָר שֶׁהוּא מִשּׁוּם שֵׁם אֶחָד, שֶׁהוּא חַיָּב. וְעַל־מַה־נֶּחֱלְקוּ? עַל־דָּבָר שֶׁהוּא מִשּׁוּם שְׁנֵי שֵׁמוֹת, שֶׁרַבִּי אֱלִיעֶזֶר מְחַיֵּב חַטָּאת, וְרַבִּי יְהוֹשֻׁעַ פּוֹטֵר. אָמַר רַבִּי יְהוּדָה: אֲפִלּוּ

יד אברהם

Sabbath and Yom Kippur] (*Rav*).

Rambam (*Shegagos*, 8:5), however, rules in accordance with R' Yehudah that he is not liable to an *asham talui* (*Tif. Yis.*). [This is the reading in the *Kafich* edition of the *Mishnah Commentary* as well.]

3.

The following mishnah continues to elaborate on the dispute between R' Eliezer and R' Yehoshua mentioned in the previous mishnah. In addition, the mishnah focuses on a detail of the dispute not highlighted earlier — the exemption of מִתְעַסֵּק [*misassek*], *an unwitting violator.*

◆§ מִתְעַסֵּק — The Unwitting Violator

Although the Torah prescribes the *chatas* atonement for an *unintentional* transgression, it exempts a person whose sin was performed in an *unwitting* manner.

What is the difference between שׁוֹגֵג, simply *unintentional*, and מִתְעַסֵּק, *unwitting?*

שׁוֹגֵג refers to an error of judgment; מִתְעַסֵּק to unawareness. The שׁוֹגֵג is aware of what he is doing but *errs* in thinking that it is permitted. For example, one reaped on the Sabbath because he thought it was a weekday or because he thought that reaping is permitted on the Sabbath: He intentionally performed the act of reaping but erred in thinking that it was permitted. This is considered שׁוֹגֵג, an *unintentional* violation of Torah law. If, however, he intended to perform a permitted act, such as picking up a knife or cutting an already harvested vegetable and in doing so he unwittingly cut a vegetable that was still growing, although he violated a Torah prohibition, he did so by performing an act other than he intended to. This is called מִתְעַסֵּק, for the act was *unwitting*, rather than the result of erroneous judgment or ignorance (*Rashi*, *Shabbos* 72b; *Tos.* 19b cited by *Tos. Yom Tov* on mishnah 2).

An exception to the exemption of מִתְעַסֵּק is a situation in which physical pleasure is experienced. The *Gemara* (19b) states the following principle [in the name of Shmuel]: מִתְעַסֵּק בַּחֲלָבִים וַעֲרָיוֹת חַיָּב, שֶׁכֵּן נֶהֱנָה, *the one who is unwitting regarding cheilev fats and intimacies is [nonetheless] liable [to a chatas], as he experienced [physical] pleasure.* Thus, one who intended to eat a piece of permitted meat but unwittingly ate a *different* piece, which is *cheilev*, is nevertheless liable to a *chatas*. Similarly, one who intended to have relations with his wife but unwittingly cohabited with his sister instead, is likewise obligated for a *chatas*. The mishnah discusses the exemption of מִתְעַסֵּק as it is developed from the dispute between R' Eliezer and R' Yehoshua of the previous mishnah.

רַבִּי שִׁמְעוֹן שְׁזוּרִי וְרַבִּי שִׁמְעוֹן אוֹמְרִים: — *R' Shimon Shizuri and R' Shimon say:*

R' Shimon Shizuri was a disciple of R' Tarfon. He was named after the place of his residence, Shizur, a town near Kefar Anan, in Upper Galilee, in the vicinity of Safed (*Aruch HaShalem*, quoting *Seder HaDoros* p. 183). Alternatively he was called Shizuri, *spinner*, because of his occupation: a spinner [of threads] (*Rambam*).

4 **3.** R′ Shimon Shizuri and R′ Shimon say: They did not
3 disagree that concerning anything of one category he is liable. Concerning what do they differ? Concerning something of two categories, that R′ Eliezer holds [him] liable to a *chatas*, and R′ Yehoshua exempts [him].

YAD AVRAHAM

Whenever the mishnah cites R′ Shimon, with no surname, it always refers to R′ Shimon ben Yochai, the disciple of R′ Akiva (see *Yevamos* 62b).

לֹא נֶחְלְקוּ עַל־דָּבָר שֶׁהוּא מִשּׁוּם שֵׁם אֶחָד, שֶׁהוּא חַיָּב. — *They did not disagree that concerning anything of one category he is liable.*

[In the previous mishnah R′ Eliezer and R′ Yehoshua disagreed on the status of someone who certainly committed a transgression but is uncertain of which: R′ Eliezer holds him liable to a *chatas* and R′ Yehoshua says he is exempt. R′ Shimon Shizuri and R′ Shimon now add that if both transgressions in question were of the same category there is no disagreement that he is liable to a *chatas*.]

For example, one is uncertain whether he desecrated the Sabbath by picking the fruit of one fig tree or the fruit of another fig tree: Since he certainly picked the fruit of a fig tree it is immaterial which, because in either case, he transgressed the *av melachah* of קוֹצֵר, *reaping,* in the same manner. Thus he is liable to a *chatas* even according to R′ Yehoshua (*Rashi*).

Likewise, if a person's two menstruous wives or two sisters were with him and he cohabited with one of them, but he does not know which one, he is liable to a *chatas* because he is certain of the type of sin he committed (*Rav; Rambam, Comm.*).

Tos. R′ Akiva Eiger questions the latter illustration, given by *Rav* and *Rambam* concerning two menstruants or sisters. Regarding these transgressions, he argues, he would be liable even if he intended to cohabit with his wife who was *tahor* and inadvertently was intimate with another wife who was a menstruant. As explained in the prefatory remarks to the mishnah, the *Gemara* (20b) articulates the principle that מִתְעַסֵּק בַּחֲלָבִים וַעֲרָיוֹת חַיָּב, שֶׁכֵּן נֶהֱנָה, *the one who is unwitting regarding cheilev fats or intimacies is [nonetheless] liable [for a chatas], as he experienced [physical] pleasure*. Thus, one need not *intend* to cohabit with a menstruant to be liable for a *chatas*, and the issue of his cognizance of the fact is irrelevant. Thus, R′ Akiva Eiger opts for the illustration of *chillul Shabbos* cited by *Rashi* above.

וְעַל־מַה־נֶּחְלְקוּ? — *Concerning what do they differ?*

Regarding what case, then, do R′ Eliezer and R′ Yehoshua differ?

עַל־דָּבָר שֶׁהוּא מִשּׁוּם שְׁנֵי שֵׁמוֹת, — *Concerning something of two categories,*

He is uncertain which category of prohibition he transgressed or in which manner he did it. For example, he knows that he desecrated the Sabbath but is uncertain how — whether he plowed or he sowed, or whether he picked figs or picked grapes. The same, of course, applies if he intended to do one sin and he unwittingly did another (*Rashi*).

שֶׁרַבִּי אֱלִיעֶזֶר מְחַיֵּב חַטָּאת, וְרַבִּי יְהוֹשֻׁעַ פּוֹטֵר. — *that R′ Eliezer holds [him] liable to a chatas, and R′ Yehoshua exempts [him].*

R′ Yehoshua holds that, since the Torah states: אֲשֶׁר חָטָא בָּהּ, *in which he sinned*, in order to be liable to a *chatas*, he must intend to commit that particular sin and become aware of the sin that he committed. In the above cases, either he did not become aware with a certainty of the particular sin he had committed or he did not commit the sin that he had intended. Thus, he is not liable to a *chatas*. R′ Eliezer, however, understands that as long as he intends to do an act that involves a sin, and later, becomes aware that he has sinned, he is liable to a *chatas* (*Rashi*).

כריתות ד/ג

נִתְכַּוֵּן לְלַקֵּט תְּאֵנִים וְלִקֵּט עֲנָבִים, עֲנָבִים וְלִקֵּט תְּאֵנִים, שְׁחוֹרוֹת וְלִקֵּט לְבָנוֹת, לְבָנוֹת וְלִקֵּט שְׁחוֹרוֹת, רַבִּי אֱלִיעֶזֶר מְחַיֵּב חַטָּאת, וְרַבִּי יְהוֹשֻׁעַ פּוֹטֵר. אָמַר רַבִּי יְהוּדָה: תָּמֵהַּ אֲנִי אִם יִפְטֹר בָּהּ רַבִּי יְהוֹשֻׁעַ. אִם כֵּן, לָמָּה נֶאֱמַר: ,,אֲשֶׁר חָטָא בָהּ?" פְּרָט לַמִּתְעַסֵּק.

יד אברהם

אָמַר רַבִּי יְהוּדָה: אֲפִלּוּ נִתְכַּוֵּן לְלַקֵּט תְּאֵנִים וְלִקֵּט עֲנָבִים, עֲנָבִים וְלִקֵּט תְּאֵנִים, שְׁחוֹרוֹת וְלִקֵּט לְבָנוֹת, לְבָנוֹת וְלִקֵּט שְׁחוֹרוֹת, — *Said R' Yehudah: Even if he intended to pick figs and he picked grapes, [to pick] grapes and he picked figs, [to pick] black ones and he picked white ones, [or to pick] white ones and he picked black ones,*

[R' Yehudah goes a step further than R' Shimon Shizuri and R' Shimon. According to him, to be liable for a *chatas* one must fulfill his intention to sin, not only in terms of the category of the transgression but even in its physical form. Thus, R' Yehoshua exempts him even if he intended to pick one species of fruit and he in fact picked another. Although in terms of halachah, both acts are identical transgressions, the physical distinction between the two acts exempts him from a *chatas*.]

The *Gemara* (20a) explains that if indeed he did pick a fruit other than the one he intended, there is no dispute that he would be exempt. He would be considered a מִתְעַסֵּק, *an unwitting violator*, for he did not fulfill his intended act; even R' Eliezer would exempt him under those circumstances.

The *Gemara* therefore interprets R' Yehudah's qualification of the controversy between R' Eliezer and R' Yehoshua as referring to a mistake in the *order* of his actions. The mishnah's case is one in which a person had intended to first pick figs and then grapes, or to first pick black ones and then white ones. Then, unwittingly, he reversed the order (*Rav*).

רַבִּי אֱלִיעֶזֶר מְחַיֵּב חַטָּאת, — *R' Eliezer holds [him] liable to a chatas,*

Since he had intended to do both acts, the sequence is not important (*Rav*).

וְרַבִּי יְהוֹשֻׁעַ פּוֹטֵר. — *and R' Yehoshua exempts [him].*

Since each fruit that he picked is not the one he intended, he is considered a מִתְעַסֵּק, *an unwitting violator*, and he is exempt from a *chatas* (*Rav*).

Rashi (21a) explains that R' Shimon Shizuri and R' Shimon agree with R' Yehudah's statement that the controversy between R' Eliezer and R' Yehoshua is in regards to the order of his actions. They disagree with R' Yehudah only insofar as its application. They hold that should one intend to pick black and white figs, even R' Yehoshua rules that the sequence means nothing; he is liable even if it reversed. The only case in which R' Yehoshua rules that he is exempt is one in which he reverses the order of two *species* of fruit. For example, he intends to pick figs and grapes in a certain sequence, and unwittingly reverses the sequence.

אָמַר רַבִּי יְהוּדָה: תָּמֵהַּ אֲנִי אִם יִפְטֹר בָּהּ רַבִּי יְהוֹשֻׁעַ. — *[But] said R' Yehudah: I am amazed that* [lit. *if*] *R' Yehoshua exempts [him] in this case.*

R' Yehudah concludes his statement by questioning its reasoning. He, in effect, says as follows: Although it is true that I have been taught that R' Yehoshua exempted simply because he unwittingly reversed the order of his intentions, I cannot understand why (*Rashi*).

Some omit the clause אָמַר רַבִּי יְהוּדָה and read simply וְתָמֵהַּ אֲנִי, *but I am amazed* [or תְּמֵהַנִי, a contraction of the two words]

4 Said R' Yehudah: Even if he intended to pick figs and he
3 picked grapes, [to pick] grapes and he picked figs, [to pick] black ones and he picked white ones, [or to pick] white ones and he picked black ones, R' Eliezer holds [him] liable to a *chatas*, and R' Yehoshua exempts [him]. [But] said R' Yehudah: I am amazed that R' Yehoshua exempts [him] in this case. If so, why is it stated (*Lev.* 4:23): *In which he sinned?* This is to exclude an unwitting act.

YAD AVRAHAM

(*Rabbeinu Gershom, Rashi; Shitah Mekubetzes*). Others read אָמַר רַבִּי שִׁמְעוֹן, attributing this statement to R' Shimon who is in effect arguing against R' Yehudah's version of the dispute between R' Eliezer and R' Yehoshua (*Rav; Rambam Comm.*).

אִם כֵּן, — *If so,*

The anonymous mishnah now counters the previous question (*Rav*). Others explain that it is R' Yehudah who is rebutting R' Shimon's previous question [i.e., if you disagree with me and do not consider one who reversed the sequence of his actions exempt, what then do you derive from the verse אֲשֶׁר חָטָא בָּהּ?] (*Rambam Comm.*).

לָמָּה נֶאֱמַר: ,,אֲשֶׁר חָטָא בָּהּ?" — *why is it stated* (*Lev.* 4:23): *In which he sinned?*

Since R' Yehoshua does not exempt him when he sins out of the sequence he had intended, what exemption is meant by the expression: אֲשֶׁר חָטָא בָּהּ, *in which he sinned?* (*Rav; Rashi; Rambam Comm.*).

R' Shimon could have answered: Even if you find difficulty in my doubt that R' Yehoshua exempts him for sins out of sequence, nevertheless how will you account for R' Eliezer's view? R' Eliezer *surely* holds him liable to a *chatas*. [What does *he* learn from the phrase אֲשֶׁר חָטָא בָּהּ?] (*Tos. Yom Tov*).

פְּרָט לְמִתְעַסֵּק. — *This is to exclude an unwitting act.*

[The answer is that] it comes to exclude either one who had no intention at all of picking the fruit, but unwittingly did so, or one who intended to pick figs and picked grapes. In this case, when his intention was not executed at all, the Torah exempts him as מִתְעַסֵּק (*Rav*).

According to R' Eliezer, the exemption of מִתְעַסֵּק is derived from the word בָּהּ, as the mishnah here mentions. According to R' Yehoshua, the word בָּהּ teaches us that in order to be liable for a *chatas*, one must be certain which sin he committed, as discussed in mishnah 2. According to him, the exemption of מִתְעַסֵּק is the result of the Torah's requirement for מְלֶאכֶת מַחֲשֶׁבֶת, *intentional labor*. One who intended to perform one act and unwittingly did another is not considered to have done an intentional labor. [This exemption, which does not appear in the mishnah, is mentioned by the *Gemara* (10b) in the name of Shmuel] (*Rashi* 19a s.v. מיבעי לי).

Tosafos deal differently with the issue of the two exemptions mentioned in connection with מִתְעַסֵּק. They explain that the exemption intended by our mishnah from the word בָּהּ and the one intended by the *Gemara* from the concept of מְלֶאכֶת מַחֲשֶׁבֶת, are not one and the same; they refer to two different types of מִתְעַסֵּק. The exemption derived from the word בָּהּ is a general one, which mandates that a *chatas* is not brought when one unwittingly transgresses a prohibition. For example, he intended to cut a vegetable that he thought was detached from the ground and later discovered it was still growing. Although his intention to cut this vegetable was fulfilled, he did not intend to do something prohibited. [This is called נִתְכַּוֵּן לְהֶתֵּר וְעָלְתָה בְיָדוֹ איסור, *he intended [to do] a permitted [act] but unwittingly did a prohibited act.*] The exemption of מְלֶאכֶת מַחֲשֶׁבֶת, by contrast, refers even to one who intended to do a prohibition but did not execute his act in the fashion he intended, e.g., he intended to pick grapes and picked figs

כריתות [א] **דַּם** שְׁחִיטָה בִּבְהֵמָה, בַּחַיָּה, וּבָעוֹפוֹת, בֵּין טְמֵאִים וּבֵין טְהוֹרִים; דַּם נְחִירָה; וְדַם עִקּוּר; וְדַם הַקָּזָה, שֶׁהַנֶּפֶשׁ יוֹצְאָה בוֹ —

ה/א

יד אברהם

instead, or the like. This exemption is unique to the laws of the Sabbath, in which the Torah specified the required מְלֶאכֶת מַחְשֶׁבֶת. This is referred to as נִתְכַּוֵּן לְאִיסוּר וְעָלְתָה בְיָדוֹ אִיסוּר אַחֵר, *he intended to do one prohibition and did another*. Hence, the exemption mentioned in the mishnah and that mentioned in the *Gemara* are complementary rather than conflicting[1] (*Tos.; Shabbos* 72b).

Chapter 5

1.

The following mishnah deals with the prohibition of eating blood, listed above (1:1) among those transgressions punishable by *kares*.

דַּם שְׁחִיטָה — *Slaughter-blood*

[This refers to blood shed during the course of slaughtering.]

בִּבְהֵמָה, בַּחַיָּה, וּבָעוֹפוֹת, — *of cattle, of* ***beasts****, or of fowl,*

בְּהֵמָה, *cattle*, is the term used for domesticated animals. It includes bulls, cows, sheep and goats which are kosher, and horses, donkeys, pigs which are not (see *Kilayim* 8:6).

חַיָּה, *beasts*, refers to undomesticated or wild animals. Included in this category are the deer, antelope, ibex, bison, giraffe, which are kosher; and the wild donkey, elephant, monkey, which are not (see *Deut.* 14:5; *Chullin* 59b; and *Kilayim* loc. cit.).

Blood shed in the course of the slaughter of any of these animals [is prohibited by the Torah and is punishable by *kares*] (*Rashi*).

The prohibition against the consumption of blood states (*Lev.* 7:26): וְכָל־דָּם לֹא תֹאכְלוּ . . . לָעוֹף וְלַבְּהֵמָה, *you shall not eat any blood whether of fowl or of cattle.* The blood of fowl and cattle are mentioned explicitly; that of beasts is included in the word בְּהֵמָה, as is taught in the maxim, חַיָּה בִּכְלַל בְּהֵמָה, *beasts can be included in the term* בְּהֵמָה (*Chullin* 71a, *Bava Kamma* 54b et al.) (*Tos. Yom Tov*).

בֵּין טְמֵאִים וּבֵין טְהוֹרִים; — *whether unclean or clean;*

[The blood is prohibited regardless of whether or not these aforementioned creatures are clean, i.e., permitted to be eaten by the Torah, or not.]

It is derived by exegesis that the terms לָעוֹף וְלַבְּהֵמָה, *whether of fowl or of cattle*, refers to all creatures in these categories, both permissible and forbidden (*Tos. Yom Tov*, from *Gem.* 21a).

Tos. R' Akiva Eiger argues that it is not necessary to resort to exegesis to come to this conclusion; the terms עוֹף and בְּהֵמָה in themselves include both clean and unclean species. The exegesis mentioned in the *Gemara* is used, rather, to include a כְּוִי, an animal of doubtful status, which may be in a category by itself, neither cattle nor beast.

דַּם נְחִירָה; — *blood [shed as a result] of piercing;*

נְחִירָה is stabbing the animal in the neck, thereby piercing the windpipe which ends with the nostrils. This is a method of slaughter which is not valid for *shechitah* (*Tif. Yis., Rav, Chullin* 5:3; cf. *Rashi* and *Rav, Bava Kamma* 7:5; *Mussaf HeAruch*).

The term נְחִירָה is sometimes rendered as *choking* (*Rashi, Chullin* 85b). This, however,

1. See *Responsa Rabbi Akiva Eiger* (I), Responsa 8, for an amplification of this distinction.

5
1 **1.** Slaughter-blood of cattle, of beasts, or of fowl, whether unclean or clean; blood [shed as a result] of piercing; or blood [shed as a result] of tearing; or the blood of bloodletting, by which life escapes — they

YAD AVRAHAM

cannot apply to our mishnah, which obviously refers to an action that causes bleeding.

וְדַם עִקּוּר; — *or blood [shed as a result] of tearing;*

עִקּוּר, *tearing*, is a form of an invalid *shechitah*. It describes a situation where the throat organs involved in *shechitah* [viz., trachea and esophagus] were *torn* from their place of attachment (*Rav*).

Alternatively, it means that the organs were severed by a knife that had a nick [called a *pegimah*], resulting in a slight *tearing* rather than a smooth slicing. This, too, is an invalid *shechitah* (*Tif. Yis.*).

In the context of the laws of *shechitah*, the term *ikkur* refers to one of the five invalidating factors which are derived from an oral tradition [*halachah l'Moshe miSinai*]. There, too, there is a dispute regarding what is meant: According to *Rashi* it means slaughtering with a nicked knife; according to *Halachos Gedolos* it means slaughtering organs which were detached from their place in the jaw [see *Tosafos Chullin* 9a; ArtScroll Mishnah *Chullin*, prefatory remarks to 1:1].

If, in the context of our mishnah, we are to follow the latter interpretation of the term *ikkur*, we must explain that the blood in question was emitted as a result of the *slaughter* of the detached organs, not simply the detachment itself. The detachment of the organs in itself does not render the animal *treifah*. It is simply the slaughter of such organs which is considered invalid (*Tos.* 20b).

Others, though, disagree, holding that detachment of the organs does indeed render the animal *treifah* (*Ramban*).

Tos. Yom Tov suggests that, in the context of our mishnah, *ikkur* means simply slaughtering the animal by tearing out its organs rather than using a knife. The blood that issues forth as a result of this slaughter is indeed lifeblood but is distinct from the previously mentioned blood of slaughtering or blood of stabbing. (See at length his commentary to *Chullin* 5:3.)

וְדַם הַקָּזָה, שֶׁהַנֶּפֶשׁ יוֹצְאָה בוֹ – — *or the blood of bloodletting, by which life escapes* —

If someone, for the purpose of bloodletting [which was commonly practiced for therapeutic reasons], opened the arteries of an animal or fowl until the lifeblood issued forth, he is liable to *kares* for the consumption of that blood (*Tif. Yis.*).

Blood issues forth in three stages. At the time of the incision, the blood simply oozes out without any force, at first black in color then turning red. Later, the blood issues forth as a stream. Then, as the victim weakens, the flow of blood is reduced to a trickle. The lifeblood, then, is the middle blood — that which is emitted in a stream. The blood that oozes initially is simply דַּם מַכָּה, *the blood of a wound;* the blood that oozes while the animal is dying is no longer the lifeblood (*Rav* from *Gem.* 22a according to R' Yochanan; *Tos. Yom Tov, Rambam, Hil. Maachalos Asuros* 6:3).

Tosafos (20b s.v. דם), explain that the quality of דַּם שֶׁהַנֶּפֶשׁ יוֹצְאָה בוֹ is critical to the *kares* punishment for all of the above-mentioned cases, i.e., the consumption of blood of slaughter, piercing or stabbing is punishable by *kares* only if it was the lifeblood. It is however mentioned specifically in connection with the case of bloodletting because it is not usual for one to perform bloodletting to the extent that the lifeblood issues forth. Therefore, the mishnah must mention specifically that the blood of the bloodletting must be of the lifeblood variety.

Rambam (*Maachalos Asuros* 6:3) disagrees. In his view it is only the blood of bloodletting that must be דַּם שֶׁהַנֶּפֶשׁ יוֹצְאָה בוֹ in order for the *kares* punishment to take effect. This is because the blood involved is really דַּם הָאֵבָרִים, *blood of the limbs*, not blood of the life-giving arteries. Were it to be the blood of slaughter [or tearing or stabbing], he would be liable for *any* blood as long as it is red. Since the blood issues from a wound inflicted in the

כריתות ה/א

חַיָּבִים עָלָיו. דַּם הַטְּחוֹל; דַּם הַלֵּב; דַּם בֵּיצִים; דַּם דָּגִים; דַּם חֲגָבִים; דַּם הַתַּמְצִית – אֵין חַיָּבִין עֲלֵיהֶן. רַבִּי יְהוּדָה מְחַיֵּב בְּדַם הַתַּמְצִית.

יד אברהם

vital arteries [esophagus or trachea], it is considered דַּם הַנֶּפֶשׁ regardless of the nature of the flow. Thus, the clause שֶׁהַנֶּפֶשׁ יוֹצְאָה בוֹ, *by which life escapes*, qualifies only the instance of דַּם הַקָּזָה, *bloodletting* (*Tos. Yom Tov*).

חַיָּבִים עָלָיו. — *they are liable for it.*

If one consumes a *kezayis* of any of these varieties of blood, he is liable to *kares*[1] (*Rav; Rashi*).

[A *kezayis* of blood in its fluid state means the amount of blood displaced by an olive's bulk of solid.]

The reason that the *kezayis* measure is used even for blood in its liquid state [rather than the *reviis* measure usually used in connection with fluids] is that the Torah phrased the prohibition in terms of eating by stating (*Lev.* 17:26): וְכָל דָּם לֹא תֹאכֵלוּ, *Do not eat any blood.* Thus the measurement used is *kezayis*, just as it is when food is involved (*Aruch HaShulchan, Yoreh Deah* 66:1*ff*).

As explained previously, the *kares* penalty applies only to דם הנפש, *lifeblood*. Other blood, known as דַּם הָאֵבָרִים, *blood of the limbs*, is in the category of a negative prohibition, prohibited by Torah law but punishable only by *malkus*. The mishnah now proceeds to list the types of blood that are not punishable by *kares*. [Morever, some of the types of blood mentioned are not prohibited at all. This will be explained in the course of the mishnah.]

דַּם הַטְּחוֹל; דַּם הַלֵּב; — *The blood of the spleen; the blood of the heart;*

The blood contained in these organs is considered דַּם הָאֵבָרִים, *blood of the limbs*, prohibited by a negative commandment for which there is a penalty of *malkus*, but not *kares* (*Rav*).

Although due to their numerous veins and blood vessels, the heart and the spleen consist mostly of blood, the halachah regarding the blood contained in them is the same as that regarding blood of other organs: As long as it is part of the organ it is permitted; once it is removed or becomes clotted from a blow or the like it is prohibited by a negative commandment but not punishable by *kares* (*Tif. Yis.* from *Tur Yoreh Deah* 67).

Regarding the heart, this leniency applies only to the blood of the walls of the heart, contained in the arteries which run through the organ. The blood of the heart cavity (which is pumped to the rest of the body) is considered in the דַּם הַנֶּפֶשׁ, *lifeblood*, category, the consumption of which is punishable by *kares*. Because the animal draws this blood from the throat at the time it is being slaughtered, it is deemed שֶׁדַּם שֶׁהַנֶּפֶשׁ יוֹצְאָה בוֹ, *blood by which life escapes* (*Rav* from *Gem.* 22a).

This ruling follows our reading of the *Gemara*, as explained by *Rashi* and *Rabbeinu Gershom*. *Tosafos* (*Chullin* 111a) add that even the blood in the blood vessels of the liver or in the bronchia of the lungs bears a penalty of *kares* because it is also drawn from the throat during *shechitah*.

There is, however, another reading of the *Gemara* which leads to just the opposite conclusion: One is liable to *kares* only for the blood found in the walls of the heart, not for the blood of the heart cavity. It is the latter which is drawn from the throat at the time of slaughter (*Rif, Chullin* ch. 8; *Rosh*, ibid. 1:5; *Rambam, Maachalos Asuros* 6:3ff; see *Tif. Yis.*).

דַּם בֵּיצִים; — *the blood of eggs;*

According to one explanation (followed in our translation) this refers to the blood found in a hen's egg. According to another explanation it means blood of the

1. Some say that this is true as well for any prohibition regarding liquids (such as a non-*Kohen* consuming *terumah* fluids), unless the Torah specifically used the term drinking in its phraseology (*Sedei Chemed*, Vol. IV letter *shin* #97).

5
1 are liable for it. The blood of the spleen; the blood of the heart; the blood of eggs; the blood of fish; the blood of locusts; or the blood that oozes out — they are not liable for it. R' Yehudah holds [one] liable for the blood that oozes out.

YAD AVRAHAM

testicles of bulls, rams, and he-goats (*Rav; Rashi*).

דַּם דָּגִים; דַּם חֲגָבִים; — *the blood of fish; the blood of locusts;*

[The blood of these forms of life are permitted because regarding the prohibition of blood the Torah (*Lev.* 7:26) makes mention only of לָעוֹף וְלַבְּהֵמָה, *of fowl or of cattle*.]

דַּם הַתַּמְצִית — *or the blood that oozes out* —

This refers to the blood that oozes out during the slaughter or after it [as opposed to the blood that gushes forth in a steady stream] (*Rav; Tif. Yis.*).

.אֵין חַיָּבִין עָלֶיהָן — *they are not liable for it.*

There is no *kares* for these types of blood because the Torah placed this penalty only for consuming the lifeblood of an animal, not the blood of its limbs or organs. Therefore, for the blood of the spleen, the heart, or the kidneys, or the blood that oozes, there is no *kares*. The consumption of the blood of the limbs or the organs is nevertheless prohibited by the negative commandment (*Lev.* 7:26): וְכָל־דָּם לֹא תֹאכְלוּ, *And no blood shall you eat*. There is therefore a penalty of *malkus* for eating it.

The blood of reptiles or rodents is not prohibited under the category of blood but is prohibited under the prohibition against שְׁרָצִים, *creeping things*, and as such is punishable by *malkus*.

The blood of kosher fish and locusts is permissible to be eaten provided that there are scales in the vessel from which the blood is being drunk, to avoid suspicion that it is the blood of animals or fowl.

The blood of non-kosher fish is also prohibited but not as blood or as שֶׁרֶץ הַמַּיִם, *creatures that swarm in the waters*. It is prohibited because it is an extract of the bodies of the non-kosher fish, similar to milk of non-kosher animals. There is, therefore, no *malkus* for the blood of non-kosher fish or locusts (*Rambam Comm; Melachos Asuros* (6:1) cited by *Tos. Yom Tov*).

.רַבִּי יְהוּדָה מְחַיֵּב בְּדַם הַתַּמְצִית — *R' Yehudah holds [one] liable for the blood that oozes out.*

[As already explained, דַּם הַתַּמְצִית is the blood which trickles out after the slaughtering. In the context of the sacrificial process, this blood is invalid to be thrown on the Altar and cannot effect atonement. Only lifeblood is effective for atonement, as derived from the verse (*Lev.* 17:11): כִּי־הַדָּם הוּא בַּנֶּפֶשׁ יְכַפֵּר, *for it is the blood that will atone through life*, i.e., only lifeblood is valid for atonement.]

R' Yehudah holds that the words וְכָל־דָּם, *and any blood* (ibid. 7:26), teach that eating any blood, even blood that cannot be used for atonement, is punishable by *kares* (*Tos. Yom Tov* from *Gem.* 22a).

The halachah is in accordance with the *Tanna Kamma* (*Rav; Rambam Comm.*).

2.

The following mishnayos resume the discussion of the preceding chapters, which dealt with the laws of *asham talui*, the offering which atones for a doubtful, inadvertent transgression of prohibitions in the *kares*-bearing category.

The subject of the following mishnah is that of מְעִילָה, *me'ilah*, which means inadvertent misappropriation from the Temple treasury, either of items to be offered on the Altar or of the property of the Temple. As described in the Torah, the

רַבִּי עֲקִיבָא מְחַיֵּב עַל סְפֵק מְעִילוֹת אָשָׁם תָּלוּי, וַחֲכָמִים פּוֹטְרִים. וּמוֹדֶה רַבִּי עֲקִיבָא, שֶׁאֵין מֵבִיא אֶת־מְעִילָתוֹ עַד שֶׁתִּתְוַדַּע לוֹ, וְיָבִיא עִמָּהּ אָשָׁם וַדַּאי. אָמַר רַבִּי טַרְפוֹן: מַה לָּזֶה מֵבִיא שְׁתֵּי אֲשָׁמוֹת? אֶלָּא, יָבִיא מְעִילָה וְחֻמְשָׁהּ, וְיָבִיא אָשָׁם בִּשְׁנֵי סְלָעִים וְיֹאמַר: „אִם וַדַּאי מָעַלְתִּי, זוֹ מְעִילָתִי וְזֶה אֲשָׁמִי״; וְאִם סָפֵק, הַמָּעוֹת

inadvertent transgression of this prohibition calls for restitution of the property value with the addition of a fifth and the offering of an *asham.*

The discussion of our mishnah focuses on the procedure governing a situation of *doubtful* misappropriation of Temple property, i.e., he is unsure whether or not he inadvertently used sacred property for his own benefit.

רַבִּי עֲקִיבָא מְחַיֵּב עַל סְפֵק מְעִילוֹת אָשָׁם תָּלוּי, — *R' Akiva holds [one] liable to an asham talui for a doubtful case of me'ilah,*

[R' Akiva rules that the obligation for an *asham talui* applies also to] a person who was in doubt whether he benefited from consecrated objects (*Rav*).

For instance, if one had two pieces of meat before him — one sacrificial for which there is a penalty of *me'ilah*, and the other ordinary meat — and, unaware of the situation, he ate one. Now when he learns that one of them was consecrated, he is uncertain which piece he ate.

Although as a rule, the *asham talui* is brought only for a doubtful transgression punishable by *kares*, for which the atonement for a definite inadvertent transgression is a *chatas*, R' Akiva holds that the doubtful transgression of *me'ilah* is likewise cause for an *asham talui*, despite the fact that for the definite inadvertent transgression the required atonement is an *asham [me'ilos]*, not a *chatas* (*Rabbeinu Gershom*).

R' Akiva derives his ruling from the fact that the portion in the Torah dealing with *asham talui* immediately follows the portion dealing with *me'ilah*, and the two portions are connected with the letter *vav*, meaning *and*. Thus, the *me'ilah* portion is considered a continuation of the above *asham talui* portion, indicating that there is a liability to an *asham talui* for a doubtful case of *me'ilah* as well as the doubtful transgressions of *kares* mentioned earlier by the Torah (*Tos. Yom Tov* from *Gem.* 22b).

וַחֲכָמִים פּוֹטְרִים. — *but the Sages exempt [him].*

The Sages reason that one is liable to an *asham talui* only for a doubtful case of a sin for which there is a penalty of *kares* for a willful transgression and a *chatas* for an unintentional transgression. The *me'ilah* transgression, however, is subject to neither. For an unintentional transgression, one is liable to an *asham*, not a *chatas*; for a willful *me'ilah* transgression there is no *kares* (*Rav* from *Gem.* 22b).

The Sages, too, acknowledge the *vav* joining the two sections as an indication that there is a connection between the *asham talui* and the *asham me'ilos*. However, they interpret the connection differently. They maintain that the Torah teaches us that the offerings are the same in terms of their required value. Regarding the *asham me'ilos*, the Torah states (*Lev.* 5:15) that it must be worth at least two *selaim*. The connecting *vav*, therefore, teaches us that the *asham talui*, too, must be purchased at a minimum of two

5
2

2. R' Akiva holds [one] liable to an *asham talui* for a doubtful case of *me'ilah*, but the Sages exempt [him]. R' Akiva agrees, however, that he does not bring his restitution until it becomes known to him, and he [then] accompanies it with the unconditional *asham*. Said R' Tarfon: Why should this [person] bring two *ashamos*? Rather, let him bring restitution and its fifth, and let him bring an *asham* for two *selaim* and say, "If I am surely guilty of *me'ilah*, let this be my restitution and this my *asham*"; and if it is doubtful, the money is

YAD AVRAHAM

selaim[1] (*Tos. Yom Tov* from *Gem.* ad loc.).

[The Biblical shekel was known as a *selah* in mishnaic nomenclature, see below (6:6) and *Shekalim* (1:6).]

וּמוֹדֶה רַבִּי עֲקִיבָא, שֶׁאֵין מֵבִיא אֶת־מְעִילָתוֹ — *R' Akiva agrees, however, that he does not bring his restitution*

[As explained above, the atonement for *me'ilah* consists of two components: (a) restitution of the principal, plus one fifth; (b) the atonement of an *asham*. Although R' Akiva maintains that an *asham* is brought even in a situation of doubt, the same does not apply to the restitution of the principal and the additional fifth.]

As long as he is uncertain whether or not he misappropriated Temple property, R' Akiva concedes that he need not repay the amount he may have taken from the Temple treasury (*Rav; Rashi*).

עַד שֶׁתִּתְוַדַּע לוֹ, וְיָבִיא עִמָּהּ אָשָׁם וַדַּאי. — *until it becomes known to him, and he [then] accompanies it with the unconditional asham.*

Until it becomes known to him that he definitely committed *me'ilah* [at which point he makes the restitution accompanied by the required *asham me'ilos*] (*Tif. Yis.*).

אָמַר רַבִּי טַרְפוֹן: מַה לָּזֶה מֵבִיא שְׁתֵּי אֲשָׁמוֹת? — *Said R' Tarfon: Why should this [person] bring two ashamos?*

Why should we require this uncertain sinner to bring first an *asham talui* and then, when he becomes aware of his sin, to bring an unconditional *asham*? (*Rav*).

אֶלָּא, יָבִיא מְעִילָה וְחֻמְשָׁהּ, — *Rather, let him bring restitution and its fifth,*

Let him simply repay the principal value of his misappropriation plus a fifth (*Rav*).

וְיָבִיא אָשָׁם בִּשְׁנֵי סְלָעִים — *and let him bring an asham for two selaim*

And, at the same time, let him bring as an *asham*, a ram the value of two *selaim*, as required by the Torah (*Lev.* 5:15): אַיִל תָּמִים מִן־הַצֹּאן בְּעֶרְכְּךָ כֶּסֶף־שְׁקָלִים בְּשֶׁקֶל־הַקֹּדֶשׁ, *an unblemished ram from the flock, with a value of [two] silver shekels, according to the shekel of the Sanctuary* (*Rav*).

וְיֹאמַר: „אִם וַדַּאי מָעַלְתִּי, זוּ מְעִילָתִי וְזֶה אֲשָׁמִי״; — *and say, 'If I am surely guilty of*

1. This requirement is unique to the *asham*; a *chatas* or any other offering has no minimum required value. In the context of the requirement of an *asham talui*, this law creates a paradox, for it means that the atonement for a doubtful transgression [the *asham talui*] is, in terms of cost, more stringent than the atonement for a definite transgression [the *chatas*] (see *Zevachim* 48a). This ruling is rationalized by *Rama* at the end of laws of Rosh Hashanah (*Orach Chaim* 603), by noting that a person is more likely to feel remorse for a definite transgression than for one that he is not certain that he committed. Therefore, the Torah required a more elaborate offering for the questionable transgression, to emphasize that one must make greater effort for the questionable transgression than for the certain transgression (*Tos. Yom Tov*).

נְדָבָה וְאָשָׁם תָּלוּי, שֶׁמִּמִּין שֶׁהוּא מֵבִיא עַל־הוֹדַע, מֵבִיא עַל־לֹא הוֹדַע.

[ג] **אָמַר** לוֹ רַבִּי עֲקִיבָא: נִרְאִים דְּבָרֶיךָ בְּמְעִילָה מְעוּטָה. הֲרֵי שֶׁבָּא עַל־יָדוֹ סָפֵק מְעִילָה בְּמֵאָה מָנֶה, לֹא יָפֶה לוֹ שֶׁיָּבִיא אָשָׁם בִּשְׁתֵּי סְלָעִים וְאַל יָבִיא סְפֵק מְעִילָה בְּמֵאָה מָנֶה?

יד אברהם

me'ilah, let this be my restitution and this my asham';

He can fulfill his obligation by merely bringing one offering and the equivalent of the value of the misappropriated item plus its fifth, stipulating as follows: 'If indeed I am guilty of *me'ilah,* then let this money serve as my restitution plus its fifth and let the offering count as an *asham me'ilos.'*

וְאִם סָפֵק, — *and if it is doubtful,*

There is no question that the person is presently uncertain of his transgression. What the mishnah means by the statement *if it is doubtful,* then, is that if it will *remain* doubtful [and the liability for an *asham me'ilos* never materializes] (*Rav* from *Gem.* 22b).

הַמָּעוֹת נְדָבָה וְאָשָׁם תָּלוּי, — *the money is a donation and the asham is an asham talui,*

[The money equaling the principal and the fifth shall instead be a donation to the Temple treasury and the *asham* shall be an *asham talui.*]

This phrase is the concluding clause of R' Tarfon's statement, i.e., if it is never determined whether he committed *me'ilah,* the money will be considered a donation and the offering an *asham talui* (*Rambam Comm.*). He need not stipulate that the money should be a donation or that the *asham* should be an *asham talui.*

שֶׁמִּמִּין שֶׁהוּא מֵבִיא עַל־הוֹדַע, מֵבִיא עַל־לֹא הוֹדַע. — *for, from the [same] species from which he brings for an obligation of doubt, he brings for an obligation of certainty.*

Since both the offerings for a definite transgression and for a doubtful transgression consist of the same animal — a ram — he is able to bring one offering [and stipulate that it should serve as an *asham talui,* if need be].

Unlike the *chatas,* in R' Akiva and R' Tarfon's view, the *asham* needs no awareness of the transgression prior to bringing the offering for it to be effective. Therefore, should it later become known that he, in fact, was guilty of *me'ilah,* he need not bring another *asham.* The original *asham,* brought as an *asham talui,* can in retrospect serve as an *asham me'ilos* because there is no requirement that he be aware of his sin at the time of the offering (*Tos. Yom Tov* from *Gem.* 22b).

We have learned previously that one who is doubtful whether he inadvertently transgressed a *kares*-punishable prohibition must bring an *asham talui.* However, the *asham talui* is effective for as long as there is doubt regarding the transgression; when he subsequently learns that he did indeed commit the sin, he must bring a *chatas* in addition to the *asham talui* already brought.

One may therefore ask: Why can the duplication of offerings not be avoided in the same manner as it is in our mishnah? Let him bring one animal and stipulate as he does in this case: 'If I sinned let this animal be a *chatas* and if I remain uncertain the animal will be an *asham talui.'*

One reason for this difference is that the animals are not the same. A *chatas* is a female, whereas an *asham* is a male. Moreover, a *chatas* requires knowledge of the sin before

5
3 a donation and the *asham* is an *asham talui*, for, from the [same] species from which he brings for an obligation of doubt, he brings for an obligation of certainty.

3. Replied R' Akiva to him: Your words are acceptable in the case of a small *me'ilah*. [But] what if he is guilty of a doubtful case of *me'ilah* of one hundred *maneh*, is it not better for him that he bring an *asham* for two *selaim* and not bring a doubtful restitution of

YAD AVRAHAM

sacrificing it, whereas according to R' Tarfon and R' Akiva an *asham* does not. Therefore, a *chatas* cannot be brought simply on the chance that he sinned.

The halachah, however, does not follow R' Tarfon and R' Akiva on this point. An *asham*, too, requires prior knowledge of the transgression in order to be effective (*Tif. Yis.*).

The halachah is in accordance with the Sages that there is no *asham talui* for a doubtful case of *me'ilah* (*Rav; Rambam Comm.*).

3.

אָמַר לוֹ רַבִּי עֲקִיבָא: נִרְאִים דְּבָרֶיךָ בִּמְעִילָה מְעוּטָה. — *Replied R' Akiva to him: Your words are acceptable in the case of a small me'ilah.*

R' Akiva reasoned with R' Tarfon: I understand that by allowing him to bring one *asham* and stipulate accordingly you wish to make it easier for the person who is uncertain whether or not he committed *me'ilah*. However, your ruling is effective only if the case involves a *me'ilah* of a small monetary value. For example, the misappropriation in question involved only the amount of one *perutah* or two *perutos* (the copper coin which was the smallest monetary denomination in mishnaic terms. See *Kiddushin* 1:1). In such a situation it is indeed to his advantage to pay the small amount in question and bring one *asham*, with the accompanying stipulation (*Rabbeinu Gershom*).

הֲרֵי שֶׁבָּא עַל־יָדוֹ סָפֵק מְעִילָה בְּמֵאָה מָנֶה, — *[But] what if he is guilty of a doubtful case of me'ilah of one hundred maneh,*

[But what if the possible *me'ilah* involved a large amount, such as one hundred *maneh?* How does your ruling make it easier for him then?]

The *maneh* was one hundred *dinarim* (or *zuz*) or twenty-five *selaim* (see *Kiddushin* 12a; *Toras Kohanim* on *Lev.* 5:17). One hundred *maneh*, then, is an enormous sum, as two *maneh* (200 *zuz*) is considered a minimum yearly income (see *Peah* 8:8).

לֹא יָפֶה לוֹ שֶׁיָּבִיא אָשָׁם בִּשְׁתֵּי סְלָעִים וְאַל יָבִיא סָפֵק מְעִילָה בְּמֵאָה מָנֶה? — *is it not better for him that he bring an asham for two selaim and not bring a doubtful restitution of one hundred maneh?*

As mentioned above, the requirement for any *asham*, including the *asham me'ilos*, is a ram costing at least two *selaim*, as in *Lev.* 5:15 (*Rav*). [Since each *maneh* consists of twenty-five *selaim*, the two *selaim* required for an *asham* are considerably less than the one hundred *maneh* involved in the restitution of the *me'ilah* involved in this case.]

Thus, R' Akiva reasons with R' Tarfon: In this case is it not better for him to first bring an *asham talui* [without a restitution] and if he finds out that he

הָא מוֹדֶה רַבִּי עֲקִיבָא לְרַבִּי טַרְפוֹן בִּמְעִילָה מוּעֶטֶת.

הָאִשָּׁה שֶׁהֵבִיאָה חַטַּאת הָעוֹף סָפֵק: אִם עַד שֶׁלֹּא נִמְלְקָה נוֹדַע לָהּ שֶׁיָּלְדָה וַדַּאי, תַּעֲשֶׂנָּה וַדַּאי, שֶׁמִּמִּין שֶׁהִיא מְבִיאָה עַל לֹא הוֹדַע, מְבִיאָה עַל הוֹדַע.

[ד] **חֲתִיכָה** שֶׁל־חֻלִּין וַחֲתִיכָה שֶׁל־קֹדֶשׁ, אָכַל אַחַת מֵהֶן, וְאֵין יָדוּעַ אֵיזוֹ מֵהֶן אָכַל — פָּטוּר. רַבִּי עֲקִיבָא מְחַיֵּב

sinned, to bring another *asham* rather than pay one hundred *maneh* because of his uncertainty of whether he benefited from consecrated objects? It is obviously a greater stringency to pay the larger amount now than to risk an extra *asham*, which costs merely two *selaim*, later. Perhaps he will never definitely determine for certain that he committed the *me'ilah* and thus be spared the additional *asham* [and the restitution] (*Rabbeinu Gershom*).

It is not possible, though, to simply bring one *asham* without the money and make the above-mentioned stipulation, then wait to bring the money until it is determined that he sinned. If he stipulates that the ram should be an *asham me'ilos* in the event that it becomes known that he sinned, he must make restitution immediately for he may not bring the *asham* before making restitution (*Tif. Yis.*).

הָא מוֹדֶה רַבִּי עֲקִיבָא לְרַבִּי טַרְפוֹן בִּמְעִילָה מוּעֶטֶת. — *R' Akiva [then] agrees with R' Tarfon in the case of a small me'ilah.*

The *Tanna* now concludes that R' Akiva's statement to R' Tarfon indicates that he agrees with him in the case of a small *me'ilah* [that one ram may be brought with the stipulation that it be either an *asham* or *asham talui*] (*Rabbeinu Gershom*).

Others dispute this contention, concluding that in reality R' Akiva does not agree with R' Tarfon at all. See *Tif. Yis.* cited in following mishnah.

הָאִשָּׁה שֶׁהֵבִיאָה חַטַּאת הָעוֹף סָפֵק: — *[If] a woman brought a bird chatas of doubt:*

As explained at length in chapter 1, the birth of a child necessitates the offering of two offerings: an *olah* lamb and a *chatas* bird. When there is uncertainty whether an aborted fetal substance meets the requirement for childbirth [see mishnah 1:4], then the following procedure is followed: The *olah* is brought with the stipulation that if the aborted substance was not a fetus the *olah* should be considered a *nedavah* [voluntary offering].

The *chatas*, which cannot be brought as a *nedavah*, is referred to as חַטַּאת הָעוֹף סָפֵק, *a bird chatas of doubt*. It is brought in order to fulfill the woman's sacrificial obligation but it may not be eaten, because the procedure for the slaughter of a bird offering calls for *melikah* [nipping the neck with a thumbnail] rather than the usual *shechitah*. Thus, in the event that the woman is *not* obligated to bring the *chatas*, the bird is prohibited as *neveilah* [ritually unslaughtered meat] (*Rav; Rashi*).

Actually the basis for חַטָּאת הַבָּאָה עַל הַסָּפֵק, *the chatas brought out of doubt*, is Scriptural

one hundred *maneh*? R′ Akiva [then] agrees with R′ Tarfon in the case of a small *me'ilah*.

[If] a woman brought a bird *chatas* of doubt: If it became known to her before its neck was nipped that she had definitely given birth, she must make it an unconditional [*chatas*], for, from the [same] species from which she brings for an obligation of doubt, she brings for an obligation of certainty.

4. [If there was] a piece of ordinary [meat] and a piece of sanctified [meat], [if] he ate one of them, but it is not known which of them he ate — he is exempt. R′

YAD AVRAHAM

[similar to the *asham talui*, which is likewise brought for a situation of doubt]. As such, it is a valid offering which should be eaten. However, because of the resemblance to *neveilah*, it is Rabbinically forbidden to be eaten (*Tif. Yis.*).

אִם עַד שֶׁלֹּא נִמְלְקָה נוֹדַע לָהּ שֶׁיָּלְדָה וַדַּאי, תַּעֲשֶׂנָּה וַדַּאי, — *If it became known to her before its neck was nipped that she had definitely given birth, she must make it an unconditional [chatas],*

If before the *melikah* she learned that what she aborted is considered a birth, and she is definitely liable to an offering, then she should offer the bird as regular *chatas* offering which may be eaten by the *Kohanim* like other *chataos* (*Rav; Rashi*).

שֶׁמִּמִּין שֶׁהִיא מְבִיאָה עַל לֹא הוֹדַע, מְבִיאָה עַל הוֹדַע. — *for, from the [same] species from which she brings for an obligation of doubt, she brings for an obligation of certainty.*

For either offering the requirement is the same: either a young pigeon or a turtledove. [Therefore, just as in the case of the *asham me'ilos* mentioned earlier, the same offering can serve as either an offering for doubt or an offering of certainty] (*Rav*).

4.

חֲתִיכָה שֶׁל־חֻלִּין וַחֲתִיכָה שֶׁל־קֹדֶשׁ, אָכַל אַחַת מֵהֶן, וְאֵין יָדוּעַ אֵיזוֹ מֵהֶן אָכַל — *[If there was] a piece of ordinary [meat] and a piece of sanctified [meat], [if] he ate one of them, but it is not known which of them he ate —*

[If a person had two pieces of meat lying before him, one a piece of ordinary meat which is permitted and the other a prohibited piece of sacrificial meat, e.g., the meat of an *olah* or of the *eimurin* of other offerings, and he inadvertently ate one of the pieces, not realizing that there was sacrificial meat present. The doubt now exists whether he transgressed by inadvertently eating the sacrificial meat.]

פָּטוּר. — *he is exempt.*

[Although this is the classical situation of doubt for which one is liable to an *asham talui*, nonetheless, he is exempt because the prohibition involved is that of *me'ilah*. As we learned in mishnah 2, the view of the Sages is that a doubtful transgression of *me'ilah* does not call for an *asham talui* because a definite transgression calls for an *asham* rather than a *chatas*].

בְּאָשָׁם תָּלוּי. אָכַל אֶת־הַשְּׁנִיָּה, מֵבִיא אָשָׁם וַדַּאי. אָכַל אֶחָד הָרִאשׁוֹנָה, וּבָא אַחֵר וְאָכַל אֶת־הַשְּׁנִיָּה — זֶה מֵבִיא אָשָׁם תָּלוּי, וְזֶה מֵבִיא אָשָׁם תָּלוּי; דִּבְרֵי רַבִּי עֲקִיבָא. רַבִּי שִׁמְעוֹן אוֹמֵר: שְׁנֵיהֶם מְבִיאִים אָשָׁם אֶחָד. רַבִּי יוֹסֵי אוֹמֵר: אֵין שְׁנַיִם מְבִיאִים אָשָׁם אֶחָד.

[ה] **חֲתִיכָה** שֶׁל־חֻלִּין וַחֲתִיכָה שֶׁל־חֵלֶב,

יד אברהם

רַבִּי עֲקִיבָא מְחַיֵּב בְּאָשָׁם תָּלוּי. — *R' Akiva holds [him] liable to an asham talui.*

As we also learned in the two previous mishnayos, R' Akiva differs with the Sages and is of the view that a doubtful transgression of *me'ilah* is liable for an *asham talui* (*Rav; Rashi; Rambam Comm.*).

In the previous mishnah it was stated by R' Tarfon that the procedure regarding the doubtful transgression of *me'ilah* is to bring one offering as an *asham* and stipulate that it should be either an *asham me'ilos* or an *asham talui*.

Furthermore, the mishnah there states that when the amount of *me'ilah* involved is minimal, R' Akiva agrees to this procedure. This leads *Tiferes Yisrael* to question why this procedure is not followed in the case described by our mishnah, which involves the possible *me'ilah* of only one piece of meat, the value of which is certainly minimal.

Tiferes Yisrael concludes, therefore, that in fact, R' Akiva does *not* agree with R' Tarfon regarding a doubtful situation of *me'ilah*. For his part, he holds that an *asham* cannot be effective if the occurrence of the transgression has not been established prior to bringing the offering. Bringing one *asham* with a stipulation to cover the possibilities of both transgressions is ineffective, therefore, because as long as he never determined with certainty that he transgressed *me'ilah*, the *asham* will not atone for him.

His statement in the previous mishnah was intended only according to R' Tarfon's reasoning. R' Akiva argued with R' Tarfon on the latter's own terms, saying in effect: 'Even according to you, R' Tarfon, the effectiveness of stipulation is limited to a case of a small *me'ilah*.' As far as R' Akiva's own opinion is concerned, stipulation is ineffective in *any* case. [There is a basis for this conclusion from *Rashi* in *Shabbos* 71b s.v. למ״ד.]

אָכַל אֶת־הַשְּׁנִיָּה, מֵבִיא אָשָׁם וַדַּאי. — *[If] he ate the second [piece], he must bring an unconditional asham.*

If the same person then ate the second piece, he brings an *asham me'ilos* since it is now certain that he ate sacrificial meat (*Rabbeinu Gershom*).

אָכַל אֶחָד הָרִאשׁוֹנָה, וּבָא אַחֵר וְאָכַל אֶת הַשְּׁנִיָּה — — *[If] one [person] ate the first [piece], and another [person] came and ate the second [piece] —*

[The two pieces were eaten by two different people. We are thus certain that the sacrificial meat was eaten by one of them, but we cannot determine by whom. Each of these individuals is now in doubt whether he transgressed.]

זֶה מֵבִיא אָשָׁם תָּלוּי, וְזֶה מֵבִיא אָשָׁם תָּלוּי; דִּבְרֵי רַבִּי עֲקִיבָא. — *this one must bring an asham talui, and that one must bring an asham talui; [these are] the words of R' Akiva.*

[As explained before, R' Akiva's view is that an uncertain situation of *me'ilah* calls for an *asham talui*. Thus, each of these individuals brings an *asham talui* for the possibility that it was he who transgressed.]

Earlier (4:1), we explained the mishnah according to the view that the *asham talui*

5
5 Akiva holds [him] liable to an *asham talui*. [If] he ate the second [piece], he must bring an unconditional *asham*. [If] one [person] ate the first [piece], and another [person] came and ate the second [piece] — this one must bring an *asham talui*, and that one must bring an *asham talui*; [these are] the words of R' Akiva. R' Shimon says: They both bring one *asham*. R' Yose says: Two do not bring one *asham*.

5. [If there was] a piece of ordinary [meat] and a piece

YAD AVRAHAM

obligation depends on a situation described as חֲתִיכָה אַחַת מִשְּׁתֵּי חֲתִיכוֹת, *one of two pieces*. In other words, one brings an *asham talui* only if there were two pieces in front of him, one prohibited and one permissible, and he inadvertently ate one but is now uncertain which. Eating one piece of questionable meat, however, is not the type of doubtful situation for which one brings an *asham talui*. Thus, it may be asked that in this case, when the second person ate the remaining piece of meat, there was only *one* piece of questionable meat present. Accordingly, only the first person in our case should be liable to an *asham talui*!

The mishnah can be explained, though, according to the reasoning given previously for the requirement of two pieces, viz. the principle of אִיקְבַּע אִסוּרָא, *the prohibition must be established*. In other words, one is liable to an *asham talui* only if there was a doubt which involved the unquestioned presence of a prohibition. In our case, too, the fact that at one time there was surely a piece of prohibited meat suffices to create a situation of אִיקְבַּע אִסוּרָא. Therefore, although technically the second person found only one piece of meat, in principle the doubt was created by two pieces. Thus he is liable to an *asham talui* (*Tos. Yom Tov*).

רַבִּי שִׁמְעוֹן אוֹמֵר: שְׁנֵיהֶם מְבִיאִים אָשָׁם אֶחָד. — *R' Shimon says: They both bring one asham.*

They bring jointly an unconditional *asham*, and each one stipulates to the other, 'If it was you who ate the prohibited piece, I relinquish my share in this animal to you, and the entire *asham* is yours' (*Rav; Rashi, Rabbeinu Gershom*).

רַבִּי יוֹסֵי אוֹמֵר: אֵין שְׁנַיִם מְבִיאִים אָשָׁם אֶחָד. — *R' Yose says: Two do not bring one asham.*

R' Yose does not subscribe to the principle of stipulation in offerings. Therefore, according to the Sages, both are exempt, and according to R' Akiva, each one must bring an *asham talui* (*Rav; Rashi*).

Others say that the statement of the Sages who — in the beginning of our mishnah, rule that there is no *asham talui* for an uncertain case of *me'ilah* — follows the view of R' Yose (*Rambam Comm.*). [See below, end of mishnah 7 and *Tos. Yom Tov* there.]

We have already stated above that the halachah is in accordance with the Sages (*Rav; Rambam, Comm.*).

The following mishnayos, until the end of the chapter, list the various possibilities for the *asham talui* obligation, beginning with the elementary case of the permitted and prohibited pieces of meat, and becoming progressively more complex. The order of this sequence is described below (mishnah 8).

5.

חֲתִיכָה שֶׁל־חֻלִּין וַחֲתִיכָה שֶׁל־חֵלֶב, — *[If there was] a piece of ordinary [meat] and a piece of cheilev,*

[One had two pieces of meat lying

אָכַל אַחַת מֵהֶן, וְאֵין יָדוּעַ אֵיזוֹ מֵהֶן אָכַל, מֵבִיא אָשָׁם תָּלוּי. אָכַל אֶת־הַשְּׁנִיָּה, מֵבִיא חַטָּאת. אָכַל אֶחָד אֶת־הָרִאשׁוֹנָה, וּבָא אַחֵר וְאָכַל אֶת־הַשְּׁנִיָּה — זֶה מֵבִיא אָשָׁם תָּלוּי, וְזֶה מֵבִיא אָשָׁם תָּלוּי. דִּבְרֵי רַבִּי עֲקִיבָא. רַבִּי שִׁמְעוֹן אוֹמֵר: שְׁנֵיהֶם מְבִיאִים חַטָּאת אַחַת. רַבִּי יוֹסֵי אוֹמֵר: אֵין שְׁנַיִם מְבִיאִים חַטָּאת אַחַת.

[ו] **חֲתִיכָה** שֶׁל־חֵלֶב וַחֲתִיכָה שֶׁל־קֹדֶשׁ, אָכַל אֶת־אַחַת מֵהֶן, וְאֵין יָדוּעַ אֵיזוֹ מֵהֶן אָכַל, מֵבִיא אָשָׁם תָּלוּי. אָכַל אֶת הַשְּׁנִיָּה, מֵבִיא חַטָּאת וְאָשָׁם וַדַּאי. אָכַל אֶחָד אֶת־

יד אברהם

before him; one was *shumman* (permitted fat) taken from an ordinary animal, the other was *cheilev* (forbidden fat), also from an ordinary animal.]

The permitted meat here is obviously *shumman*, the permitted type of fat which can easily be confused with *cheilev*, as explained. The mishnah refers to it simply as *chullin* [ordinary meat] to contrast it to the case of the following mishnah which deals with the confusion of *cheilev* and *sanctified* meat. Indeed, *Rambam* (*Hil. Shegagos* 8:9) appears to have read in our mishnah: חֲתִיכָה שֶׁל־שׁוּמָן, *a piece of shumman [and a piece of cheilev]* (*Tos. Yom Tov*).

אָכַל אַחַת מֵהֶן, וְאֵין יָדוּעַ אֵיזוֹ מֵהֶן אָכַל, מֵבִיא אָשָׁם תָּלוּי. — *[if] he ate one of them, and it is not known which one of them he ate, he must bring an asham talui.*

This is a classic case of a doubtful transgression for which all agree that he must bring an *asham talui.* He *may* have eaten something for which [there is a penalty of *kares* and] he would be obligated for a *chatas* if there was no doubt surrounding the occurrence of a transgression (*Rabbeinu Gershom*).

אָכַל אֶת־הַשְּׁנִיָּה, — *[If] he ate the second [piece],*

If after he ate the first piece and brought an *asham talui,* he inadvertently ate the other one (*Rambam, Hil. Shegagos* 8:9).

מֵבִיא חַטָּאת. — *he must bring a chatas.*

Since he knows definitely that one of the pieces he ate was *cheilev*, although he is unsure which, he is liable to a *chatas* (*Tif. Yis.*).

אָכַל אֶחָד אֶת־הָרִאשׁוֹנָה, וּבָא אַחֵר וְאָכַל אֶת־הַשְּׁנִיָּה — זֶה מֵבִיא אָשָׁם תָּלוּי, וְזֶה מֵבִיא אָשָׁם תָּלוּי. — *[If] one person ate the first [piece], and another came and ate the second [piece] — this one must bring an asham talui, and that one must bring an asham talui.*

[As explained above (mishnah 4), the second one must bring an *asham talui* although, when he ate the second piece, there was only one doubtful piece.]

דִּבְרֵי רַבִּי עֲקִיבָא. — *[These are] the words of R' Akiva.*

[This clause is omitted in the mishnah printed with the *Gemara,* and in many manuscripts.] It is unnecessary to ascribe this statement only to R' Akiva. Only where the doubtful transgression involves *me'ilah* is R' Akiva involved in the dispute, as above mishnah 4. [Indeed, the *Gemara* attrib-

5
6

of *cheilev*, [if] he ate one of them, and it is not known which one of them he ate, he must bring an *asham talui*. [If] he ate the second [piece], he must bring a *chatas*. [If] one person ate the first [piece], and another came and ate the second [piece] — this one must bring an *asham talui*, and that one must bring an *asham talui*. [These are] the words of R' Akiva. R' Shimon says: They both bring one *chatas*. R' Yose says: Two do not bring one *chatas*.

6. [If there was] a piece of *cheilev* and a piece of sanctified [fat], [if] he ate one of them and it is not known which of them he ate, he must bring an *asham talui*. [If] he ate the second [piece], he must bring a *chatas* and an unconditional *asham*. [If] one person ate

YAD AVRAHAM

utes this statement to R' Yose] (*Meleches Shlomo*).

רַבִּי שִׁמְעוֹן אוֹמֵר: שְׁנֵיהֶם מְבִיאִים חַטָּאת אַחַת. — *R' Shimon says: They both bring one chatas.*

As explained above (mishnah 4), they jointly buy one animal and stipulate that each one relinquishes his share in the animal to the one who, in truth, ate the *cheilev* (*Rav; Rashi*).

רַבִּי יוֹסֵי אוֹמֵר: אֵין שְׁנַיִם מְבִיאִים חַטָּאת אַחַת. — *R' Yose says: Two do not bring one chatas.*

Each, however, brings an *asham talui*. Thus, R' Yose agrees with the previous statement of the mishnah. In fact, this is the point of the mishnah: The view that each brings an *asham talui* is that of R' Yose (*Rav; Tos. Yom Tov* from *Gemara* 23a).

6.

חֲתִיכָה שֶׁל־חֵלֶב וַחֲתִיכָה שֶׁל־קֹדֶשׁ, — *[If there was] a piece of cheilev and a piece of sanctified [fat],*

One had before him two pieces of meat; one was *cheilev* of an ordinary animal and the other was not *cheilev*, but was from a sacrificial animal for which there is a prohibition of *me'ilah* (*Tif. Yis.*).

[Unlike the situation of the previous case, both pieces here are prohibited but one is in the *me'ilah* category for which there is neither *kares* nor a *chatas*.]

אָכַל אֶת־אַחַת מֵהֶן, וְאֵין יָדוּעַ אֵיזוֹ מֵהֶן אָכַל, מֵבִיא אָשָׁם תָּלוּי. — *[if] he ate one of them, and it is not known which of them he ate, he must bring an asham talui.*

The chance that he may have eaten the piece which is *cheilev* is itself sufficient reason to obligate him for an *asham talui*. Thus, he brings an *asham talui* although normally for a doubtful case of *me'ilah* there is no *asham talui*, according to the Sages [mishnah 2 and 3] (*Rav; Rabbeinu Gershom*).

R' Akiva (ad loc.), for his part, holds that either side of the question is enough for an *asham talui;* perhaps he ate *cheilev* or perhaps he committed *me'ilah*. Yet one *asham talui* is sufficient, for in either case he is liable to only one *asham talui* (*Tos. Yom Tov* from *Rambam Comm., Rashi*).

אָכַל אֶת־הַשְּׁנִיָּה, מֵבִיא חַטָּאת וְאָשָׁם וַדַּאי. — *[If] he ate the second [piece], he must bring a chatas and an unconditional asham.*

הָרִאשׁוֹנָה, וּבָא אַחֵר וְאָכַל אֶת־הַשְּׁנִיָּה — זֶה מֵבִיא אָשָׁם תָּלוּי, וְזֶה מֵבִיא אָשָׁם תָּלוּי. רַבִּי שִׁמְעוֹן אוֹמֵר: שְׁנֵיהֶם מְבִיאִים חַטָּאת וְאָשָׁם. רַבִּי יוֹסֵי אוֹמֵר: אֵין שְׁנַיִם מְבִיאִים חַטָּאת וְאָשָׁם.

[ז] **חֲתִיכָה** שֶׁל־חֵלֶב וַחֲתִיכָה שֶׁל־חֵלֶב קֹדֶשׁ, אָכַל אֶת־אַחַת מֵהֶן, וְאֵין יָדוּעַ אֵיזוֹ מֵהֶן אָכַל, מֵבִיא חַטָּאת. רַבִּי עֲקִיבָא אוֹמֵר: מֵבִיא אָשָׁם תָּלוּי. אָכַל אֶת־הַשְּׁנִיָּה, מֵבִיא שְׁתֵּי חַטָּאוֹת וְאָשָׁם וַדַּאי. אָכַל אֶחָד אֶת־הָרִאשׁוֹנָה, וּבָא אַחֵר וְאָכַל אֶת־הַשְּׁנִיָּה — זֶה מֵבִיא חַטָּאת, וְזֶה מֵבִיא חַטָּאת.

יד אברהם

After he subsequently ate the other piece it is certain that he transgressed both the prohibition of eating *cheilev* and the prohibition of *me'ilah.* Thus he must bring a *chatas* for eating *cheilev* and an *asham me'ilos* for eating the consecrated meat (*Rav*).

אָכַל אֶחָד אֶת־הָרִאשׁוֹנָה, וּבָא אַחֵר וְאָכַל אֶת־הַשְּׁנִיָּה — זֶה מֵבִיא אָשָׁם תָּלוּי, וְזֶה מֵבִיא אָשָׁם תָּלוּי. — *[If] one person ate the first [piece], and another came and ate the second [piece] — this one must bring an asham talui, and that one must bring an asham talui.*

[As above, each one brings an *asham talui* since it is he who may have eaten the *cheilev* (see mishnah 4).]

רַבִּי שִׁמְעוֹן אוֹמֵר: שְׁנֵיהֶם מְבִיאִים חַטָּאת וְאָשָׁם. — *R' Shimon says: They both bring a chatas and an asham.*

[Instead of each bringing a separate *asham talui* they can absolve their obligation by sharing a *chatas* and an *asham.* In this manner, even if it is determined later who ate the *cheilev,* he is not obligated to bring a *chatas* because he already brought one.]

They bring the two offerings jointly, and each one stipulates: 'If I ate *cheilev,* and you ate the *kodesh* meat [and thus I must bring a *chatas* and you an *asham*], my share in the *asham* is relinquished to you, and your share in the *chatas* shall be relinquished to me. If, however, I ate the *kodesh* meat, and you ate the *cheilev,* my share in the *chatas* is relinquished to you, and your share in the *asham* shall be relinquished to me' (*Rav; Rashi*).

רַבִּי יוֹסֵי אוֹמֵר: אֵין שְׁנַיִם מְבִיאִים חַטָּאת וְאָשָׁם. — *R' Yose says: Two do not bring a chatas and an asham.*

Instead, each one brings an *asham talui,* as the *Tanna Kamma* rules. Here, too, the mishnah is indicating with this statement that the *Tanna Kamma* of this mishnah is R' Yose (*Rav* from *Gem.* 23a).

7.

חֲתִיכָה שֶׁל־חֵלֶב וַחֲתִיכָה שֶׁל־חֵלֶב קֹדֶשׁ, — *[If there was] a piece of cheilev and a piece of sanctified cheilev,*

[There was one piece of *cheilev* from an

the first [piece], and another came and ate the second [piece] — this one must bring an *asham talui*, and that one must bring an *asham talui*. R' Shimon says: They both bring a *chatas* and an *asham*. R' Yose says: Two do not bring a *chatas* and an *asham*.

7. [If there was] a piece of *cheilev* and a piece of sanctified *cheilev*, [if] he ate one of them, and it is not known which of them he ate, he must bring a *chatas*. R' Akiva says: He must bring an *asham talui*. [If] he ate the second [piece], he must bring two *chataos* and an unconditional *asham*. [If] one person ate the first [piece], and another came and ate the second [piece] — this one must bring a *chatas*, and that one must bring a *chatas*.

YAD AVRAHAM

ordinary animal and one piece of *cheilev* from a sacrificial animal. This case is different from the previous one in the respect that not only are both pieces prohibited, but they actually share the same *cheilev* prohibition. One piece, however, also has the additional prohibition of *me'ilah.*]

אָכַל אֶת־אַחַת מֵהֶן, וְאֵין יָדוּעַ אֵיזוֹ מֵהֶן אָכַל, מֵבִיא חַטָּאת. — *[if] he ate one of them, and it is not known which of them he ate, he must bring a chatas.*

R' Akiva agrees with the *Tanna Kamma* that he must bring a *chatas*. R' Akiva adds, however, that since it is certain that in any case, he inadvertently ate *cheilev*, he must bring a *chatas* (*Rav*).

רַבִּי עֲקִיבָא אוֹמֵר: מֵבִיא אָשָׁם תָּלוּי. — *R' Akiva says: He must bring an asham talui.*

Since he may have eaten the *cheilev* which was *kodesh*, there is a chance that he may have committed *me'ilah*. In R' Akiva's view [mishnah 2ff] this is grounds for an *asham talui*. Therefore he must bring an *asham talui* in addition to the *chatas* mentioned by the *Tanna Kamma* (*Rav; Shitah Mekubetzes*).

[Indeed, in the mishnah text printed in the *Gemara* the reading is אַף אָשָׁם תָּלוּי, *also an asham talui.*]

אָכַל אֶת־הַשְּׁנִיָּה, מֵבִיא שְׁתֵּי חַטָּאוֹת — *[If] he ate the second [piece], he must bring two chataos*

If he subsequently also ate the second piece of meat he must bring two *chataos*, for it is now certain that he ate two pieces of *cheilev*.

This applies only if he ate the pieces in two lapses of awareness; that is, he reminded himself in the interim that it was *cheilev* and subsequently forgot again. Thus, each *he'elam* [lapse of awareness] necessitates a separate *chatas*. Should he eat them both in one lapse of awareness, he is liable to only one *chatas* as above [3:2] (*Rav*).

וְאָשָׁם וַדַּאי. — *and an unconditional asham.*

Since it is now certain that he ate the *cheilev* which was *kodesh*, he is liable to an *asham me'ilos* (*Tif. Yis.*).

אָכַל אֶחָד אֶת־הָרִאשׁוֹנָה, וּבָא אַחֵר וְאָכַל אֶת־הַשְּׁנִיָּה — זֶה מֵבִיא חַטָּאת, וְזֶה מֵבִיא חַטָּאת. — *[If] one person ate the first [piece], and another came and ate the second [piece] — this one must bring a chatas, and that one must bring a chatas.*

[Since they both unquestionably ate *cheilev*, each one must bring a *chatas.*]

כריתות ה/ח

רַבִּי עֲקִיבָא אוֹמֵר: זֶה מֵבִיא אָשָׁם תָּלוּי, וְזֶה מֵבִיא אָשָׁם תָּלוּי. רַבִּי שִׁמְעוֹן אוֹמֵר: זֶה חַטָּאת וְזֶה חַטָּאת, וּשְׁנֵיהֶם מְבִיאִים אָשָׁם אֶחָד. רַבִּי יוֹסֵי אוֹמֵר: אֵין שְׁנַיִם מְבִיאִין אָשָׁם אֶחָד.

[ח] **חֲתִיכָה** שֶׁל־חֵלֶב וַחֲתִיכָה שֶׁל־חֵלֶב נוֹתָר, אָכַל אֶת־אַחַת מֵהֶן, וְאֵין יָדוּעַ אֶת־אֵיזוֹ מֵהֶם אָכַל, מֵבִיא חַטָּאת וְאָשָׁם תָּלוּי. אָכַל אֶת־הַשְּׁנִיָּה, מֵבִיא שָׁלֹשׁ חַטָּאוֹת. אָכַל

יד אברהם

רַבִּי עֲקִיבָא אוֹמֵר: זֶה מֵבִיא אָשָׁם תָּלוּי, וְזֶה מֵבִיא אָשָׁם תָּלוּי. — *R' Akiva says: This one must bring an asham talui, and that one must bring an asham talui.*

In R' Akiva's view, as has been repeatedly mentioned, a doubtful transgression of *me'ilah* calls for an *asham talui.* Thus, in addition to the *chatas* that each one brings for eating *cheilev,* he must bring an *asham talui* for the uncertain case of *me'ilah* (*Rav*).

רַבִּי שִׁמְעוֹן אוֹמֵר: זֶה חַטָּאת וְזֶה חַטָּאת, וּשְׁנֵיהֶם מְבִיאִים אָשָׁם אֶחָד. — *R' Shimon says: This one [brings] a chatas and that one [brings] a chatas, and both must bring one asham.*

[Albeit that each must bring a separate *chatas,* but the duplication of the *asham talui* can be avoided. They can share one *asham me'ilos.*] They can bring it jointly and stipulate that it should be sacrificed for the one who ate the *cheilev* of *kodesh* and is guilty of *me'ilah* (*Rav*).

רַבִּי יוֹסֵי אוֹמֵר: אֵין שְׁנַיִם מְבִיאִין אָשָׁם אֶחָד. — *R' Yose says: Two do not bring one asham.*

Here, too, the mishnah indicates that the *Tanna Kamma* is R' Yose (*Rav*).

Tos. Yom Tov challenges this assertion: R' Yose states only that they cannot jointly bring an *asham me'ilos,* whether or not the alternative is that they each bring an *asham talui* for the questionable *me'ilah* or merely a *chatas* for the certain transgression of *cheilev* is an issue that is not addressed by R' Yose. What R' Yose holds vis-a-vis the dispute of R' Akiva and the Sages regarding the issue of an *asham talui* for a questionable *me'ilah* seems to be a matter of conjecture, for which the *Gemara* makes no statement. [*Rambam Comm.* on mishnah 4, though, likewise asserts that R' Yose disagrees with R' Akiva on this issue.]

8.

חֲתִיכָה שֶׁל־חֵלֶב וַחֲתִיכָה שֶׁל־חֵלֶב נוֹתָר, — *[If there was] a piece of cheilev and a piece of cheilev that was nossar,*

A person had two pieces of *cheilev* before him; one was from an ordinary animal and one was *nossar, leftover* [the meat of a sacrificial animal left over after the allotted time for consumption or offering on the Altar].

[In the case of *cheilev,* which must be burnt on the Altar, it means that it remained unoffered the entire night after the offering was slaughtered.] Eating of *nossar* is a prohibition which is punish-

R' Akiva says: This one must bring an *asham talui*, and that one must bring an *asham talui*. R' Shimon says: This one [brings] a *chatas* and that one [brings] a *chatas*, and both must bring one *asham*. R' Yose says: Two do not bring one *asham*.

8. [If there was] a piece of *cheilev* and a piece of *cheilev* that was *nossar*, [if] he ate one of them, and it is not known which of them he ate, he must bring a *chatas* and an *asham talui*. [If] he ate the second [piece], he must bring three *chataos*. [If] one person ate the first

YAD AVRAHAM

able by *kares* and hence in the category of a *chatas* offering for inadvertent transgression, as above 1:1.

This case presents yet another scenario: Both pieces of meat were prohibited with the same *kares*-punishable prohibition but one was prohibited with an *additional* prohibition which is also punishable by *kares*. Thus there is no question that *one* transgression occurred, but it (the second one [the *nossar*]) is of questionable status.

As noted above, the foregoing series of mishnayos present a progressive sequence of *asham talui* possibilities. In each case there are two pieces of meat of increasingly stringent status: mishnah 4 — one permitted piece of ordinary meat (חֻלִּין) and one piece of sanctified meat (קָדָשִׁים); mishnah 5 — one permitted piece and one piece of *cheilev;* mishnah 6 — one piece prohibited by *kares* and one piece prohibited by *me'ilah*; mishnah 7 — one piece prohibited by *kares* and one by *me'ilah* and *kares;* mishnah 8 — one piece prohibited by *kares* and one piece prohibited by two *kares* prohibitions.

אָכַל אֶת־אַחַת מֵהֶן, וְאֵין יָדוּעַ אֶת־אֵיזוֹ מֵהֶם אָכַל, — *[if] he ate one of them, and it is not known which of them he ate,*

[If he ate one of these two pieces of *cheilev* but it is not known whether he ate the one that was also *nossar*, or the one that was merely *cheilev* from the ordinary animal.]

מֵבִיא חַטָּאת — *he must bring a chatas*

Since he unquestionably ate *cheilev*, he must bring a *chatas* (*Rav*).

וְאָשָׁם תָּלוּי. — *and an asham talui.*

Since he may have eaten *nossar*, a prohibition which bears a penalty of *kares*, he must bring an *asham talui* (*Rav*).

The fact that the piece is prohibited because of *nossar* although it was already prohibited as *cheilev* is not inconsistent with the dictum of אֵין אִיסּוּר חָל עַל אִיסּוּר, *a prohibition cannot take effect on another [pre-existing] prohibition* [discussed at length earlier (3:4)]. The *nossar* prohibition is more inclusive then the *cheilev* prohibition because *nossar* is prohibited for the Altar as well as for human consumption. This then is considered אִיסּוּר מוֹסִיף, *an additive prohibition,* which takes effect even on a previously existing prohibition. Thus, just as the piece becomes prohibited for sacrificial purposes, it becomes prohibited for human consumption as well (*Rav; Tos. Yom Tov; Tif. Yis.*).

אָכַל אֶת־הַשְּׁנִיָּה, מֵבִיא שָׁלֹשׁ חַטָּאוֹת. — *[If] he ate the second [piece], he must bring three chataos.*

[If he ate the second piece after having eaten the first piece, he must bring three *chataos*:] two for the two pieces of *cheilev* and one for *nossar*. As mentioned above, he is liable to two *chataos* for the two pieces of *cheilev* only if he realized in the interim that they were *cheilev*. Oth-

כריתות ה/ח

אֶחָד אֶת־הָרִאשׁוֹנָה, וּבָא אַחֵר וְאָכַל אֶת־הַשְּׁנִיָּה — זֶה מֵבִיא חַטָּאת וְאָשָׁם תָּלוּי, וְזֶה מֵבִיא חַטָּאת וְאָשָׁם תָּלוּי. רַבִּי שִׁמְעוֹן אוֹמֵר: זֶה חַטָּאת וְזֶה חַטָּאת, וּשְׁנֵיהֶם מְבִיאִים חַטָּאת אַחַת. רַבִּי יוֹסֵי אוֹמֵר: כָּל חַטָּאת שֶׁהִיא בָאָה עַל־חֵטְא, אֵין שְׁנַיִם מְבִיאִים אוֹתָהּ.

ו/א

[א] **הַמֵּבִיא** אָשָׁם תָּלוּי, וְנוֹדַע לוֹ שֶׁלֹּא חָטָא: אִם עַד שֶׁלֹּא נִשְׁחַט, יֵצֵא וְיִרְעֶה

יד אברהם

pieces, and another ate the second piece, and it is not known who ate the piece of *nossar.*]

זֶה מֵבִיא חַטָּאת וְאָשָׁם תָּלוּי, וְזֶה מֵבִיא חַטָּאת וְאָשָׁם תָּלוּי. — *this one must bring a chatas and an asham talui, and that one must bring a chatas and an asham talui.*

Each must bring a *chatas* since, regardless of which piece he ate, he transgressed the prohibition of *cheilev.* In addition, each one must bring an *asham talui* due to the possibility that he ate *nossar* (*Tif. Yis.*).

רַבִּי שִׁמְעוֹן אוֹמֵר: זֶה חַטָּאת וְזֶה חַטָּאת, וּשְׁנֵיהֶם מְבִיאִים חַטָּאת אַחַת. — *R' Shimon says: This one [brings] a chatas and that one [brings] a chatas, and both must bring a [third] chatas.*

While R' Shimon agrees that each must bring a separate *chatas* for their respective transgressions for eating *cheilev,* he holds that they can jointly bring an additional *chatas* and stipulate that it should be for the one who ate the *nossar* (*Tif. Yis.*).

רַבִּי יוֹסֵי אוֹמֵר: כָּל חַטָּאת שֶׁהִיא בָאָה עַל־חֵטְא, אֵין שְׁנַיִם מְבִיאִים אוֹתָהּ. — *R' Yose says: Any chatas that comes for sin, two may not bring it.*

R' Yose qualifies his previous state-

erwise, one *chatas* is sufficient for both pieces. He is, however, not liable to an *asham me'ilos* for eating the *cheilev* of *nossar* because *me'ilah* is only for using something with a monetary value and *nossar,* not being fit for any use, is considered valueless (*Rav* from *Gem.* 23a).

It will be recalled that above (3:4) the mishnah stated that for eating *cheilev* which is *nossar* one is liable to an *asham me'ilos* as well as *chatas.* Apparently, then, there *is* a monetary value to *nossar.* Why, then, does our mishnah exempt him from an *asham me'ilos?*

The *Gemara* 23a answers that our mishnah is discussing a case of someone who ate a large volume of the *nossar.* In quantity, the *nossar* is probably worth a *perutah.* The mishnah above, however, refers to someone who ate only a *kezayis* as stated clearly there. The small quantity is not worth a *perutah,* hence he is exempt from an *asham me'ilos.* Alternatively, the *nossar* is worth something only in the winter when it remains preserved. In the summer, when the fat will become rancid, the *nossar* is not worth a *perutah* (*Tos. Yom Tov* from *Gem.,* loc. cit.).

אָכַל אֶחָד אֶת־הָרִאשׁוֹנָה, וּבָא אַחֵר וְאָכַל אֶת־הַשְּׁנִיָּה — *[If] one person ate the first [piece] and another came and ate the second [piece]* —

[If one person ate the first of these two

5 [piece] and another came and ate the second [piece] —
8 this one must bring a *chatas* and an *asham talui*, and
that one must bring a *chatas* and an *asham talui*. R'
Shimon says: This one [brings] a *chatas* and that one
[brings] a *chatas*, and both must bring a [third] *chatas*.
R' Yose says: Any *chatas* that comes for sin, two may
not bring it.

6 **1.** [If] one brings an *asham talui*, and then discovers
1 that he has not sinned: If it has not yet been
slaughtered, it may go forth and graze with the flock;

YAD AVRAHAM

ments, telling us that only a *chatas* that comes to expiate sin may not be brought jointly. A *chatas* of a woman who has given birth, however, may be brought jointly and stipulated that the one liable to this *chatas* shall be given credit for it, as above [1:4] (*Rav; Rashi*).

The halachah, however, is that no *chatas* can be brought jointly (*Rav; Rambam Comm.*).

Chapter 6

1.

As we have seen repeatedly throughout this tractate, the *asham talui* is an atonement only for a doubtful transgression. If it is eventually determined that he did sin, he is liable to a *chatas* even if he already brought an *asham talui.*

Our mishnah discusses a case where he is obligated to bring an *asham talui*, but later determines that he did *not* sin.

הַמֵּבִיא אָשָׁם תָּלוּי, — *[If] one brings an asham talui,*

[One was in doubt whether or not he inadvertently committed a sin, in the manner which calls for an *asham talui*, as described above (4:1ff). So he designated an animal to be brought as his *asham*.]

וְנוֹדַע לוֹ שֶׁלֹּא חָטָא: — *and then discovers that he has not sinned:*

The doubt was created by the presence of two pieces of meat, one forbidden *cheilev* and one permitted *shumman*. He ate one of the pieces while unaware that either it or the other pieces was *cheilev*. Upon discovery that one of the pieces was *cheilev*, he designated an *asham talui* for his doubtful transgression. Later, the remaining piece was analyzed and discovered to be *cheilev*. Thus he determined that the piece he had eaten was *shumman*, and his *asham talui* is actually unnecessary (*Rabbeinu Gershom*; see *Meleches Shlomo*).

אִם עַד שֶׁלֹּא נִשְׁחַט, יֵצֵא וְיִרְעֶה בָּעֵדֶר; — *If it has not yet been slaughtered, it may go forth and graze with the flock;*

If prior to the animal's slaughter it was determined that no sin had transpired, the animal may be sent to graze with the flock, i.e., it is not considered consecrated in any way (*Rabbeinu Gershom; Rav; Rashi*).

כריתות ו/א

בָּעֵדֶר; דִּבְרֵי רַבִּי מֵאִיר. וַחֲכָמִים אוֹמְרִים: יִרְעֶה עַד שֶׁיִּסְתָּאֵב; וְיִמָּכֵר, וְיִפְּלוּ דָמָיו לִנְדָבָה. רַבִּי אֱלִיעֶזֶר אוֹמֵר: יִקְרַב, שֶׁאִם אֵינוֹ בָא עַל חֵטְא זֶה, הֲרֵי הוּא בָא עַל חֵטְא אַחֵר.

אִם, מִשֶּׁנִּשְׁחַט, נוֹדַע לוֹ, הַדָּם יִשָּׁפֵךְ, וְהַבָּשָׂר יֵצֵא לְבֵית הַשְּׂרֵפָה. נִזְרַק הַדָּם, הַבָּשָׂר יֵאָכֵל. רַבִּי

יד אברהם

.דִּבְרֵי רַבִּי מֵאִיר — *[these are] the words of R' Meir.*

R' Meir reasons that a person who consecrates an *asham talui* does so only in order to bring it when there is a doubt whether he sinned. Since this person determined with certainty that he did not sin and the *asham talui* is not required, it is regarded in retrospect as if he never consecrated the animal (*Rav* from *Gem.* 23b).

וַחֲכָמִים אוֹמְרִים: יִרְעֶה עַד שֶׁיִּסְתָּאֵב; וְיִמָּכֵר, וְיִפְּלוּ דָמָיו לִנְדָבָה. — *The Sages [however] say: It must graze until it develops a blemish; then it is sold and the proceeds deposited for a voluntary offering.*

The Sages reason that the sanctity which was initially invested in the animal remains despite the fact that reason for the sanctification is no longer valid. When a person designates an *asham talui,* he does so because he is beset by fear that he may have sinned. Since his designation takes place when he is not sure that he sinned, he thereby consecrates the animal unequivocally. The mere apprehension that he *may* have sinned is sufficient grounds for his designation of an offering (*Gem.* 23b, *Rambam Comm., Pesulei HaMukdashin* 4:19).

The fact that it is now clear that he did not sin does not render his initial designation an error. At the time that he designated it, he was aware that he may not have sinned, yet he designated it out of fear that he may have sinned. Thus his dedication of the offering is not contingent on his sin actually having taken place (*Rabbeinu Gershom*).

The *kedushah* (sanctity) of the *asham* remains even after it is clear that it was not necessary. But since the animal can no longer be brought for the purpose for which it was designated, it must be redeemed and the proceeds used for an *olah.* Since a sacrificial animal without a blemish cannot be redeemed, it must graze until it develops a blemish, after which it may be sold. The proceeds are then deposited in one of the chests in the Temple which were designated for money earmarked for the purchase of animals for an עוֹלַת נְדָבָה, *voluntary olah*[1] (*Rav*).

The halachah is in accordance with the Sages (*Rav; Rambam, Comm.*).

רַבִּי אֱלִיעֶזֶר אוֹמֵר: יִקְרַב, שֶׁאִם אֵינוֹ בָא עַל חֵטְא זֶה, הֲרֵי הוּא בָא עַל חֵטְא אַחֵר. — *R' Eliezer says: It is sacrificed, for, if it is not brought for this sin, it may be brought for another sin.*

R' Eliezer holds that the animal itself can be brought for an *asham talui*, the purpose for which it was consecrated. Although it is now clearly determined in this instance that no sin has occurred, he can bring it just in case he sinned some

1. The mishnah (*Shekalim* 6:5) states that there were thirteen collection chests in the Temple, of which six were designated for *olos nedavah* (donative offerings) (6:6). The second of these six chests was for מוֹתַר אֲשָׁמוֹת, *money remaining from asham offerings.* That is the one referred to here by the Sages.

6 [these are] the words of R′ Meir. The Sages [however]
1 say: It must graze until it develops a blemish; then it is sold and the proceeds deposited for a voluntary offering. R′ Eliezer says: It is sacrificed, for, if it is not brought for this sin, it may be brought for another sin.

If, after it is slaughtered, it becomes known to him, the blood must be spilled, and the meat must be removed to the place of burning. [If] the blood had

YAD AVRAHAM

other time. R′ Eliezer's view is that one can bring an *asham talui* simply out of fear that he may have sinned, even if he has no clear-cut doubt to that effect. Thus, R′ Eliezer maintains [in mishnah 3] that if one so desires, he may offer an *asham talui* every day, to suspend retribution just in case he sinned (*Tos. Yom Tov* from *Gem.* 27b).

אִם, מִשֶּׁנִּשְׁחַט, נוֹדַע לוֹ, — *If, after it is slaughtered, it becomes known to him,*

[If the offering was already slaughtered as an *asham talui* and then he determined that there is no necessity for atonement as he definitely committed no sin.]

הַדָּם יִשָּׁפֵךְ, — *the blood must be spilled,*

[As the reason for this offering is no longer valid,] its blood must be spilled into the stream that flows through the Temple court (*Rav; Rashi*). [See *Middos* 2:6.]

In the beginning of the mishnah, the Sages rule that a person who consecrates an *asham talui* does so unequivocally, and therefore, when he determines that he did not sin, must properly convert it into an *olah*. Yet they do not disagree with this ruling which finds that an unnecessary *asham talui* is considered invalid and its blood spilled. Once it is slaughtered it cannot be converted into an *olah*. Only the *proceeds* of the blemished-designated *asham* are fit to be used for an *olah*, not the sacrifice itself. Additionally, since at the time of the animal's *shechitah* the owner still had doubts that he may have sinned, it was slaughtered as an *asham talui*. After the *shechitah*, he may not offer it up as an *olah* (*Tos. Yom Tov* from *Tos.*).

וְהַבָּשָׂר יֵצֵא לְבֵית הַשְּׂרֵפָה. — *and the meat must be removed to the place of burning.*

[An offering that becomes invalidated must be burnt (*Temurah* 7:6).] Once it has been determined that the doubtful transgression for which this offering was intended to suspend Divine punishment never occurred, this animal, too, is similar to an offering which became invalidated [after the *shechitah*]. Therefore it must be burnt (*Rav*).

The mishnah in *Temurah* (7:4,6) delineates: Offerings which become invalidated are burnt; *chullin*, animals which by error were slaughtered in the Temple yard (חוּלִּין שֶׁנִּשְׁחֲטוּ בָּעֲזָרָה), are buried. In our case, the offering which was slaughtered as an *asham talui* is considered an offering that was invalidated and therefore burnt, as explained above (ibid.). According to the view of the Sages this ruling is self-understood: A person who designates an *asham talui* does so even for the eventuality that he did not sin. This, then, is a bona fide offering which subsequently became invalidated. According to R′ Meir, however, it must be clarified why this offering is not considered in the category of חוּלִּין שֶׁנִּשְׁחֲטוּ בָּעֲזָרָה. Since R′ Meir holds that his original consecration was contingent on the existence of the doubt of his willful transgression, it should follow that, in retrospect, this animal was never sanctified. Why, then, is it considered an invalid offering?

One answer to this question is that although R′ Meir holds his original consecration was equivocal, he agrees that after the *shechitah* the offering must be burnt, for it *resembles* an invalidated offering (*Rashash;* cf. *Tos. Yom Tov; Gemara* 24b).

Others go so far as to suggest that even according to R′ Meir the animal actually *is* an invalidated offering, for R′ Meir agrees that

יוֹסֵי אוֹמֵר: אֲפִלּוּ הַדָּם בַּכּוֹס, יִזָּרֵק, וְהַבָּשָׂר יֵאָכֵל.

[ב] **אָשָׁם** וַדַּאי אֵינוֹ כֵן. אִם עַד שֶׁלֹּא נִשְׁחַט, יֵצֵא וְיִרְעֶה בָעֵדֶר. מִשֶּׁנִּשְׁחַט, הֲרֵי זֶה יִקָּבֵר. נִזְרַק הַדָּם, הַבָּשָׂר יֵצֵא לְבֵית הַשְּׂרֵפָה.

יד אברהם

once it was slaughtered he consigns it for an offering regardless of whether or not he sinned (*Tos.* cited by *Tos. Yom Tov*).

נִזְרַק הַדָּם, — *[If] the blood had [already] been thrown,*

If the blood has already been thrown on the Altar wall before he ascertained that he did not sin (*Rav; Rambam Comm.*).

In any sacrificial process, it is the *zerikah* ['throwing' or 'applying' the blood to the Altar wall] that consummates the atonement process (see Intro. to ArtScroll *Zevachim*). Thus, once the *zerikah* has taken place, the offering is completed as an *asham talui*, for at that time the status of the transgression was still in doubt. The question remains only whether the meat may be eaten, for now that there is no longer any doubt of his transgression, the offering can no longer be considered a bona fide *asham talui*.

הַבָּשָׂר יֵאָכֵל. — *the meat may be eaten.*

This is a valid *asham talui*, because at the time of the *zerikah* the doubt that he committed a sin still existed.

רַבִּי יוֹסֵי אוֹמֵר: אֲפִלּוּ הַדָּם בַּכּוֹס, יִזָּרֵק, וְהַבָּשָׂר יֵאָכֵל. — *R' Yose says: Even if the blood is [still] in a vessel, it may be thrown, and the meat may be eaten.*

[According to R' Yose, even if, at the time he ascertained that he did not sin, the blood was not yet applied but merely in a state of readiness for *zerikah*, the *zerikah* may take place and the meat subsequently eaten. He disagrees, then, with the earlier ruling that if the absence of sin was determined after the *shechitah*, the blood must be spilled out.]

R' Yose holds that כְּלֵי שָׁרֵת מְקַדְּשִׁין אֶת הַפָּסוּל לִיקָּרֵב לְכַתְּחִלָּה, *klei shareis (vessels used in sacrificial service) consecrate even things unfit for sacrifice.*[1] Accordingly, once the blood was received in the vessel, it became consecrated to be thrown on the Altar. Furthermore, R' Yose subscribes to the view that כָּל הָעוֹמֵד לִיזָּרֵק כְּזָרוּק דָּמֵי, *whatever is ready to be thrown is adjudged as though it has already been thrown.* [Thus it is as if the *zerikah* took place as soon as the blood is received in the *kli shareis*. Consequently, this offering has the same status as one whose blood was sprinkled before the doubt of sin was eliminated.] The blood may be thrown and the meat eaten (*Rav* from *Gem.* 24b).

1. As described in *Zevachim* (9:1), the Altar has sanctification properties, which, in some cases, extend even to invalid offerings. Therefore, once the *eimurin* [sacrificial parts] of certain types of disqualified offerings have been placed on the Altar they are not removed, even though they should not have been placed there in the first place [see ArtScroll *Zevachim*, Introduction IV f].

Whether this principle applies to the blood of an invalid offering which was received in a *kli shareis* is the subject of an inquiry in the *Gemara* (*Zevachim* 87a). According to some *Rishonim* this means that the blood of this category of invalid offerings may be thrown on the Altar if it was received in a *kli shareis* (*Rashi, Zevachim* loc. cit.; *Rambam, Pesulei HaMukdashin* 31:19). Others strongly disagree (*Tos.; Zevachim* loc. cit.). See Introduction to ArtScroll *Zevachim* V-e; comm. to mishnah 9:2, s.v. ושקבלו; 9:7 s.v. כשם.

The principle articulated by R' Yose in this mishnah is, however, not related to the above [already] been thrown, the meat may be eaten. R' Yose says: Even if the blood is [still] in a vessel, it may be thrown, and the meat may be eaten.

2. An *asham vaddai* is unlike this. If it had not yet been slaughtered, it may go forth and graze with the flock. [If] it had already been slaughtered, it must be buried. [If] the blood had been thrown, the meat must be removed to the place of burning.

YAD AVRAHAM

2.

אָשָׁם וַדַּאי אֵינוֹ כֵן. — *An asham vaddai is unlike this.*

The *asham* offerings which atone for transgressions that occurred without any doubt are dissimilar to the *asham talui* in regard to the situation described above: If it was determined that the transgression in actuality never occurred, the designated *asham* offering can revert back to its non-sanctified status. This is true even according to the Sages' opinion that an *asham talui* in this situation must be converted to an *olah*, as will now be explained (*Rav*).

אִם עַד שֶׁלֹּא נִשְׁחַט, — *If it had not yet been slaughtered,*

If before the *asham* was slaughtered, it was discovered that the person had not sinned (*Tif. Yis.*).

יֵצֵא וְיִרְעֶה בָּעֵדֶר. — *it may go forth and graze with the flock.*

Above, the Sages reason that since his conscience plagues him over the doubt that he may have sinned, he consecrates the animal unconditionally. Regarding the *asham vaddai*, however, his consecration is contingent on his having sinned. He consecrates an *asham vaddai* only because he is under the impression that he has indeed sinned, e.g., witnesses told him that he had eaten consecrated food. When it is discovered that the witnesses were false, or the supposedly consecrated food was ordinary, it turns out that his consecration was done in error and is therefore invalid (*Rav; Rashi*).

מִשֶּׁנִּשְׁחַט, הֲרֵי זֶה יִקָּבֵר. — *[If] it had already been slaughtered, it must be buried.*

If the determination that he did not sin occurred after the offering had already been slaughtered, it has the status of חוּלִין שֶׁנִּשְׁחֲטוּ בָּעֲזָרָה, *an ordinary animal that was slaughtered in the Temple courtyard.* Since it is now known that it was consecrated in error, it must be buried in accordance with the halachah for this type of error (as in *Temurah* 7:4).

נִזְרַק הַדָּם, הַבָּשָׂר יֵצֵא לְבֵית הַשְּׂרֵפָה. — *[If] the blood had been thrown, the meat must be removed to the place of burning.*

[If, by the time it was discovered that the transgression in fact never took place, the *zerikah* had already been performed, then the offering is invalid and must be

question. Although he states that the fact that the blood of invalid offerings which was received in a *kli shareis* renders it fit to be offered, the same does not apply to unnecessary offerings. The *asham talui* designated for a doubtful transgression which was subsequently determined not to have transpired is, in this sense, not an invalid offering; it is merely an unnecessary one. Thus, once its blood was received in the *kli shareis* it can, in R' Yose's opinion, be thrown on the Altar (*Tos.*).

שׁוֹר הַנִּסְקָל אֵינוֹ כֵן. אִם עַד שֶׁלֹּא נִסְקַל, יֵצֵא וְיִרְעֶה בָעֵדֶר. מִשֶּׁנִּסְקַל, מֻתָּר בַּהֲנָאָה. עֶגְלָה עֲרוּפָה אֵינָהּ כֵּן. אִם עַד שֶׁלֹּא נֶעֶרְפָה, תֵּצֵא וְתִרְעֶה בָעֵדֶר. מִשֶּׁנֶּעֶרְפָה, תִּקָּבֵר בִּמְקוֹמָהּ,

יד אברהם

burnt in accordance with the requirement for such instances.]

This is an apparent contradiction to the immediately preceding clause, which states that if it was discovered after the slaughter, the meat must be buried, not burnt. Indeed, these two clauses must be attributed to different *Tannaim:* The previous *Tanna* holds that since it is ordinary meat, in the category of חולין שֶׁנִּשְׁחֲטוּ בָּעֲזָרָה, it requires burial because its initial consecration was conditional. This *Tanna,* however, holds that it is like an unfit offering and must, therefore, be burnt (*Rav* from *Gem.* 24b).

Others reconcile the two segments of the mishnah by reasoning that although the sacrifice is actually *chullin* and should be buried, nevertheless, if the *zerikah* took place before the discovery of his innocence, it must be burnt because it *appears* like an unfit offering (*Tos. Yom Tov* citing *Tos.* in explanation of Rav Ashi's opinion in *Gem.* ibid., cf. *Rambam Comm.; Rashash*).

שׁוֹר הַנִּסְקָל אֵינוֹ כֵן. — *An ox which is [to be] stoned is unlike this.*

[The term שׁוֹר הַנִּסְקָל [*shor haniskal*] refers to an ox (or any other animal) that killed a person. The Torah (*Exodus* 21:28ff) requires that the animal be stoned to death and any benefit from its carcass is prohibited.]

The law of a *shor haniskal* that was subsequently proven to be innocent is different from the law of the *asham talui* after the innocence of the person has been determined. The mishnah now details the differences (*Rav*).

אִם עַד שֶׁלֹּא נִסְקַל, — *If it had not yet been stoned,*

Before it was stoned, it was discovered that its designation as a *shor haniskal* was in error. This can occur if, for example, the testifying witnesses were proven false (*Tif. Yis.*).

יֵצֵא וְיִרְעֶה בָעֵדֶר. — *it may go forth and graze with the herd.*

Regarding the *shor haniskal* the law is undisputed: The ox [whose innocence has been determined] is completely permissible. It may graze with the herd like any other ordinary ox (*Rav; Rashi*).

מִשֶּׁנִּסְקַל, מֻתָּר בַּהֲנָאָה. — *If it had already been stoned, it is permissible to derive benefit from it.*

[If its innocence was discovered after it had already been stoned it may not, of course, be eaten since it was not ritually slaughtered. Its carcass may, however, be put to other use, e.g., the meat may be sold to gentiles and the skin may be processed into leather.]

עֶגְלָה עֲרוּפָה אֵינָהּ כֵּן. — *A calf that is [to be] decapitated is unlike this.*

[The reference is to the rite of עֶגְלָה עֲרוּפָה [*eglah arufah*], *the decapitated calf.* As delineated in *Deut.* 21:1-9, if a victim of an unknown murderer be found outside of a city in *Eretz Yisrael,* the elders of the nearest city must take a calf and decapitate it in a rock-hard valley. The carcass of this calf is then prohibited from any use.]

The *eglah arufah,* too, is not like an *asham talui.* [Although both are designated out of doubt, they differ regarding a situation where the doubt was eliminated before the animal was slaughtered, as will be explained] (*Rav; Rashi*).

Rambam Comm., however, explains that

6 An ox which is [to be] stoned is unlike this. If it had
2 not yet been stoned, it may go forth and graze with the herd. If it had already been stoned, it is permissible to derive benefit from it.

A calf that is [to be] decapitated is unlike this. If it had not yet been decapitated, it may go forth and graze with the herd. [After the calf] has been decapitated, it must be buried at its site, for it originally came [to atone] for a

YAD AVRAHAM

the contrast is between the *eglah arufah* and the *shor haniskal* mentioned earlier. This approach will be explained at the end of the mishnah.

אם עד שֶׁלֹּא נֶעֶרְפָה, תֵּצֵא וְתִרְעֶה בָעֵדֶר. — *If it had not yet been decapitated, it may go forth and graze with the herd.*

If the murderer was discovered before the calf had been decapitated, the animal may graze with all other animals, for it maintains no status of prohibition (*Rav; Rashi*).

As was explained, once the rite has been performed with the calf, it becomes forbidden from all benefit. This prohibition, however, does not take effect until after the calf has been decapitated. Thus, if the murderer is identified before the decapitation takes place — even though the calf has already been designated for use as an *eglah arufah* and has been brought to the decapitation site — the calf maintains its non-prohibited status and may be returned to the flock [i.e., may be used for any purpose] (*Meiri* to *Sotah* 9:7).

Elsewhere (*Kiddushin* 57a) the *Gemara* cites a view that יְרִידָתָהּ לְנַחַל אֵיתָן אוֹסַרְתָּה, *its descent to the rock-hard valley makes it prohibited*. According to this view then, the prohibition begins even while the animal is still alive, from the time it is taken down to the valley where it will be decapitated. Thus, the law formulated in our mishnah is not unanimous. Our *Tanna* holds that the beheading creates the prohibition on the *eglah*; should the doubt be resolved prior to that, the *eglah* remains permitted. The other *Tanna* maintains that the *eglah* becomes prohibited while still alive. Accordingly, in our case the calf would not be permitted to return to the herd [but would be left to die and then be buried] (*Gem.* 25a; *Rashi* ad loc. and *Sotah* 47a).

Others, though, explain that our mishnah is independent of the dispute regarding the point at which the calf becomes forbidden. They reason that even according to the view that the calf becomes forbidden as soon as it is brought down into the valley, this is so only if the murderer is not found. Should the murderer be found, however, the calf retroactively reverts to its non-prohibited status, because its designation as an *eglah arufah* was originally made on the assumption that the murderer's identity would not be discovered before the decapitation would take place (*Tos. Yom Tov* from *Kesef Mishneh, Rotzeach* 10:6; see *Keren Orah*, *Sotah* loc. cit.). However, if the murderer is not discovered, so that the rite is required, then the animal becomes forbidden as soon as it is brought down to the valley. Consequently, even if it should die before being decapitated, its carcass is still forbidden for benefit and must be buried instead. Thus, the view stated in our mishnah is consistent with both sides in the dispute regarding when the calf becomes forbidden (*Meiri;* based on *Rambam, Rotzeach* 10:6,8).

מִשֶּׁנֶּעֶרְפָה, תִּקָּבֵר בִּמְקוֹמָהּ, — *[After the calf] has been decapitated, it must be buried at its site,*

[Once the calf has been decapitated, it becomes prohibited and cannot revert to its former state. Therefore, even if the murderer is subsequently found, the calf is prohibited and must be buried. The mishnah continues with the rationale behind this ruling.]

שֶׁעַל סָפֵק בָּאָה מִתְּחִלָּתָהּ — כִּפְּרָה סְפֵקָהּ וְהָלְכָה לָהּ.

[ג] **רַבִּי** אֱלִיעֶזֶר אוֹמֵר: מִתְנַדֵּב אָדָם אָשָׁם תָּלוּי בְּכָל־יוֹם וּבְכָל־שָׁעָה שֶׁיִּרְצֶה, וְהִיא נִקְרֵאת אֲשַׁם חֲסִידִים. אָמְרוּ עָלָיו עַל בָּבָא בֶּן בּוּטִי, שֶׁהָיָה מִתְנַדֵּב אָשָׁם תָּלוּי בְּכָל־יוֹם, חוּץ מֵאַחַר יוֹם הַכִּפּוּרִים יוֹם אֶחָד. אָמַר: הַמָּעוֹן הַזֶּה!

יד אברהם

שֶׁעַל סָפֵק בָּאָה מִתְּחִלָּתָהּ — כִּפְּרָה סְפֵקָהּ וְהָלְכָה לָהּ. — *for it originally came [to atone] for a doubtful situation — [once] it has atoned for its doubt, its purpose has been fulfilled* [lit., *it has gone on its way*].

The purpose of the *eglah arufah* rite is to gain atonement for the local court and the local citizenry for the murder which took place in their proximity, for which the proper atonement would be the bringing of the murderer to justice. Since at the time of the decapitation of the *eglah arufah* the murderer had not yet been identified, the *eglah arufah* was needed and served its purpose. Thus, its forbidden status properly took effect and therefore remains, just as it does with any animal brought for atonement (*Rav;* cf. *Rashi*).

According to the above interpretation of the mishnah, both cases cited are in contrast to the *asham talui,* i.e., unlike the *asham talui,* neither the *shor haniskal* nor the *eglah arufah* retains any of its prohibition status after the initial doubt has been eliminated.

According to *Rambam,* however, the mishnah is a sequence: Each segment of the mishnah is a contrast with the immediately preceding one. The flow of the mishnah is as follows: The *shor haniskal* is not like the *asham vaddai.* The *asham vaddai,* which was slaughtered before it was discovered that the person did not sin, must be buried. The *shor haniskal*, by contrast, is not prohibited if it was discovered to be innocent of killing a Jew after having been stoned. The *eglah arufah,* though, in this respect is not like the *shor haniskal.* Whereas the *shor haniskal*, which was discovered to have been innocent after its stoning, is permissible for any benefits, regarding the *eglah arufah,* however, if the murderer is discovered after the calf has been decapitated, it is still prohibited and must be buried in its place (*Rav* from *Rambam Comm.*).

3.

In general terms, offerings fall into two categories: קָרְבְּנוֹת נְדָבָה, *voluntary offerings,* and קָרְבְּנוֹת חוֹבָה, *obligatory offerings.* The former category includes such offerings as the *olah,* the *shelamim* and the *minchah.* These may be donated on an entirely voluntary basis, whenever a person is inspired to offer them. The category of obligatory offerings includes the *chatas* and the *asham.* Since their function is to bring atonement, they may be brought only if a transgression was committed.

The question of the following mishnah is the status of the *asham talui.* Do we consider it as an obligatory offering since its purpose is to suspend Divine punishment for a possible transgression? Or do we consider it in the category of voluntary offerings because it does not conclusively provide atonement?

6 doubtful situation — [once] it has atoned for its doubt,
3 its purpose has been fulfilled.

3. R' Eliezer says: A person may donate an *asham talui* any day or any time that he wishes, and this is called the *asham* of the pious. It was said concerning Bava ben Buti that he would donate an *asham talui* every day, except one day after Yom Kippur. He said: By this Temple! Were they to permit

YAD AVRAHAM

רַבִּי אֱלִיעֶזֶר אוֹמֵר: מִתְנַדֵּב אָדָם אָשָׁם תָּלוּי בְּכָל־יוֹם וּבְכָל־שָׁעָה שֶׁיִּרְצֶה, וְהִיא נִקְרֵאת אֲשַׁם חֲסִידִים. — *R' Eliezer says: A person may donate an asham talui any day or any time that he wishes, and this is called the asham of the pious.*

As we have seen repeatedly, the *asham talui* does not provide conclusive atonement. If a person, having already brought an *asham talui*, learns that he did indeed commit a transgression, he must subsequently bring a *chatas*. This leads R' Eliezer to assert that an *asham talui* is really a קָרְבַּן נְדָבָה, *voluntary offering.* Were it to be an obligatory offering, he reasons, he would not have to bring a *chatas* after having previously brought an *asham talui* (*Rav* from *Gem.* 25a).

R' Eliezer concludes that the function of the *asham talui* is not to atone. Thus it may be brought as a *nedavah* [voluntary offering] (*Tos. Yom Tov* from *Rambam Comm.*).

R' Eliezer deliberately used the redundant phrase *any day or any time that he wishes* to indicate that not only may he bring an *asham talui* any *day* that he wishes but even *any time* during the day, i.e., even more than once a day. In R' Eliezer's view, the *asham talui* is wholly a donative offering, as is the *olah* or the *shelamim*, and there are no restrictions on the number of times that it may be offered (*Aruch LaNer*).

אָמְרוּ עָלָיו עַל בָּבָא בֶּן בּוּטִי, שֶׁהָיָה מִתְנַדֵּב אָשָׁם תָּלוּי בְּכָל־יוֹם, — *It was said concerning Bava ben Buti that he would donate an asham talui every day,*

Together with R' Eliezer, Bava ben Buti was a disciple of Beis Shammai (*Tif. Yis.*). [Both shared the view that the *asham talui* can be brought without conclusive grounds for a doubt.]

חוּץ מֵאַחַר יוֹם הַכִּפּוּרִים יוֹם אֶחָד. — *except one day after Yom Kippur.*

On Yom Kippur, all sins are forgiven. There is, therefore, no reason to bring an *asham talui* until, at least, one day has passed (*Rav*).

The question can still be raised: Why did he not bring an *asham talui* towards evening of the day following Yom Kippur for any sins that he may have committed throughout that day?

Some explain that the sanctity of Yom Kippur prevented him from sinning the entire day following it (*Minchas Yitzchak*).

Others explain that Bava ben Buti did bring an *asham talui* towards evening on the day following Yom Kippur. What the mishnah means is that he did not bring an *asham talui* after Yom Kippur *for* Yom Kippur. In other words, he would bring an *asham talui* for sins committed on every day of the year, including Sundays and the days following festivals for the sins committed the previous day [as above]. For the one day of Yom Kippur, however, he did not find it necessary to bring an *asham talui* (*Ner Tamid*).

A variant reading punctuates the mishnah differently.... חוּץ מִיּוֹם הַכִּפּוּרִים. יוֹם אֶחָד אָמַר. [*He would bring an asham talui every day*] *except for Yom Kippur. One day he said ...* (*Meleches Shlomo*). This, too, is explained as above — he would bring an *asham talui* on the day following Yom Kippur but not in the morning to atone for Yom Kippur (*Zera Yitzchak*).

אָמַר: הַמָּעוֹן הַזֶּה! — *He said: By this Temple!*

אִלּוּ הָיוּ מַנִּיחִים לִי, הָיִיתִי מֵבִיא, אֶלָּא אוֹמְרִים לִי: הַמְתֵּן עַד שֶׁתִּכָּנֵס לְסָפֵק. וַחֲכָמִים אוֹמְרִים: אֵין מְבִיאִין אָשָׁם תָּלוּי אֶלָּא עַל־דָּבָר שֶׁזְּדוֹנוֹ כָּרֵת וְשִׁגְגָתוֹ חַטָּאת.

[ד] **חַיָּבֵי** חַטָּאוֹת וַאֲשָׁמוֹת וַדָּאִין, שֶׁעָבַר עֲלֵיהֶן יוֹם הַכִּפּוּרִים, חַיָּבִין לְהָבִיא לְאַחַר יוֹם הַכִּפּוּרִים. חַיָּבֵי אֲשָׁמוֹת תְּלוּיִין

יד אברהם

This is an expression of oath (*Tif. Yis.*), as if to say, 'I swear by the Temple (or its utensils) [that if I were allowed to I would bring an *asham talui* even on the day following Yom Kippur]' (see *Rav* above 1:7 and *Tos. Yom Tov Kesubos* 2:9). Alternatively, it is not really an oath, but an affirmative statement of emphasis similar to an oath (*Tif. Yis., Boaz;* see *Shoshannim LeDavid* above 1:7).

אִלּוּ הָיוּ מַנִּיחִים לִי, הָיִיתִי מֵבִיא, — *Were they to permit me, I would bring it,*

I would bring it immediately after Yom Kippur [i.e., the morning after Yom Kippur for Yom Kippur] (*Tif. Yis.*).

The above interpretation, of Bava ben Buti's statement of course, follows the explanation above that Bava ben Buti did bring an *asham talui* at the end of the day following Yom Kippur, albeit not in the morning. Otherwise, his statement simply meant that, if permitted, I would bring an *asham talui* on the day after Yom Kippur.

אֶלָּא אוֹמְרִים לִי: הַמְתֵּן עַד שֶׁתִּכָּנֵס לְסָפֵק. — *but they tell me: Wait until you come into a doubt.*

On any other day of the year, an *asham talui* can be brought because he may have committed a sin during the period following the *asham talui* offering of the previous day. But since Yom Kippur itself provides atonement for any doubtful transgression, the next day does not leave enough room for doubt of a transgression [as explained in the following mishnah], for a full day has not passed during which he may have sinned (*Tif. Yis.*).

In principle, Bava ben Buti's colleagues subscribe to the ruling that an *asham talui* may be brought voluntarily. They insisted, however, that he wait a day after Yom Kippur only to allow a reasonable amount of time to pass for a doubt to be created.

It should be noted that this is a departure from the view stated by R' Eliezer at the outset of the mishnah, in which he considered the *asham talui* as a voluntary offering. The Sages, for their part, maintain that R' Eliezer did not mean that it is a wholly voluntary offering; it must be brought to atone for some possible sin. However, even they hold that the *asham talui* can be brought for *any* possible sin, such as eating *neveilah* [ritually unslaughtered meat] or the like, even though there is no *kares* involved (*Tevuos Shor, Yoreh Deah* 5:8 cited by *Tos. R' Akiva Eiger*, see *Gem.* 25b).

There are, then, three views expressed in the mishnah: (1) R' Eliezer's opinion is that the *asham talui* is a wholly donative offering, just as the *olah* or the *shelamim.* He supports this by citing the example of Bava ben Buti who, for his part, wanted to offer an *asham talui* even on the morrow of Yom Kippur. (2) The Sages, who remonstrated with Bava ben Buti to wait at least a day after Yom Kippur before offering the *asham talui,* hold that there must be at least some possibility of the commission of a sin — albeit a minor one — in order to allow the offering of the *asham talui.* (3) The Sages mentioned in the following segment of the mishnah hold that an *asham talui* is only to suspend

6
4

me, I would bring it, but they tell me: Wait until you come into a doubt. But the Sages say: We may not bring an *asham talui* except for something which, if intentional, [bears a penalty of] *kares* and, if unintentional, [is liable to a] *chatas*.

4. Those liable to *chataos* or unconditional *ashamos*, for whom Yom Kippur passed, are liable to bring them after Yom Kippur. Those liable to conditional

YAD AVRAHAM

atonement in the event of a doubtful transgression. In their view the *asham talui* is wholly a קָרְבַּן חוֹבָה, *obligatory offering*, as is the *chatas* and the *asham vaddai* (*Aruch LaNer*).

וַחֲכָמִים אוֹמְרִים: אֵין מְבִיאִין אָשָׁם תָּלוּי אֶלָּא עַל־דָּבָר שֶׁזְּדוֹנוֹ כָּרֵת וְשִׁגְגָתוֹ חַטָּאת. — *But the Sages say: We may not bring an asham talui except for something which, if intentional, [bears a penalty of] kares and, if unintentional, [is liable to a] chatas.*

The Sages rule that an *asham talui* may not be brought as a donation. It may be brought only if there are grounds to believe that one may have unintentionally committed a sin for which the intentional transgression bears the penalty of *kares*. The fact that he must still bring a *chatas* if he discovers that he indeed sinned is, however, no indication that the *asham talui* is considered a *nedavah*. It is rather brought to temporarily suspend any Divine punishment (*Rav* from *Gem.* 25a).

The *asham talui*, then, does not atone for the sin. It merely relieves him from the constant fear of having transgressed (*Rambam Comm., Kafich* ed.).

The halachah follows the view of the Sages (*Rav; Rambam Comm.; Shegagos* 8:1).

In *Chullin* (2:10), the mishnah states that there is a Rabbinic injunction against eating the meat of a non-sacrificial animal slaughtered for the expressed purpose of a donative sacrifice, such as an *olah* or a *shelamim*. If it was slaughtered for the purpose of an obligatory offering, (such as a *chatas*) however, it may be eaten. In that context, the mishnah mentions *asham talui* as a donative offering, an inclusion which is ascribed by the *Gemara* (41b) as the view of R' Eliezer. *Rosh* (ad loc.) and *Tur* (*Yoreh Deah* 5) cite this ruling, indicating that the halachah follows R' Eliezer.

Rambam (*Shechitah* 2:17) does not include the *asham talui* in his listing of donative offerings. This is consistent with his view, cited above, that the halachah follows the Sages of our mishnah.

This difference of opinion is reflected in the rulings of *Shulchan Aruch*, and *Rama* (*Yoreh Deah* 5:1), who rule according to *Rambam* and *Rosh* respectively[1] (*Beur HaGra, Yoreh Deah loc. cit.*).

4.

חַיָּבֵי חַטָּאוֹת וַאֲשָׁמוֹת וַדָּאִין, שֶׁעָבַר עֲלֵיהֶן יוֹם הַכִּפּוּרִים, חַיָּבִין לְהָבִיא לְאַחַר יוֹם הַכִּפּוּרִים. — *Those liable to chataos or unconditional ashamos, for whom Yom Kippur passed, are liable to bring them after Yom Kippur.*

[If before Yom Kippur someone committed a sin for which he was liable to a

1. Another application of practical halachah stemming from the dispute between R' Eliezer and the Sages involves the recitation of the part of the daily morning prayers known as

כריתות ו/ה פְּטוּרִים. מִי שֶׁבָּא עַל יָדוֹ סְפֵק עֲבֵרָה בְּיוֹם הַכִּפּוּרִים, אֲפִלּוּ עִם חֲשֵׁכָה, פָּטוּר, שֶׁכָּל־הַיּוֹם מְכַפֵּר.

[ה] **הָאִשָּׁה** שֶׁיֵּשׁ עָלֶיהָ חַטַּאת הָעוֹף סָפֵק, שֶׁעָבַר עָלֶיהָ יוֹם הַכִּפּוּרִים, חַיֶּבֶת לְהָבִיא לְאַחַר יוֹם הַכִּפּוּרִים מִפְּנֵי שֶׁמַּכְשַׁרְתָּהּ לֶאֱכוֹל בַּזְּבָחִים. חַטַּאת הָעוֹף הַבָּאָה עַל־סָפֵק — אִם מִשֶּׁנִּמְלְקָה נוֹדַע לָהּ — הֲרֵי זוֹ תִּקָּבֵר.

יד אברהם

chatas or an unconditional *asham* and failed to bring it before Yom Kippur, he must nonetheless bring his atonement after Yom Kippur as will be explained further. Yom Kippur does not serve in lieu of an offering to expiate for sins which are known to the transgressor.]

חַיָּבֵי אֲשָׁמוֹת תְּלוּיִין פְּטוּרִים. — *Those liable to conditional ashamos are exempt.*

If, however, one was liable to an *asham talui,* and did not bring it before Yom Kippur, he is exempt from his obligation.

The *Gemara* (25b) bases this on the Torah's phrase regarding Yom Kippur (*Lev.* 16:30): מִכֹּל חַטֹּאתֵיכֶם לִפְנֵי ה׳ תִּטְהָרוּ, *from all your sins before Hashem, shall you be purified.* This denotes that Yom Kippur atones for those sins which are לִפְנֵי ה׳, *before God,* i.e., known only to God, but not for those sins which are known to the transgressor. Therefore, one liable to an *asham talui* is exempt after Yom Kippur, for the *asham talui* is brought for a doubtful transgression, which is a situation in which it is known only to God whether a sin was committed. One liable to a *chatas* or an *asham vaddai* remains liable even after the passage of Yom Kippur, since he is aware that he committed a sin (*Rav*).

מִי שֶׁבָּא עַל יָדוֹ סְפֵק עֲבֵרָה בְּיוֹם הַכִּפּוּרִים, אֲפִלּוּ עִם חֲשֵׁכָה, פָּטוּר, — *One for whom a doubtful situation of sin occurred on Yom Kippur, even at dusk, is exempt,*

One who, on Yom Kippur, committed an act which may have involved the unintentional transgression of a *kares*-bearing sin is exempt from subsequently bringing an *asham talui,* even if this doubtful transgression took place at the very end of Yom Kippur (*Tif. Yis.*).

שֶׁכָּל־הַיּוֹם מְכַפֵּר. — *for the entire day atones.*

korbanos (offerings), which consists of the selected sections of the Torah dealing with the various offerings. *Tur* (*Orach Chaim* 1) recommends that after the recitation of the sections dealing with donative offerings [*olah, minchah, shelamim, todah*], one should conclude with the prayer יְהִי רָצוֹן מִלְּפָנֶיךָ שֶׁיְּהֵא זֶה חָשׁוּב וּמְקוּבָּל לְפָנֶיךָ כְּאִלּוּ הִקְרַבְתִּי עוֹלָה וכו׳, *May it be Your will that this [recitation] be worthy and accepted before You as if I brought an olah, etc.* For the obligatory offerings (*chatas, asham*) this prayer cannot be said, for they cannot be brought unless the obligatory circumstances exist. *Beis Yosef* (ibid.) indicates that the *asham talui* also is in this category. According to the view of the *Tur* and *Rosh* cited above, though, the prayer can be recited after the section of an *asham talui,* for they rule according to R' Eliezer, that the *asham talui* is a donative offering (*Magen Avraham* 1:11). Others disagree (*Shach, Y.D.* 1:7).

ashamos are exempt. One for whom a doubtful situation of sin occurred on Yom Kippur, even at dusk, is exempt, for the entire day atones.

5. A woman who was obligated to bring a bird *chatas* of doubt, for whom Yom Kippur passed, is obligated to bring [it] after Yom Kippur since it renders her fit to eat of the offerings. A bird *chatas* that is brought because of a doubt — if, after its neck was nipped, it became known to her — must be buried.

YAD AVRAHAM

[It is not necessary for the full day of Yom Kippur to pass to provide atonement. Even one moment of Yom Kippur has the power to atone for sins.]

5.

הָאִשָּׁה שֶׁיֵּשׁ עָלֶיהָ חַטַּאת הָעוֹף סָפֵק, — *A woman who was obligated to bring a bird chatas of doubt,*

A woman aborted a fetus of doubtful status, i.e., it is not known whether it was considered a birth or not, as above [1:4] (*Rav*).

שֶׁעָבַר עָלֶיהָ יוֹם הַכִּפּוּרִים, — *for whom Yom Kippur passed,*

[She aborted before Yom Kippur, and then Yom Kippur passed before she brought her offerings. The question the mishnah addresses is whether the obligation to bring her *chatas* offering still exists. Do we say that since Yom Kippur provides atonement for situations of doubt, the woman's offering, the purpose of which is atonement, is no longer necessary? Or is the purpose of the woman's offering something other than simple atonement?]

חַיֶּבֶת לְהָבִיא לְאַחַר יוֹם הַכִּפּוּרִים — *is obligated to bring [it] after Yom Kippur*

[Although this is an obligation known only to God, she is nonetheless obligated to bring it after Yom Kippur. This is unlike an *asham* for a doubtful sin, as the mishnah now explains.]

מִפְּנֵי שֶׁמַּכְשַׁרְתָּה לֶאֱכֹל בַּזְּבָחִים. — *since it renders her fit to eat of the offerings.*

As we learned in 2:1, a woman after childbirth is prohibited from partaking of any offering until she brings her purification offerings. Thus she must bring her offerings even after Yom Kippur, because Yom Kippur provides only atonement, which can serve in lieu of offerings that expiate sin; it does not, however, replace offerings which enable a person to partake of sanctified foods (*Tif. Yis.* from *Gem.* 26a).

חַטַּאת הָעוֹף הַבָּאָה עַל־הַסָּפֵק — אִם — מִשֶּׁנִּמְלְקָה נוֹדַע לָהּ — *A bird chatas that is brought because of a doubt — if, after its neck was nipped, it became known to her —*

If a woman brought a bird *chatas* for a birth of doubtful status and, after the *melikah* [nipping the bird's neck], it was determined that her miscarriage was not legally regarded as a birth (*Rav*).

הֲרֵי זוּ תִקָּבֵר. — *must be buried.*

[Burial is the form of disposal of prohibited material which have no status of sanctity. As listed in *Temurah* (7:4), an ordinary animal that was erroneously slaughtered in the Temple yard (חוּלִּין שֶׁנִּשְׁחֲטוּ בָּעֲזָרָה) is in this category. Thus

הַמַּפְרִישׁ שְׁתֵּי סְלָעִים לְאָשָׁם, וְלָקַח בָּהֶן שְׁנֵי אֵילִים לְאָשָׁם: אִם הָיָה אֶחָד מֵהֶן יָפֶה שְׁתֵּי סְלָעִים, יִקְרַב לַאֲשָׁמוֹ, וְהַשֵּׁנִי יִרְעֶה עַד שֶׁיִּסְתָּאֵב; וְיִמָּכֵר, וְיִפְּלוּ דָמָיו לִנְדָבָה. לָקַח בָּהֶן שְׁנֵי אֵילִים לְחֻלִּין, אֶחָד יָפֶה שְׁתֵּי סְלָעִים וְאֶחָד יָפֶה עֲשָׂרָה זוּז — הַיָּפֶה שְׁתֵּי סְלָעִים

יד אברהם

the burying of the *chatas* of doubt in this case is because the bird is viewed as חוּלִין שֶׁנִּשְׁחֲטוּ בָּעֲזָרָה, since once the doubt of birth has been resolved to the negative, the basis of its initial sanctification has been proven groundless.]

According to the *Gemara* (26b), the requirement for burial in this instance is only Rabbinic in nature. By Torah law, benefit from this *chatas* should be permitted because it is, in retrospect, not an offering at all. Furthermore, the restriction against *chullin* slaughtered in the Temple yard does not apply because it was slaughtered through *melikah* (nipping) rather than *shechitah*.[1] The Rabbis, nonetheless, decreed that it be buried because since, in any event, the *chatas* of doubt may not be eaten [as above 1:4], it resembles invalidated *kodashin*, that are prohibited (*Rav; Rashi*).

Others suggest a different reason why this bird is not really in the category of חוּלִין שֶׁנִּשְׁחֲטוּ בָּעֲזָרָה. Since the doubt of birth was resolved only after the offering process was performed, it retains its initial sanctified status. This is analogous to an *asham talui* brought for a doubtful transgression which was later determined not to have transpired, which retains its offering status [as above mishnah 1]. Thus, here too, the *chatas* should be treated as a *chatas* of doubt, which is burned (*Temurah* ibid.). Nonetheless, the *chatas* is buried because of its resemblance to *chullin* slaughtered in the Temple yard, as explained above (*Tif. Yis.*).

6.

The following sequence of mishnayos, which closes the tractate, presents a discussion on the laws governing the purchase or designation of animals for various categories of offerings. This mishnah discusses *asham*, an offering unique in that it must be worth two silver shekels (or, in the mishnah's phrase two *selaim*). [The *asham* brought by a *nazir* and by a *metzora* as part of their purification processes are exceptions to this rule.]

הַמַּפְרִישׁ שְׁתֵּי סְלָעִים לְאָשָׁם, — *[If] one sets aside two selaim for an asham,*

As explained above, for most of the categories of *asham* required by the Torah, a ram worth two shekels of silver must be brought.

The Torah's שְׁקָלִים is rendered by *Targum Onkelos* as סְלָעִין. Hence the mishnaic expression, *selaim*, instead of shekalim (*Rav*).

1. This premise is questioned by many commentaries, who cite a *Gemara* (*Nazir* 29) which states that an ordinary bird which was nipped in the Temple yard *is* considered as חוּלִין שֶׁנִּשְׁחֲטוּ בָּעֲזָרָה. The process of *melikah* of a fowl is analogous to the *shechitah* of an animal. Indeed, this line of reasoning is apparent in the remarks of *Rashi* and *Rav* in the first chapter (mishnah 4). See *Tos. Chadashim* here; *Shitah Mekubetzes; Aruch LaNer* 7b, s.v. שם בא״ד; *Shaar HaMelech, Hil. Shechitah* 2:1.

6
6

6. [If] one sets aside two *selaim* for an *asham*, and he purchases with them two rams for an *asham*: If one of them became worth two *selaim*, it may be offered for his *asham*, and the second must graze until it develops a blemish; then it is sold, and its proceeds are deposited for a voluntary offering. [If] he purchased with them two rams for ordinary meat, one became worth two *selaim* and one became worth ten *zuz* — the

YAD AVRAHAM

וְלָקַח בָּהֶן שְׁנֵי אֵילִים לְאָשָׁם: — *and he purchases with them two rams for an asham:*

[Instead of purchasing one ram for the two *selaim*, as the Torah requires, he purchased two; each one being worth less than the required amount.]

אִם הָיָה אֶחָד מֵהֶן יָפֶה שְׁתֵּי סְלָעִים, יִקָּרֵב לַאֲשָׁמוֹ. — *If one of them became worth two selaim, it may be offered for his asham,*

[The price of the animals rose so that one of the rams is now worth two *selaim*.]

Although at the time of the purchase neither ram was worth two *selaim*, since one is worth two *selaim* at the time of offering, it is fit for an *asham*.

Since the rise in price occurred after the animal was designated for an *asham*, it is actually tantamount to an increase in the value of *hekdesh*, [consecrated] property. Nevertheless, the person may use it for his atonement as if it were his own property that appreciated in value (*Rambam, Pesulei HaMukdashin* 4:24 from conclusion of *Gemara* 26a, cited by *Tos. Yom Tov*).

The *Gemara* does add, though, that the person should pay the extra *sela* to the Temple treasury to avoid giving the impression that he used an *asham* whose value was less than two *selaim*. It is puzzling that *Rambam* omits this detail (*Lechem Mishneh* ad loc.).

וְהַשֵּׁנִי יִרְעֶה עַד שֶׁיִּסְתָּאֵב; — *and the second must graze until it develops a blemish;*

Since the second ram, which is not worth two *selaim*, was nonetheless purchased with money designated for an **asham**. Although it is invalid for an *asham*, it bears sanctity and cannot be treated as an ordinary animal. Therefore it must graze until it develops a blemish (*Rav*).

וְיִמָּכֵר, וְיִפְּלוּ דָמָיו לִנְדָבָה. — *then it is sold, and its proceeds are deposited for a voluntary offering.*

Since it is the remainder of a guilt offering, it is deposited in the chest designated for such monies, from which they would buy *olah* offerings (*Rav*). See above, mishnah 1.

לָקַח בָּהֶן שְׁנֵי אֵילִים לְחֻלִּין, — *[If] he purchased with them two rams for ordinary meat,*

[By error, he used his designated two *selaim* to purchase two rams for non-sacrificial purposes.]

By taking consecrated funds to purchase animals for his own use, he is guilty of *me'ilah* and the money loses its sanctity (*Rav*).

As a result of his error, there now are three obligations which he must fulfill: First, he must pay for the *me'ilah* he committed by making restitution of the two *selaim* plus a fifth. Then he must bring an *asham me'ilos* to atone for the *me'ilah*. In addition, he must still bring the *asham* for which he was originally liable (*Rambam Comm., Tif. Yis.*).

אֶחָד יָפֶה שְׁתֵּי סְלָעִים וְאֶחָד יָפֶה עֲשָׂרָה זוּז — *one became worth two selaim and one became worth ten zuz* —

[As in the previous case, the value of the rams which he purchased for the two *selaim* rose. Now one of them is in itself worth two *selaim* (the equivalent of eight *zuz*) and the other is one worth ten *zuz*.]

כריתות ו/ו

יִקְרַב לַאֲשָׁמוֹ, וְהַשֵּׁנִי לִמְעִילָתוֹ. אֶחָד לְאָשָׁם וְאֶחָד לְחֻלִּין — אִם הָיָה שֶׁל־אָשָׁם יָפֶה שְׁתֵּי סְלָעִים, יִקְרַב לַאֲשָׁמוֹ, וְהַשֵּׁנִי לִמְעִילָתוֹ, וְיָבִיא עִמָּהּ סֶלַע וְחֻמְשָׁהּ.

[ז] **הַמַּפְרִישׁ** חַטָּאתוֹ, וָמֵת, לֹא יְבִיאֶנָּה בְּנוֹ

יד אברהם

A *sela* consists of four *zuz;* ten *zuz* equal two *selaim* plus two *zuz.* The animal worth ten *zuz* is the equivalent of the two *selaim* for which he is guilty of *me'ilah* plus a fifth (*Rav*).

The two *zuz*, which are actually a fourth of the *sela*, are called a fifth, since this amount is a fifth of *the total* of the restitution with the additional amount added. This is called חוֹמֶשׁ מִלְּבַר, *a fifth from the outside*, i.e., a fifth of the total after the addition. Whenever the Torah refers to a fifth, this is how it is calculated (*Tos. Yom Tov*). See *Bava Metzia* 4:8, *Arachin* 8:1, ArtScroll *Menachos* 7:1 footnote 1.

הַיָּפֶה שְׁתֵּי סְלָעִים יִקְרַב לַאֲשָׁמוֹ, — *the one worth two selaim should be offered for his asham,*

Since the one animal is worth two *selaim* it can be used for the original *asham* he was obligated to bring. This is the *asham* for which the money he misappropriated was originally designated (*Rav*).

וְהַשֵּׁנִי לִמְעִילָתוֹ. — *and the other for his me'ilah.*

The other ram (which is worth ten *zuz*) equals the amount of restitution to which he is liable, in addition to the fifth [as explained]. Therefore, he gives this second ram to the treasurer of the Temple to restore his *me'ilah.* He must still bring yet another ram for the *asham* required to atone for the *me'ilah* (*Rav*).[1]

Others interpret the mishnah in just the opposite manner: The ten-*zuz* ram is sacrificed for the original *asham.* In this manner, he fulfills his obligation of restoring to the Temple the amount he misappropriated and its fifth. Since his *me'ilah* consisted of taking money that was designated for an offering, his restitution thereof is brought on the altar in lieu of the original *asham.* The second ram, which is worth two *selaim*, is brought as an *asham me'ilos* to atone for his sin of *me'ilah.* He is, therefore, not liable to a third *asham* since he has made his restitution for the *me'ilah* and has brought an *asham me'ilos* as well (*Rambam Comm.* and *Hil. Me'ilah* 4:7; *Rashi; Tif. Yis.*; see *Mishneh LaMelech* on *Rambam* loc. cit.).

אֶחָד לְאָשָׁם וְאֶחָד לְחֻלִּין — — *One for his asham and one for ordinary [meat]* —

If, with the two *selaim* that he had designated for an *asham*, he purchased two rams, one for an *asham* and one for

1. The key point of *Rav's* commentary is that it is the two-*selaim* ram that is used to replace the *asham* for which the two *selaim* were originally designated. The phrase וְהַשֵּׁנִי לִמְעִילָתוֹ, *and the other one for his me'ilah*, then, refers to the ten-*zuz* ram which is donated to the Temple treasury as restitution for his misappropriated two *selaim.* This, of course, still leaves him with the obligation to bring yet another ram for an *asham me'ilos.*

This explanation is strongly questioned by the commentaries, who regard it as a novelty which has no basis in the *Gemara* or *Rishonim.* For, according to this approach the result is that he is actually restoring his *me'ilah* twice — once by giving the ten-*zuz* ram to the Temple treasury and again by replacing it with the other *asham*! Therefore, the classical commentators accept the other interpretation of the mishnah (*Mishneh LaMelech, Me'ilah* 4:7; *Bircas HaZevach;* cf. *Aruch LaNer*)

6
6

one worth two *selaim* should be offered for his *asham*, and the other for his *me'ilah*. One for his *asham* and one for ordinary [meat] — if the one for the *asham* became worth two *selaim*, it should be offered for his *asham*, and the second for his *me'ilah*, and he must bring with it a *sela* and its fifth.

7. [If] one sets aside his *chatas*, then dies, his son may

YAD AVRAHAM

ordinary meat for his own consumption. He is now guilty of committing *me'ilah* with only the one *sela* [that he used for himself] (*Rav; Rashi*).

אִם הָיָה שֶׁל־אָשָׁם יָפֶה שְׁתֵּי סְלָעִים, יִקְרַב לַאֲשָׁמוֹ, — *if the one for the asham became worth two selaim, it should be offered for his asham,*

If the animal purchased for an *asham* is now worth two *selaim* it should be brought for the original *asham*, for which the money was designated (*Rav; Rashi; Rambam Comm.*).

וְהַשֵּׁנִי לִמְעִילָתוֹ, — *and the second for his me'ilah,*

If the second ram, which he purchased for use as ordinary meat, is also worth two *selaim*, it should be offered as his *asham me'ilos*. Should it be worth less than two *selaim*, he may not offer it, since the minimum value of an *asham me'ilos* is two *selaim*, as explained in the prefatory remarks to this mishnah (*Rav*).

It should be noted that the word מְעִילָה in this clause means the *me'ilah* offering whereas the same word in the previous clause means the *me'ilah* restitution. In the previous situation, the ten-*zuz* animal can serve as a restitution, whereas regarding the situation described in this clause the animal itself does not serve as the restitution, which is paid separately, as the mishnah now specifies (*Tos. Yom Tov* from *Gem.* 27a).

וְיָבִיא עִמָּהּ סֶלַע וְחֻמְשָׁהּ. — *and he must bring with it a sela and its fifth.*

The *sela* is for the restitution, since he is guilty of *me'ilah* involving one *sela*, and one more *zuz*, which is the fifth required for the *me'ilah* of a four-*zuz sela* (*Rav*). Although the ram purchased for that *sela* is now worth two *selaim*, he is not liable for that much, since, at the time of the *me'ilah*, it was worth only one *sela* (*Rashi*).

Although the ram is now worth the originally designated two *selaim* he is nonetheless liable to make restitution, for it is *hekdesh* property that rose in value. When he bought it, it was worth only one *sela* so that he still owes the Temple treasury one *sela* and its fifth (*Rashi, Rav;* and *Aruch LaNer;* cf. *Sfas Emes*).

In view of the fact that the other animal has been offered as his *asham*, the *sela* that he is restoring has the status of מוֹתַר אֲשָׁמוֹת, *the remainder of an asham*, because it is now, in fact, money left over after an *asham* was brought. Therefore, had the *me'ilah* not occurred, the *sela* would have had to be used for purchasing *olos nedavah* (donative *olos*), as explained above. Accordingly, the restitution and the fifth that are to be paid to the Temple are likewise to be utilized for the same purpose (*Tif. Yis.*).

7.

הַמַּפְרִישׁ חַטָּאתוֹ, וָמֵת, — *[If] one sets aside his chatas, then dies,*

[One was liable to a *chatas* for a sin he had committed, and designated an animal

אַחֲרָיו, וְלֹא יְבִיאֶנָּה מֵחֵטְא עַל חֵטְא, אֲפִלּוּ עַל חֵלֶב שֶׁאָכַל אֶמֶשׁ, לֹא יְבִיאֶנָּה עַל־חֵלֶב שֶׁאָכַל הַיּוֹם, שֶׁנֶּאֱמַר: ,,קָרְבָּנוֹ... עַל־חַטָּאתוֹ,'' שֶׁיְּהֵא קָרְבָּנוֹ לְשֵׁם חֶטְאוֹ.

[ח] **מְבִיאִין** מֵהֶקְדֵּשׁ כִּשְׂבָּה שְׂעִירָה; מֵהֶקְדֵּשׁ שְׂעִירָה כִּשְׂבָּה; מֵהֶקְדֵּשׁ כִּשְׂבָּה וּשְׂעִירָה תּוֹרִין וּבְנֵי יוֹנָה; מֵהֶקְדֵּשׁ תּוֹרִין וּבְנֵי יוֹנָה

יד אברהם

for that purpose, but died prior to actually offering it.]

לֹא יְבִיאֶנָּה בְּנוֹ אַחֲרָיו, — *his son may not bring it after him,*

Even if the son is likewise guilty of a sin for which he is liable to a *chatas*, he may not bring his father's *chatas* to atone for his own sin (*Rav*).

It goes without saying that he may not bring it to atone for his father's sin, since there is no atonement [through offerings] after death (*Rashi*). In addition, it cannot be brought for the father's sin because, as such, it is in the category of חַטָּאת שֶׁמֵּתוּ בְּעָלֶיהָ, *a chatas whose owner died*, regarding which the halachah dictates that it be allowed to die, as explained in *Temurah* 4:1 and *Me'ilah* 3:1 (*Rambam Comm.*; see *Tos. Yom Tov*).

וְלֹא יְבִיאֶנָּה מֵחֵטְא עַל חֵטְא, — *and he may not bring it from one sin to another,*

If someone designated an animal for a *chatas* to atone for a specific sin (e.g., eating *cheilev*), he may not bring it to atone for another sin (e.g., eating blood) (*Tif. Yis.* from *Gem.* 27b).

אֲפִלּוּ עַל חֵלֶב שֶׁאָכַל אֶמֶשׁ, לֹא יְבִיאֶנָּה עַל־חֵלֶב שֶׁאָכַל הַיּוֹם, — *even [if it was set aside] for cheilev that he had eaten yesterday, he may not bring it for the cheilev he ate today,*

[Although the two sins are identical, one may bring the *chatas* only to atone for that sin for which it was initially designated.]

שֶׁנֶּאֱמַר: ,,קָרְבָּנוֹ... עַל־חַטָּאתוֹ,'' שֶׁיְּהֵא קָרְבָּנוֹ לְשֵׁם חֶטְאוֹ. — *for it is stated* (*Lev.* 4:28): *'his offering ... for his sin,' that is, his offering shall be for his sin.*

[The full passage reads: וְהֵבִיא קָרְבָּנוֹ שְׂעִירַת עִזִּים תְּמִימָה נְקֵבָה עַל־חַטָּאתוֹ אֲשֶׁר חָטָא, *and he shall bring his offering, an unblemished female goat, for his sin that he sinned.*]

This indicates that the animal can atone only for the sin for which it was designated originally (*Rabbeinu Gershom*).

The verse is cited only to explain the invalidation of the first two cases, in which the animal was designated either for the father's sin or for his own sin of a different category. In either of these cases, the invalidation is מִדְּאוֹרַיְתָא, *of Torah origin*, and the offering cannot atone even if it is brought. The injunction regarding the situation of the *chatas* designated for the previous day's sin, however, is only Rabbinical in origin and, if the *chatas* was, in fact, brought for a later sin, it can atone (*Rambam, Shegagos* 3:3, as explained by *Mahari Korkus* cited by *Kesef Mishneh* ad loc., cf. *Lechem Mishneh* loc. cit.; *Tos. Yom Tov*).

8.

In mishnah 7, the laws of altering the designation of a *chatas* from one sin to the next were discussed. Now the mishnah states the law of replacing the animal designated for a *chatas* with another animal.

not bring it after him, and he may not bring it from one sin to another, even [if it was set aside] for *cheilev* that he had eaten yesterday, he may not bring it for the *cheilev* he ate today, for it is stated (*Lev.* 4:28): *his offering . . . for his sin*, that is, his offering shall be for his sin.

8. From funds consecrated for a ewe lamb we may bring a she-goat; from funds consecrated for a she-goat [we may bring] a ewe lamb; from funds consecrated for a ewe lamb or a she-goat [we may bring] turtledoves or young pigeons; from funds consecrated for turtledoves or young pigeons [we may bring] a tenth of

YAD AVRAHAM

The קָרְבָּן עוֹלֶה וְיוֹרֵד, *variable sin offering*, has been mentioned several times in this tractate (see General Introduction and above 2:3,4). Essentially, it is a *chatas* that 'fluctuates,' making allowance for the sinner's financial circumstances. This *chatas* calls for a ewe lamb or a she-goat for the rich and a pair of birds (one for a *chatas* and one for an *olah*) for the poor.[1] For some sins, the Torah provides for yet a less expensive offering for the poorest of the poor — a flour offering called *minchas chotei* (the sinner's *minchah*).

מְבִיאִין מֵהֶקְדֵּשׁ כִּשְׂבָּה שְׂעִירָה; — *From funds consecrated for a ewe lamb we may bring a she-goat;*

If one set aside money to purchase a ewe lamb for his *chatas*, he may instead purchase a she-goat if he so wishes (*Rav; Rashi*).

Alternatively, one who designated money for the ewe offering, but then finds that he needs the money for some other purpose, may use a she-goat instead. He thus transfers the sanctity of the money to the goat, and thereby releases the money of its sanctity which he may then use for his personal needs (*Rambam, Hil. Shegagos* 10:9).

מֵהֶקְדֵּשׁ שְׂעִירָה כִּשְׂבָּה; — *from funds consecrated for a she-goat [we may bring] a ewe lamb;*

[Likewise, if one set aside money to purchase a she-goat for his *chatas*, he may use a ewe-lamb instead.]

מֵהֶקְדֵּשׁ כִּשְׂבָּה וּשְׂעִירָה תּוֹרִין וּבְנֵי יוֹנָה; — *from funds consecrated for a ewe lamb or a she-goat [we may bring] turtledoves or young pigeons;*

[If one set aside money towards the purchase of either a ewe lamb or a she-goat for a *chatas*, he may use these funds to purchase turtledoves or young pigeons, one for an *olah* and one for a *chatas*, as will be explained below.]

מֵהֶקְדֵּשׁ תּוֹרִין וּבְנֵי יוֹנָה עֲשִׂירִית הָאֵיפָה. — *from funds consecrated for turtledoves or young pigeons [we may bring] a tenth*

1. The rich and poor category is determined by his ability to purchase the offering in question: if one has sufficient funds to pay for a sheep or a goat, he must buy one of these; if not, he may purchase birds; but if he does not have enough for birds, he may bring a flour offering (*Chinuch, Mitzvah* 123). *Minchas Chinuch* (ad loc.) raises the question of whether affordability is determined by the amount of money one has left after his basic needs have been taken care of (similar to the status of poverty in regards to the laws of charity) or by the fact that he has funds or possessions at hand, even if they don't cover his basic needs. See *Aruch LaNer* 27b.

עֲשִׂירִית הָאֵיפָה. כֵּיצַד? הִפְרִישׁ לְכִשְׂבָּה אוֹ לִשְׂעִירָה, הֶעֱנִי, יָבִיא עוֹף; הֶעֱנִי, יָבִיא עֲשִׂירִית הָאֵיפָה. הִפְרִישׁ לַעֲשִׂירִית הָאֵיפָה, הֶעֱשִׁיר, יָבִיא עוֹף. הֶעֱשִׁיר, יָבִיא כִּשְׂבָּה וּשְׂעִירָה. הִפְרִישׁ כִּשְׂבָּה אוֹ שְׂעִירָה, וְנִסְתָּאֲבוּ, אִם רָצָה, יָבִיא

יד אברהם

of an ephah.

[If one set aside money towards the purchase of two birds, one for an *olah* and one for a *chatas*, he may use this money to purchase a tenth of an *ephah* of fine wheat flour for a *minchas chotei*, the meal offering of a sinner, as will be explained below.]

כֵּיצַד? — *How so?*

In what case may the money designated for a ewe lamb or a she-goat be used for turtledoves or young pigeons? And in what case may the money designated for turtledoves and young pigeons be used for a tenth of an *ephah?* (*Tif. Yis.*).

הִפְרִישׁ לְכִשְׂבָּה אוֹ לִשְׂעִירָה, — *[If] he set aside [money] for a ewe lamb or a she-goat,*

If any of those liable to the variable sin offering set aside money to purchase a ewe lamb or a she-goat for a *chatas* (*Rav; Rashi*).

הֶעֱנִי, יָבִיא עוֹף; — *and then became poor, he may bring birds;*

With [part of] the money that he designated for the lambs or the goat for his *korban*, he buys birds. The remainder may obviously be used for his own benefit. Otherwise, this leniency would be of no avail to the poor person (*Rav; Rashi; Rambam Comm.*). He does this by transferring the sanctity of the money to the birds, thus releasing the remainder of the money for *chullin* (mundane) use (*Rambam, Pesulei HaMukdashin* 5:7 cited by *Tos. Yom Tov*). As a rule, the remainder of money designated for a *chatas* or an *asham* must be used for donative *olos*, as stated in *Shekalim* (2:5). However, regarding the variable sin offering [if part of the money is used for a different form of the same offering], the remainder of the money may be used for personal benefit (*Tos. Yom Tov*).

Others explain that he set aside *part* of the money for a ewe or a goat. He can subsequently use this money for a bird instead of adding the rest of the cost of the ewe or goat (*Rabbeinu Gershom*; cf. *Aruch LaNer; Sfas Emes*).

This is derived from the Torah's wording regarding the ewe lamb or the goat of the variable sin offering (*Lev.* 5:6): וְכִפֶּר עָלָיו הַכֹּהֵן מֵחַטָּאתוֹ, *and the Kohen shall provide him atonement for his sin.* Because of the prefixed letter מ [which usually means *from* or *of*], the word מֵחַטָּאתוֹ is interpreted to mean part *of* his *chatas*, i.e., he can atone for himself by using only a part *of* the originally designated money (*Rav* from *Gem.* 27b).

הֶעֱנִי, יָבִיא עֲשִׂירִית הָאֵיפָה. — *[if] he became [still] poorer, he may bring a tenth of an ephah.*

If he is so poor that he can no longer afford to bring even a bird offering, he may bring a tenth of an *ephah* from [part of] of the money previously set aside for the bird offerings.

Regarding bird offerings too, the Torah states (ibid. 10) מֵחַטָּאתוֹ, thus denoting that part of the money designated for the bird offerings may be used for a tenth of an *ephah*, and the rest is *chullin*, ordinary money (*Rav* from *Gem.* 27b).

Although the Torah already stated this

6 an *ephah*. How so? [If] he set aside [money] for a ewe
8 lamb or a she-goat, and then became poor, he may bring birds; [if] he became [still] poorer, he may bring a tenth of an *ephah*. [If] he set aside [money] for a tenth of an *ephah*, and then became prosperous, he must bring birds. [If] he became [still] more prosperous, he must bring a ewe lamb or a she-goat. [If] he set aside a ewe lamb or a she-goat, and it developed a blemish, if he wishes, he may

YAD AVRAHAM

ruling regarding the ewe lamb and the she-goat, it was, nevertheless, necessary to state it as regards the bird offering as well. Otherwise, we might believe that, in this case, since the tenth of an *ephah* has no blood to place on the Altar, it cannot serve as an alternate use of the money initially designated for bird offerings. The *minchah* would then have to be purchased from other money and the money originally set aside towards the purchase of the bird offering would be deposited in a donative-offering chest. Therefore, the Torah specifies that in this case, too, although there is no blood placed on the Altar, the money designated for the *chatas* and *olah* birds may be used for the *minchah* offering (*Tos. Yom Tov* from *Gem.* 27b).

הִפְרִישׁ לַעֲשִׂירִית הָאֵיפָה, הֶעֱשִׁיר, יָבִיא עוֹף. — *[If] he set aside [money] for a tenth of an ephah, and then became prosperous, he must bring birds.*

When he had sinned, he was in the category of דַּלֵּי דַלּוֹת, *the poorest of the poor*, and had set aside money to purchase flour for his *minchah.* When he subsequently prospers and is liable for the higher category of *chatas*, he must add to the money he had previously designated for the *minchah* and purchase birds (*Rambam Comm.*).

The ruling [that money designated for the *minchah* may be used towards the purchase of the birds] is derived from another verse in the passage of the variable sin offering (*Lev.* 5:13): וְכִפֶּר עָלָיו הַכֹּהֵן עַל־חַטָּאתוֹ, *and the Kohen shall atone for him for his sin.* The phrase עַל־חַטָּאתוֹ used in connection with the *minchah* form of the variable sin offering [as opposed to the phrase מֵחַטָּאתוֹ, *from his sin*, used regarding two earlier forms] is interpreted as *in addition to*, i.e., on occasion he *adds* to his previously designated money and brings birds instead of a *minchah* (*Rav* from *Gem.* 27b; *Rashi* to *Lev.* 5:13).

הֶעֱשִׁיר, יָבִיא כִּשְׂבָּה וּשְׂעִירָה. — *[If] he became [still] more prosperous, he must bring a ewe lamb or a she-goat.*

If he became so prosperous that he can now afford a ewe lamb or a she-goat, he should add to the set-aside money and purchase an animal.

Although the Torah does not state עַל־חַטָּאתוֹ, *upon his chatas*, in reference to the bird offering [as it does for the *minchah*], we derive the same ruling by means of a *kal vachomer:* If the Torah permits bringing a bird offering from the money designated for a tenth of an *ephah*, although the latter offering has no blood placed on the Altar and the other does, then surely money designated for a bird offering may be taken for an animal offering, for both have their blood placed on the Altar (*Tos. Yom Tov* from *Gem.* 27b).

הִפְרִישׁ כִּשְׂבָּה אוֹ שְׂעִירָה, וְנִסְתָּאֲבוּ, — *[If] he set aside a ewe lamb or a she-goat, and it* [lit., *they*] *developed a blemish,*

This final segment of the mishnah does not appear in the mishnah printed with the *Gemara*. It does, however, appear in the

בְּדְמֵיהֶן עוֹף. הִפְרִישׁ עוֹף וְנִסְתָּאֵב, לֹא יָבִיא בְדָמָיו עֲשִׂירִית הָאֵיפָה, שֶׁאֵין לָעוֹף פִּדְיוֹן.

[ט] רַבִּי שִׁמְעוֹן אוֹמֵר: כְּבָשִׂים קוֹדְמִין לְעִזִּים, בְּכָל־מָקוֹם. יָכוֹל מִפְּנֵי שֶׁהֵן מֻבְחָרִין מֵהֶן. תַּלְמוּד לוֹמַר: ,,וְאִם־כֶּבֶשׂ יָבִיא קָרְבָּנוֹ לְחַטָּאת.״ מְלַמֵּד שֶׁשְּׁנֵיהֶם שְׁקוּלִין. תּוֹרִין קוֹדְמִין לִבְנֵי יוֹנָה, בְּכָל־מָקוֹם. יָכוֹל מִפְּנֵי

יד אברהם

Gemara, as a *Baraisa.*

[Unlike the previously discussed cases, in which he merely designated money for an offering, in this case he actually purchased the animal and designated it as his required offering. An unblemished consecrated animal, of course, may not be exchanged for another (*Lev.* 27:10). In the event, however, that the animal develops a blemish which invalidates it from being brought as an offering, it must be redeemed and another offering bought from the proceeds.]

אִם רָצָה, יָבִיא בִדְמֵיהֶן עוֹף. — *if he wishes, he may bring birds from their proceeds.*

[He can transfer the funds to buy the birds, which is his offering] if he became poor[1] (*Rav*).

It goes without saying that if he is still rich, he cannot bring birds from the proceeds of the blemished sheep because a rich man who brings a poor man's offering does not discharge his obligation (*Tif. Yis.*).

הִפְרִישׁ עוֹף וְנִסְתָּאֵב, — *[If] he set aside a bird and it became blemished,*

[He was a poor man who set aside birds for his offering and they subsequently became blemished. He then became further impoverished to the extent that he may bring a tenth of an *ephah* for his offering. He wants to exchange the birds for money and use it for the purchase of the *minchah.*]

Only the loss of a limb, such as the withering of a wing or the like, is a blemish that disqualifies a bird for sacrificial purposes. Other blemishes do not disqualify a bird, as stated in *Temurah* 6:4 (*Tif. Yis.; Beis David*).

לֹא יָבִיא בְדָמָיו עֲשִׂירִית הָאֵיפָה, שֶׁאֵין לָעוֹף פִּדְיוֹן. — *he may not bring for its proceeds a tenth of an ephah, for a bird has no redemption.*

[He cannot redeem them by bringing a tenth of an *ephah* with the money because a disqualified bird cannot be redeemed.] This is derived exegetically from the verse (regarding the redemption of blemished animals) which states (*Lev.* 27:11): וְהֶעֱמִיד אֶת־הַבְּהֵמָה לִפְנֵי הַכֹּהֵן, *and he will 'present' the animal before the Kohen.* The emphasis of the word בְּהֵמָה, *animal,* excludes all other types of consecrated objects: birds, wood, frankincense, and vessels used for the Temple service

1. *Chinuch* (*Mitzvah* 123) states that a poor person who brings the offering of a rich person does not fulfill his obligation . [The commentators regard this as a novel ruling whose basis is questionable. In fact, from the mishnah (*Negaim* 14:12) it would appear that this ruling is incorrect (*Perashas Derachim; Derech Mitzvosecha*).] *Rambam* (*Shegagos* 10:13) rules that a poor person can dispense his obligation with the offering of a rich person.

6
9

bring birds from their proceeds. [If] he set aside a bird and it became blemished, he may not bring for its proceeds a tenth of an *ephah*, for a bird has no redemption.

9. R' Shimon says: Everywhere, lambs are mentioned before goats. I would think [that this is] because they are preferable to them. [Therefore,] Scripture states (*Lev.* 4:32): *And if he bring a lamb for a chatas*. This teaches [us] that both are equal.

Everywhere, turtledoves are mentioned before young

YAD AVRAHAM

(*Rav; Rambam Comm.* from *Sifra* ad loc.).

[Although if he set aside money he can go to a lower level (from lamb to birds to flour), the bird itself cannot be redeemed.]

9.

רַבִּי שִׁמְעוֹן אוֹמֵר: כְּבָשִׂים קוֹדְמִין לְעִזִּים, בְּכָל־מָקוֹם. — *R' Shimon says: Everywhere, lambs are mentioned before goats.*

Wherever the Torah mentions sheep and goats, sheep are mentioned first. Some examples are: מִן־הַכְּבָשִׂים וּמִן־הָעִזִּים תִּקָּחוּ, *You shall take from the lambs or from the goats* [for the *pesach* offering] (*Exodus* 12:5); and אוֹ־לַשֶּׂה בַכְּבָשִׂים אוֹ בָעִזִּים, *or for the young of the lambs or from the goats* [the libation offerings are ...] (*Numbers* 15:11; *Rav; Rashi*).

יָכוֹל מִפְּנֵי שֶׁהֵן מְבְחָרִין מֵהֶן. — *I would think [that this is] because they are preferable to them.*

From the fact that the mention of lambs always precedes that of goats, I would think that lamb offerings are more meritorious than goat offerings. Consequently, if one vows to bring an *olah* [without specifying from which species], I would conclude that preferably he should bring a lamb rather than a goat (*Rav; Rashi*).

תַּלְמוּד לוֹמַר: ,,וְאִם־כֶּבֶשׂ יָבִיא קָרְבָּנוֹ לְחַטָּאת." — *[Therefore], Scripture states* (*Lev.* 4:32): *'And if he bring a lamb for a chatas.'*

Prior to this verse the Torah states (ibid. 4:28): וְהֵבִיא קָרְבָּנוֹ שְׂעִירַת עִזִּים, *He shall bring a she-goat for a chatas.* Thus, in this one instance, the goat is mentioned before the lamb (*Rav*).

Although the mishnah begins with the categorical statement that the mention of lambs *always* precedes that of goats, it is not inconsistent with the fact that in this one instance goats are mentioned before lambs. The pattern is that regarding the mention of *males*, lambs are always mentioned first. In the verse just cited, the reference is to a female goat (*Aruch LaNer*).

מְלַמֵּד שֶׁשְּׁנֵיהֶם שְׁקוּלִין. — *This teaches [us] that both are equal.*

Therefore, he may bring whichever he wishes [to fulfill his vow] (*Rav*).

Although the verse mentioned refers to females, there is no ground to distinguish between males and females regarding the order of precedence of their offering (*Aruch LaNer*).

תּוֹרִין קוֹדְמִין לִבְנֵי יוֹנָה, בְּכָל־מָקוֹם. — *Everywhere, turtledoves are mentioned before young pigeons.*

שֶׁהֵן מֻבְחָרִין מֵהֶן. תַּלְמוּד לוֹמַר: ,,וּבֶן־יוֹנָה אוֹ־תֹר לְחַטָּאת.״ מְלַמֵּד שֶׁשְּׁנֵיהֶן שְׁקוּלִין.

הָאָב קוֹדֵם לָאֵם בְּכָל־מָקוֹם. יָכוֹל שֶׁכְּבוֹד הָאָב עוֹדֵף עַל כְּבוֹד הָאֵם. תַּלְמוּד לוֹמַר: ,,אִישׁ אִמּוֹ וְאָבִיו תִּירָאוּ.״ מְלַמֵּד שֶׁשְּׁנֵיהֶם שְׁקוּלִים. אֲבָל אָמְרוּ חֲכָמִים: הָאָב קוֹדֵם לָאֵם, בְּכָל־מָקוֹם, מִפְּנֵי שֶׁהוּא וְאִמּוֹ חַיָּבִין בִּכְבוֹד אָבִיו. וְכֵן בְּתַלְמוּד תּוֹרָה: אִם זָכָה הַבֵּן לִפְנֵי הָרַב, קוֹדֵם אֶת־הָאָב

יד אברהם

In almost every verse in which the Torah mentions turtledoves and young pigeons in regard to offerings, the turtledoves appear first (*Rav; Rashi*).

יָכוֹל מִפְּנֵי שֶׁהֵן מֻבְחָרִין מֵהֶן. — *I would think [that this is] because they are preferable to them.*

[Were this conclusion true, a vow for bird offerings would preferably be fulfilled with turtledoves rather than young pigeons.]

תַּלְמוּד לוֹמַר: ,,וּבֶן־יוֹנָה אוֹ־תֹר לְחַטָּאת.״ — *[Therefore,] Scripture states (Lev. 12:6): 'And a young pigeon or a turtledove for a chatas.'*

[Regarding the woman who has given birth, who brings her offerings at the conclusion of the days of her purification, the Torah states that she must bring a young pigeon or a turtledove for a *chatas.*]

מְלַמֵּד שֶׁשְּׁנֵיהֶן שְׁקוּלִין. — *This teaches [us] that both are equal.*

[Therefore, whenever one is obligated to bring a bird offering, he may bring either turtledoves or pigeons.]

הָאָב קוֹדֵם לָאֵם בְּכָל־מָקוֹם. — *Everywhere, the father is mentioned before the mother.*

Whenever the Torah speaks of filial duties, the father is mentioned first, for example: כַּבֵּד אֶת־אָבִיךָ וְאֶת־אִמֶּךָ, *Honor your father and your mother* (*Exodus* 20:12); וּמַכֵּה אָבִיו וְאִמּוֹ מוֹת יוּמָת, *Whosoever strikes his father or his mother shall be put to death* (ibid. 21:15); וּמְקַלֵּל אָבִיו וְאִמּוֹ מוֹת יוּמָת, *Whosoever curses his father or his mother shall be put to death* (ibid. v. 17).

יָכוֹל שֶׁכְּבוֹד הָאָב עוֹדֵף עַל כְּבוֹד הָאֵם. — *I would think that the father's honor exceeds the mother's honor.*

[This arrangement may lead us to conclude that one must honor his father more than his mother or, if a conflict between the two obligations arises, the father's honor takes precedence.]

תַּלְמוּד לוֹמַר: ,,אִישׁ אִמּוֹ וְאָבִיו תִּירָאוּ.״ מְלַמֵּד שֶׁשְּׁנֵיהֶם שְׁקוּלִים. — *[Therefore,] Scripture states (Lev. 19:3): 'Every man shall fear his mother and his father.' This teaches [us] that both are equal.*

Regarding the command to fear parents, the Torah mentioned the mother first to indicate that the honor due the mother is equal to the honor due the father (*Tif. Yis.*).

אֲבָל אָמְרוּ חֲכָמִים: הָאָב קוֹדֵם לָאֵם, בְּכָל־מָקוֹם, — *But the Sages said: Everywhere, the father takes precedence to the mother,*

The Rabbis ordained that the father takes precedence to the mother (*Tif. Yis.*).

Although the Torah equated the honor of the mother with that of the father, the Rabbis interpreted this only in regard to pigeons. I would think [that this is] because they are preferable to them. [Therefore,] Scripture states (*Lev.* 12:6): *And a young pigeon or a turtledove for a chatas*. This teaches [us] that both are equal.

Everywhere, the father is mentioned before the mother. I would think that the father's honor exceeds the mother's honor. [Therefore,] Scripture states (*Lev.* 19:3): *Every man shall fear his mother and his father.* This teaches [us] that both are equal. But the Sages said: Everywhere, the father takes precedence to the mother, because [both] he and his mother are obligated to honor his father. And so it is with the study of Torah: If the son gained much [while sitting] before the teacher, he precedes the father in all matters, because [both] he and

YAD AVRAHAM

the reward gained by respecting each parent. However, in terms of whose honor takes precedence, the father's respect precedes that of the mother's (*Rabbeinu Gershom*). Thus, if, for example, each parent requests a glass of water, but he can only bring one at a time, he should serve his father first (*Kiddushin* 31a).

מִפְּנֵי שֶׁהוּא וְאִמּוֹ חַיָּבִין בִּכְבוֹד אָבִיו. — *because [both] he and his mother are obligated to honor his father.*

Certain services (such as bringing water) are included among the duties to which a woman is obligated, by her marriage contract, to perform for her husband (*Kesubos* 5:5). Regarding such services the Rabbis placed one's father's honor before his mother's. Should, however, the father and mother's conflicting requests involve a type of service that a woman is not required to do for her husband, it appears that both the father and mother are equal, and one may grant precedence to either parent's request (*Pischei Teshuvah, Yoreh Deah* 240:9).

Likewise, should the parents be divorced, and thus the mother is not obligated to the father, the honor due each parent is the same, and the son may honor whichever one he prefers first (*Yoreh Deah* 240:14).

וְכֵן בְּתַלְמוּד תּוֹרָה: — *And so it is with the study of Torah:*

[The previous case illustrated the principle that when there is an obligation to honor two parties (e.g., father and mother), precedence is given to one (the father) on the basis of the fact that the other party (the mother) is also obligated to honor him. The same applies with the honor due to one's master in Torah scholarship, viz., the honor due to a master takes precedence over the honor due to a father, because the father, too, must honor a Torah scholar, as will be explained.]

אִם זָכָה הַבֵּן לִפְנֵי הָרַב, — *If the son gained much [while sitting] before the teacher,*

This refers to a רַב מוּבְהָק, *outstanding master*, i.e., the person from whom he learned most of the Torah knowledge that he possesses (*Rav, Bava Metzia* 2:11), be it Scripture, Mishnah or *Gemara* (*Rashi, Bava Metzia* 33a, cf. *Tos. Yom Tov, Bava Metzia* loc. cit.).

קוֹדֵם אֶת־הָאָב בְּכָל־מָקוֹם, — *he precedes the father in all matters* [lit., *everywhere*],

[Whenever there is a conflict between

בְּכָל־מָקוֹם, מִפְּנֵי שֶׁהוּא וְאָבִיו חַיָּבִין בִּכְבוֹד רַבּוֹ.

יד אברהם

the demands of honoring a teacher and those of honoring a father, the teacher's honor takes precedence.] For example, if someone finds items lost by both his father and his teacher, he must first return the article belonging to his teacher before returning the article belonging to his father. The same applies to ransoming them from captivity, or providing them with support, or helping them if they are both carrying burdens; he must always first help his teacher and then his father (*Rav*).

מִפְּנֵי שֶׁהוּא וְאָבִיו חַיָּבִין בִּכְבוֹד רַבּוֹ. — *because [both] he and his father are obligated to honor his teacher.*

Since the father is obligated to honor

his father are obligated to honor his teacher.

YAD AVRAHAM

every Torah scholar including, of course, his son's teacher, the son's obligation to honor his teacher takes precedence over the obligation to honor his father (cf. *Shoshannim LeDavid*). However, if the father, too, is a Torah scholar, the son must give his honor precedence, even if he is not as erudite as the master (*Rav* from *Bava Metzia* 2:11).

Some distinguish between returning a lost article and relieving him of a burden or redeeming him: Regarding the former, the master always takes precedence unless the father is an equally erudite scholar; regarding the latter, as long as the father is a scholar he takes precedence over the master (*Rosh* quoted by *Tur Yoreh Deah* 242; cf. *Beis Yosef* ad loc.; and *Tos. Yom Tov*, *Bava Metzia* 2:11; *Yad Avraham* comm. ad loc.).